THE BLUE GUIDES

England
Ireland
Scotland
Wales
London
Cathedrals and Abbeys of England and Wales
Channel Islands
Literary Britain and Ireland
Museums and Galleries of London
Oxford and Cambridge
Victorian Architecture in Britain

Austria

Belgium and Luxembourg

China*

Cyprus

Egypt

France
Paris and Environs

Corsica

Germany

Greece
Crete

Holland

Florence
Northern Italy
Rome and Environs
Southern Italy
Sicily
Venice

Mexico*

Boston and Cambridge
New York

Moscow and Leningrad

Yugoslavia*   *in preparation

The Dome of the Rock (courtesy of John Prag)

BLUE GUIDE

JERUSALEM

Kay Prag

Atlas, maps and plans by John Flower

A & C Black
London

W W Norton
New York

First edition 1989

Published by A & C Black (Publishers) Limited
35 Bedford Row, London, WC1R 4JH

© A & C Black (Publishers) Limited 1989

Published in the United States of America by
W W Norton & Company, Inc
500 Fifth Avenue, New York, NY 10110

Published simultaneously in Canada by
Penguin Books Canada Limited
2801 John Street, Markham, Ontario, LR3 1B4

British Library Cataloguing in Publication Data
Pray, Kay
  Jerusalem. — (Blue guide).
  1. Jerusalem — Description — Guide-books
  I. Title   II. Series
  915.694′40454 DS109

  ISBN 0-7136-2944-4

ISBN 0-393-30480-9   >$19.95   USA

Biographical Note

Kay Prag studied Near Eastern archaeology at the Universities of
Sydney, London and Oxford, and has carried out archaeological
excavation and field survey work in Jordan, Iran, Lebanon and Italy.
She has taught and worked in the museums of several British universities. She is currently engaged in writing and research work, and is
conducting excavations in Jordan.

ACKNOWLEDGEMENTS

A number of people have been most generous with their time and knowledge of Jerusalem, and I should like to acknowledge and to thank in particular Professor Edmund Bosworth for his patient help with many questions and for producing a consistent transliteration of the Arabic; Dr Michael Burgoyne who kindly responded to a number of questions, and both him and Dr Donald Richards, for the debt to their book *Mamluk Jerusalem* will be obvious to anyone who reads this guide; Dr John Kane for guidance to the tombs and stylistic developments of the Hellenistic and Roman monuments in Jerusalem and for reading a section of the text; Dr Denys Pringle who has been immensely patient and generous with his knowledge of the Crusader period; Dr Philip Alexander; Dr Simon Lloyd; Dr Gillian Clark for kind last minute help; and Dr John Prag for impressing some sense and consistency on the English. No errors remaining in the text should, however, be attributed to them. I would also like to thank the Palestine Exploration Fund and the John Rylands Library of the University of Manchester for access to their splendid libraries.

For my own part the writing of this guide has been the beginning of an attempt to answer all those questions about Jerusalem which are hardly answered on the spot, and often not even asked until a few layers of ignorance have been surmounted. Very few people are expert on every period of Jerusalem's history: I might claim to be an expert on Jerusalem during one century in the late third millennium, and can therefore well play the role of one with many questions to ask. The book is only the beginning of an answer, for there is still much for me to find out, and excavation, research and publication reveals fresh insights every year to balance the destruction which tends to occur with development. Those who visit Jerusalem often return with a strong feeling for the city and its people. I first went as a student of the British School of Archaeology in Jerusalem to work on Kathleen Kenyon's excavations of the ancient city, and even the first view of the city remains vivid in my mind. The opportunities to strengthen the bond in the following years were provided largely through the British School and friends met within its walls; and stimulated by the many congenial people who accompanied me on Swans Art Treasures Tours. To all these I willingly acknowledge a debt and offer thanks.

Acknowledgements (in addition to those in captions) for use of illustrations: courtesy of Oxford University Press and of The British Library for p. 123; of the Palestine Exploration Fund (PEF), London for pp. 146, 150 and 282; of the École Biblique et Archéologique Française, Jerusalem and of the PEF for p. 159;   and of the Institute of Archaeology, Hebrew University, Jerusalem and of the PEF for p. 244.

CONTENTS

PRACTICAL INFORMATION

ROUTES

MAPS AND PLANS

8   CONTENTS

INTRODUCTION

Jerusalem, A. *al-Quds*, H. *Yerushalayim*, Greek and Latin *Hierosolyma*, has been the de facto capital of the State of Israel since 5 December 1949 (though this status is not formally recognised by the UN, and many foreign ambassadors still reside in the first capital, Tel Aviv). It consists of two parts, West Jerusalem, part of the state of Israel since the latter's establishment in 1948, consisting of modern suburbs dating mostly to the 19C and 20C; and East Jerusalem, part of the Hashemite Kingdom of the Jordan from 1948 until 1967, and formally annexed by Israel on 28 June 1967 (a status also not recognised by the UN), which consists of the ancient and medieval cities of Jerusalem and extensive modern suburbs to the N, mostly also of 19C and 20C date.

Jerusalem is situated at latitude 31° N, longitude 35° E, c 52km from the Mediterranean Sea. It lies on the limestone watershed of the hill country, at c 780m above sea level, with ancient agricultural terraces and modern afforestation to the W and N, and the starkly barren hills of the Judaean wilderness to the E and S.

The Old City of Jerusalem in its present roughly quadrilateral shape is enclosed by walls of local limestone built by Sulaiman the Magnificent in the 16C, mostly on pre-existing lines and much repaired and restored since. For the visitor the medieval walls are the first focus of attention. The Old City, covering c 82 hectares (c 200 acres) only in part overlies the smaller ancient city to the SE, which was first occupied around 6000 years ago. The area of occupation shifted in the course of centuries according to the demands of strategy and population growth and decline. Although the Old City is by custom divided into four quarters based on religious and ethnic factors, the most important points are the Church of the Holy Sepulchre to the W, and the Herodian Temple platform with the Dome of the Rock, the Aqsa Mosque and the Western or Wailing Wall to the E. Between these points, the focus of millions of pilgrims, lies a dense and bewildering mass of buildings and people packed into a small space which can reward weeks rather than days of exploring to begin to uncover the historical, religious, architectural and ethnic layers of this revered place.

To the Jews it is the focal point of their religion, the site of the Temple built by Solomon in the 10C BC; it is the centre of the Christian world, as the site of the Crucifixion and the Resurrection of Christ in the 1C AD; and to the Muslims it is the sacred city of the Prophets and location of the Prophet Muhammad's Night Journey (7C AD), the third holiest city in the Muslim world and the second most important place of pilgrimage after Mecca.

The area around the N and W sides of the Temple platform still forms one of the best preserved medieval Muslim urban complexes in the world.

The dominant impression in the unrestored parts of the Old City is of the fine local limestone used for the old domed houses and for the narrow stepped streets, the stones of which are polished by centuries of pedestrian traffic. The stone in the Jerusalem area often has a reddish vein, and reflects the changes of light throughout the day, looking fresh and yellow in the early morning, grey-whitish in the harsh mid-day sunshine, with deeper, subtler shades of gold and pink emerging in the late afternoon and evening. The Old City of Jerusalem has amazing variety to offer the wanderer at all hours. The

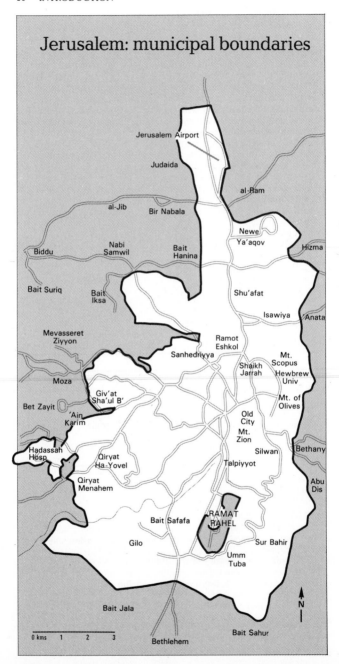

Jerusalem: municipal boundaries

Jerusalem Airport

Judaida

al-Ram

al-Jib

Bir Nabala

Newe
Ya'aqov

Hizma

Biddu

Nabi
Samwil

Bait
Hanina

Bait Suriq

Bait
Iksa

Shu'afat

Isawiya

Anata

Mevasseret
Ziyyon

Ramot
Eshkol

Sanhedriyya

Mt.
Scopus

Moza

Shaikh
Jarrah

Hebrew
Univ

Bet Zayit

Giv'at
Sha'ul B'

Mt. of
Olives

'Ain
Karim

Old
City

Mt.
Zion

Silwan

Bethany

Hadassah
Hosp

Qiryat
Ha-Yovel

Talpiyyot

Abu
Dis

Qiryat
Menahem

Bait Safafa

RAMAT
RAHEL

Sur Bahir

Gilo

Umm
Tuba

Bait Jala

N

0 kms   1   2   3

Bait Sahur

Bethlehem

mellowness of masonry which in much of the Muslim Quarter has stood for 500 and sometimes 1000 years, and in some places elsewhere for as much as 2000 years, gives Jerusalem a timeless visual quality.

To accommodate the increase in population, the W suburbs were developed outside the walls of the Old City in the mid-19C, expanded rapidly in the early 20C and again from 1948; the N suburbs followed a similar but somewhat slower pattern. More recent expansion to the S and E has resulted in the almost complete encirclement of the Old City by modern building. The new suburbs were built with local stone by custom during the Turkish period, and by law during the British Mandate period, but that by-law had to be set aside to keep pace with housing demands in Israel in later years. Today there is an attempt to continue and preserve this visual image, both in new building and particularly in restoration. The new W city, with its parliament and other civic buildings, is built on modern European and American models.

Population. The population of Jerusalem has shown extremes of change during the last two millennia. The effects of political change in the past have been countered to some extent by the tendency of elements in the population to leave the city in times of stress and to return under more propitious circumstances; and by the demographic process by which urban populations are 'refuelled' from the surrounding countryside. In addition the Holy City has always attracted a large foreign element. Since the 1860s the older pattern has been submerged in the tide of Jewish immigration to the city. In the early 12C the population was entirely Christian, both local Orthodox and Western Latins. The Muslims and Jews had been massacred or expelled, and some (Jacobite) Christians had fled to Egypt. This situation was radically changed by the Muslim reconquest in 1187.

In 1267 Nachmanides recorded a population of c 2000 consisting of 1700 Muslims, 300 Christians and two Jews. The Muslim population was augmented by immigrants from the E Islamic world, and North Africa. Some Christian sects (particularly the Georgians) were favoured, the Latins were barely present. The early Ottoman archives for 1525/6 record 934 households in Jerusalem, of which 616 were Muslim, 199 were Jewish and 119 were Christian. From the 16C the Jewish population increased by immigration, but in the mid-19C the total population was still very small, c 15,000, of whom c 7000 were Jewish, c 5000 were Muslim and c 3000 Christian. By 1912 the population had grown to 70/80,000. In 1987 it stands at 442,000, of whom 330,000 are Jewish, 100,000 are Muslim and 12,000 are Christian.

Geology. The plateau upon which the city is built occupies c 1000 acres on the E flank of the Judaean anticline. It consists mainly of Tertiary limestones. There were many caves and karst clefts which were utilised anciently for burial, occupation, or water storage. The local limestones have been much quarried and several varieties provide excellent building material. The different types have a variety of local Arabic names: 1. *Mizzi* is a fine-grained, hard, compact limestone. A variety with reddish veining which occurs in Jerusalem and Bethlehem is called *mizzi ahmar*. The *mizzi* limestone occurs mainly in the upper strata on the W side of Jerusalem and is a Cenomanian deposit. There are also some outcrops of dolomite of the same date. 2. *Malaki*, meaning 'royal', is fine and hard and much

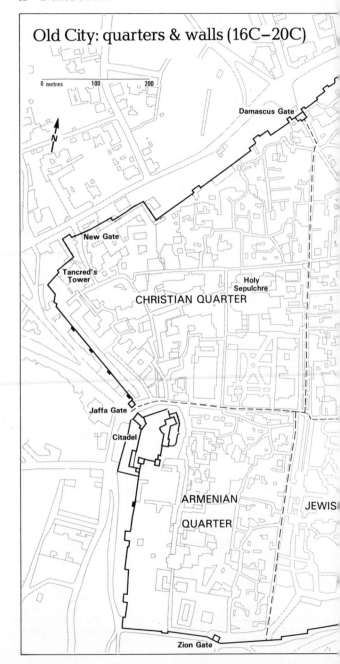

Old City: quarters & walls (16C–20C)

0 metres 100 200

N

Damascus Gate

New Gate

Tancred's Tower

Holy Sepulchre

CHRISTIAN QUARTER

Jaffa Gate

Citadel

ARMENIAN QUARTER

JEWIS

Zion Gate

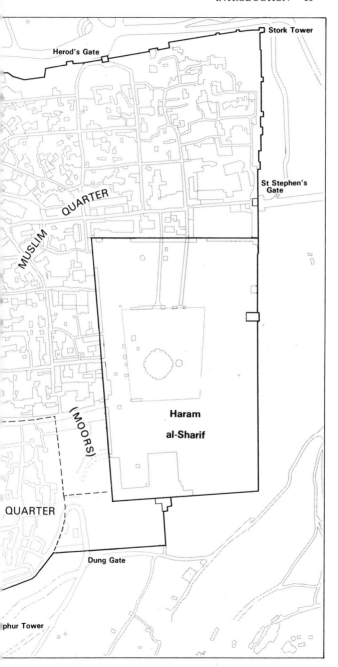

Stork Tower

Herod's Gate

St Stephen's Gate

QUARTER

MUSLIM

(MOORS)

Haram

al-Sharif

QUARTER

Dung Gate

phur Tower

used in the past, usually underlies the *mizzi*, and is not as hard; tombs were often cut in it. It is a Turonian deposit and occurs mostly in the lower strata to the W of Jerusalem; outcrops were quarried to the N of the Old City, at Solomon's Quarries and in the Kidron Valley. 3. *Nari* is a friable limestone, convenient for dressing and working, but not much used for monumental contructions after the Iron Age. It is of Quaternary deposition and occurs on the E and S sides of the city, particularly on the top of the Mount of Olives and at Abu Tor. 4. *Qa'qule* (Tertiary, Senonian) and *huwar* are soft chalky limestones with bands of flint, easy to cut, in which tombs were sometimes excavated, which to tend collapse in the course of time. They also outcrop on the Mount of Olives and at Abu Tor. The valleys contain alluvium, much being of recent deposition.

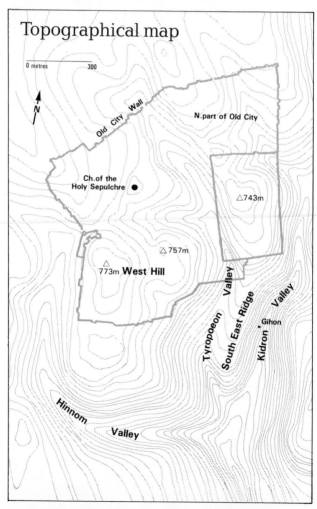

Topographical map

0 metres — 300

N

Old City Wall

N.part of Old City

Ch.of the Holy Sepulchre ●

△743m

△757m

△773m **West Hill**

Tyropoeon Valley

South East Ridge

Kidron Valley

Gihon

Hinnom Valley

Topography (see map). Jerusalem, located on the Judaean watershed, on a series of hills or ridges intersected by deep valleys, has a complex terrain. The SE ridge (c 700m above sea level) is lower than the area of the medieval city but was chosen as the site of the first city because it was adjacent to a permanent water source, the spring Gihon, and to the fertile gardens in the Kidron Valley. This ridge was divided from the higher W hill (c 770m above sea level) by a once deep valley, the Central or Tyropoeon (Cheesemakers') Valley, which extended northwards up to the area of the modern Damascus Gate. The Temple was located on the high point (c 743m) of the E ridge, to the N of the most ancient city. Occupation only spread to the W hill in the 8C BC, and in Herodian and Roman times to the N area. The Church of the Holy Sepulchre is in this area of late settlement, and was outside the city in the time of Christ. Other lesser valleys are known to have existed, though now filled in by centuries of occupation debris. The city is bounded to the W and S by the Hinnom Valley. Strategically the least defensible approach was from the higher ground to the N.

HISTORY

Little is known of the earliest history of Jerusalem. Palaeolithic and Mesolithic finds have been made in the areas to the E, W and SW of the city but the first known town was located on the SE ridge above the spring of Gihon. This steep ridge, with narrow crest and uneven bedrock, contained natural caves in the limestone. The earliest remains discovered date to the Chalcolithic period and to Early Bronze Age I, perhaps also Early Bronze Age II (c 4000–2800 BC). The Chalcolithic remains are limited to potsherds and flints, including fragments of chalices and churns, mostly preserved in pockets of earth on bedrock on the slopes SW of the spring (Shiloh) and on the crest of the ridge above (Parker). In the latter area tomb groups of Early Bronze IA and IB were discovered by Parker (1909–11) in natural caves near the crest of the ridge and by Macalister (1923–24). Some stratified remains of the same date, and possibly Early Bronze II, including a typical broad roomed building with bench (Shiloh, Area E1), have been found on the slopes to the SW and to the W (Kenyon, Area A) of the spring and seem to belong to an unwalled settlement (Shiloh, 1984). Nothing of the later Early Bronze Age has as yet been discovered in the town area, but a cemetery of c 2000 BC has been excavated (Saad, 1961; Kenyon, 1965) on the higher S and E slopes of the Mount of Olives.

Middle and Late Bronze Ages. The first walled town seems to date to c 1800 BC (MBA I–II transition). Remains of a stone-built defence wall, 2m–3m in width, have been found mid-way down the W slope of the SE ridge (Kenyon, Area A, 1961–67; Shiloh, Area E, 1978–82). A few poor-quality house walls climbing the steep slopes have been found inside these walls, but the extent of the MBA town has not yet been traced. Unstratified MBA sherds have been found in places S of the Temple area, but one MBA I–II tomb, found in Macalister's 'Field 5' near the crest of the ridge, suggests that Macalister and Kenyon may have been right in suggesting that the northern limit of the town at this time lay not far N of the spring.

Little is known of the town's history in the succeeding two hundred years. Some fine MBA II pottery was found S of the spring (Shiloh) and on the Mount of Olives in 1868 (Warren) which almost certainly derives from tombs, and one late MBA II tomb is published (Saller, 1954, at Dominus Flevit) from the W slope of the Mount of Olives, which was clearly one of the major locations for Bronze Age and later burials in Jerusalem. The town seems to have undergone a major rebuilding in the 14C and 13C BC.

Literary sources for the second millennium are sparse. The earliest mention of Jerusalem is in a list of enemies of Egypt (Execration Texts, Luxor, Egypt, Sesostris III c 1850–1810 BC) and refers to *Urushalimmu*=Shalim has founded (Shalim=Canaanite deity manifest in the evening star, known from the Ras Shamra texts). Two rulers of Jerusalem are listed: *Yaqir-'ammu* and *Shayzanu*. Both names are of West Semitic/Amorite type. It has been suggested that the plurality of rulers listed for Jerusalem (and other places), and indications of tribal structure in the personal names, represent a relatively non-sedentary type of society which seems to coincide with the period just pre-dating the building of the first walled town. It is surmised that the occupants were West Semites, either Canaanites, or Amorites who dwelt in the hill country.

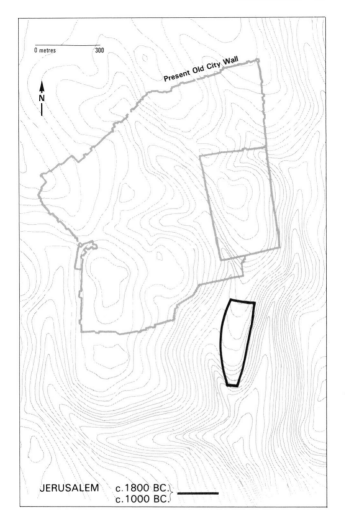

0 metres   300

N

Present Old City Wall

JERUSALEM   c.1800 BC.
             c.1000 BC.

The gap which follows in the literary and largely in the archaeological records exists till the 14C BC, when the town is mentioned in
the Amarna Letters (c 1350 BC, state archives of Akhenaten,
Amarna, Egypt) when the ruler of *Urushalimmu* was Abdi-Khipa
(worshipper of Khipa, a Hurrian goddess venerated especially in
Anatolia) whose name might suggest the man was of non-Semitic
ethnic origin. Six letters survive which were sent to the Egyptian
king by Abdi-Khipa. The letters depict him as a petty hereditary ruler
of a small state, confirmed in his office by the Egyptian king, to whom
he was vassal and paid tribute. Jerusalem supported an Egyptian
garrison of Kashi (Cushite, Sudanese) mercenaries of whose

behaviour he complained. Abdi-Khipa would have been subordinate to the Egyptian Resident or Governor in Gaza, at a time when Egyptian officials and messengers travelled between the towns of Canaan. His duties included enforcement of Egyptian policy and the furnishing of porters and escorts for Egyptian caravans. Nonetheless he engaged in disputes with his neighbouring rulers, and was at war with marauding bands of *'apiru*, unsettled peoples or refugees of uncertain origins, who were sometimes employed as mercenaries, and from among whom the Hebrews may in part have originated. He was allied with three other rulers of Canaanite towns in fighting these peoples, one of whom sent a contingent of fifty chariots; they appealed for more help from the Egyptian army. No rulers of Jerusalem are mentioned during the remaining 14C–13C BC under the strong rule of such Egyptian kings as Seti I and Ramses II, and Egyptian influence over Jerusalem may well have continued well into the 12C BC.

It is during this period, of some stability imposed by the Egyptians, and rather limited prosperity, that major rebuilding is indicated in Jerusalem. Preserved on the crest of the SE ridge, directly above the spring, are massive terraces of rubble-filled compartments which raised the surface of the slopes some 10m above bedrock in Area G (Shiloh) and 4.75m in adjacent Area A (Kenyon). Traces of the terracing were also found in Area P (Kenyon) just to the N, and just to the W in the area dug by Macalister, but very little elsewhere on the ridge. This massive terracing probably supported a strong and high citadel on the crest above the spring, as it added a flat area of c 200m^2 to the top of the hill. Because so little else has been found, it is not clear whether the MBA city wall was still in use surrounding a residential quarter or lower city to the S; neither is it certain when the first water system for the town was built. It seems likely that from the 18C to the 10C BC the town wall or citadel overlooked a defended gate and path to the spring below; but the presence of 14C–13C BC sherds in the silt in 'Warren's Shaft' (see Rte 10) and evidence for use of rock-cut water reservoirs in the LBA (at for example Hazor, but also in Jerusalem itself at the old Government House site and perhaps at Dominus Flevit), leaves open the possibility that a series of tunnels and shafts gave defended access to the water from within the walls as early as the 13C BC.

In addition to the mammoth terrace and fortress above the spring, the 14C–13C BC occupation of Jerusalem is attested by several excavated burial caves in the vicinity: at Dominus Flevit just to the E; in a large rock cut tomb with many imported vases, discovered in 1933 in the modern suburb of Nahalat Ahim (2km to the W), and in a cistern-like cave in the grounds of the old Government House (2km to the SSE).

The Old Testament adds considerable detail to our picture of Jerusalem, though sometimes of uncertain date and historical weight. The earliest reference, Gen. 14:18–19, is the least reliable source. It refers to Melchizedek, king of Salem (Shalim) who was 'priest of God Most High', and gave a blessing to Abraham; and then also to Adoni-zedek, King of Jerusalem (Jos. 10:1,3), who led a coalition of five Amorite kings against Gibeon and was defeated by Joshua and the invading Israelites perhaps in the late 13C or 12C (cf. Abdi-Khipa and his three allies against the *'apiru* in the 14C). The names of these kings of Jerusalem are again of 'Amorite' type but at a time when the inhabitants of Jerusalem are also described in the Old Testament as Jebusites (Jos. 15:63). Whether or not the Jebusites had links with the Hittites or Hurrians, they are closely allied with the peoples called Amorites and Canaanites.

Iron Age I. Although the Old Testament claims Israelite successes against the town and its Jebusite inhabitants in the time of the Israelite conquest, it is clear that the Jebusites remained entrenched in their citadel in Jerusalem until conquered by David early in the 10C BC. Various translations of II Sam. 5:8 suggest that entry was gained either by the drain or gutter, or by grappling irons, and according to I Chr. 11:6 Joab was the first to enter the citadel. This has given rise to the theory that the citadel was entered by way of 'Warren's Shaft'. David did not completely drive out the Jebusites,

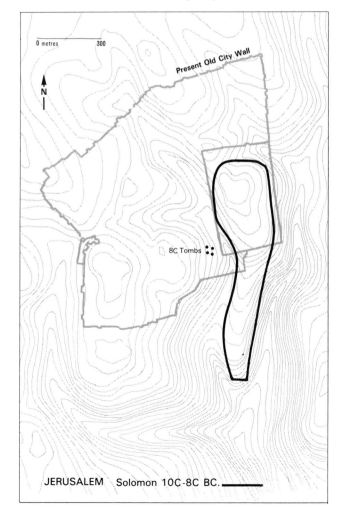

0 metres   300

Present Old City Wall

N

8C Tombs

JERUSALEM Solomon 10C-8C BC.

who continued to live alongside the Israelites at Jerusalem (Jos. 15:63; Judges 1:21) but he made it his capital.

Very few remains of the 12C–11C BC have been uncovered so far on the SE ridge of Jerusalem. Such remains are found sparsely in Sites A and P (Kenyon) and Sites E1 and D1 (Shiloh). The latter finds indicate the lower town as well as the citadel was occupied at the time.

A fragment of a bronze statuette (Shiloh, Area G) of a type usually associated with Canaanite deities, and remains which may be those of a Canaanite style cult area (Shiloh, Area E) were discovered in the succeeding Davidic/Solomonic level at Jerusalem. It reinforces the hypothesis that Jerusalem was a focus of Canaanite cult (of deities in addition to Shalim, as the element SDQ=zedek or Zadok might indicate). The Old Testament compilers may well have assimilated earlier Jebusite traditions after the capture of the town by David. Melchizedek, Adoni-zedek and the line of High Priests beginning with Zadok under David, suggest a cultic link or an historical gloss in the stories of Abraham's relations with the ancient Jebusite king and priest of Shalim, though in later texts Zadok is listed in the Hebrew genealogy of the priest Aaron. David purchased a threshing floor from Arauneh the Jebusite (the name may imply a Jebusite ruler or baron) on which Solomon built the Temple, and the site was linked with Mount Moriah, where the patriarch Abraham had offered the sacrifice of his son Isaac. A thousand years later Josephus wrote (War VI:438) 'But he who first built (Jerusalem) was a potent man among the Canaanites, and is in our tongue called (Melchizedek) the Righteous King for such he really was; on which account he was the first priest of God, and first built a temple and called the city Jerusalem'.

Iron Age II. The establishment of the town as the religious and political capital of the new united kingdom of Israel ushers Jerusalem into the full light of history. The choice of a site midway between the northern and southern Israelite tribal territories, neutral but accessible, and on the most strategic N–S route through the hill country, was politically astute despite the relative poverty of the agricultural and economic resources of Jerusalem's territory. At all times, Jerusalem's economic importance increased only when it had a significant political or religious role. Undoubtedly much of the old Canaanite town, population and customs survived, and this influence is seen in many aspects of the life of the city in the succeeding centuries.

David occupied the stronghold of Jerusalem and built the city, starting at the Millo and working inwards (II Sam. 5:9–12). Hiram, King of Tyre, sent cedar logs, carpenters and stonemasons to build David's palace: a sizeable building to accommodate his harem, large court and a picked guard of thirty. David brought the Ark of the Covenant to Jerusalem from Kirjath-jearim, housed it in a tented shrine and appointed Abiathar of the Shiloh priesthood and Zadok to be the high priests. Jerusalem became the central and only legitimate focus of cult and thus played an immensely important role in unifying the Israelite tribes. All this activity was undoubtedly funded by David's tremendous military ability. During his reign he built an empire covering most of Palestine except for a small Philistine state on the coast. He held all the kingdoms of Transjordan, and for a short time most of south and central Syria as far as the Euphrates river to the NE, and the boundary with Tyre to the NW; from this empire he must have drawn considerable tribute. The Davidic town at Jerusalem probably covered about 4.5 hectares (11 acres).

His successor, Solomon, was annointed king by the High Priest Zadok at the spring Gihon. Much of the territory gained by David was lost during Solomon's reign, but his wisdom, administrative capacity and building work are famous. In Jerusalem he built lavishly: the Temple, his palace, the House of the Forest of Lebanon, his Judgement Hall, a palace for the daughter of the Egyptian Pharaoh who was one of his wives, again Millo and the wall of Jerusalem (I Kings 9). He maintained the alliance with the King of Tyre, and also had Phoenician craftsmen to aid in his construction works. The lavish and expensive decoration of his buildings is carefully described. He consolidated the Temple as the one legitimate shrine, as the eternal dwelling of the God of Israel, and the focus of Israel's faith and covenant with God for all time. The temple and the palace alone took twenty years to build, but virtually nothing of any of his work is known to have survived.

The archaeological evidence indicates that the Jebusite terraces were repaired and rebuilt with a massive stepped revetment (Kenyon and Shiloh). To the N (Kenyon, Site H) parts of a casemate wall were found and perhaps mark the Solomonic extension of the city along the ridge to the N. It is assumed that Solomon's new buildings were located in an area called the Ophel, between the old Jebusite fortress and the new Temple on the high point of the E ridge to the N of the town. This increased the size of the town to c 12.8 hectares (c 32 acres). To the S there are some traces of occupation in the lower city, and to this period are usually attributed the first of the defensive water systems, 'Warren's Shaft' (Shiloh), and also a canal/tunnel system down the W side of the Kidron Valley, constructed to irrigate the garden plots and store water in reservoirs and pools below the S end of the ridge.

With the death of Solomon c 928 BC, the defection of the northern tribes and thus the loss of all the rich lands and tax of the northern territory, Jerusalem was reduced in economic status, in political status (the capital of the southern kingdom of Judah only), and in religious status (the establishment of rival cult centres in the north). Jerusalem survived in this role until 586 BC but took a relatively minor place in history. A list of rulers is given in the Books of the Kings, and their relations with neighbouring states are described. Uzziah, Hezekiah and Manasseh are all credited with improving the fortifications of Jerusalem during this period.

8C–6C BC Jerusalem is however rather better preserved than the earlier towns. Two major events affected its growth and shape. The city expanded considerably in the 8C BC, probably after an influx of refugees following the destruction of the northern kingdom of Israel by Sargon II in 722/1 BC. In face of the renewed threat from Assyria and the invasion of Judah by Sennacherib in 701 BC, Hezekiah took drastic steps to refortify the city.

On the SE ridge, on or near the old Middle Bronze Age wall line, a new E fortification wall was built mid-way down the slope. A number of large 7C BC houses are preserved, cut into the older terraces above. The ruins include stepped alleys, drainage channels and lavatories. Hezekiah also built a new water system ('Hezekiah's Tunnel'), which took the water of the Gihon Spring underground beneath the E ridge to a reservoir in the central valley; and there may well have been additional reservoirs in the lower Tyropoeon Valley.

On the W hill, a population explosion in the 8C BC led to the first

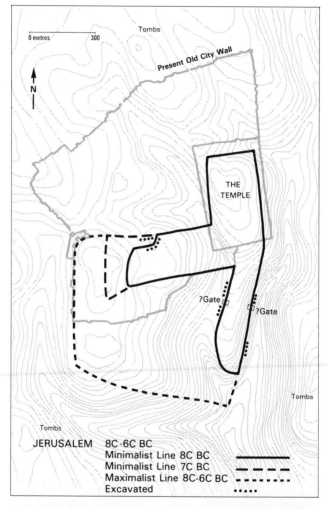

settlement of this area, at first unwalled, and then massively fortified,
probably by Hezekiah. Parts of this wall have been found in the
Jewish Quarter of the Old City (see Rte 7). Most of its precise line is
not determined: some archaeologists hold the view that the whole of
the Western Hill and the Tyropoeon Valley were included within the
walls which enclosed the Misneh (or Second Quarter) and the
Makhtesh (or Commercial Quarter), thus enclosing the reservoirs at
the lower end of Hezekiah's Tunnel (Avigad and Shiloh). Others
believe that this fortification covered only part of the Western Hill
(Tushingham), and the Tyropoeon valley was still not occupied
except by a hidden subterranean reservoir and overflow channel or
tunnel (Kenyon). Although strategically the former explanation

would make better sense (if there was manpower to defend such an extended line of wall), no finds of this date have yet been made within the Tyropoeon valley; and extensive and presumably extra-mural quarrying is found around the N and W of the area. The Kenyon view could fit Isaiah's description of Hezekiah's actions: 'between the two walls you made a cistern for the waters of the Old Pool' (Isaiah 22:8–11). The maximalist view would vastly increase the size of Jerusalem (c 60 hectares or 150 acres) during the 8C BC (Avigad). A later phase of defensive walls of this period was found in the same area of the Jewish Quarter, perhaps built by Manasseh or just before the Babylonian destruction. It is probable that Kenyon's quarry with its 7C BC fill (Site C, outside the 8C BC walls to the N in Christian Quarter) results from this construction work.

A number of tombs (c 8C BC) have been found in the upper area of the Tyropoeon valley, near the SW corner of the Haram, which must pre-date the enclosure of the area; there are also tombs along the E side of the Kidron valley, especially among the houses of the modern village of Silwan, on the W side of the Hinnom Valley and to the N of the Old City. The increasing size of the city is indicated by the ring of burials around it. The fall of the Assyrian Empire in 612 BC was followed by a struggle for supremacy between Egypt and Babylonia, with Judah supporting the Egyptians. The Babylonian success was marked by the surrender of Jerusalem in 597 BC and the deportation of king Jehoiachin, the queen mother and leading citizens, and the exaction of a great plunder. Nine years later the Babylonian army came again and in January 588 BC Jerusalem came under siege. The city held out for nearly 18 months: in July 587 BC the Babylonians breached the walls, the ruler Zedekiah fled, was captured, had his sons executed in front of him before he was blinded and taken to Babylon in chains, where he died. Other officials were executed, and further deportations were made. Shortly after the fall of the city the walls were levelled and the city burnt.

The temple built by Solomon was destroyed by the Babylonians and the rest of its treasures taken. Much of what had originally been placed there by Solomon must have been seriously depleted prior to this event, given the looting by the Egyptian king Shishak c 923 BC, the high tribute exacted in the time of Ahaz in the later 8C BC, and again in 597 BC.

Post-Exilic and Persian Periods. Only a remnant of the population of Jerusalem survived in the ruined city amid a foreign population of deportees brought from other parts of the Babylonian Empire. The leading citizens remained in Babylon after the fall of the Babylonian Empire in 539 BC. Recovery of the city began with the edict of Cyrus in 538 BC when the Persian ruler permitted Sheshbazzar, as ruler of Judah, and Zerubbabel son of Shealtiel, to return to Jerusalem to rebuild the Jewish Temple on the same site as previously (c 537–515 BC). It is possible that part of the present E wall of the temple platform, in a Persian style of masonry, marks this rebuild (Kenyon), though others think it is Seleucid (Tsafrir) or Herodian (Avi-Yonah) and part even Solomonic (Warren and Wilson, Laperrousaz). Poverty and schism amongst the small Jewish population and pressures from the 'foreign' population meant a slow revival as part of the Persian province of Yehud, but there was an improvement in the time of Ezra, the priest and scribe, with the return of more exiles (457–428 BC). Under Nehemiah, governor of Yehud c 445 BC, the city walls were rebuilt. These were restricted to a very small area on the crest of the SE ridge and the temple area. Nehemiah describes the rubble still littering the surface following the Babylonian destruction of 142 years previously, and the co-operative effort lasting 52 days by which the new walls were constructed. Parts of this wall survive at the top of the SE ridge. The W hill was not re-occupied from 587 till the 2C BC (Avigad).

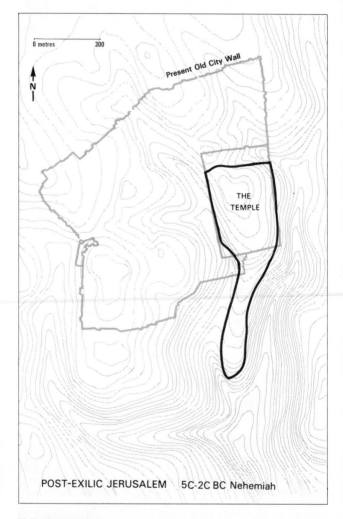

POST-EXILIC JERUSALEM   5C-2C BC Nehemiah

Hellenistic Period

Early Hellenistic period. Jerusalem became part of the Hellenistic world following Alexander the Great's conquest in 332 BC. After Alexander's death, the city was first the possession of the Ptolemies from c 301 BC and then from 198 BC of the Seleucids under

Antiochus III. His successor Antiochus IV Epiphanes made a severe and antagonising effort to Hellenise the Jews, which included the renaming of the city Antiochia, the desecration of the temple by building an altar to Zeus and sacrificing a pig on it—the event referred to as 'the abomination of desolation'. The Seleucids also built a fort in 168 BC, called the Akra, to control the temple area. It is not certain whether this fort overlooked the Temple area from the S or from the W.

Late Hellenistic period. Extreme intolerance on both sides led to the Revolt of the Maccabees in 167 BC led by the Hasmonean family of Mattathias and his five sons. One of these, Judas Maccabee, recaptured Jerusalem from the Seleucids in 164 BC (commemorated at Hannukah, the Jewish Festival of Lights) although the Akra remained in Seleucid hands till 141 BC. The Hasmonean rulers, with the status of High Priests, followed this up with a number of military successes. Their territory extended from the Upper Jordan valley to Beersheba, and included much of Transjordan, especially under Alexander Janneus (103–76 BC). However the state suffered from bitter religious dissension between the Pharisees and the more conservative Sadducee sect (Sadducee from Zadok, David's High Priest).

Remains of Hasmonean Jerusalem (c 164–63 BC) reflect the expansion of the kingdom. On the E side of the city there was little growth, with Nehemiah's wall on the crest of the ridge continuing in use with the addition above Gihon of towers and an earth and gravel glacis to consolidate the steep slopes below (Shiloh). There are traces of lesser walls and terraces on the slopes just to the S, and probably reservoir pools at the S end of the Tyropoeon Valley. The growth of the city is again shown by the reoccupation of the W hill, though most of the house remains have been destroyed in subsequent building operations and it is usually only the cisterns and baths cut into the bedrock that survive. The wall described by Josephus as the First North Wall of Jerusalem was built during this period, probably towards the end of the 2C BC and along the same line as the broad wall of the 8C BC. The whole W hill seems to have been fortified (Tushingham claims that the citadel/Armenian garden on the extreme W was not yet enclosed) and there is still some dispute as to whether the whole Tyropoeon valley was enclosed (Avigad and Shiloh) or whether the wall skirted its upper W slopes (Kenyon). It is possible that it extended to enclose the lower Tyropoeon area and its pools, but if so, much of the space within the walls cannot have been built up, as nothing pre-dating the 1C AD has yet been found in the lower W slopes of the Tyropoeon.

During the 1C BC the main occupation began to shift to the Upper City on the W hill, away from the Lower City on the SE ridge. The site of the Hasmonean Palace mentioned by Josephus has not been identified, nor has the site of the 'Syrian Akra' on which the palace may have been built. The tower called Baris was built by the Hasmoneans in the early 2C BC at the NW corner of the Temple enclosure and provided with water from an extra-mural rock cut pool called the Struthion Pool. The Great Pools (Bethesda) to the N of the temple are attributed to the Seleucid period, said to have been constructed by the High Priest Simon c 200 BC (Sir. 50:3). Other large open cisterns may also have originated at this time, but the archaeological evidence is still lacking. Impressive tomb monuments began to be constructed beyond the walls, including the Tomb of the Bene Hezir in the Kidron Valley and the Tomb of Jason on the W. Avigad suggests that the Hasmonean city was laid out according to a Hippodamian plan, but there is little certainty about this.

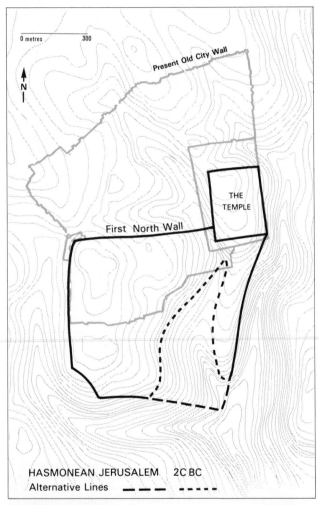

HASMONEAN JERUSALEM   2C BC
Alternative Lines

The Roman Period. As civil war grew more bitter, Hyrcanus II, prompted by Antipater of Idumea (who was married to a Nabataean), called the Nabataean king Aretas III to his aid. As the conflict spread, Rome seized the opportunity to intervene. In 64 BC Pompey had annexed the Seleucid Empire. In 63 BC he besieged and took Jerusalem, and entered but did not destroy the Temple. He broke up the Hasmonean kingdom into a series of petty states, confirmed the Hasmonean Hyrcanus II as High Priest in Jerusalem, but entrusted the administration of the kingdom to Antipater of Idumea. Pompey thus ushered in the Roman period of Jerusalem's history, an era of more intense Hellenisation, which saw the rise of the Idumean family of Antipater (Idumeans were Edomites who moved westwards into Judah following the depopulation by the Babylonians). Antipater, under Roman favour, became the client ruler of most of the former Hasmonean territory. He made his elder son, Phasael, governor of Jerusalem, and his younger son, Herod, governor of Galilee. After Antipater's murder in 43 BC the two sons became rulers of Judaea. Surviving various revolts by his Jewish citizens, who disliked both his foreign origins and his extermination of the Hasmonean dynasty, Herod became sole ruler by 37 BC.

As Herod the Great (37–4 BC) he built on a flamboyant scale. In Jerusalem he built the great temple platform, a large part of which still survives; he rebuilt Zerubbabel's temple on a grand scale: almost nothing remains, but it was undoubtedly on the same site as its predecessor; he built a magnificent palace, full of trees, canals and frescoes, on the Western Hill, with three massive towers to fortify its N end: much of one of these towers survives, though little except foundations and fragments of his palace have been found; he fortified a new suburb in the N part of the city (enclosed by the Second North Wall of Josephus, which ran from the Gate Gennath to the Antonia).

He built, and named for his friend Mark Anthony, the Antonia, a strong fortress on the site of the Hasmonean tower Baris. It stood on the rock at the NW corner of the Temple enclosure and also utilised the water of the adjacent Struthion Pool. He also added to the city's amenities such Hellenistic amusements as a theatre and a hippodrome, the sites of which are lost, though Josephus says the hippodrome was to the S of the temple area.

Undoubtedly there was a considerable increase in the population, with a new suburb and so much building work, and considerable additions to the city's water supply were necessary. The spring Gihon would long have been inadequate to the city's needs. From the 14C BC rock-cut cisterns for collecting rainwater became important priorities in urban complexes. Jerusalem's water system had been extended before the time of Herod by a series of aqueducts and pools to which Herod added. The Lower Pool in the Tyropoeon probably existed in Israelite times, and the Upper Tyropoeon Pool (Siloam) was probably constructed by Hezekiah. The northern of the two pools of Bethesda may have been cut in Israelite times and served the temple area by conduit (White Fathers at St. Anne's). The various other large open pools in the Old City and the aqueducts which supplied them were probably in use or date in large part to Herod's time, and if so were apparently mostly outside the walls. The evidence suggests that the Tyropoeon Pools, the Struthion, Bethesda and Israel pools were in use in Herod's time, and probably the Pool of the Patriarch's Bath also. Herod is credited with building the Pool of Israel immediately to the N of the temple enclosure, which then supplied his vast new temple area. The Mamilla Pool, in the same system as the Pool of the Patriarch's Bath, certainly existed by the early 7C AD and may be earlier, and the same applies to the Sultan's Pool in the Hinnom valley, which certainly existed in the 12C but which fits readily into systems of the time of Herod or the 1C AD.

Some impressive tombs of this period and the following century ring the city, including the 'Tomb of Absalom' in the Kidron Valley, and the 'Tombs of the Sanhedrin', and the Tomb of Helena of Adiabene on the N side. Private architecture also flourished. The ruins of fine villas have been found on the W hill, with frescoes,

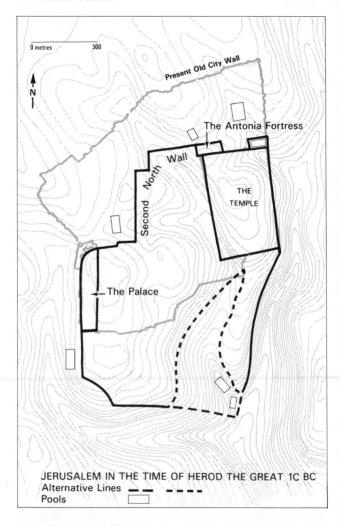

JERUSALEM IN THE TIME OF HEROD THE GREAT 1C BC
Alternative Lines
Pools

stucco and mosaic decoration. Some think Herod laid out the city at this time according to a new grid plan of Hellenistic or Hippodamian type, aligned in the W on his palace, and on the E on his new temple enclosure (Wilkinson). Others see little evidence for it among the villas on the W hill (Avigad). The plan of the city was therefore much as in Hasmonean times, but with extensive extra-mural additions like pools and theatres; there are some uncertainties about the line of the S wall, and the new walled northern suburb, which some think went as far as the area of the present Damascus Gate.

This was the plan of Jerusalem in the time of Christ, whose life span (perhaps 4 BC–AD 29/30) probably fell almost within the reign of Herod's successor, Herod Antipas (4 BC–AD 39). Herod's temple was still brand new (indeed not quite finished) and stood in an enlarged and beautified city.

The weakness of the successors of Herod the Great led to the installation of a series of Roman governors, first Prefects, then Procurators, from AD 6 onwards, of whom Pontius Pilate (AD 26–36) was one. During the reign of the most capable of the later Herods, Herod Agrippa I, more building work was carried out. He is credited with the construction of the Third North Wall by Josephus, who also says he did not complete it for fear of the Romans. To him is credited by some the Triple Gate flanked by towers on the site of the present Damascus Gate (see Rte 1), of which the E pedestrian entrance is still almost complete. The Ecce Homo arch is also attributed to him (Blomme) as a city gate rather than a triumphal or monumental arch. According to Josephus the Third North Wall of the city enclosed a new quarter in the N, Bezetha, or the New City. A new paved street on the W hill leading towards the SW corner of the temple platform, and a paved street, drain, houses and shops down the Tyropoeon valley are dated to the 1C AD (Avigad and Kenyon). Kenyon suggested that this was the first period at which the S wall of the city enclosed the whole of the Tyropoeon valley. If Herod Agrippa's wall enclosed the modern Christian Quarter of the Old City, as well as Bezetha and the Tyropoeon, all the major pools except that in the central Hinnom could have been within the walls at this time. On the other hand, Kenyon's excavations in the Muristan (Site C) do not show any evidence of building before the 2C AD, so she may be right in excluding the NW quarter of the Old City from the enclosed area in Herod Agrippa's time, and suggesting that the line of the city wall ran southwards directly E from the Damascus Gate.

With Roman rule growing more severe, and sectarian resentment increasing, with fears especially among the Pharisee and Zealot sects of further acts of desecration in the Temple, events led to the First Jewish Revolt AD 66–73, in the reign of Agrippa II and the Pro-curatorship of Gessius Florus (AD 64–66). By August 66 Jerusalem was in the hands of the Jews, a government had been set up and silver coinage of the Revolt was being minted. At this time many Judaean Christians moved away from the Zealots in Jerusalem, to Pella down in the Jordan Valley. According to Josephus, during the Revolt the Antonia, much of the Upper City and Herod's Palace were burnt by the Jewish insurgents. In the first attempt to quell the revolt Cestius Gallus pitched camp on Mount Scopus in November 66, set fire to the suburb of Bezetha and very nearly took the Temple from the N before making a disastrous retreat (War II:528–55). By AD 67 the Romans were moving to counter-attack, and had regained Galilee. In AD 68 Vespasian reached Jerusalem. The final assault was organised by his son Titus, who built a siege wall around the city. A detailed account is given by Josephus of the hideous sectarian strife among the Jews within the walls, of the famine and of the preparations for the assault by the Romans. Titus destroyed Jerusalem in AD 70, including the complete demolition of the Herodian Temple. The signs of destruction in the villas on the western hill (the Burnt House, see Rte 7), and in the houses, shops and street in the Tyropoeon valley are immense; great slabs of masonry were overthrown, the valley was clogged metres deep in ash, rubble and human bones, all giving realism to Josephus' description of the horror of the event. Though the Romans were shocked by the numbers who had died of famine during the siege,

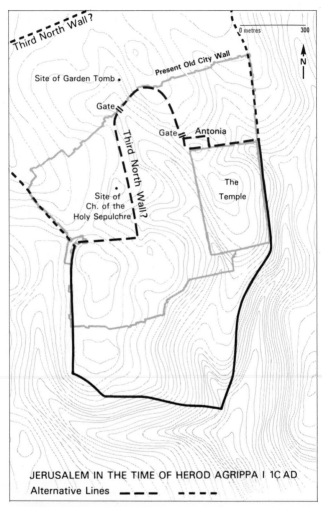

JERUSALEM IN THE TIME OF HEROD AGRIPPA I 1C AD

Alternative Lines

yet they showed no mercy to the living, whom they pursued and slew till the lanes of the city ran with blood.

By Roman decree all inhabitants of Jerusalem were taken captive and the city was levelled. The SE ridge, ancient Jerusalem, never regained its importance. Herod's temple and porticoes were thrown down, massive rubble littered the surface of the platform and the ground below. The temple area lay in ruins or as open space until the Islamic conquest in 638. The 10th Roman Legion (Fretensis) was stationed in Jerusalem, and its camp lay on the W hill in the former area of Herod's palace. Very little trace of this camp survives, except for roof tiles, bricks and a few inscriptions.

A Jewish remnant again remained in or returned to Jerusalem despite the Roman decree that Jews should no longer live there; and these and the Jewish inhabitants of Judaea mounted the Second Jewish Revolt (131/2–35). The cause of this second revolt was in part the Roman plan to set up a colonia (a strategically placed Roman colony populated partly by Roman veterans) on the site of Jerusalem. The rebels forced the retreat of the 10th Legion from Jerusalem which again became the Jewish capital for a short period. In Year 4 of the revolt (in the summer of 135) the rebels were again forced out of Jerusalem by Hadrian and Septimius Severus.

Hadrian then continued with his plans for the founding of the Colonia Aelia Capitolina. The Roman work is marked by extensive levelling of the landscape in the NW quarter and an almost completely new layout of the city, on which the present plan of the Old City is based. Jews were forbidden to dwell in Aelia, which was a

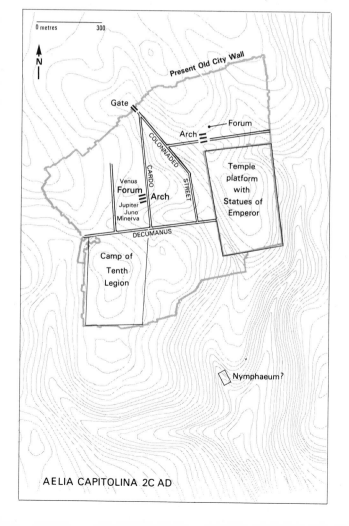

0 metres 300

N

Present Old City Wall

Gate

Forum

Arch

COLONNADED STREET

CARDO

Venus
Forum

Arch

Jupiter
Juno
Minerva

Temple
platform
with
Statues of
Emperor

DECUMANUS

Camp of
Tenth
Legion

Nymphaeum?

AELIA CAPITOLINA 2C AD

relatively insignificant place, as the capital of the Roman province of Judaea was at Caesarea on the coast. The layout of the city walls is uncertain. There may have been none, apart from the defences of the Legionary camp. The Roman gates at the Damascus Gate and at Ecce Homo were in use, perhaps as triumphal arches like that at the new forum.

The layout of the town itself is clear. It was typically Roman, with a cardo maximus running S from the present Damascus Gate, on the line of the present Suq Khan al-Zait; and a decumanus running E from the modern Jaffa Gate on the line of David St and the Street of the Chain. A column in honour of Hadrian and Antoninus Pius stood just inside the N gate ornamenting the open area at the top of the cardo and the columned street running SE along the line of the modern Tariq al-Wad. This column was still in existence in Byzantine times and is the origin of the modern Arabic name of the Damascus Gate (Bab al-Amud, the Gate of the Column). In the NW quarter, most of which was now included within the city, the Tripartite temple of Jupiter Capitolinus, Juno and Minerva, the temple of Venus and the forum with Triumphal Arch were laid out as part of the monumental scheme connected with the cardo; another parallel paved road has been found to the W under Christian Quarter St. In the NE section, as well as a columned street on the line of the Tariq al-Wad, the Triumphal Arch which may have been built as a city gate by Herod Agrippa I (see Ecce Homo, Rte 3) now stood on a magnificent pavement (the Lithostratos) which covered over the old Hasmonean and Herodian Struthion Pool. The camp of the 10th Legion and a secondary barracks area were still sited in the SW quarter, of which little remains. The Legion was eventually posted S to Elath at the end of the 3C. The cardo, at least in monumental form, does not seem to have extended S of the line of the decumanus at this time. A Byzantine source, the 'Chronicon Pascale', says Hadrian built two public baths, a theatre, the *Trikameron* (the Temple of Jupiter, Juno and Minerva), the *Tetranymphon* (at Siloam?), the *Dodekapylon* (the colonnade formerly known as the *Anabathmoi*, the Steps) and the *Kodra* (the square podium of the Temple Mount?). The Roman period lasted until 324.

The Byzantine Period. Judaean Christians in the early years were a part of the Jewish community participating in synagogal worship. In the first generation the disciples met in a house at the S end of the Western Hill, and the site of the tomb of Christ was venerated by the community. Gentile conversion began at an early date. Differences in the beliefs of Jews and Jewish Christians increased during the First Revolt, when, not sharing in the Jewish messianic and political aspirations, many Christians moved away from the areas of Zealot fanaticism. According to Eusebius, who admits that it was a partly oral tradition, of which he could find no written chronology, there were 15 bishops in Jerusalem before the Second Jewish Revolt, all of whom were short-lived, of Jewish descent and circumcised. The first was James, the brother of the Lord. Not until after the Second Revolt, when Jews were no longer permitted to live within the city of Aelia were the first gentile bishops consecrated there (Marcus). The split widened during the Second Revolt and the centre of Palestinian Christianity became Caesarea, where a famous school and community built up around the writings and teachings of such men as Origen, Pamphilius and Eusebius. Many Christians suffered in periods of Roman persecution and a considerable list of martyrs is commemorated. Alexander Flavian came to Jerusalem from Cappadocia as a pilgrim and was persuaded to remain as bishop, c 212–51, dying in prison a martyr in the persecution under the Emperor Decius.

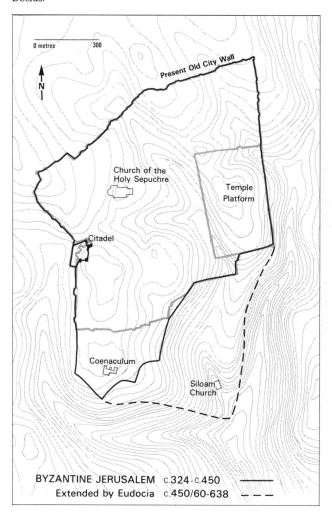

0 metres   300

N

Present Old City Wall

Church of the
Holy Sepuchre

Temple
Platform

Citadel

Coenaculum

Siloam
Church

BYZANTINE JERUSALEM c.324-c.450
Extended by Eudocia c.450/60-638

In 313 the Imperial Edict of Milan made Christianity a legitimate religion within the Empire, and even more relevant to Jerusalem, in 324 the Emperor Constantine brought Palestine within the Christian Eastern Roman Empire. In the same year Makarios, Bishop of Jerusalem, got permission at the Council of Nicaea to remove the Roman Temple of Venus from the site which tradition then strongly maintained was that of the Holy Sepulchre. The Tomb of Christ, with other tombs of 1C AD date, was discovered, and Eusebius describes its location beneath the Roman temple.

In 326 Helena, mother of the Emperor Constantine, visited the Holy Land and according to a later tradition, found the True Cross in a cave or cistern adjacent to the tomb. Constantine had the Church of the Holy Sepulchre built over the sites of the Rock of the Crucifixion, of the location of the True Cross and of the Tomb. His church was dedicated in 335. Helena was responsible for many buildings erected on sites venerated for their traditional association with Christ's ministry. The Bordeaux Pilgrim left an account of many of the holy sites he visited in 333, and his description of leaving Jerusalem to climb Mount Zion implies that the Tyropoeon Valley was not then enclosed. Jerusalem became the centre of the Christian world and at the Council of Ephesus in 431 the city was raised to the status of a Patriarchate of the Orthodox church.

From 438 Eudocia, wife of the Emperor Theodosius II, was responsible for many more buildings, including an Episcopal palace on the NW side of the precinct of the Church of the Holy Sepulchre. She also rebuilt the walls of Jerusalem to enclose the Tyropoeon valley and built new churches on the site of Pentecost (Visitation of the Holy Spirit at Pentecost), on the site of the House of Caiaphas, and also a church dedicated to the Virgin at the Pool of Siloam. A martyr's shrine was also built outside the N gate of the city (the Damascus Gate) on the site of the later basilica of St. Stephen. At this time it is clear that Jews were again permitted to live in the city (Avigad) and some had made pilgrimage to the site of the Temple since the period following Hadrian's death in 138. Precisely when a Jewish community re-established itself in Jerusalem is not known.

Jerusalem reached its peak of development in the Byzantine period under the Emperor Justinian (527–65). The Madaba mosaic map of the mid-6C shows this stage of the city's development. Justinian built the great Nea church, and the southern continuation of the monumental Roman Cardo Maximus to lead up to the church and to the Nea Gate (Avigad). The Madaba map shows many of the existing buildings, but is broken at its SE edge and does not extend as far as Eudocia's Church at the Pool of Siloam, though it does show some buildings on the Haram platform, including the Golden Gate at the E side of the Temple Platform (Avigad). It shows the great Church of Mount Zion, called 'the mother of all churches' on the SW hill, with the nearby Church of St. Peter on the House of Caiaphas. Two colonnaded streets run S from the column inside the N gate. The façade of the Church of the Holy Sepulchre opened onto the cardo; St. Anne's church lay in the NE with porticoes around the Pools of Bethesda. Outside the wall to the E was the Church of St. Mary in the Valley of Jehoshaphat. Theodosius the pilgrim counted 24 churches on the Mount of Olives at this time.

The eastern Orthodox church at this time was divided on many issues and the great church councils were busy discussing and condemning heresies in many forms. The split between eastern and western Christianity was a contributory weakness in the Byzantine defence against first the Sassanians and then the Arabs, in addition to the friction between the Jews and Christians within Palestine itself. Within Palestine, the Samaritan Revolt of 529 had created further tensions.

The Sassanian Empire was pushing W and S in the second half of the 6C. In 613 the Sassanian army reached Damascus, and the Samaritans and Jews co-operated with the Persian invasion of

Palestine in the following years. In 614 Jerusalem fell, despite the efforts of the Patriarch Zacharias to negotiate a surrender. The ensuing massacre and destruction was horrendous, and it is said that 33,000 died. The Christian monuments were devastated and tradition locates the slaughter of Christian prisoners by the Jews and Persians at the Mamilla Pool. The Sassanian ruler, Khosroes II, in due course permitted some reconstruction of Christian monuments, which was undertaken by Modestus of the Monastery of St. Theodosius (see Rte 17).

The Emperor Heraclius (610–41) negotiated a peace, obtained the restoration of the venerated fragments of the True Cross found by Helena, which had been seized by the Persians, and duly celebrated their return with a solemn procession which entered the city by the Golden Gate, led across the Temple Platform and ended at the Church of the Holy Sepulchre on 21 March 631.

However the city was a shadow of its former self: hardly any Christian monument surviving this devastation fails to show the cracks and scars of destruction; Byzantines and Persians alike were exhausted; the various factions were still antagonistic and willing to welcome new rulers to the scene. The whole area of Palestine fell to the Arab advance, despite last desperate battles by the Christians. Jerusalem itself surrendered in 638.

Many remains of the Byzantine city have been found, but they are remarkably poor compared with the monuments that once existed. The Church of the Holy Sepulchre forms an excellent example in that parts of the once glorious Constantinian structure do still exist as battered and burnt remnants incorporated in the fabric of not just the present church, but in neighbouring buildings also. Many other existing churches incorporate such ruined fragments. The houses were mostly not so well built or monumental, and were destroyed or reduced to fragments which are often poorly recorded when found. Such fragments of houses have been found in many places, including the Jewish Quarter, and especially in the upper Tyropoeon Valley, and S of the Temple area; fragments of a bath house exist in the Jewish Quarter. It is difficult to put together the fragments so widely distributed and found in both archaeological and building work but the evidence suggests that:

1. The earliest Byzantine Jerusalem had its walls and street plan on the lines of the Roman Aelia, and contained the Church of the Holy Sepulchre and many other churches, including the 'Mother of all churches' and the Coenaculum on Mount Zion, the sites of which were enclosed some time before 333.

2. Eudocia built the episcopal palace, the churches of Pentecost, and Caiaphas, and of the Virgin at the Siloam Pool c 450–60. She also extended the city wall to enclose Siloam and the S end of the Tyropoeon valley. The wall followed the line of the earlier walls up the E side of the SE ridge.

3. Justinian's town lay within the lines of Eudocia's walls, but included a grand layout, with the extension of the cardo in monumental form S to the Nea Church and Gate. The paved streets and stepped roads excavated on the SE slopes of the Western Hill probably belong to the time of Justinian.

The Early Islamic Period. The Prophet Muhammad died in 632, his teachings accepted through most of Arabia. The sanctity of Jerusalem was subsequently ensured by the traditional identification of the 'furthest place of prayer' of the Koran with the Aqsa mosque in

Jerusalem. His successors, the 'orthodox' caliphs, four elected leaders all related by marriage to the Prophet, carried on the spread of Islam. Under brilliant military leadership, the Arab armies, usually in extended Bedouin-like raids, sometimes in set battles, cut with incredible speed through the divided and weakened Byzantine and Sassanian empires. Persia, Iraq, Syria, Palestine and Egypt fell to them in the first twenty years after his death, with Jerusalem itself surrendering to the second caliph, 'Umar in 638. Under the terms of this surrender the Christians retained their sanctuaries; Jews and Christians became subject to a poll-tax and to an Arab administration broadly based on the previous Byzantine one.

Madaba Map mid-6C

The Muslim population of Jerusalem immediately following the conquest was small. There were some settlers from Medina and the Yemen. Jerusalem was called Iliya (Aelia). The prominent temple area was still largely empty, for very few Byzantine structures seem to have been built on the ruins of the 1C AD Roman destruction and this prominent but empty area was the obvious place for the new rulers to occupy, given their rigorous observance of the treaty to respect the Christian sanctuaries (which were mainly in the NW quarter of the city). 'Umar is said to have built his mosque at the site of the Holy Rock, but the first Arab structure to be described (by the Christian pilgrim Arculf c 680), was a congregational mosque built at the S end of the Temple Platform and oriented towards the S, which could hold 3000 people. The main Arab occupation seems to have been in the area of destroyed Byzantine houses and perhaps hospices immediately to the S of the Temple area, where the greatest quantity of distinctively Umayyad remains known from Jerusalem have been uncovered. The Christian population continued to live in the area of the Church of the Holy Sepulchre, and remains of this period have been discovered nearby.

The Umayyad Dynasty. 'Abd-al-Malik (685–705) built the first major Islamic structure in Jerusalem, the shrine or place of pilgrimage called the Dome of the Rock (691–92) on the Rock which was then remembered to be the site of the Solomonic temple. Though much restored and repaired, the present building retains the essence of the original mosaic-encrusted building put up in the same Byzantine martyrium tradition as the nearby Church of the Holy Sepulchre, and the Chapel of the Ascension on the Mount of Olives, but with 7C innovations including mathematically harmonious proportions, and distinctively fresh decoration.

By this time the Muslim population was increasing, and c 710

Walid I (or just possibly his predecessor 'Abd-al-Malik) rebuilt the congregational Aqsa Mosque on a grand scale. Its principal approach was by the old Herodian stepped tunnels from the S. Very little of the Umayyad period survives in Jerusalem, except for the Domes of the Rock and of the Chain, the rebuilt Aqsa Mosque and the recently excavated Umayyad palaces to the S. The latter seem to have been destroyed in the very severe earthquake of 747/8, and not rebuilt but succeeded by rather poor houses. The city walls were more or less on the present line of the Old City walls, though they extended further S. Pilgrims in the 9C could still discern the line of Eudocia's walls, which were finally pulled down by the Fatimid caliph al-'Aziz in 975.

Jerusalem was not at this time the capital, even of the administrative province of Filastin in which it lay. The provincial capital was at Ramla on the coastal plain, founded by Sulaiman at the beginning of the 8C. The Umayyad caliphs resided in Damascus and in a series of palaces in the Transjordanian and Syrian deserts, and in the Jordan Valley.

The Abbasid Dynasty. In the mid-8C the Umayyads were succeeded by the Abbasid Dynasty whose capital lay at Baghdad. During this time Jerusalem was a relatively poor religious centre in the provinces. At the beginning of the 9C in the time of Harun al-Rashid negotiations with Charlemagne resulted in more building and endowment of Christian churches.

The Fatimid Dynasty. This dynasty established itself in Cairo in 969 and shortly after included Syria and Palestine in its territory. Though this dynasty was Shi'ite, most of their subjects in Palestine were of the Sunni persuasion. The Fatimids for the most part showed tolerance to Christians and Jews, apart from a brief interlude in the reign of the caliph al-Hakim who with crazed anti-Christian fanaticism destroyed the Church of the Holy Sepulchre and the tomb itself in 1009. The rotunda was partially restored by 1048. Numerous buildings to serve the Muslim community were constructed, including hospitals, baths, places of ablution and improvements to the water supply. The mosques and gates of the Haram were beautified with mosaics. The city walls, for the most part on the present line, were improved in 1033 and 1063, but the main surviving monuments are parts of the arcades ornamenting the stairs to the upper platform of the Dome of the Rock. During the 9C–11C Jerusalem suffered from the raids and extortions of bedouin and Turcoman groups. By this time many traditions had grown up connecting Jerusalem with the scene of the Last Judgement and Resurrection and with Muhammad's Night Journey to the Aqsa. The impoverished town, the main exports of which were oil, cheese, cotton and fruit, also suffered from earthquakes. In 1071 the Turcoman warlord Atsiz captured Jerusalem, then the Seljuqs in 1078; the Fatimids retook the city after a forty-day bombardment in 1098. Hardly had the Fatimids regained the city than the armies of the First Crusade arrived at Jerusalem in 1099. The Fatimid dynasty was finally overthrown in Egypt by Saladin in 1171.

The Crusader Period (1099–1291). The eruption of the Norman Christian West into the Muslim East during these two centuries was as unexpected as it was influential in politics, commerce, religion and architecture. The Crusader period left its mark on Jerusalem as elsewhere in the Near East in fine secular and ecclesiastical buildings and in hardened secular and religious attitudes.

The First Crusade was launched in 1095, partly to regain and protect the holy places and protect the Eastern Christians, and culminated in the capture of Jerusalem in 1099. The Frankish army arrived before the walls on 7 June. An attack mounted on 13 June failed and the army set about the construction of siege engines. A solemn procession around the city took place on 8 July; and the final attack began on 13 July. By the evening of the 14th Raymond of Toulouse had got his siege tower up to the walls on the SW side of Mount Zion, but failed to enter. In the morning of the 15th the siege engine of Godfrey of Bouillon was got up against the NE wall not far from the present Herod's Gate, where Robert of Normandy and Robert of Flanders were stationed. At midday Godfrey and his brother Eustace of Boulogne got to the top of the wall, and were followed by Tancred, who went on take the Haram. The Fatimid Governor Iftikar held out in the S until early afternoon, and then retreated to the Tower of David, and sued for terms. Apart from the garrison, almost every other Muslim and Jew in the city was slaughtered in the ensuing massacre, which profoundedly shocked even many Christians at the time.

In all, eight major military expeditions were sent out by the western kings and nobles, from France, Germany, Italy and England in particular. The triumphs of the Franks (so called because predominantly French speaking) included the establishment of the Kingdom of Jerusalem in 1100, which reached its greatest expansion by 1112 and included at that time not just Jerusalem but all the coastal cities S from Beirut except Ascalon and Tyre, most of Palestine to the Jordan River, extended to Krak des Chevaliers in S Syria, and included most of Transjordan as far as the Gulf of Aqaba. The territory was defended by lines of magnificent castles; and some 300 ecclesiastical buildings (churches, chapels, convents and shrines) are listed for west Palestine alone (Pringle) which reflect the religious as opposed to the territorial aspects of the Crusader conquest. These for the most part were buildings in fine masonry and Romanesque style.

The most notable disasters of the Crusader period were the Battle of the Horns of Hattin and the surrender of Jerusalem to Saladin in 1187, when virtually the whole kingdom was lost. Jerusalem was regained by diplomacy in 1229, but was finally lost in 1244. Another low point was the capture in Egypt of Louis IX of France who was ransomed in 1250. The final blows to the Crusader establishment in Palestine were delivered by the Mamluk ruler Baybars and his successors in the 13C, and ended with the fall of Acre in 1291. Hostilities were still continued against Egypt until 1365, and the last tremors of the Crusades in the West finally died in the 15C.

Crusader building in Jerusalem itself included 61 ecclesiatical buildings, some of which survive almost intact, notable examples being the Church of the Holy Sepulchre dedicated on 15 July 1149, and the Church of St. Anne. The great suq in the centre of the Old City is largely Crusader work. The powerful monastic orders established at this time, the Hospitallers, the Templars and the Teutonic Order in particular, were responsible for a great deal of construction work. The Dome of the Rock was converted into a church or Christian prayer hall, the Aqsa Mosque became temporarily the palace of the king and was then converted into the headquarters of the Templar Order. Plans as well as monuments of Crusader Jerusalem survive.

Crusader Jerusalem (12C)

The Later Islamic Period. *The Ayyubid Dynasty (1169–1250 in Egypt)*. Salah-al-Din (Saladin), as the real founder of this dynasty, ended Fatimid rule in 1171 and captured Jerusalem 16 years later. The dynasty was Sunni Muslim, as were the majority of the Muslim inhabitants of Palestine, and extended toleration to Jews and Christians. Even the Latin Christians were ransomed or sold into slavery rather than massacred immediately following the capture of the city. Many Crusader buildings in Jerusalem were converted to Muslim use; for example St. Anne's church was converted to a Muslim school, the great Hospital and church of the Knights' Hospitallers was converted into a Muslim hospital, mosque and religious school.

The buildings in the Haram reverted to their original purposes of mosque and shrine. At least 24 buildings of this period survive in and around the Old City. As well as a rebuilding of the city wall, many structures such as gates, porticoes, schools, fountains, libraries, mausolea and convents can be seen. Domestic structures probably of this period have been excavated in the Upper and Lower Tyropoeon valley (Crowfoot, 1927 and Shiloh, Area A1, 1978–82). In 1219 due to the political instability occasioned by the advent of the Fifth Crusade, al-Malik al-Mu'azzam decided to dismantle strategic sections of the city walls, in case they should be retaken by the Crusaders. They remained in this condition until 1537. Under the Peace Treaty of 1229 between al-Malik al-Kamil and Frederick II of Germany, the Crusaders again took possession of Jerusalem, and though the Muslims retained their shrines, Christians were permitted to pray in the Haram. This arrangement was shortlived, for in 1244 the Khwarizmian Turks took the city. Dispossessed of their own homeland by the Mongols, they in turn were defeated in 1246. By 1247 al-Malik al-Salih Ayyub was in control of Jerusalem. Some damage was sustained during this turbulent period, and very little was built.

The Bahri Mamluk Dynasty (1250–1390). The Mamluks, the former slave guard of the Ayyubid rulers, came to power in Egypt in 1250. These were mostly of South Russian, Qipchaq Turkish and Mongol origin, converted to the Sunni branch of the Muslim faith. They established good relations with both the West and Byzantium, and many pilgrims came to Jerusalem during this time. The most capable soldier and probably the best known ruler was Baybars I (1260–77) who claimed successes against Crusaders and Mongols. The high point of the dynasty came under al-Nasir Muhammad (c 1294–1340). Fortification works, ceramics and metalwork flourished along with a widespread commercial network extending to the Far East. Jerusalem remained an unwalled city, but during this period a great number of pious Muslim foundations were built all along the W and N boundaries of the Haram, which today give the Old City much of its character. In particular, tombs of notables were located adjacent to the Haram, within the city walls, where they had not previously been permitted. 55 monuments of the period have been recorded. Rabbi Nachmanides (c 1194–1270) describes Jerusalem as in a very poor state early in the Mamluk period, with 2000 inhabitants, all Muslim except for 300 Christians and two Jews. It was a flourishing period for the Georgian Christians, who had good relations with rulers coming from the same area. Conditions improved considerably during the 14C. The Franciscans (a Latin Catholic Order), who had withdrawn from Palestine at the fall of Acre in 1291, returned in 1335 and settled in a house on Mount Zion. Their Custodian of the Holy Places cared for the welfare of Latin pilgrims and merchants. With the onset of plague in the mid-14C conditions again began to decline.

The Burji Mamluks (1382–1517 in Palestine, 1811 in Egypt), had a similar history in that they began as slave guards but were mostly of Circassian origins. Under their rule the pattern of building continued in Jerusalem with more caravanserais, palaces, schools and devotional and teaching foundations, completing one of the finest surviving medieval complexes in the Islamic world. 24 monuments of this period have been recorded in Jerusalem. The 15C was a period of relative social and economic decline following the ravages of the Black Death in the 14C. Agriculture as well as trade shrank, taxation was heavy, and there were greater problems with bedouin infiltration and lack of security. The dynasty had little continuity, and power was divided among numerous strong amirs. Rabbi Obadiah of Bartenura wrote in 1488 that Jerusalem was desolate, with no walls, and the tiny Jewish community especially wretched.

The Ottoman Dynasty, in Jerusalem 1517–1917. The dynasty was at its peak in the 16C when Selim the Grim (1512–20) conquered Syria and divided the former territories of the Mamluks into pashaliks of the Ottoman Empire. His successor, Sulaiman II 'the Magnificent' (1520–66) was responsible for a considerable programme of work in Jerusalem, including the rebuilding of the walls of the Old City as we see them today. They are mostly on the same lines as those of the Fatimid period. He also restored and beautified the Haram. Jerusalem became the seat of a Turkish governor of a district or *sanjaq* but in the 16C and 17C it was a fairly low grade posting, and only increased in status in the 19C. Very few Ottoman Turks actually lived in Jerusalem. During the later 17C there was civil unrest owing to a weak government, plague in Jerusalem, riots, and tension among the Christian sects, which was exacerbated by heavy taxation. In 1685 the few remaining Georgian Christians finally departed, under a heavy burden of debt. Local Arab families became prominent in the administration and leadership of the city.

Not all areas within the city walls were built up: for example there was an arable field in the Muristan area c 1850 and the number of inhabitants, who suffered great hardships during the First World War, declined sharply through emigration and disease. The water supply system in particular had declined by 1860, with aqueducts out of use or in poor repair, and cisterns not regularly cleaned. By the end of each summer fever was endemic in the city. Generally speaking the town was considerably decayed by the later 19C, and contemporary etchings show that the stonework was in a poor state, with cactus, caper bush and other weeds growing in the cracks. Thirty-five diverse monuments of the Ottoman period are recorded in Jerusalem. From the end of the Crimean War much greater European interest in the city developed, and many new buildings were constructed outside the walls to the W. The Ottoman period ended with the Turkish surrender of the city on 10 December 1917 and the entry of General Allenby and the British forces into Jerusalem the next day.

British Mandate Period (1920–48). A civil administration was set up on 1 July 1920 and a League of Nations British Mandate in 1922. Not all areas within the city walls were built up, and vegetables were still being cultivated within the NE quarter of the Old City in 1927. The Mandate Government much improved the supply of piped water to the city, from Solomon's Pools in 1918 and from the springs at Ras al-'Ain on the coastal plain in 1934. Both pipe lines served the Romema Reservoir in the NW of the city. The population of Jerusalem increased greatly, and many administrative and service buildings were constructed in the new W suburbs. In 1921 the Jewish National Council and the Muslim Supreme Council were set up, in 1929 the Jewish Agency and in 1936 the Higher Arab Committee, which were based in Jerusalem. Increasing Arab anxiety at increased Jewish immigration, land purchase and nationalistic aspirations led to a state of terrorism and civil war. The Mandate ended with the departure of all British troops from Jerusalem on 14 May 1948.

Recent times. The battle for the city between the Arab and Israeli forces began on the following day. From 1948–67 the city was partitioned, with the W suburbs administered by Israel, and the Old City and the northern suburbs by Jordan. On 22 June 1967 following the Six Day War, the Israeli parliament enacted a law bringing East Jerusalem within the confines of West Jerusalem which was brought into effect on 28 June. New immigration centres, expropriation of land, building and industrial projects in east Jerusalem were rapidly developed to inhibit any future separation.

ANNOTATED BIBLIOGRAPHY

This is a very selective guide to further reading on Jerusalem. Many books about the city are out-of-print, some also being rare and difficult to obtain scholarly works. The following list refers to some of these, but mostly to those which are reasonably accessible. Many contain extensive additional bibliographies.

The fundamental guide to Jerusalem is of course, *The Bible*. It is a truism that there can be small perception of the Holy City without some acquaintance with the Jewish, Christian and Muslim holy books. The Old Testament (which achieved its final written form in the last centuries BC) offers the traditional story of ancient Jebusite and Jewish Jerusalem, and the New Testament contains all the foundations for any Christian pilgrimage to the city. Though the King James' version remains the classic translation for many English readers, the Blue Guide also uses the New English Bible. In the Guide translations from *The Koran* are taken mainly from J.M. Rodwell, in the Everyman edition of 1913, but other translations into English are available. Though written down after Muhammad's death in AD 632 the teachings of the Prophet not only form the basis of Islam, but also contain the seeds of Muslim attitudes to Jerusalem which developed and expanded in the centuries following the Muslim conquest of Jerusalem in AD 638.

Among the earliest surviving secular accounts relating to the history of Jerusalem are the books of Flavius Josephus written in the late 1C AD. His more important book is *The Jewish War*, a somewhat polemical account of the First Revolt by a Jew in the Roman camp, which nonetheless is a vivid and often first-hand acount of considerable accuracy, and has much to say about contemporary Jerusalem. His *Jewish Antiquities*, in 20 books, though interesting, is generally less useful, containing the traditional view current in his day of the history of the Jewish people from the Creation to the First Jewish Revolt. Translations in the Guide are those of H. St. J. Thackeray in the Loeb edition.

Many accounts written by early Christian pilgrims survive. The collected texts of numerous visitors to the city were published in the volumes of the Palestine Pilgrim's Text Society. Those of many Christian pilgrims are now readily available in the recent translations of J. Wilkinson, *Egeria's Travels to the Holy Land* (rev. ed. Ariel, Jerusalem, 1981); and, *Jerusalem Pilgrims before the Crusades* (Aris and Philips, Warminster, 1977). Important source material for medieval Jerusalem survives in the works of a number of Arab writers, particularly in that of two natives of Jerusalem: Mujir al-Din whose account of Hebron and Jerusalem was written in 1495, and al-Muqaddasi whose geographical treatise was written c AD 985. The Guide also refers to the work of the Persian poet Nasir-i Khusraw who wrote an account of his pilgrimage through Syria and Palestine in c 1047. There are no recent translations of these works available in English.

Travellers' accounts particularly in the 19C are almost too numerous to mention, but the relevant sections of A. W. Kinglake, *Eothen* (London, 1844) and R. Curzon, *Visits to Monasteries in the Levant* (London, 1850) are fascinating reading and can be enjoyed in conjunction with the engravings in David Roberts' beautiful folios, *The Holy Land, Syria, Idumea, Arabia, Egypt and Nubia* (London 1842–49). A very extensive bibliography of travellers to Jerusalem from the 17C onwards is given in Gilbert Martin, *Jerusalem. Illustrated History Atlas* (2nd ed. Steimatzky's Agency, Jerusalem, 1978). Modern recording in Jerusalem began around the middle of the 19C, with such notable publications as those of E. Pierotti, *Jerusalem Explored* (London and Cambridge, 1864), M. de Vogüé, *Le Temple de Jérusalem* (Paris, 1864), C.W. Wilson, *Ordnance Survey of Jerusalem 1864/5* (reprinted, Ariel, Jerusalem, 1980) and, *The Recovery of Jerusalem* (1871). Wilson and C. Warren produced, *Underground Jerusalem* in 1876.

Warren and C.R. Conder were attached to the Survey of Western Palestine and sent out by the Palestine Exploration Fund to excavate, survey and produce the first accurate maps of the locality. The Jerusalem volume of the *Survey of Western Palestine* (London, 1884) is still a basic source of information about Jerusalem before the great surge of development in the later 19C, as are C. Clermont-Ganneau, *Archaeological Researches in Palestine during the years 1873–1874* (Vol. I, London, 1899) and the compilation by H. Vincent and F.-M. Abel, *Jérusalem. Recherches de Topographie, d'Archéologie et d'Histoire* (5 Fascicules, Paris, 1912–26). The main collection of Arabic inscriptions was published by Max van Berchem in, *Matériaux pour un Corpus Inscriptionum Arabicarum* (Second Part, 3 vols., Cairo 1920–27).

More recent and available works include a number of atlases, encyclopaedias and histories which provide the geographical setting and historical background to the city.

Aharoni, Y.: *The Land of the Bible* (Philadelphia, 1974).

Aharoni, Y. and Avi-Yonah, M.: *The Macmillan Bible Atlas* (2nd ed., Collier Macmillan, London, 1977).

Ben-Arieh, Y.: *A City Reflected in its times: Jerusalem in the Nineteenth Century*. Part I. *The Old City* (Jerusalem, 1977).

Duncan, Alistair: *The Noble Sanctuary* (Longman, London, 1972).

Encyclopaedia Judaica.

Encyclopaedia of Islam.

Ehrenkreutz, A.S.: *Saladin* (Albany State University of New York, 1972).

Eisenstadt, S.N.: *Israeli Society* (Weidenfeld, London, 1967).

Eisenstadt, S.N.: *The Transformation of Israeli Society: an Essay in Interpretation* (Weidenfeld, London, 1985).

Gray, John: *A History of Jerusalem* (Hale, London, 1969).

Jerusalem (*Israel Pocket Library*, Keter Books, Jerusalem, 1973). This is particularly useful for information on the Jewish community, and the recent history of the city, and is compiled from material originally published in the *Encyclopaedia Judaica*.

Guillaume, A.: *Islam* (Penguin, London, 1954).

Hitti, P.K.: *History of the Arabs* (10th ed., Macmillan, London, 1970).

Le Strange, G.: *Palestine Under the Moslems* (London, 1890, reprinted by Khayats, Beirut, 1965).

Lewis, B. (ed.): *The World of Islam. Faith, People, Culture* (Thames and Hudson, London and New York, 1976).

Lucas, N.: *The Modern History of Israel* (Weidenfeld and Nicholson, London, reprinted 1975).

May, H.G. (ed.): *Oxford Bible Atlas* (3rd ed., Oxford University Press. Oxford. 1984).

Peters, F.E.: *Allah's Commonwealth. A History of Islam in the Near East 600–1100 A.D.* (Simon and Schuster, New York, 1973).

Peters F.E.: *Children of Abraham: Judaism/Christianity/Islam* (Princeton U.P., 1982).

Peters, F.E.: *Jerusalem: the Holy City in the eyes of chroniclers...* (Princeton U.P., 1985).

Prawer, J.: *The Latin Kingdom of Jerusalem: European colonialism in the Middle Ages* (London, 1972).

Runciman, S.: *A History of the Crusades*. Vols. I-III (Pelican, Cambridge, 1951–54).

Rogerson, J.: *The New Atlas of the Bible* (Macdonald, London, 1985).

Sacher, H.: *Israel: The Establishment of a State* (London, 1952).

Schacht. J. and Bosworth C.E. (eds.): *The Legacy of Islam* (Oxford University Press, 1974, now in paperback).

Ware, T.: *The Orthodox Church* (Penguin, London, 1963).

Wilkinson, John: *Jerusalem as Jesus Knew It* (Thames and Hudson, London, 1978).

Books with accounts of recent archaeological discoveries in Jerusalem include the following:

Avigad, N.: *Discovering Jerusalem* (Oxford, 1984).

Kenyon, K.M.: *Digging Up Jerusalem* (Ernest Benn, London, 1974).

Kenyon, K.M.: *Jerusalem. Excavating 3000 Years of History* (Thames and Hudson, London, 1967).

Tushingham, A.D.: *Excavations in Jerusalem 1961–1967*. Vol. I (Royal Ontario Museum, Toronto, 1985).

Shiloh, Y.: *Excavations at the City of David* (QEDEM Vol. 19, Jerusalem, 1984).

Yadin, Y.: *Jerusalem Revealed. Archaeology in the Holy City 1968–1974 (Israel Exploration Society and Yale University Press, 1976).*

A number of journals are published which regularly contain news of recent discoveries in Jerusalem. These include the following, but the list is by no means exhaustive:

Biblical Archaeologist (American Schools of Oriental Research, Cambridge, Mass.)

Bulletin of the American Schools of Oriental Research.

Israel Exploration Journal (Israel Exploration Society, Jerusalem).

Levant (British School of Archaeology in Jerusalem and British Institute at Amman for Archaeology and History, London).

Liber Annuus (Studium Biblicum Franciscanum, Jerusalem).

Palestine Exploration Quarterly (Palestine Exploration Fund, London).

Revue Biblique (École Biblique, Paris).

Zeitschrift des Deutschen Palästina-Vereins (German Evangelical Institute, Weisbaden).

There are numerous books dealing with the architecture of the city. Foremost among these are:

Creswell, K.A.C.: *Early Muslim Architecture*. 2 Vols. (Oxford, 1932–1969).

Burgoyne, M.H.: *Mamluk Jerusalem* (WIFT and BSAJ, London, 1987).

Coüasnon, Charles: *The Church of the Holy Sepulchre in Jerusalem* (British Academy, London, 1972).

Hamilton, R.W.: *The Structural History of the Aqsa Mosque* (Oxford, 1949).

A selection relating to other topics includes:

Amiran, Ruth: *The Ancient Pottery of the Holy Land* (Brunswick, 1970).
Carswell, J. and Dowsett, C.J.F: *Kütahya Tiles and Pottery from the Armenian Cathedral of St. James, Jerusalem* (Oxford, 1972).
Grabar, O.: *The Formation of Islamic Art* (Yale U.P., Conn, 1973).
Narkiss, Bezalel: *Armenian Art Treasures of Jerusalem* (Masada Press, Jerusalem, 1979).
Polunin, O. and Huxley, A.: *Flowers of the Mediterranean* (Chatto and Windus, London, 1981).

CHRONOLOGICAL TABLES

Archaeological Periods in Palestine

Prehistoric

700,000–15,000 BC	*Palaeolithic* (Old Stone Age)
15,000–8300	*Mesolithic* (Middle Stone Age)
8300–4500	*Neolithic* (New Stone Age)
4500–3100	*Chalcolithic* ('Copper Age')

Bronze Age

3150–2850	Early Bronze Age I
2850–2650	Early Bronze Age II
2650–2350	Early Bronze Age III
2350–2200	Early Bronze Age IV
2200–2000	Middle Bronze Age I
2000–1750	Middle Bronze Age IIA
1750–1550	Middle Bronze Age IIB
1550–1400	Late Bronze Age I
1400–1300	Late Bronze Age IIA
1300–1200	Late Bronze Age IIB

Iron Age

1200–1000	Iron Age I
1000–900	Iron Age IIA
900–800	Iron Age IIB
800–586	Iron Age IIC
586–332	Babylonian and Persian Periods
332–152	Hellenistic I
152–37	Hellenistic II (Hasmonaean)
37 BC–AD 70	Roman I (Herodian)
AD 70–180	Roman II
180–324	Roman III
324–451	Byzantine I
451–640	Byzantine II
640–1099	Early Islamic
1099–1291	Crusader
1187–	Later Islamic

King Lists (relevant to Jerusalem)

Rulers of Jerusalem

c 1850–1810 BC	Yaqir-'ammu and Shayzanu
c 1350 BC	Abdi-Khipa

Kings of Judah and Israel

The United Kingdom

c 1020–1004 BC	Saul
1004–965	David
965–928	Solomon

Judah		*Israel*	
928–911	Rehoboam	928–907	Jeroboam
911–908	Abijam	907–906	Nadab
908–867	Asa	906–883	Baasha
867–846	Jehoshaphat	883–882	Elah
846–843	Jehoram	882	Zimri
843–842	Ahaziah	882–871	Omri
842–836	Athaliah	871–852	Ahab
836–798	Joash	852–851	Ahaziah
798–769	Amaziah	851–842	Jehoram
769–733	Uzziah	842–814	Jehu
758–743	Jotham	814–800	Jehoahaz
733–727	Ahaz	800–784	Jehoash
727–698	Hezekiah	784–748	Jeroboam
698–642	Manasseh	748	Zechariah
641–640	Amon	748	Shallum
640–609	Josiah	747–737	Menahem
609	Jehoahaz	737–735	Pekahiah
609–598	Jehoiakim	735–733	Pekah
597	Jehoiachin	733–724	Hoshea
596–586	Zedekiah		

The Hasmoneans

152–142 BC	Jonathan
142–134	Simeon
134–104	John Hyrcanus
104–103	Aristobulus
103–76	Alexander Jannaeus
76–67	Salome Alexandra
67–63	Aristobulus II
63–40	Hyrcanus II
40–37	Matthias Antigonus

The Herods

37–4 BC	Herod the Great
4 BC–AD 6	Archelaus
4 BC–AD 39	Herod Antipas
4 BC–AD 34	Philip
AD 37–44	Herod Agrippa I
53–100(?)	Agrippa II

Roman Procurators

c AD 6–9	Coponius
9–12	M. Ambibulus
12–15	Annius Rufus
15–26	Valerius Gratus
26–36	Pontius Pilatus
36–37	Marcellus
41–46	Cuspius Fadus
46–48	Tiberius Alexander
48–52	Ventidius Cumanus
52–60	Antonius Felix
60–62	Porcius Festus
62–64	Albinus
64–66	Gessius Florus

Seleucid Kings

311–281 BC	Seleucus I Nicator
281–261	Antiochus I Soter
261–246	Antiochus II Theos
246–225	Seleucus II Callinicus
225–223	Seleucus III Soter
223–187	Antiochus III the Great
187–175	Seleucus IV Philopator
175–164	Antiochus IV Epiphanes
163–162	Antiochus V Eupator
162–150	Demetrius I Soter

150–145	Alexander Balas
145–140	Demetrius II Nicator
145–138	Antiochus VI Epiphanes
138–129	Antiochus VII Sidetes
129–125	Demetrius II Nicator
126	Cleopatra Thea
125–121	Cleopatra Thea and Antiochus VIII Grypus
125	Seleucus V
121–96	Antiochus VIII Grypus
115–95	Antiochus IX Cyzicenus
96–95	Seleucus VI Epiphanes Nicator
95–88	Demetrius III Philopator
95–83	Antiochus X Eusebes
94	Antiochus XI Philadelphus
94–83	Philip I Philadelphus
87–84	Antiochus XII Dionysus
69–64	Antiochus XIII
67–65	Philip II

Ptolemies

304–282 BC	Ptolemy I Soter
285–246	Ptolemy II Philadelphus
246–221	Ptolemy III Euergetes
221–204	Ptolemy IV Philopator
204–180	Ptolemy V Epiphanes
180–145	Ptolemy VI Philometor
145–144	Ptolemy VII Neos Philopater
145–116	Ptolemy VIII Euergetes II
116–107	Ptolemy IX Soter II
107–88	Ptolemy X Alexander I
88–81	Ptolemy IX Soter II (restored)
80	Ptolemy XI Alexander II
80–51	Ptolemy XII Neos Dionysos
51–30	Cleopatra VII Philopator
51–47	Ptolemy XIII
47–44	Ptolemy XIV
44–30	Ptolemy XV

Roman and Byzantine Emperors

27 BC–AD 14	Augustus
AD 14–37	Tiberius
37–41	Gaius Caligula
41–54	Claudius
54–68	Nero
68–69	Balba
69	Otho
69	Vitellius
69–79	Vespasian
79–81	Titus
81–96	Domitian
96–98	Nerva
98–117	Trajan
117–138	Hadrian
138–161	Antoninus Pius
161–180	Marcus Aurelius
161–169	Lucius Verus
180–192	Commodus
193	Pertinax
193	Didius Julianus
193–194	Pescennius Niger
193–197	Clodius Albinus
193–211	Septimius Severus
211–212	Geta
211–217	Caracalla
217–218	Macrinus
218	Diadumenianus
218–222	Elagabalus
222–235	Alexander Severus

235–238	Maximian I
238	Gordianus I
238	Gordianus II
238	Balbinus
238	Pupienus
238–244	Gordianus III
244–249	Philip Senior
247–249	Philip Junior
249–251	Trajanus Decius
251–253	Trebonianus Gallus
251	Hostilianus
251–253	Volusian
253–260	Valerian
253–268	Gallienus
268–270	Claudius Gothicus
270–275	Aurelian
275–276	Tacitus
276–282	Probus
282–283	Carus
283–284	Carinus
283–284	Numerianus
284–305	Diocletian
286–305	Maximianus Herculius
293–306	Constantius I
293–311	Galerius
306–307	Severus
306–312	Maxentius
308–324	Licinius
308–313	Maximinus II
308–337	Constantine the Great
337–361	Constantius II
337–350	Constans
361–363	Julian
363–364	Jovian
363–375	Valentinian I
367–383	Gratian
375–392	Valentinian II
364–378	Valens
378–395	Theodosius I
383–408	Arcadius
383–423	Honorius
402–450	Theodosius II (and Eudocia)
425–455	Valentinian III
450–457	Marcian
457–474	Leo I
467–472	Anthemius
474–491	Zeno
491–518	Anastasius I
518–527	Justin I
527–565	Justinian I
565–578	Justin II
578–582	Tiberius II
582–602	Tiberius Maurice
602–610	Focas
610–641	Heraclius
641–668	Constans II

Early Islamic Caliphs

Orthodox Caliphs (AD 632–661; AH 11–40)

632–634	Abu-Bakr
634–644	'Umar b. al-Khattab
644–656	'Uthman b. 'Affan
656–661	'Ali b. Abi-Talib

Umayyad Caliphs (AD 661–750; AH 41–132)

661–680	Mu'awiya I b. Abi-Sufyan
680–683	Yazid I
683–684	Mu'awiya II
684–685	Marwan I b. al-Hakam
685–705	'Abd-al-Malik
705–715	al-Walid I
715–717	Sulaiman
717–720	'Umar b. 'Abd-al-'Aziz
720–724	Yazid II
724–743	Hisham
743–744	al-Walid II
744	Yazid III
744	Ibrahim
744–750	Marwan II al-Himar

'Abbasid Caliphs
*(in Iraq and Baghdad: AD 749–974; AH 132–363; note: the Dynasty continued
to AD 1258; AH 656)*

749–754	al-Saffah
754–775	al-Mansur
775–785	al-Mahdi
785–786	al-Hadi
786–809	Harun al-Rashid
809–833	al-Amin
813–817	al-Ma'mun
817–819	Ibrahim b. al-Mahdi (in Baghdad)
833–842	al-Mu'tasim
842–847	al-Wathiq
847–861	al-Mutawakkil
861–862	al-Muntasir
862–866	al-Musta'in
866–869	al-Mu'tazz
869–870	al-Muhtadi
870–892	al-Mu'tamid
892–902	al-Mu'tadid
902–908	al-Muktafi
908–932	al-Muqtadir
932–934	al-Qahir
934–940	al-Radi
940–944	al-Muttaqi
944–946	al-Mustakfi
946–974	al-Muti'

Fatimid Caliphs
*(Egypt and Syria: AD 975–1171; AH 365–567; note: the Dynasty commenced in
AD 909; AH 297)*

975–996	al-'Aziz
996–1021	al-Hakim
1021–1036	al-Zahir
1036–1094	al-Mustansir
1094–1101	al-Musta'li
1101–1130	al-Amir
1130–1131	interregnum; al-Hafiz as Regent
1131–1149	al-Hafiz as Caliph
1149–1154	al-Zafir
1154–1160	al-Fa'iz
1160–1171	al-'Adid

Crusader Dynasty (1099–1291)
(sovereignty in Jerusalem ended in 1187 and occupation ended in 1244)

1099–1100	Godfrey of Bouillon, Defender of the Holy Sepulchre
1100–1118	Baldwin I
1118–1131	Baldwin II
1131–1161	Melisande (married Fulk of Anjou, died 1143)
1143–1163	Baldwin III
1163–1174	Almaric I
1174–1185	Baldwin IV (had leprosy; Raymond of Tripoli, Regent)
1185–1186	Baldwin V (child)
1186–1192	Sybil (married Guy of Lusignan)
1192	Isabel and Conrad of Montferrat
1192–1197	Isabel and Henry of Champagne
1197–1205	Isabel and Amalric II (Aimery of Lusignan)
1206	Isabel
1206–1212	Mary La Marquise
1210–1212	John of Brienne
1212–1225	John of Brienne (as Regent)
1225–1228	Frederick II of Hohenstaufen
1228–1254	Conrad I
1254–1268	Conrad II
1269–1284	Hugh I (Hugh III of Cyprus)
1284–1285	John I
1285–1291	Henry I

Later Islamic Caliphs

Ayyubid Caliphs
(in Egypt; AD 1169–1252; AH 564–650)

1169–1193	al-Malik al-Nasir I Salah-al-Din (Saladin)
1193–1198	al-Malik al-'Aziz 'Imad-al-Din
1198–1200	al-Malik al-Mansur Nasir-al-Din
1200–1218	al-Malik al-'Adil I Sayf-al-Din
1218–1238	al-Malik al-Kamil I Nasir-al-Din
1238–1240	al-Malik al-'Adil II Sayf-al-Din
1240–1249	al-Malik al-Salih Najm-al-Din Ayyub
1249–1250	al-Malik al-Mu'azzam Turan-Shah
1250–1252	al-Malik al-Ashraf II Muzaffar-al-Din

Ayyubid Caliphs
(in Damascus; AD 1186–1260; AH 582–658)

1186–1196	al-Malik al-Afdal Nur-al-Din 'Ali
1196–1218	al-Malik al-'Adil I Sayf-al-Din
1218–1227	al-Malik al-Mu'azzam Sharaf-al-Din
1227–1229	al-Malik al-Nasir Salah-al-Din Da'ud
1229–1237	al-Malik al-Ashraf I Muzaffar-al-Din
1237–1238	al-Malik al-Salih 'Imad-al-Din (first reign)
1238	al-Malik al-Kamil I Nasir-al-Din
1238–1239	al-Malik al-'Adil II Sayf-al-Din
1239	al-Malik al-Salih Najm-al-Din Ayyub (first reign)
1239–1245	al-Malik al-Salih 'Imad-al-Din (second reign)
1245–1249	al-Malik al-Salih Najm-al-Din Ayyub (second reign)
1249–1250	al-Malik al-Mu'azzam Turan-Shah (with Egypt)
1250–1260	al-Malik al-Nasir II Salah-al-Din

Bahri Mamluk Caliphs
(in Egypt and Syria; AD 1250–1390; AH 648–792)

1250	Shajar al-Durr
1250–1257	al-Mu'izz 'Izz-al-Din Aybak
1257–1259	al-Mansur Nur-al-Din 'Ali
1259–1260	al-Muzaffar Sayf-al-Din Qutuz
1260–1277	al-Zahir Rukn-al-Din Baybars I al-Bunduqdari
1277–1280	al-Sa'id Nasir-al-Din Baraka Khan
1280	al-'Adil Badr-al-Din Salamish
1280–1290	al-Mansur Sayf-al-Din Qala'un al-Alfi
1290–1294	al-Ashraf Salah-al-Din Khalil
1294–1295	al-Nasir Nasir-al-Din Muhammad (first reign)
1295–1297	al-'Adil Zayn-ad-Din Kitbugha
1297–1299	al-Mansur Husam-al-Din Lajin
1299–1309	al-Nasir Nasir-al-Din Muhammad (second reign)
1309	al-Muzaffar Rukn-al-Din Baybars II al-Jashankir
1309–1340	al-Nasir Nasir-al-Din Muhammad (third reign)
1340–1341	al-Mansur Savf-al-Din Abu-Bakr
1341–1342	al-Ashraf 'Ala'-al-Din Kujuk
1342	al-Nasir Shihab-al-Din Ahmad
1342–1345	al-Salih 'Imad-al-Din Isma'il
1345–1346	al-Kamil Sayf-al-Din Sha'ban I
1346–1347	al-Muzaffar Sayf-al-Din Hajji I
1347–1351	al-Nasir Nasir-al-Din al-Hasan (first reign)
1351–1354	al-Salih Salah-al-Din Salih
1354–1361	al-Nasir Nasir-al-Din al-Hasan (second reign)
1361–1363	al-Mansur Salah-al-Din Muhammad
1363–1376	al-Ashraf Nasir-al-Din Sha'ban II
1376–1382	al-Mansur 'Ala'-al-Din 'Ali
1382	al-Salih Salah-al-Din Hajji II (first reign)
1382–1389	al-Zahir Sayf al-Din Barquq
1389	Hajji II (second reign, with honorific title al-Muzaffar or al-Mansur)

Burji Mamluk Caliphs
(in Egypt and Syria; AD 1382–1517; AH 784–922)

1382–1389	al-Zahir Sayf-al-Din Barquq (first reign)
1389–1390	Hajji II (second reign)
1390–1399	al-Zahir Sayf-al-Din Barquq (second reign)
1399–1405	al-Nasir Nasir-al-Din Faraj (first reign)
1405	al-Mansur 'Izz-al-Din 'Abd-al-'Aziz
1405–1412	al-Nasir Nasir-al-Din Faraj (second reign)
1412	al-'Adil al-Musta'in ('Abbasid Caliph, proclaimed Sultan)
1412–1421	al-Mu'ayyad Sayf-al-Din Shaikh
1421	al-Muzaffar Ahmad
1421	al-Zahir Sayf-al-Din Tatar
1421–1422	al-Salih Nasir-al-Din Muhammad
1422–1437	al-Ashraf Sayf-al-Din Barsbay
1437–1438	al-'Aziz Jamal-al-Din Yusuf
1438–1453	al-Zahir Sayf-al-Din Jaqmaq
1453	al-Mansur Fakhr-al-Din 'Uthman
1453–1461	al-Ashraf Sayf-al-Din Inal
1461	al-Mu'ayyad Shihab-al-Din Ahmad
1461–1467	al-Zahir Sayf-al-Din Khushqadam
1467	al-Zahir Sayf-al-Din Bilbay
1467–1468	al-Zahir Timurbugha
1468–1496	al-Ashraf Sayf-al-Din Qa'it Bay
1496–1498	al-Nasir Muhammad
1498–1500	al-Zahir Qansuh
1500–1501	al-Ashraf Janbalat
1501	al-'Adil Sayf-al-Din Tuman Bay
1501–1516	al-Ashraf Qansuh al-Ghawri
1516	al-Ashraf Tuman Bay

Ottoman Rulers (AD 1512–1918; AH 918–1336)
(from the conquest of Jerusalem)

1512–1520	Selim I Yavuz ('the Grim')
1520–1566	Sulaiman II Qanuni ('the Law-giver', also known in the West as 'the Magnificent')
1566–1574	Selim II
1574–1595	Murad III
1595–1603	Muhammad III
1603–1617	Ahmad I
1617–1618	Mustafa I (first reign)
1618–1622	'Uthman II
1622–1623	Mustafa I (second reign)
1623–1640	Murad IV
1640–1648	Ibrahim
1648–1687	Muhammad IV
1687–1691	Sulaiman III
1691–1695	Ahmad II
1695–1703	Mustafa II
1703–1730	Ahmad III
1730–1754	Mahmud I
1754–1757	'Uthman III
1757–1774	Mustafa III
1774–1789	'Abd-al-Hamid I
1789–1807	Selim III
1807–1808	Mustafa IV
1808–1839	Mahmud II
1839–1861	'Abd-al-Majid I
1861–1876	'Abd-al-'Aziz
1876	Murad V
1876–1909	'Abd-al-Hamid II
1909–1918	Muhammad V Rashad

British Mandate 1920–1948

PRACTICAL INFORMATION

Travel to and within Jerusalem

General Information. *Information* may be had from many airlines and travel agents. The Israeli Government Tourist Offices in the UK are at 18 Great Marlborough St, London W1V 1AF (tel. 01–434 3651); the Israel Information Centre, 57 Leicester Rd, Salford M7 ODA (tel. 061–792 6072); in the USA at: 350 Fifth Avenue, New York. NY 10118 (tel. [212] 560 0650); 6380 Wilshire Boulevard, Los Angeles, California 90048 (tel. [213] 658 7462); 5 South Wabash Ave, Chicago, Illinois 60603 (tel. [312] 782 4306); 4151 Southwest Freeway, Houston, Texas 77027 (tel. [713] 850 9341); 420 Lincoln Road Building, Lincoln Rd, Miami Beach, Florida (tel. [305] 673 6862); in Canada at: 180 Bloor St West, Toronto, Ontario M5S 1M8 (tel. [416] 964 3784); in South Africa at: 73 Market St, Johannesburg (tel. 23 8931 2); in Jerusalem at: 24 King George St (Ha-Melekh George), Jerusalem (tel. [02] 241281/2); inside the Old City at the Jaffa Gate (tel. [02] 282295/6); in Bethlehem at Manger Square (tel. [02] 742591).

Leaflets and maps with tourist information, newspapers with current events, information on tours and guided walks, bus maps and items of general interest are available.

The Jerusalem Municipal Tourist Information Office is at: 34 Jaffa (Yafo) Rd (tel. [02] 228844). The local opening hours are Sun–Thu 8.30–17.00, Fri and days preceding Jewish holidays 8.30–14.00, Sat and religious holidays closed. For walking tours of the excavations below the Temple Mount, see the Lifshitz Information Centre, 34 Habad St, Old City.

Opening times of the various places vary from year to year, as do the precise dates of some religious holidays, and these should be checked before arrangements are made. Numerous travel agents advertise package tours, charter flights and hotel information. These may offer substantial reductions on scheduled flights.

Accommodation in a range of hotels, self-catering apartments and holiday villages is available (see below).

Passports are required (**not** British Visitor's Passports); no visa is required for UK nationals for a stay of up to three months; Australian, Canadian, New Zealand, South African and US nationals can be issued with a free visitor's visa at the point of entry. It is possible to travel to and from Israel via Jordan and Egypt but careful enquiry concerning regulations and visas at the time should be made at the relevant embassies prior to booking. Those intending to visit an Arab country should request to have their Israeli entry form (AL 17) rather than their passport stamped on arrival, as passports with Israeli visas or entry stamps are not accepted in Arab countries. The Israeli entry visa must be retained until departure from Israel. Passports will be stamped if an extension of stay is obtained from the Ministry of the Interior.

There are *no vaccination* requirements for entry to Israel.

Travelling Arrangements. The international airport is the **Ben Gurion International Airport** N of Lod on the coastal plain at c 50km NW of Jerusalem. It is served by 18 international airlines.

Public transport between the airport and Jerusalem is by Egged service bus (approximately every 20 minutes from 6.15–19.00), by sharut or service taxis (set rate for a seat in a taxi), and by ordinary taxi. The journey takes up to one hour; few buses run at night, and intending travellers should check availability of any transport on the eve of Jewish religious holidays and on religious holidays. Nesher Taxi Service (21 King George St) offers a 24-hour taxi service to the airport at fixed fares but requires at least 24 hours' advance booking, tel. (02) 231231.

An airport tax (in 1987 this is c £7 per person) is levied on departure, when a two-hour check-in is normal.

Security checks, baggage and personal searches are applied. *Remove film from cameras.*

Flights should be confirmed within 72 hours of departure.

There is a branch of the **Government Tourist Office** at the Airport.

The domestic airport for Jerusalem is **Atarot (Qalandia)** c 10km N of Jerusalem. It serves some international charter flights and mainly domestic flights to Tel Aviv, Haifa, Rosh Pinna and Eilat.

The entry point from Jordan is by the Allenby Bridge approximately 40km E of Jerusalem, usually open from Sun to Thu 9.00–13.00; Fri and eves of religious holidays 8.00–11.00 and closed on Saturdays and Jewish religious holidays.

Tourists may cross from Jordan to Israel and back again to Jordan, or from Israel to Jordan but *not* back again to Israel. Israeli visas should be obtained in advance by those requiring them, as visas are not obtainable in any Arab country except Egypt and they are not granted at the Allenby Bridge. Arrangements for a visit in Jerusalem should be made in advance as it is not possible to make bookings from an Arab country. A sharut taxi service is available from the Damascus Gate to the Allenby Bridge. Private tourist vehicles and bicycles are not permitted to cross the bridge. On entry a strict baggage search is carried out and cameras checked by requesting one exposure. An Israeli transit tax is payable on departure. Visitors departing to Jordan should obtain a Jordanian visa and Jordanian bridge permit in advance of their visit to Israel.

The entry points from Egypt are at Nitzana (open 8.00–16.00), Rafiah (open 9.00–17.00), Netafim (open 24 hours) and Taba (open 7.00–21.00, visa obtainable) and are open daily except at Yom Kippur and the first day of the Id al-Adha. Except at Taba entry visas should be obtained in advance. Private vehicles may be taken across this border, but obtain the necessary documentation from local automobile clubs in the country of origin in advance.

Rented vehicles are *not* permitted to cross the frontier. The Egged Bus Company has a regular service from Tel Aviv to Cairo.

Ports. The principal port is Haifa which is served by car ferries mainly from Italy, Greece and Cyprus. Information on prices, timetables, routes, customs and other formalities can be obtained from tourist offices; a branch of the Israeli Government Tourist Office is located at Haifa Port. Cars can be imported by foreign visitors for up to one year, and without duty for up to three months. Two other deep-water ports are located at Ashdod and Eilat.

Local Travel. *Local bus services* are frequent and cheap; maps of the Jerusalem city routes are available from the tourist offices; the Central Bus Station (for Jerusalem and serving other towns) is in the Jaffa (Yafo) Rd, in the W section of the town at Romema; Egged buses do not operate on Friday evening or Saturday, other days most services are at approximately 15-minute intervals from 6.00–24.00. The Damascus Gate Bus Station serves the E side of the town and country areas of the West Bank. These services operate daily. For information about touring bus services tel. (02) 248144; for bus travel between towns, tel. 551866; discount and 'runabout tickets' can be purchased from Egged Tour Offices at Zion Square, at Bait Tannous opposite the Jaffa Gate and at the Central Bus Station.

Taxis. There are numerous taxi firms in the city. Meters should be displayed; tariff rate 1 operates 5.30–20.59; a higher (+25 per cent) tariff rate 2 operates 21.00–5.29 and on Saturday. Tipping is not customary. The sharut or service taxis which run on fairly set routes in and mainly beyond the city are inexpensive and usually quicker and more comfortable than buses. Individual seats (enquire cost locally) can be taken; between cities these can be booked in advance through a travel agent. Local advice is necessary for costs, routes etc. The main departure points are from near the Central Bus Station, and in Rabbi Kook St, opposite Zion Square.

Car hire is also available through local firms (Yourent, 5 Pines St, opposite Central Hotel, tel. (02) 383903/383883; Eldan, tel. (02) 636183; Splendid, 10 King David St, tel. (02) 242553/242556 and nearly all international firms have offices in Jerusalem (Avis; Budget Rent-a-Car, 14 King David St, tel. (02) 248991/3; Hertz; InterRent).

It is worth comparing prices to obtain better rates. Drivers require either an international driving licence, or a national driving licence issued by a country which recognises the Israeli licence and is printed in English or French (other languages must be accompanied by a certificate of confirmation in Hebrew).

Cycling. Cyclists can contact The Jerusalem Cyclists Club, P.O. Box 7281, Jerusalem (tel. (02) 248238/412522).

The Railway Station lies to the S of the Old City of Jerusalem at Kikkar Remez (tel. (02) 717764 for information); the passenger line to Tel-Aviv follows a scenically attractive route and provides an agreeable if slower alternative to road travel; seats may be booked in advance for a small extra charge; no trains on Saturday or Jewish religious holidays; connections to Haifa and Nahariyya; freight services only to Ascalon, Ashdod, Beersheba and S of Dimona.

Climate and Timing of Visit

Jerusalem, in the hill country, has an agreeably dry Mediterranean climate, and lacks the humidity of the coastal resorts. Generally the winters are moderately cold and wet, the summers dry and hot. The average rainfall is 560mm but can rise to 1059mm (1877/8) and be as little as 210mm (1959/60); rainfall is mainly from November to March. The wettest months are January and February when rainfall averages 120mm per month. Average January temperature is 8.8°C (48°F) and frost and snow (average two days per year) are possible.

Average August temperature is 23.8°C (75°F), but can rise to over 30°C (86°F).

Spring in the surrounding countryside, though brief, can be very beautiful if the winter and spring rains have been good. Easter is a popular time when the climate is very pleasant (10°–23°C, 50°–73°F)—warm and with the likelihood of only light showers. Many people go at this time because it is the main pilgrimage season and much of interest occurs; but then Jerusalem can be very crowded. The temperature and conditions may also be affected at this season by hot desert winds (al-hamsin). The autumn from October (15°–27°C, 59°–81°F) is also a good and less crowded time to visit.

The evenings in Jerusalem at all times of year can be cool, and in addition to clothes suitable to the season, it is useful to have a light coat or jacket for summer evenings. Sun-glasses and hats are recommended for the summer, and strong shoes with good grips at all times of the year: the stone paved streets of Jerusalem can be very slippery. People of either sex wearing shorts and short-sleeved garments may be refused entry at the holy places.

Accomodation

Hotels exist in large numbers in all classes to serve the busy tourist trade. Information can be obtained from tourist offices and travel agents. The following is only a selection of hotels in Jerusalem:

☆☆☆☆☆Intercontinental (tel. (02) 282551/7)
☆☆☆☆☆Jerusalem Hilton (tel. (02) 536151)
☆☆☆☆☆King David (tel. (02) 221111)
☆☆☆☆American Colony (tel. (02) 282421/3)
☆☆☆☆Ariel (tel. (02) 719222)
☆☆☆YMCA (tel. (02) 227111)
☆☆☆YMCA (East) (tel. (02) 282375/6)
☆☆☆YWCA (tel. (02) 282593)
☆☆Har Aviv (tel. (02) 521515)
☆☆New Regent (tel. (02) 284540)
☆New Imperial (tel. (02) 272400)
☆Savoy (tel. (02) 283366)

Youth hostels. A number are located in the city or on the outskirts and are affiliated to the International Youth Hostel Association. In the Old City there is the Moreshet HaYahadut on Harat Dawaiyya between the Syrian Monastery and Christ Church in the Armenian Quarter (tel. (02) 288611); Bet Bernstein near the centre of the new city at 2 Keren HaYessod (tel. (02) 228286); several on the W edges of the city, at ʿAin Karim (tel. (02) 416282), on the S edge of the Jerusalem Forest overlooking ʿAin Karim for groups booked in advance (tel. (02) 416060), and the Louise Waterman Wise Hostel near Mount Herzl at Baʿit WeGan, buses 6, 12, 17, 18, 20, 23, 27 (tel. (02) 423366, 420990).

Camping. Israel Camping Union, P.O. Box 53, Nahariyya, and information from Tourist Offices. The camp site at En Hemed lies 11km W of Jerusalem.

Church hospices. Most denominations operate hospices. The Armenian Catholic hospice (tel. (02) 284262), the Casa Nova (Roman Catholic, tel. (02) 282791), Christ Church (Anglican, tel. (02) 282082), Dom Polski (Roman Catholic, tel. (02) 282077), Ecce Homo (Sisters of Sion, Roman Catholic, tel. (02) 282445) and the German Evangelical Hospice (tel. (02) 282120) are all in the Old City.

In the N part of the new city are St. George's Hostel (Anglican, tel. 283302), Notre Dame de France (tel. (02) 289723) and the White Sisters (tel. (02) 282633).

In the W are St. Andrew's (Scottish Church, tel. (02) 717701), the Sisters of the Rosary (tel. (02) 228529) and Notre Dame de Sion at 'Ain Karim (tel. (02) 415738).

Language

The official languages of the State of Israel are modern Hebrew and Arabic. Information for tourists and most main and tourist road signs are also given in English.

Modern Hebrew is distinct from classical or biblical Hebrew though based on the same alphabet of 22 letters and is written from right to left. Classical Hebrew is used for liturgical purposes. The development of a language suited to the needs of the modern world took place from the 19C, particularly under the instigation of Eliezer ben-Yehuda (1852–1922) who emigrated to Israel in 1881 and compiled the first modern Hebrew dictionary. Hebrew was recognised as an official language under the Mandate Government. The Academy of the Hebrew Language was established in 1953.

Many Jews still speak the forms of Hebrew developed in medieval times: Yiddish which is basically a mixture of German and Hebrew and is spoken by Ashkenasi groups; and Ladino which incorporates much Spanish and is spoken by some Sephardi communities.

Arabic is also a Semitic language, linked to the older Aramaic and adopted widely since the Islamic conquest in the 7C. It has 28 letters and is also written from right to left. It is the language of the Muslim and Christian Arab communities.

Owing to the very high percentage of Jewish immigrants from all over the world, many Israelis speak at least one other language.

Currency

The Israeli unit of currency is the *shekel* (after the ancient Syro-Palestinian weight measure for silver; in Israel in the time of David a royal standard of c 12 grams was set (heavier than the local common shekel of c 9.87 grams) which had declined to c 11.34 grams by the end of the Judaean monarchy. A silver shekel coin was minted during the First Revolt).

The modern shekel (IS) is issued in banknotes of various denominations and is divided into 100 *agorot*. Coins for 1, 5, 10 agorot, $^1/_2$ and 1 shekel are minted, and banknotes for higher denominations of shekels.

Many prices are advertised in dollars and often tax can be avoided by paying in foreign currency. Sterling Travellers' cheques may only be converted into Israeli currency. In recent times the inflation rate has also made it advisable for visitors to buy only small amounts of shekels for small daily purchases, fares etc. There is no limit on the import of foreign currency, but no more than is declared on entry may be exported; the number of shekels which can be exported is also limited.

Banks. Normal opening times are Sun, Tue, Thu 8.30–12.30, 16.00–17.30, Mon 8.30–12.30; Wed and Fri 8.30–12.00; closed Sat and Jewish religious holidays.

Israel Discount Bank, 62 King George St. (tel. (02) 637902); Barclays Discount Bank, 64 Jaffa Rd. (tel. (02) 224241).

Miscellaneous Services

Post Offices. Most main post offices are open from 8.00–18.00. Branch offices are open 8.00–12.30, 15.30–18.00 daily except Wed 8.00–14.00.

Postal services are marked by a sign with a **white stag on a blue ground**.

The main post office in West Jerusalem is near the E end of the Jaffa Rd, in East Jerusalem at the corner of Sulaiman and Salah al-Din Streets, opposite Herod's Gate. Stamps can also be obtained from bookstalls etc. and big hotels. Telegrams can be sent from all post offices and hotels, or by dialling 171. Tokens (*asimonim*) for public telephones can be purchased at post offices and some news stands. International calls are best made from main post offices. A public telephone centre from which direct dialling abroad is possible is at 1 Koresh St (behind the main post office) Sun-Thurs 7.00-20.30, Fri and holiday eves 7.00-13.30, Sat closed.

Police. Emergency calls dial 100. Headquarters is at the Russian Compound, Jaffa Road.

Ambulance. Emergency calls dial 101. This contacts Magen David Adom, the Israeli equivalent of the Red Cross. The central First Aid Post is near the Central Bus Station in Romema in West Jerusalem; another is located near the Dung Gate on the S side of the Old City.

Fire Brigade. Emergency calls dial 102.

Travel Agents. In West Jerusalem, Travex Ltd., 8 Shamai St, (tel. (02) 223211); in East Jerusalem, Albina Tours, 24 Salah al-Din St (tel. (02) 283397); ISSTA (Israel Student Travel Association), student flights tel. 231418.

Airline Offices. British Airways, 33 Jaffa Rd tel. (02) 233602; El Al, 12 Rechov Hillel, tel. (02) 233333; KLM, 33 Jaffa Rd, tel. (02) 232881; Olympic Airways, 33 Jaffa Rd, tel. (02) 234538.

Shipping Offices. The Adriatica and Hellenic Mediterranean lines operate car ferry and other services to Israel. Check at travel agents.

Embassies, Legations and Consulates. UK Embassy, 192 Hayarkon St, Tel Aviv (tel. (03) 249171); Consulate-General: Tower House, Harakevet St, West Jerusalem (tel. (02) 717724); Shaikh Jarrah, East Jerusalem (tel. (02) 282481). US Embassy, 71 Hayarkon St, Tel Aviv (tel. (03) 254338); Consulate-General: 18 Agron St, West Jerusalem (tel. (02) 234271); Nablus Rd, East Jerusalem (tel. (02) 282231). Australian Embassy: 185 Hayarkon St, Tel Aviv (tel. (03) 243152; Canadian Embassy, 220 Hayarkon St, Tel Aviv (tel. (03) 228122).

Major Religious Festivals and Holidays

Because of the varied ethnic and religious communities in the Holy Land the number and variety of religious festivals is very complex. Because different calendars (solar and lunar) are employed by the different communities, the dates of the festivals vary slightly from year to year and the intending traveller is well advised to check the dates of major holidays when making travel plans.

Jewish Festivals

The Hebrew calendar is lunar and adapted by leap years to a solar cycle so that religious holidays based on seasonal events fall at the right time of year. The Hebrew year dates from the Traditional Year of the Creation c 3761 BC, so that AD 1984/5 = the Jewish Year 5745.

Rosh Hoshana (New Year, a two day public holiday; the start of a ten-day fast; Jews visit the Pool of Siloam where sins are symbolically cast into the water); September/October.
Yom Kippur (the most important holiday, on the ancient Day of Atonement (Exodus 30:10), ends the ten-day New Year fast, a public holiday); September/October.
Succoth (The Feast of Tabernacles, seven days of which the first is a public holiday. A harvest festival, and the building of booths and tents in gardens commemorates the wanderings of the Exodus); September/October.
Simhath Torah (Rejoicing for the law (the Torah) at the end of Succoth, a public holiday); September/October.
Hanukkah (The Festival of Lights, celebrates the Maccabean capture of Jerusalem from the Seleucids in 164 BC); November/December.
Tu Be Shevat (Feast of the Trees, spring, tree-planting); January/February.
Purim (Festival of Queen Esther who thwarted a massacre of Persian Jews in the 5C BC); February/March.
Pesach (Passover, Feast of the Unleavened Bread, the Israelites spared before the Exodus from Egypt, public holiday at beginning and at end); March/April.
Independence Day (foundation of the State of Israel, a public holiday); April/May.
Lag Ba'Omer (commemorates no deaths on the 33rd day of a 1C epidemic); April/May.
Jerusalem Day (Capture of West Jerusalem); May/June.
Shabnoth (Feast of Weeks, ends the period of mourning after Passover, a public holiday); May/June.
Tish B'av (Mourning for the destruction of the Temple in 587 BC and AD 70, a public holiday); July/August.

Muslim Festivals

The Muslim calendar is lunar but not adapted to the solar calendar so that the years recede by 10 or 11 days annually. The festivals are not linked to the seasons. The Muslim year dates from AD 622 when Muhammad moved from Mecca to Medina. In the Muslim calendar AD 1984/5 = the year 1405 of the Hegira (Flight).

New Year.
Maulid (Muhammad's birthday).
Beginning of Ramadan (the ninth month is a month of fasting when Muslims may not eat, drink or smoke between dawn and dusk).
Leilat al-Kadr (26th day of Ramadan, Koran given to mankind).
Id al-Fitr (last three days of Ramadan).
Id al-Adha (Sacrificial Celebrations).

Christian Festivals

Based on a 365-day year adjusted by a leap year every four years, the calendar is calculated from the traditional birthdate of Christ.

Christmas (birth of Christ): Western churches, 24/25 December; Eastern Churches, 7 January.
New Year: Western Churches, 1 January; Eastern Churches, 14 January.
Easter (Resurrection of Christ); March/April.
Lent, Easter, Ascension, Pentecost and some other feasts are moveable, being calculated according to the old calendar.

Churches. For information, the Christian Information Office, opposite the Jaffa Gate, Old City (tel. (02) 287647). (Times of some English language services on Sunday are listed below).

Orthodox: Greek Orthodox, Church of the Holy Sepulchre, Old City (tel. (02) 284202).
Roman Catholic: Latin Patriarchate, near the Jaffa Gate, Old City (tel. (02) 282323); Chapel of the Flagellation, Via Dolorosa, Old City (tel. (02) 282936); Sisters of Sion (Ecce Homo) Church, Via Dolorosa (at 18.00).
Protestant: St. George's Cathedral (Anglican), Salah al-Din St (tel. (02) 282146) (at 8.00, 11.00, 18.00); Christ Church (Anglican) opposite the Jaffa Gate in the Old City (tel. (02) 282082) (at 8.00, 11.00 and 18.45); St. Andrew's Church (Church of Scotland), Harakevet St (tel. (02) 714659) (at 10.00); Baptist Tourist Chapel, 6 Rasheed St (at 11.00); Baptist Church, 4 Narkis St (tel. (02) 225942); Garden Tomb Church (Inter-denominational), Nablus Rd (tel. (02) 283402) (at 9.00); Church of the Redeemer (Lutheran), Muristan, Old City (tel. (02) 282543).

Principal Mosques. Aqsa Mosque, Old City; Khanqah Mosque, Old City; Mosque of 'Umar, Old City; Shaikh Jarrah Mosque, Nablus Rd.

Principal Synagogues. Hekal Shlomo, 58 King George St (tel. (02) 635212). Sephardic Synagogues, Jewish Quarter, Old City (tel. (02) 226773).

Restaurants

Restaurants in Jerusalem offer considerable variety, both international and local on all levels, including many informal eating places. Many advertise in the tourist information newspapers. Jewish restaurants often reflect the origin of the owner; those with East European background may offer bagels, bortsch, goulash, strudels, blintzes, schnitzel and gefilte fish on the menu; or one with a North African or Moroccan background may offer chicken with rich sauces; there are also restaurants with Yemeni dishes; most are kosher, which indicates that the food has been prepared according to religious dietary laws, with meat correctly slaughtered, no prohibited foods such as pork, shell-fish, game etc., as proscribed in the Bible (e.g. Levit. 11 and Deut. 14 which mostly reflect ancient health safeguards). Strictly applied this means also a refusal to serve meat and dairy products at the same meal—e.g. no milk in coffee for about five hours after eating meat.

Other eating places typical of Jewish sections of the city are dairy restaurants (milk, cream and egg dishes, pancakes and blintzes, ice cream and salads), delis (hamburger, pastrami, sandwiches, salad, fries etc.), fish, vegetarian and, increasingly, health food restaurants (vegetarian quiches, casseroles and pies, tofu, grains, fruit juices).

Muslim cooking is mainly available in East Jerusalem where restaurants feature mezze (starters with 25 or more varieties), kebabs and chicken dishes (mainly near Herod's Gate, just outside the Old City: National Palace Restaurant, al-Zahira St, tel. (02) 282246; Hassan Effendi, 3 Rashid St, tel. (02) 283599)

International styles of cookery abound: there are French, Hungarian, Indian, Italian, Mexican, Rumanian, Chinese, Lebanese, Kurdish, Iraqi and Japanese restaurants which are sometimes also kosher. Luxury hotels offer a high standard of international catering—the Hilton in West Jerusalem, the American Colony and Intercontinental in East Jerusalem.

Some local cheap and good foods include falafel (deep fried balls of ground seasoned chickpeas), humous (creamy purée of chickpeas, oil and lemon), tahina (sesame cream purée) and many salads; kebabs (lamb minced or cut, grilled on a skewer); shawarma (sliced lamb cooked on a spit); pitta bread sandwiches and yogurt. If buying at a street stall choose one that is clearly popular and has a rapid-turnover with freshly-cooked food. Apart from the pitta bread, the rings of bread covered with sesame seeds are very good; among the Arabs bread is often eaten with a seasoning of herbs, spices and oil, and bread sellers will often have small portions of such seasoning available. A few old-style bread bakeries still exist.

Wines and beers are available, both imported and local. The cheaper local varieties, Cremisan and Latroun, have been produced for many years by Christian communities living south and west of Jerusalem.

Shopping, Entertainment, Sport

Shops are normally open 8.30–13.00, 16.00–19.00, but times vary. Jewish shops are closed Friday afternoon and Saturday; Muslim shops are closed on Friday; Christian shops are closed on Sunday. Most requirements can be met daily by going to different areas of the city.

If buying antiquities the legal safeguard and guarantee against fakes is to buy at shops displaying the sign of two figures carrying a bunch of grapes (which indicates that it is licensed by the Ministry of Tourism) but an export permit is required and there is a fee of 10 per cent of the purchase price. Otherwise the export of antiquities (defined as objects fashioned by man pre-dating AD 1700) is strictly prohibited.

Booksellers. There are numerous booksellers in West Jerusalem and a good bookshop in the foyer of the Israel Museum; in East Jerusalem booksellers are mainly located on Salah al-Din St. A biennial Book Fair is held in Jerusalem and every spring Hebrew Book Week is marked by numerous book markets.

Learned Institutions and libraries: W.F. Albright Institute of Archaeological Research, Salah al-Din St, East Jerusalem; American Institute of Holy Land Studies, Mount Zion; British Council, Shaikh Jarrah, East Jerusalem; British School of Archaeology in Jerusalem, Ramallah Rd, Sheikh Jarrah, East Jerusalem; École Biblique et Archéologique de St. Étienne, Nablus Rd, East Jerusalem; German Institute of Archaeology, Old City; Institute of Archaeology, Hebrew University, Mount Scopus; Israel Exploration Society; Nelson Glueck School of Biblical Archaeology, Hebrew Union College—Jewish Institute of Religion; Pontifical Biblical Institute, Paul Emile Botta St; Schocken Institute of Jewish Research, 6 Balfour St.

Theatres, Concerts, and Cultural Festivals. Tickets for concerts etc. can be bought from ticket agencies: Cahana-On, 1 Dorot Rishonim St (at the corner of Ben Yahuda St) (tel. (02) 222831, 234006); Klaim Agency, 8 Shamai St (tel. (02) 240896, 234061); at Ben Naim, 38 Jaffa Road (tel. (02) 224008).

Concerts are given by the Israel Philharmonic Orchestra and by the Jerusalem Symphony Orchestra of the Israel Broadcasting Authority are given at various places including the Jerusalem Theatre in Chopin St, the Mitchell Auditorium in Strauss St, the Israel Museum and the concert hall at the Binyené HaUmma; master classes for young Israeli musicians are held at the Jerusalem Music Centre.

Information on the Israel Festival (the spring festival of music, theatre and dance held annually in April) may be obtained from the information offices; folk dancing is also popular and numerous performances are given by the Bat Sheva Dance Company and the Bat Dor Dance Company; regular evenings with the Khan Theatre Group and the Jerusalem Dance Company are held at the Khan Centre near the Railway Station, the YMCA and other centres.

There are numerous cinemas: local and foreign films usually have sub-titles.

Sport. Tennis is available at the Israel Tennis Centre, 5 Elmaliach St, Katamon Quarter, (tel. (02) 413866) and various hotels, particularly the YMCA; sport and recreation facilities at Bet HaHistradut, Strauss

St; the Jerusalem Sports Club (HaZefira, tel. (02) 632125) and the Hapoel Sports Grounds in 'Emeq Refa'im; at the sports centre at Ramat Rahel Kibbutz; swimming at 'Emeq Refa'im Swimming Pool, Qiryat HaYovél Swimming Pool (Bus 23); and Ramat Rahel (Bus 7).

Abbreviations

A. = Arabic
b. = ibn (son of)
c = circa
C = century
H. = Hebrew
km = kilometre
m = metre
R = Room
Rd = Road
Rte = Route
St = Street
St. = Saint

Glossary

AMBULATORY a place for walking, often covered.

AMIR (A.) prince, military commander.

'AQABA (A.) slope or lane.

ARCHITRAVE the lowest part of the entablature, the beam resting on the capital; ornamental moulding around the exterior of an arch.

ARCHIVOLT the under curve of an arch from impost to impost; the mouldings which decorate the curve.

ARCOSOLIUM term used for a rock-cut trough or bench burial with arched opening above it.

ASHLAR squared stone laid in regular courses.

ATRIUM in early Christian and medieval churches, the colonnaded forecourt.

BAB (A.) gate.

BASILICA Roman hall of justice and commerce; Christian church with nave, aisles and clerestory.

BIMAH platform in a synagogue for the reading of the Torah (the Law).

BIR (A.) well.

BIRKAT (A.) pool or reservoir.

CAVETTO a hollowed moulding whose profile is the quadrant of a circle.

CHAMFER to bevel or channel an edge.

CIBORIUM a canopy raised over the high altar in a church.

CORBEL projecting or overlapping stone blocks supporting a vault.

CORNICE projecting upper section of an entablature, or a horizontal moulded projection crowning a building or some part of it.

CRENELLATIONS battlements, embrasures.

CUPOLA dome, especially a miniature dome on a lantern.

CYMA MOULDING the outline of a moulding consisting of a concave and a convex line, an ogee.

DAR (A.) house.

DAIR (A.) Christian monastery.

DARAJ (A.) steps.

DEREKH (H.) road.

DENTILS teeth-like row of small rectangular blocks under a cornice.

DIGLYPHS a block with two grooves between metopes in a Doric frieze.

DIKKA (A.) platform for prayer repeater in a mosque.

DIWAN a room open at one side, often with raised floor, where judgments were given and councils held in Ottoman practice.

DOSSERET extra stone set above the capital to level columns of varying height.

ELBOW CONSOLES or BRACKETS engaged angled columns supporting a capital.

FIRMAN (Persian) royal decree.

GADROONED VOUSSOIRS voussoirs decorated with sets of convex curves at right angles to the architrave.

GIV'AH (H.) hill.

GUTTAE stone pegs beneath the triglyphs in a Doric entablature.

HAMMAM (A.) bath house.

HANAFI one of the four canonical law schools of Islam.

HANBALI one of the four canonical law schools of Islam.

HAR (H.) mount.

HARAM (A.) a sanctuary, as in Haram al-Sharif, the Noble Sanctuary.

HYPOGEUM an underground chamber or vault.

ICONOSTASIS the screen in Orthodox churches separating the sanctuary from the main body of the church, on which icons are hung.

IMPOST upper (projecting) course of a pillar or abutment, often decorated, on which the foot of an arch rests.

IWAN vaulted hall with a large arched opening.

JAMI' (A.) congregational mosque in which the Friday prayers are said (as in Masjid al-Jami').

JOGGLED VOUSSOIRS voussoirs joined by notches and corresponding projections.

KHAN (A.) caravanserai, or hostel providing accommodation for merchants and other visitors.

KHANQAH (A.) Muslim monastery for Sufi mystics.

KIKKAR (H.) square.

KOKHIM (H.) term for rock-cut burial places of the Roman period, which are roughly oven-shaped.

LANTERN a structure with (glazed) apertures on top of a dome or room, which admits light and ventilation.

LOGGIA a gallery or arcade having one or more sides open to the air.

MACHICOLATION opening between the corbels supporting the parapet (often above a gate) through which combustibles, molten lead, stones and other objects were dropped upon attackers.

MADFAN (A.) a burial place.

MADRASA (A.) religious school for teaching the principles of orthodox Islam.

MAKTAB (A.) a Muslim primary school.

MALAKI (A.) fine local limestone much used for building in Jerusalem.

MALIKI one of the four canonical law schools of Islam.

MAR (A.) Christian saint.

MASTABA a raised platform, particularly an open-air prayer place in the Haram.

MATHARA place of ablution.

MAWAZIN in Jerusalem specifically the 'scales', or arcades on the platform of the Dome of the Rock.

MAZAR (A.) a shrine visited by pilgrims.

METOPE space between two triglyphs in a Doric frieze.

MIHRAB (A.) niche (normally in a mosque) marking the direction of prayer.

MINARET (A. manara) tower from which the call to prayer is made.

MINBAR (A.) stepped pulpit, normally inside the mosque, from which the Friday sermon is given.

MISHNAH Jewish law.

MIZZI (A.) hard local limestone used for building in Jerusalem.

MIZZI AHMAR (A.) red-veined variety of limestone used for building in Jerusalem.

MOULDINGS projecting or recessed bands used to ornament walls, arches etc.

MUEZZIN (A.) official who gives the call to prayer for the mosque.

MUQARNAS DECORATION stalactite carving, usually ornamenting the vault of a semi-dome or a corbel and much used in Mamluk times in Jerusalem.

MUSALLA (A.) open place for performing the Muslim prayer.

OSTRAKA (Greek) an inscribed potsherd.

PALMETTE an ornament with narrow radiating divsions, somewhat resembling a palm-leaf.

PENDENTIVE a section of masonry forming a spherical triangle supporting a dome above a rectangular base.

PILASTER rectangular engaged column.

QANATIR (A.) arcade, especially the arched colonnades on the platform of the Dome of the Rock.

QIBLA (A.) the direction of prayer.

QUBBA (A.) dome.

REHOV (H.) street.

RIBAT (A.) in medieval Jerusalem a hospice where pilgrims were given free accommodation.

RIWAQ portico, in Jerusalem the arcade around the north and west sides of the Haram.

SABIL fountain founded for the free supply of water for drinking and ablution.

SARAY (A.) palace.

SEDEROT (H.) boulevarde, avenue.

SHA'AR (H.) gate.

SHAFI'I one of the four canonical law schools of Islam.

SHAIKH (A.) elder, tribal chief.

SHARI'A (A.) street.

SHI'A the minority Islamic group, adherents of the cause of the Caliph 'Ali and his descendants.

SIQAYA (A.) drinking fountain, water for ablutions.

SOFFIT the under surface of a lintel, vault or arch.

SPANDREL triangular space between two arches, or between an arch and a wall.

SPRINGERS architecturally, the supports or imposts from which an arch springs.

SQUINCH a straight or arched support constructed across an angle to support a superstructure.

STRING COURSE a horizontal course in a facade, sometimes ornamental.

STUCCO coating of (ornamental) plaster or cement.

SUFI a Muslim mystic.

SUNNI the mainstream Orthodox group of Islam.

SUQ (A.) market or bazaar.

TALMUD interpretation of the Misnah.

TARIQ (A.) road.

TEMENOS (Greek) sacred area around a temple, sacred enclosure or precinct.

TIE-BEAMS structural, and often ornamental, beam linking the tops of capitals in an arcade.

TRIGLYPH a block with three vertical grooves between metopes on a Doric frieze.

TURBA(T) (A.) mausoleum.

TYMPANUM in medieval architecture the space between the lintel and the arch above it.

VOUSSOIRS wedge-shaped stone blocks forming an arch.

WALI (A.) Muslim saint or holy man.

WAQF, pl. AWQAF (A.) endowment(s) for pious purposes.

YAD (H.) memorial.

YESHIVA (H.) rabbinical seminary.

YISHUV older Jewish population established in Jerusalem by the early 20th century.

ZAWIYA (A.) 'corner', a place for devotion, often the dwelling and later burial place of a pious Muslim.

ZUQAQ (A.) alley.

1   The Walls and Gates of the Old City

Introduction. For the history of the walls of ancient Jerusalem, see p. 13ff. Sections of the present walls are on the line of those built at earlier periods, which were dismantled by al-Malik al-Muʿazzam in 1219. They were rebuilt in their present form by Sulaiman the Magnificent in 1537–41. The walls embrace a circuit of 4018m (N=1281m, W=875m, S=1100m, E=762m) and today have seven gates open to passage. The SW, W and NW walls served a defensive purpose from 1948–67 when they formed the Jordanian front line on the Armistice Line of 1948, and still bear scars from the fighting at that time. Though quite inadequate to the demands of defence against artillery, the walls have retained their symbolic status. The walls, of fine local stone of mellow colour, enhance the concept of the medieval city they were built to defend, and enclose the densely packed houses and streets, nearly all of which retain the narrow stepped crookedness of the medieval town. Cars can only enter where gates and walls have been breached for this purpose at the Jaffa, Dung and St. Stephen's Gates.

Visit. A pleasant walk with views can be had along the top and around the outer footing of the entire circuit of the walls, except the S and E wall of the Haram. Entrance to the **Rampart Walk** is from **St. Stephen's, Damascus** and **Jaffa Gates**; exits from most other gates; a small admission fee is charged; open 9.00–17.00 daily, Fri 9.00–15.00. The distance from St. Stephen's Gate to the Damascus Gate is 1150m; from Damascus Gate to Jaffa Gate is 1000m. The following description of the walls and gates runs S from the Jaffa Gate.

The Jaffa Gate, H. *Shaʿar Yafo*, A. *Bab al-Khalil* or *Gate of the Friend* (Abraham, the Friend of God, and thus by association also the Hebron Gate for the shrine of the Prophet Abraham at Hebron); in Crusader times the Gate of David. Built by Sulaiman II in 1538, the gate retains its early Ottoman form with a curved joggled lintel bearing the builder's inscription, set within a higher pointed arch. The entry contains a left-angled turn; restored machicolation and parapet above the gate. The original gate is still used for pedestrian entrance, but the curtain wall to the S was demolished and the citadel moat filled in 1898 by order of Sultan ʿAbd-al-Hamid II to allow Kaiser Wilhelm II of Germany to ride into the city in a carriage. It was also the point of entry for Allenby and the British army in December 1917.

Wall: Jaffa to Zion Gate. Immediately S of the gate is the *Citadel* (see Rte 5), the W wall of which is mostly Mamluk work, but a gate and outer bailey of Sulaiman II are visible. The wall S of the Citadel is a fine stretch of parapeted curtain wall with a series of external rectangular offsets. It is the work of Sulaiman, and the footings have been cleared to bedrock as part of the scheme for the National Park to preserve the character of the Old City. A path for pedestrians to view the remains follows the wall, and parts of the earlier Ayyubid, Crusader and Herodian or Hasmonean *city wall foundations* can be seen beneath the present wall. To the W is the Hinnom valley (see Rte 15), with the *Montefiore Windmill* and the modern city above (Route 14). From the rectangular off-set at the SW angle of the Old City is a fine view of the *Church of the Dormition* and the *Tower of David* (see Rte 8).

The Zion Gate, H. *Sha'ar Ziyyon*, A. *Bab al-Nabi Da'ud* or *Gate of the Prophet David*, was built by Sulaiman II in 1540. The gate was badly damaged in the fighting in 1948 and a flat concrete lintel replaces the original flat joggled voussoirs with a shallow relieving arch. The entrance is set within a pointed arch with machicolation above, with small gadrooned arches and ornamental panels at the sides. The gate-chamber has a right-angled turn. A re-used inscription of the Third Roman Legion (Cyrenaica) dedicated to Jupiter Serapis and Trajan (c 115–117) built into the gate was noted in 1894.

Wall: Zion to Dung Gate. A fine stretch of wall runs down the hill to the **Dung Gate**, the footings of which have also been cleared and landscaped for the National Park since 1967. The *Ottoman wall* appears to follow the course of the earlier 11C–13C wall very closely in this section. Following the outer face of the wall down the hill and past the first off-set in the wall, one can see part of a square *Ayyubid tower* projecting from the wall footings. Its N side and central pier were discovered against the inside face of the wall (Avigad, 1969–83). It was built in 1212 and dismantled by order of al-Malik al-Mu'azzam in 1219. Just inside the wall to the E of the Ayyubid tower a stretch of the *Crusader wall*, 2.5m in width, was uncovered. Continuing E outside the city wall, the main projection on the outer face of the wall on this stretch of the defences is the **Sulphur Tower**, A. *Burj al-Kibrit*, built in 1540 (inscription on S face). Part of an earlier large tower (11C–13C) of mixed masonry projects beneath it. A fragment of the *Lower Aqueduct* which brought water from *Solomon's Pools* to the Temple area can be seen nearby. It was built in the 1C BC and with many repairs, including the insertion of the ceramic pipes now visible, was still in use early this century. A small path leads up along the wall face at this point to remains of a 6C *hospice*(?) built by Justinian, which was probably connected with his great Nea Church (Rte 7). A fragment of the SE apse of the Nea Church is visible just 50m N of the Sulphur Tower. Here four courses of very large drafted blocks with rough bosses preserved to a height of 3m project from beneath the angle of the city wall. The upper course is restored. Descending from the high path, the next salient in the city wall to the E also has an earlier 11C–13C tower of small masonry projecting beneath its foundations. The adjacent area contains the cuttings of many baths and cisterns of the 1C AD. Just W of the Dung Gate a *massive tower* in rusticated masonry also of 11C–13C date is perhaps to be identified with the fortification adjacent to the *Crusader Gate of the Leatherworkers*. Steps on the W side lead into the interior of the tower. Note how steeply the rock scarp rises from here to the W. Running S from below the foundations of the tower is a fine stretch of a *paved Byzantine road*.

The Dung Gate, H. *Sha'ar ha-Ashpot*, A. *Bab al-Maghariba* or *Gate of the Moors* because it gave onto the now destroyed Maghariba quarter, was built in 1540–41, and was probably a small Ottoman postern gate with pointed arch. The gate was enlarged and the long concrete lintel inserted during Jordanian times to permit the entry of motor trafffic after the Jaffa Gate was closed in 1948.

   For the wall between the Dung Gate and St. Stephens Gate, see Rte 2A.

St. Stephen's Gate, dating to 1538, has a particularly confusing set of names: A. *Bab Sitti Maryam* or St. Mary's Gate, as it leads out towards the Church and Tomb of the Virgin Mary in the Valley of Jehoshaphat. In Sulaiman's time, *Bab al-Ghor* or *Gate of the Valley*

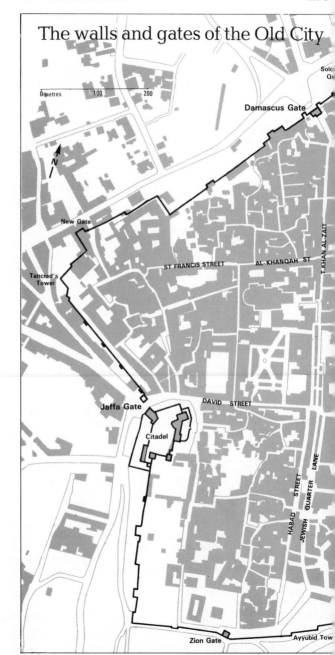

The walls and gates of the Old City

Damascus Gate

0 metres 100 200

New Gate

Tancred's Tower

ST FRANCIS STREET

AL-KHANQAH ST

T. KHAN AL-ZAIT

Jaffa Gate

DAVID STREET

Citadel

HABAD STREET

JEWISH QUARTER LANE

Zion Gate

Ayyubid Tow

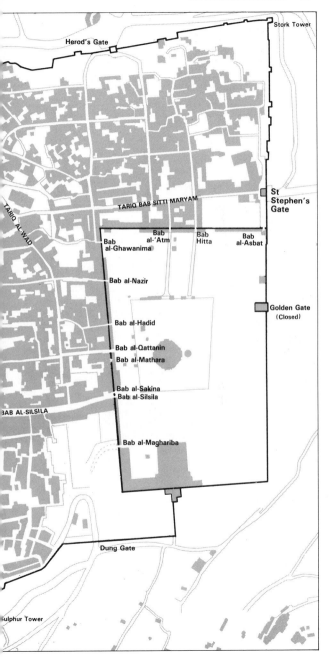

Stork Tower

Herod's Gate

TARIQ AL WAD

St Stephen's Gate

TARIQ BAB SITTI MARYAM

Bab al-'Atm

Bab Hitta

Bab al-Asbat

Bab al-Ghawanima

Bab al-Nazir

Golden Gate
(Closed)

Bab al-Hadid

Bab al-Qattanin
Bab al-Mathara

Bab al-Sakina
Bab al-Silsila

BAB AL-SILSILA

Bab al-Maghariba

Dung Gate

Sulphur Tower

(of Jordan); in Crusader times the Gate of Jehoshaphat, when the N gate was called that of St. Stephen. After 1187 the name was transferred. The H. name *Sha'ar ha-'Arayot*, the *Lions Gate*, derives from the confronted lions or panthers carved on either side of the arch, which were the armorial device of the Mamluk sultan Baybars I (1260–77), re-used by Sulaiman II. The Ottoman gate has a curved lintel (restored), with a machicolation above a pointed arch. The angled-gate chamber was removed in Mandate times to allow entry for cars. Bedrock lies c 6.1m below the gate. Just 40m to the NE of the gate was the **Pool of St. Mary** *(Birkat Sitti Maryam)* of uncertain but probably not ancient date. A built stone-lined tank of no great size, it was filled in during 1986. It was supplied by aqueduct and in recent times served the bath house just inside the gate (Rte 3). The remains of various aqueducts were explored by Warren in the area to the E of the Haram in 1868–69.

Wall: St. Stephen's to Herod's Gate. This section of the wall was particularly vulnerable to attack from the high ground to the N and had a *deep rock-cut ditch* to defend it. The wall has a large number of insets and off-sets in the section leading up to the tower at the NE angle of the city, called the *Stork Tower*, A. *Burj Laqlaq*, which dates to 1538–39 and was also built by Sulaiman II (inscription above small pointed arch in upper storey). A sheep market is held each Friday morning adjacent to this tower. Excavations by Hamilton (1937–38), and Kloner (1976), on the section of the wall between this tower and Herod's Gate indicated that the earliest foundations of a city wall on this line were not earlier than the 3C or beginning of the 4C. The Crusaders surmounted the walls and entered the city in this section, probably just to the E of Herod's Gate, at noon on 15 July 1099. The *rock outcrop of Karm al-Shaikh* opposite on the N contained many ancient rock-cut tombs (Clermont-Ganneau).

Herod's Gate, A. *Bab al-Zahra* or *Gate of Flowers* (from its decoration), *Bab al-Sahira* because it led out to the former Muslim cemetery on the hill of al-Sahira opposite. The gate was identified as that of Herod because a medieval house, the *Dair al-'Adas (Dair Abu 'Adas)*, or 'monastery of (the father of) lentils') towards the lower end of Shari'a Muhammad Darwish, near the Convent of the Flagellation (see Rte 3), was thought in medieval times to be the Palace of Herod Antipas (Abu 'Adas and Antipas sound alike) who condemned Christ. The present gate is a small one, now altered to contain a direct entrance passage, but originally it was angled with an E-facing entrance. The blocked E-facing gateway has ornamental details similar to the 16C gates of Sulaiman II, in particular the *rosette panel* above the arch compares with that at St. Stephen's Gate, and the relief boss at the apex of the arch compares with those at the Damascus Gate and the Zion Gate; there is a joggled relieving arch above the lintel, and space for a missing inscription.

Wall: Herod's Gate to the Damascus Gate. Gardens have been laid out along the base of the wall, which is here built on bed-rock. Beneath the second high scarped outcrop E of the Damascus Gate (the 'Hill of Bezetha'), is the modern entrance to **Solomon's Quarries** (sign-posted from the gardens opposite the bus station in SULAIMAN ST). Open Sun–Thu 8.00–16.00; Fri 8.00–13.00; admission charged.

This is a great cave with galleries, an ancient quarry, extending c 200m SE under the city. The quarry exploited a stratum of *malaki* limestone. It was rediscovered c 1852 or a little earlier, but is noted before the 19C. The date of the quarrying is uncertain, though it is traditionally linked with Solomon's quarry for the building of the

Temple (I Kings 5:15–17). Clermont-Ganneau found and removed a carving of a sphinx-like creature on the pier to the left of the entrance by the first gallery, which he suggested should date to the 8C–6C BC. Others have associated the quarry with the work of Herod the Great, or with that of Herod Agrippa I, and with the 'Royal Caverns' mentioned by Josephus (War V:147). In Jewish works from the 3C it appears to be called *Zedekiah's Grotto*, and this tradition is preserved in the works of al-Muqaddasi (10C) and Mujir al-Din (c 1495). Variants of the Zedekiah legend say the cave extended all the way to Jericho, and was the hidden route by which Zedekiah escaped the besieging Babylonians in 586 BC. The Old Testament account (II Kings 25:4–5; Jer. 52:7–8) describes Zedekiah as fleeing down the Kidron.

•Damascus Gate, A. *Bab al-ʿAmud* or *Gate of the Column*, reconstructed in 1537–38 on Roman foundations; H. *Shaʿar Shekhem* (leading to the SHECHEM RD). In Crusader times it was called the Gate of St. Stephen, as tradition located the stoning of St. Stephen outside this gate. The pilgrim Theodosius in the 6C called it the Galilee Gate.

History. The Arabic name of the Damascus Gate preserves the memory of the column erected in honour of the emperors Hadrian and Antoninus Pius which stood in the open place just inside the Roman gate at the top of the cardo maximus in Aelia Capitolina, from c 135. The present gate overlies the ancient gate almost exactly. The excavations of Hamilton (1937–38) and Hennessy (1964–66) indicated that the area just outside the gate was used for burials in the early part of the 1C AD and was thus outside the walls. Following recent excavation (Magen, 1980–84) it is claimed that a gate tower dating to the 1C BC underlies the present structure. In AD 40–41 Herod Agrippa I built the Third North Wall of the city and either the 1937–38 (visible) or the 1980–84 (not visible) gate could indicate that it was on the present line. Bedrock here is some 8m below the present surface.

The visible E Roman gate was either constructed or reconstructed (both views are proposed) by Hadrian for Aelia Capitolina (inscription above E gate). At that time a round-arched triple gate was flanked by two great towers with internal stairs to the ramparts above. These structures may have re-used some of the drafted stones from the Temple destroyed in AD 70. No traces of the contemporary 1C AD walls (if they existed) have yet been found. This gate complex led to a great semi-circular paved plaza with honorific column, from which in turn the cardo maximus and a second colonnaded street led SW and SE respectively. A succession of road surfaces indicated the gate continued in use through the Byzantine period. The Madaba Map of the 6C (see p. 6) shows the gate from the interior of the city, with a single round-arched gate flanked by two high towers and the honorific column still prominent. The lateral gates may therefore have been blocked by this time, and were certainly out of use in the 8C, when the flanking towers were divided into two storeys, and two large Umayyad cisterns were built which blocked the exteriors of the side gates. The E interior staircase to the ramparts was also converted into a cistern and the E guard chamber of the tower into an oil pressing area, which in turn was abandoned in the Fatimid period.

The whole gateway was remodelled in Crusader times, when the tower chamber was sealed, and an angled gate complex with E-facing entrance was thrown out to the N, much of which was discovered in 1964–66. Two rooms covered the Umayyad cisterns on either side of the gate, that on the W with frescoes of saints was certainly ecclesiastical and may have been the Church of St. Abraham, which is recorded as being just inside the gate. This complex was destroyed either by order of al-Malik al-Muʿazzam in 1219 or in the sack by the Khwarizmian Turks in 1244, when the guard chamber and gateway were filled with earth and stones. Steps were later laid over the rubble of the Crusader gatehouse, but there is little evidence for gate or wall till 1537 when Sulaiman II laid out his new gate almost precisely over the Roman gate. The lack of a gate between 1219 and 1537 is confirmed by the evidence of Rabbi Obadiah of Bartenura in 1488.

Visit. A *museum* in the Roman Gate and Plaza, which gives entrance to the City walls and Rampart Walk, is entered through the old Roman gate. Open 9.00–17.00 daily except Fri 9.00–15.00; admission charged.

The present steps and bridge to the gate are modern, built 1966–67 and subsequently. The bridge was intended as a temporary structure in a larger plan for displaying the archaeological remains. The Ottoman gate can best be viewed from the steps to the N. The smaller masonry used by the Ottomans can easily be distinguished from that of the Roman period beneath. Sulaiman built directly onto the Roman work and the present towers overlie the Roman ones. The Ottoman gate is a fine example of Sulaiman's work, with a flat lintel of joggled blocks, triangular relieving arch and inscription above. The gateway is set back within a pointed arch with decorated voussoirs. There is a wealth of fenestration, crenellation and machicolation variously restored above.

Entering the gate, the passage makes a double bend first to E, then to S through a lofty gate passage before arriving in the *Muslim Quarter* (Rte 3). The gate passage itself has been the location of money changers' shops for many years. It is in some ways the most satisfying way to enter the Old City, as it is always crowded with those passing to buy and sell in the suqs beyond. The bus and taxi stations serving the West Bank are located in the adjacent streets.

Below the bridge the *Roman and Crusader remains* are visible. Immediately E and below the modern gate level are the E tower and E gate of the *triple gate* built or rebuilt by Hadrian in 135, but perhaps begun by Herod Agrippa I in AD 40– 41. The fine masonry, large blocks dressed flat with narrow drafted margins, are probably 1C BC stones in secondary use, but note the fine mouldings of the tower. The inscribed stone above the E arch certainly dates to the time of Hadrian in 135. Some 15m N of the Roman gate the lower courses and threshold of the *Crusader gate tower* can be seen.

Descending by stairs to the W of the bridge, the remains of the *W Roman gate tower*, a few fragments of a *Crusader chapel*, perhaps dedicated to St. Abraham, with traces of the frescoed heads of saints still adhering to the walls, can be seen in the lower W area. This chapel was built above an Umayyad cistern. Passing through a café area under the bridge one notes that it stands on the *Crusader roadway* which was excavated in 1964–66, and which led directly beneath the bridge to enter the city at precisely the same spot as the present gate, but at a lower level. The central Roman Gate, and the Byzantine Gate were all located on the same spot but at a lower level. The visitor then turns right and arrives in front of the E Roman Gate.

The entrance to the City Walls and Roman remains is through the Roman Gate. Entering, turn left into the great *E tower chamber* of the Roman Gate which served as a guard chamber. It is a large and lofty rectangular chamber. The NW wall is set obliquely due to the shape of the gate tower. The jumble of masonry used, the rock cuttings, and various alterations are due to different periods of re-use. The plan is presumably that of Hadrian, with stairs up to the ramparts in the centre of the W wall; a very heavily buttressed hole and rock-cutting in the S wall is described as the entrance to the city from the guard chamber. The plan is repeated in the W Gate Tower which is not open. A second storey was inserted in the Byzantine period. The equipment for the Umayyad oil press on display indicates one period of re-use, as does the 16C vaulted ceiling. From the 13C the lower chamber was filled with rubble which has been removed in the recent excavations. The 44 steep steps of various type and date lead to the top of the Ottoman Gate, a splendid view of the Old City and the Rampart walks.

Returning to the entrance lobby, turn left to the passage to the S, which leads to the section of the *Roman and Byzantine plaza* which has been cleared and displayed beneath the present street level. The large polished ancient slabs, some ribbed, which slope gently down from the gateway for about 50m provide a magnificent setting for an interesting *photographic display* of Jerusalem's later history. Parts of a *Crusader road and sewer*, some Crusader houses built over the plaza and renovated in the Mamluk period are visible. A low annex to the W allows access to a gaming-board incised on the pavement, similar to those in the Convent of the Sisters of Sion (see Rte 3). At the S end are some vaults of the Mamluk period.

Walls: Damascus Gate to New Gate. This stretch of the Ottoman wall has numerous projections, and towards its W end has a salient extending nearly 50m to the N. Excavations (Turler, De Grot and Solar, 1979) provided evidence that this stretch of the 16C city wall lies on Byzantine foundations which may have been built not earlier than the 3C–4C.

The New Gate, H. *Sha'ar He-Hadash* lies near the NW angle of the Old City and was cut through the city wall in 1887 by the Ottoman Sultan 'Abd al-Hamid II to provide access to the new suburbs to the NW. It was sealed 1948–67. It leads into the Christian Quarter.

Walls: New Gate to Jaffa Gate. Inside the most prominent N-facing angle of the city wall a small 16C mosque, *Masjid al-Qaymari*, can be seen from the ramparts. At the NW angle of the walls are the remains of the construction known as **Tancred's Tower**, or *the Castle of Goliath*, A. *Qasr Jalut*. Most of the remains are in Christian Brothers' College inside the walls, but parts have recently been uncovered in excavations just outside the walls (Bahat and Ben-Ari, 1971–72). The square tower, with its large blocks of drafted masonry, has sometimes been identified with the Psephinus Tower of Herod Agrippa I, but although much of the masonry is re-used from some 1C AD structure, the building is probably Crusader. Attempts to date the fortifications on this line to the Herodian period, or to locate the Psephinus Tower here, cannot be substantiated. Psephinus in any case is described by Josephus as an octagonal tower (War V:160). A 12C Crusader tradition maintained that this was the spot where David slew Goliath. Tancred, after whom the ruined tower is named, played an important role in the taking of Jerusalem in 1099. He assisted Godfrey of Lorraine in the initial unsuccessful attack on the NW angle of the town on 13 June, then led an expedition to the Samaria region to get wood to build siege towers; he subsequently entered the city by the tower put up by Godfrey of Bouillon near Herod's Gate on 15 July. The association with Tancred may also favour the view that the tower was initially a Crusader building.

Excavations have shown some sherds near bedrock of 7C and 3C–2C BC date but no other walls prior to the building of the tower. The tower is 35m × 35m, built of re-used Herodian blocks with drafted edges and rough projecting bosses, with massive internal piers of which five or six courses are preserved in Christian Brothers' College. A street 3m wide separated the tower from the contemporary city wall on the N and W sides. The N wall of the tower, and the city wall to the N of it, lie outside the line of the present Ottoman city wall. These fortifications were bounded by a tremendous rock-cut ditch, 19m wide and more than 7m deep. The tower may have been destroyed c 1219 by the Ayyubid al-Malik al-Mu'azzam who ordered the demolition of the fortifications of Jerusalem. The ruins were levelled in the 16C when Sulaiman II built the present city wall over them. Some re-used Crusader capitals have been built into the lower part of the city wall.

The Ottoman wall then continues to the Jaffa Gate.

2   The Haram al-Sharif

* *Haram al-Sharif*, *the Noble Sanctuary; Bait al-Maqdis, the Holy House; H. Har ha-Moriyya, Mount Moriah or Har ha-Bayit, the Temple Mount or Beth ha-Maqdas, the Holy House.*

The western portico of the Haram (courtesy of Kay Prag).

Introduction. The Haram al-Sharif is the architectural and the visual focus of the Holy City of Jerusalem. The Haram area, raised on a great masonry platform, covers c 14 hectares (c 34 acres) which is nearly one-sixth of the total area of the Old City. The *sacred precinct*, with its gem-like central building, its open spaces, its mosques, arcades, trees, light and serenity, comes near to being one of the glories of the world. As a focus of two great religions, being the site of the Jewish Temple, as well as the second most important place of pilgrimage in the Muslim world, it has symbolic and religious overtones which add to its undoubted impact on the visitor. The platform is that built by Herod the Great to support the Jewish Temple, on the site of an earlier platform built by Solomon for the First Temple (c 961/954–586 BC) and re-used by Zerubbabel (Second Temple, c 537/515, in use until rebuilt by Herod the Great from 20 BC and then destroyed in AD 70); the present central shrine is the Muslim **Dome of the Rock**, originally built 691/2 by the Umayyad Caliph 'Abd al-Malik. The great **Aqsa Mosque** to the S, though much restored, is founded on the 8C Umayyad and Abbasid mosque probably in turn resting on an earlier mosque of 639/640. The fine buildings and porticoes which surround the Haram are principally Mamluk work of the 13C–15C but include both earlier and later structures. Remarkable survivals of early Islamic periods are housed in the *Islamic Museum* on the Haram platform.

Dimensions: Platform: N 310m; W 488.3m, S 281.20m, E 466.65m. Upper platform: N 156.15m, W 167.75m, S 128.10m, E 161.65m.

Topography. The ancient topography is largely obscured by monumental building, and exploration has been limited by the very sacredness of the site and attendant fears of desecration. The limestone E ridge of the city climbs steadily from the S to a peak at the exposed limestone bedrock located under the present Dome, approximately 743m above sea level. The surface has been almost completely covered by millennia of construction work, and altered by quarrying, but it is clear that the ridge dropped sharply on the E side to the Kidron Valley, and on the W to the Tyropoeon Valley. To the NE another deep valley running SE towards the Kidron cut across the NE corner of the Haram, but to the NW the rock rises higher than the Holy Rock to the escarpment on which Herod built the Antonia fortress. This area, like the same ridge further S, may have contained natural caves which in various periods were converted to tombs or cisterns (Gonen).

History. Tradition equates the high point of the ridge with Mount Moriah, where Abraham offered his son Isaac as a sacrifice to God (Gen. 22), with the traditional site of the threshing floor of Araunah the Jebusite, bought by David c 1000 BC as the site on which to build an altar (2 Sam. 24:18–25), and that on which his son Solomon subsequently built the first Jewish Temple.

The Solomonic Temple. According to the Old Testament (I Kings 5), Solomon began to build the Temple in the fourth year of his reign (c 961 BC) and completed it in his eleventh year, with the assistance of the Phoenician king, Hiram of Tyre, who sent cedar, pine and stonemasons to help with the work. No trace of this structure remains, but the description tells us it was a tripartite building, with an inner *Holy of Holies* in which the *Ark of the Covenant* was placed. The Temple was of stone and timber construction, and the interior was richly decorated with cedar and gold. The entrance faced E, and in front of the vestibule stood two free-standing columns named, for unknown reasons, Jachin and Boaz (I Kings 7:21). Further E in the court was an altar of unhewn stones for burnt sacrifice. It is debatable whether the altar or the Holy of Holies stood over the peak of the rock. The dimensions of the building were 60 cubits long, 20 cubits wide, 20 to 30 cubits in height, with a vestibule adding another 20 cubits to the front. The two columns were 18 cubits high, and the altar to the

E was 20 cubits square and 10 cubits high. The terrace on which the Temple stood was 5 cubits in height (the cubit being c 0.45m or a little longer). Its plan was undoubtedly similar to temple buildings of slightly later date excavated in Syria, and also seems to have had architectural ancestors among Canaanite temples (e.g. Hazor). The Solomonic Temple apparently had side chambers in the N, W and S walls which served as treasuries and storehouses for the offerings made to the Temple. The Temple stood within an inner and an outer court. Due to the narrowness of the ridge Solomon must have built a platform or terrace to support it, a smaller predecessor of the present one, which according to Josephus extended to the present E wall and had a single portico.

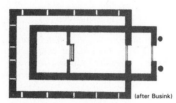

(after Busink)

Solomon's Temple
(reconstructed plan)

The Temple was looted of many of its treasures by the Egyptian Pharaoh Shishak c 923 BC (I Kings 14:25–26) and again robbed of its treasure and finally destroyed completely by the Babylonians in 586 BC. During the three and a half centuries of its existence the First Temple was regarded by the Israelites as the sole legitimate shrine of God, though other shrines were built in the northern kingdom of Israel and indeed in Judah. It is frequently mentioned in the Old Testament; most of the kings of Judah were crowned in its court.

The Post-Exilic Temple. The temple was rebuilt after the Exile by Zerubbabel in c 537–515 BC. This building was almost certainly on the same site as its predecessor, and probably built to a similar plan but lacking much of the splendour of the First Temple. The ritual was probably much as before, but the Holy of Holies was empty for the Ark was lost at the time of the Babylonian destruction and not replaced. This Second Temple was probably improved and more richly adorned during the 3C and 2C BC as the city expanded, but little is known of it.

The Herodian Temple. The Temple of Zerubbabel was completely replaced and incorporated into the massive platform and new temple built by Herod the Great, begun c 20–18 BC and completed not long before its destruction in AD 70. The magnificence of the Herodian Temple can be assessed by the remains of the platform that are still visible. The scale and perfection of the masonry of the lower part of this platform can be admired in Jerusalem, while the style of the upper wall surrounding the enclosure can be understood by looking at the smaller but better preserved temenos wall of the mosque in Hebron which was also constructed by Herod. Enough survives below ground level on the NW side of the Haram to show that the same pilastered ornament once decorated the upper enclosure wall in Jerusalem. Nothing survives in its original position of the structures on top of the platform, which were overthrown by the Romans in AD 70; but a fairly detailed account of them survives in the works of Josephus (War V:1–226, and Antiq. XV:380–425), and is supplemented and clarified by fragments found in excavation, or still preserved at foundation or subterranean level.

The *Temple enclosure* may have had nine gates. There were at least four gates on the W side, two at the courtyard level and two below; the two Hulda Gates on the S side were also below the level of the courtyard; there were probably two on the E side, including the Susa Gate used by the priests for special ceremonies only; and one on the N, the Tadi Gate which was of lesser importance. The lower gates led by way of ramps from the paved streets at ground level adjacent to the platform, up through the subterranean vaults supporting the platform to the temple courts above.

The *Herodian Temple courts* were surrounded by a portico, that on the S, the *Royal Stoa* or Portico, being of double width, with 162 monolithic columns with Corinthian capitals in four rows. This structure, occupying the S end of the

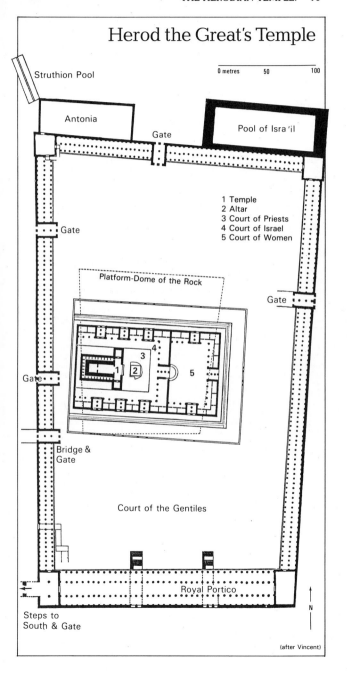

Herod the Great's Temple

Struthion Pool

0 metres 50 100

Antonia

Gate

Pool of Isra'il

1 Temple
2 Altar
3 Court of Priests
4 Court of Israel
5 Court of Women

Gate

Platform-Dome of the Rock

Gate

Gate

1 Temple
2 Altar
3 Court of Priests
4 Court of Israel
5 Court of Women

Gate

Bridge & Gate

Court of the Gentiles

Royal Portico

Steps to South & Gate

N

(after Vincent)

temple platform, was used for teaching and temple-linked activities, including shops. After the *Sanhedrin* (the Jewish Council of Elders) was expelled by the Romans from its ancient council chamber *(The Chamber of Hewn Stone)* in AD 30, it met in this stoa.

The outer court of the temple was the court of the Gentiles. Within it the sacred area was set at a higher level, surrounded by a fence and approached by stairs. At each gate into this higher area was a notice in Latin or Greek (fragments of two have been discovered) prohibiting entrance on pain of death to non-Jews. Within was first the *Court of the Women*, then beyond to the W through the *Beautiful Gate*, that of the men. Further W a fence restricted entry to the *Court of the Priests* in which lay the altar of sacrifice, probably on the peak of the rock. Most of the inner gates were plated in gold and silver. To the W, and facing towards the E was the Temple. To allay the fears of the priests Herod had all the materials prepared in advance for the rebuilding of the Temple itself, and the work was completed in 1½ years. It was based on the Solomonic plan, tripartite and with an inner Holy of Holies. The façade was covered with plates of gold, and above the enormous doors (themselves draped with multi-coloured hangings) was a golden vine from which hung bunches of grapes the height of a man. The façade was topped by a cornice. The rest of the exterior of the building was of white marble and according to Josephus the effect was of a mountain, blinding in the sunlight and capped by snow. In the main chamber were the famous altar for incense, the table with the shewbread and the golden candlestick. The inner doors were veiled by a great Babylonian curtain of linen, embroidered with blue, scarlet and purple. Within the inner room, inaccessible and inviolable, was the empty Holy of Holies. Numerous rooms, subterranean cisterns and passages restricted to the use of the priests and connected with the ritual lay in and under the adjoining courts and the terraces which supported them. Before the Temple stood the square altar of sacrifice, with corners shaped like horns. At it, Herod sacrificed 300 oxen in the celebrations which concluded the building work, and the people likewise, according to their means.

It is this temple with which Jesus is linked. It was still being built at the time of His presentation; and the money changers and usurers whom He overthrew may have been based in the Royal Stoa.

The Royal Stoa was damaged in the riots in AD 64–66 and repairs were still under way when the First Jewish Revolt started in AD 66. The complete destruction of the buildings on the platform is recorded by Josephus and the huge debris of columns, blocks, capitals, and fragments of ornamental masonry including *two sundials, friezes* and *cornices* which lay on the ground beneath the S end of the platform are mute testimony to the ferocity of the Roman destruction in AD 70.

The Temple area certainly lay in ruins for many years, at least until the founding of the Roman city of Aelia Capitolina after the Second Jewish Revolt. It seems unlikely that Bar Kosiba (Bar Kochba), the Jewish leader in the Second Revolt, had time or resources to do more than plan the rebuilding of the Temple in 132–33. The literary sources are not clear about the use to which Hadrian put the area. According to Dio Cassius the *Temple of Jupiter* was built on the site of the Temple but the text could imply that it was built in Jerusalem to replace the Jewish temple as a religious focus. It seems more likely that the tripartite temple to Jupiter, Juno and Minerva built by Hadrian would have stood near the Forum and the cardo maximus. The Chronicon Paschale (after 629) says that among other works Hadrian built the Trikameron and the Kodra; these are not listed together; the first is thought to be the tripartite temple; and the second the Temple platform. Early writers (though not contemporary ones) say Hadrian set up statues in the area of the Temple, variously mentioning statues of Hadrian on foot and on horseback, and a statue of Jupiter. The re-used base of a statue inscribed with Hadrian's name was found built into the S wall of the Temple platform above the Double Gate. Other fragments of Roman sculpture have been found amongst debris nearby, but no trace of a temple building. Thus the texts could imply the ruins were levelled, the platform itself repaired and statues set up, c 135.

In 333 the Bordeaux Pilgrim recorded only that there were two statues of Hadrian in the Temple area, an altar in front of which was a slab with the blood of Zacharias, and not far away a pierced stone at which the Jews lamented the destruction of the Temple. The precise dates at which Jews were able to return to Jerusalem, either to visit the site for pilgrimage and prayer, or to settle, are unknown. Some relaxation of the ban on settlement probably followed the death of Hadrian, either late in the 2C AD or during the 3C AD.

The platform appears not to have been built up in Byzantine times but the Madaba map in the mid-6C seems to show some structures on the perimeter of an open space, perhaps with a chapel in the SE angle; certainly the *Golden Gate* on the E side of the Haram was open, possibly from the 5C and reconstructed in 631 for the solemn procession for the rededication of the fragments of the True Cross regained from the Persians; this led from the Golden Gate across the Temple Mount W to the Church of the Holy Sepulchre. The Temple Mount had no particular significance for Christians and there is no record of the building of other structures here at this time.

The full redevelopment of the Temple Mount as a focus of veneration came with the Arab conquest in 638. It was from the first accepted as a sacred site. The building of the Aqsa Mosque from c 639/40, and then the Dome of the Rock in 691/2 (see below), began a period of centuries of Muslim construction work in and around the Haram which continued to the 19C, and which gave this part of the city its present character.

Considerable destruction was wrought by the earthquake of 747/8, and rebuilding followed. Another earthquake in 1033 led to the abandonment of the Muslim quarter to the S and the blocking of the S gates.

Changes, but fortunately not destruction, in the Haram area accompanied the conquest of Jerusalem and the setting up of the Crusader Kingdom in 1099–1100. The Dome of the Rock was converted into a Christian prayer hall, and a cross replaced the crescent on the dome. This is depicted in the seal of Baldwin I, King of Jerusalem 1100–18. The Aqsa Mosque first served as the palace of the king, and was subsequently handed over to the Templar Order as their headquarters when some alterations and extensions were made. Many traces of Crusader work remain especially in the gates of the Haram area and in the remodelling of the Aqsa. An *Augustinian convent* was built on the N side of the Haram.

After 1187 the area was restored fully to Muslim use, the Augustinian convent was torn down and many mihrabs installed; Christians were prohibited from entering. Many structures in the vicinity of the mosques date to the Ayyubid and Mamluk periods. By the end of the 15C the Haram walls were lined by fine Mamluk buildings, the high point of Mamluk construction reached under the Sultan al-Nasir Muhammad. Repairs, renovations and extensions were made in the Ottoman period.

After the schools, hospices, fountains and other religious or semi-religious institutions were built and endowed they became the responsibility of a council of the religious and civic Muslim notables, the 'ulama. The endowments and offerings are still held as a trust which is known by their Arabic name *waqf* or plural *awqaf* and it is this trust which is responsible for the gathering of revenue and the maintenance and administration of the many public institutions in its care.

During Mandate times there was some further repair to the walls, and in particular repairs to the Aqsa Mosque, damaged in the earthquake of 1927. A major restoration of this mosque was made in 1938–43.

Some damage was sustained by mortar bombing in the fighting in 1948. Major renovations of the Dome of the Rock were carried out in the 1960's when the old lead domes of both the Dome of the Rock and the Aqsa Mosque were replaced by anodised aluminium. The minbar of Salah al-Din in the Aqsa Mosque was destroyed by fire on 21 August 1969.

Excavations and studies. Very few archaeological excavations have been permitted in or near the sacred area, and the following is a summary of some work. E. Robinson first commented on the spring of the great arch which bears his name in 1838; T. Tobler, 1853; M. de Vogüé made a detailed study of the buildings in 1862; C. Wilson, Ordnance Survey 1865; C. Wilson and C. Warren investigated Wilson's Arch, and Warren also managed to excavate shafts and tunnels to bedrock around the exterior of the Haram walls revealing many details of the masonry; he also examined Solomon's Stables, 1867–70. C. Clermont-Ganneau made various discoveries in the area, including one of the inscriptions prohibiting Gentile entry to the Herodian temple, 1873–74. C. Schick reported on the Ottoman clearance of the Golden Gate, 1886-1901. M. Parker made an illegal attempt to investigate the cave under the Dome of the Rock, 1910/11. R.W. Hamilton assessed the structural history of the Aqsa, 1938–43. J. Simon, 1952; L.-H. Vincent, 1956; R. de Vaux excavated S of the Haram 1961–63; K. Kenyon excavated S of the Aqsa 1964–66; B. Mazar worked adjacent to the S wall and the SW angle from 1968. The British School of Archaeology in Jerusalem made an architectural survey of the Mamluk monuments in and adjacent to the Haram 1968–85.

Map of Route 2

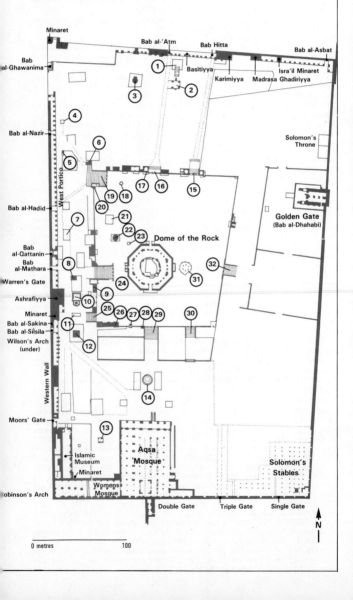

Minaret

Bab al-'Atm

Bab Hitta

Bab al-Asbat

Bab al-Ghawanima

Basitiyya

Karimiyya

Isra'il Minaret

Madrasa Ghadiriyya

Bab al-Nazir

Solomon's Throne

West Portico

Bab al-Hadid

Golden Gate
(Bab al-Dhahabi)

Dome of the Rock

Bab al-Qattanin

Bab al-Mathara

Warren's Gate

Ashrafiyya

Minaret

Bab al-Sakina

Bab al-Silsila

Wilson's Arch
(under)

Western Wall

Moors' Gate

Islamic
Museum

Minaret

Aqsa
Mosque

Solomon's
Stables

Robinson's Arch

Womens
Mosque

Double Gate

Triple Gate

Single Gate

0 metres   100

N

Approaches to the Haram. The Haram is open daily 8.00–16.00, closed Fri; the mosques are closed for midday and afternoon prayers, usually from about 11.30 and 14.30 though the times vary slightly at different seasons. *Access for non-Muslims* is from the Nazir, Chain, or Moors Gates only, though the visitor may leave by some other gates. Tickets for the Dome of the Rock, the Aqsa Mosque and the Islamic Museum should be bought at the ticket offices inside the Nazir and Moors' Gates. Group tickets are available for guided parties, who normally stay together for a visit to the three main places, the Dome of the Rock, the Aqsa Mosque and the Islamic Museum, though the Museum may be omitted from some tour itineraries. For more time to visit those monuments at present accessible to tourists it is preferable to come separately. Special permission is needed to enter some monuments and some areas are closed at present; security in the Haram is very strictly observed. It is necessary to remove outdoor shoes before entering the Dome of the Rock and the Aqsa Mosque.

Access by road to the Haram is not easy, the best approach being by the S ring road to a car park near the Dung Gate, but it is necessary to avoid festival or other busy times. Alternatively the visitor approaches on foot through the Old City to the gates open to tourists.

Tour of the Haram al-Sharif. For the visitor with only a short time available, **Rtes 2D, 2E** and **2F** on the Dome of the Rock, the Aqsa Mosque and the Islamic Museum are most relevant.

For those with more time and interest:

Rte 2A External features of the Haram platform which are visible or accessible only from outside, including the Western (Wailing) Wall and the South-west and Southern Archaeological Zones.

Rte 2B Structures built into or against the inner wall of the Haram.

Rte 2C All other subsidiary features on the Haram platform.

Rte 2D The Dome of the Rock.

Rte 2E The Aqsa Mosque.

Rte 2F The Islamic Museum.

Rte 2G Subterranean features accessible from within the Haram only, most of which are at present closed to visitors.

The descriptions will in general start at the NE corner of the Haram, and move towards the W, but the visitor can begin the tour at any point.

A.   External features of the Haram Platform

This itinerary includes the Western Wall and the South-western and Southern Archaeological Zones.

Not all features described here are readily accessible, for it is not possible to walk right round the outside wall of the Haram, as a glance at the map will indicate. The N side, and the N half of the W side, are fairly continuously built up·and the only access to the walls is where streets run up to gates. The buildings in these streets will be described in Rte 3, except for the exteriors of the Haram Gates which are included here. Access to the S half of the W wall, and to the S wall is to be had through the Jewish religious zone and the archaeological zone in the vicinity of Wilson's Arch and the Western Wall, and through the archaeological zone entered near the Dung Gate. The remains in these zones are closely connected with the Haram and its platform. The E wall is adjacent to the Muslim Cemetery where visitors may require a special permit.

The N wall of the Haram. There are three gates in the N wall. On the E is the *Bab al-Asbat*, or *Gate of the Tribes* (with the *al- Asbat*, or *Isra'il minaret*, visible to the W). There are two gates near the centre of the N wall, the *Bab Hitta*, or *Gate of Remission* and on the W the *Bab al-ʿAtm*, *Gate of Darkness*. All have rather plain pointed arches. The *Minaret of al-Ghawanima* dominates the NW corner. These gates and minarets are described in Rte 2B.

The W wall of the Haram

Most of the gates on the W are approached by lanes from the TARIQ AL-WAD (THE VALLEY ROAD), except for the *Bab al-Ghawanima*, which can also be reached from the VIA DOLOROSA. There are seven gates in the W wall; from the N, the *Bab al-Ghawanima*, the *Bab al-Nazir*, the *Gate of the Inspector* (p. 163); *Bab al-Hadid* or *Gate of Iron*; the *Bab al-Qattanin* or *Gate of the Cotton Merchants*; the *Bab al-Mathara*, the *Gate of Ablution*. The most important gate on the W side and worth visiting is a double gate, the S or main section called the *Bab al-Silsila (Gate of the Chain)*, and the closed N section the *Bab al-Sakina (Gate of the Ark)*. This gate lies at the end of the main street leading down from the Jaffa Gate, the Citadel and the great suqs, and has a minaret above it.

History. The original gate on the site may have been an Umayyad double gate constructed by ʿAbd al-Malik (Burgoyne); it was certainly important in Fatimid times when the S entrances to the Haram were blocked. Nasr-i Khusraw (1047) records that it was then elaborately decorated with mosaics, probably ordered by the caliph al-Zahir when he restored the mosaics in the Dome of the Rock (1027/8) and in the Aqsa (1034–36): surviving bonding marks may derive from this decoration; it was one of the principal entrances to the Temple (the Beautiful Gates) in Crusader times and received considerable adornment. Much of this survives on the present gate, despite a rebuilding by the Ayyubids (1187–99).

Visit. A small courtyard (Rte 3) fronts a double vestibule before the gates. The portals have fine sets of Crusader marble columns with acanthus capitals, double sets on the S and triple on the N gate. The upper range has elaborate twisted columns, the detail of which varies between the gates. The elaborate pendentives have fluted semi-domes supporting the roof domes. The entrances, with wooden doors, have flat joggled lintels and round arches. The piers and pointed arches of the porches have suffered more damage, but parts of Crusader marble columns and capitals survive on the central pier. A fountain, perhaps installed by Sultan Qaʾit Bay in 1482/3, stood here until 1871.

Returning along the TARIQ BAB AL-SILSILA one may take the steps down to the right (DARAJ AL-ʿAIN) to the underpass which continues the line of the TARIQ AL-WAD and leads directly to the **Western Wall**. (The underpass is closed at night and occasionally at other times: gate and security check; if closed continue further along the TARIQ BAB AL-SILSILA, and turn left into ʿAQABAT ABU MADYAN, a narrow angled lane with steps leading down to the plaza before the Western Wall). The underpass has some points of interest: from the N, an arch of the 8C–11C; on the right a fragment of the great paved street (2C–6C) running from the Damascus Gate to the S of the Dung Gate (Rte 1); and an earlier arch of the 1C BC–AD (see below, Wilson's Arch area). The arches support the causeway above.

The *Western Wall or Wailing Wall

H. *Ha-Kotel Ha-Ma'aravi.* This is the focus of Jewish religious activity in the Old City. An enormous space has been cleared in front of this area of the Herodian platform to allow access for prayer, for festivals and celebrations, and the scene is always busy. Access is either by the underpass from the TARIQ AL-WAD to the N; by the steps in the NW corner which lead up to the TARIQ BAB AL-SILSILA; by the steps on the W side leading up to the **Jewish Quarter**, other access points and the road in the SW corner leading up towards the Jewish Quarter and the **Zion Gate**; and through the **Dung Gate** of the Old City on the S.

Jews praying at the Wailing Wall, late 19C (courtesy of the Manchester Museum).

History. The foundation and lower courses of the Western Wall formed the lower part of the platform supporting the Jewish Temple built by Herod the Great, commencing c 20/18 BC and completed some 46 years later. In Herod's time the area adjacent to the wall may well have formed part of the structure called the *Xystos,* known from Josephus (War II:344) as an open porticoed plaza used for public assemblies with causeway and gates above it, and possibly lying on the site of an earlier Hellenistic gymnasium built by Jason (II Macc. 4:12). This area, built up in Hellenistic and Roman times on a fill above the steep bed of the Tyropoeon Valley (the present surface lies c 21m above bedrock), was used for burials in the 8C BC before the town began to expand over it.

Following the destruction of the Temple by the Romans in July AD 70 and the Roman decree prohibiting Jews to dwell in the city, only traces of bake houses, baths and other structures serving the Tenth Roman Legion which garrisoned the city in the succeeding centuries of Roman rule were found in the excavations in the vicinity. Talmudic and pilgrim accounts suggest that some time after the death of Hadrian in 138, especially in the 3C and 4C Jews began to return to the city and to come annually to lament the destruction of the Temple on 9 Ab (in the month of July). With later relaxation of the prohibition more Jews returned to settle in the city and to come to the Temple area at other pilgrimage festivals. This intermittent pilgrimage to the site continued over the centuries, increasing under favourable conditions, as in the reign of Julian the Apostate (361–63) and for a few years following the Persian Conquest (614) and declining or ceasing completely at others, such as the early Crusader Period from 1099.

After the construction of the Muslim shrines on the platform from 639 access to the Temple site itself was denied to the Jews and the Western Wall became their most accessible point of pilgrimage. After the Muslim re-conquest in 1187, al-Malik al-'Adil (the brother of Salah al-Din) endowed this area in favour of the Maghariba community (North African Muslims, Moors) c 1194; the *Afdaliyya Madrasa* for adherents of the Maliki rite was founded here, c 75m W of the Wailing Wall; it had a fine pointed-arched entrance, with gadrooned voussoirs which may have been re-used Crusader material. The interior consisted of two cross-vaulted chambers, and a central domed chamber. The dome, on a drum with four windows, rested on arched corner squinches. Further development took place in the Mamluk period, when a zawiya for the Moors was built and endowed in 1303 by Shaikh 'Umar al-Masmudi, and the *Zawiya of Abu Madyan* was founded here in 1320. Resettlement of Jews in Jerusalem began again and a small and impoverished community came regularly to the Wailing Wall from the mid-13C; the traditions and feeling of the Jewish community for the Wailing Wall increased in the 16C when the population also increased (Rte 7). Most of the area immediately W of the Haram wall continued to be occupied by the houses, shrine and mosque of the Moors. The area of the Wailing Wall frequented by the Jews was then small but adequate to the needs of a small

19C–early 20C view of the Moors' Quarter from the south: the Dome of the Rock is in the centre, the Minaret of the Chain to the left, the Minaret of al-Fakhriyya to the right (courtesy of the Manchester Museum).

community, and in the early 20C measured 47.5m in length and less than 4m in width, with five courses of Herodian masonry exposed. Against these stones the Jews leant and prayed, and there wept for the downfall of Jerusalem and their Temple, coming most frequently after 16.00 on Fridays for the beginning of the Sabbath.

In 1877 there were moves by the Jewish community to buy the land around the Wailing Wall, which came to nothing due to internal dissent within the community itself. In 1920 further discussions ended due to lack of funds. In 1930 an international committee of the League of Nations decided that the area of the Wailing Wall, the pavement, the Magharibi houses and mosque constituted a Muslim Holy Place, but Jews were to have access for religious purposes. With the division of the city after the fighting in 1948, during which the State of Israel was declared independent, the Wailing Wall area was inaccessible from Israel, but was accessible to tourists. On 10 June 1967 the whole impoverished *Moors' Quarter*, including the mosque and the shrine of Shaikh ʿAʾid (the 12C Afdaliyya Madrasa) was bulldozed to make way for the present great plaza and mass Israeli access. The official designation of the area was changed to the Western Wall.

The Government Ministry of Religions since 1968 has cleared an underground corridor to the N adjacent to the Western Wall, also known as the *Wilson's Arch area*. This is now part of the Jewish religious zone. Much of archaeological interest is exposed and work continues there. Extensive archaeological exavations have also taken place S of the Moor's Gate of the Haram since 1968 (B. Mazar) where an archaeological park has been created.

Visit. The *Wilson's Arch Area*, or the *Passageways and Arches*. Tourist access is by a gate near the NW corner of the Western Wall plaza. Open Sun, Tue, Wed 8.30–15.00; Mon, Thu 12.30–15.00; Fri 8.30–12.00; closed Sat and holidays. Passing through the series of tunnels and vaulted chambers note the plan on the adjacent wall and continue to the Jewish men's prayer hall against the face of the W wall of the Haram.

*The Herodian wall and Wilson's Arch. The Herodian wall here exhibits the same fine masonry with drafted edges seen further S, but in almost pristine condition. Directly opposite are the springers of the great Wilson's Arch.

History. This arch and the opposing pier form part of a causeway and aqueduct which originally crossed the Tyropoeon Valley and linked the Upper City on the Western Hill to the Temple and entered the court by a high level gate which is not preserved. This single arch was 22.5m high, but to the W the causeway was

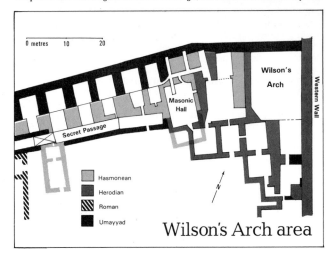

0 metres   10   20

Wilson's
Arch

Western Wall

Masonic
Hall

Secret Passage

Hasmonean

Herodian

Roman

Umayyad

N

Wilson's Arch area

supported on two tiers of vaults. The first causeway was destroyed when supporters of the Hasmonean Aristobulus in the battle against Pompey in 63 BC retreated to the Temple, cutting the causeway behind them (Josephus, War I:143; Antiq. XIV:58). The second causeway was built by Herod the Great and was destroyed in the same way by the Sicarii Zealots during the First Jewish Revolt (AD 66–70). The dating of the existing pier opposite the Herodian springers of Wilson's Arch is uncertain, as is that of the vaults on the W. The causeway and aqueduct were rebuilt or added to several times, have been beneath ground level for many centuries (though partly in use for storage and cisterns). In the 19C a water tank called the *Pool of al-Buraq* (the Prophet Muhammad's steed during the Night Journey) was located in the present prayer hall.

Remains. Three shafts cut in the floor of the present prayer hall (Warren, 1867) allow inspection of the unexposed foundation courses of the Herodian wall. The section visible is part of a total preserved height of 23m, with a further 0.86m sunk into the bedrock. It contains 21 courses of drafted stones, averaging 1.1m–1.2m in height. The principal feature visible is the springing of a great arch, known as *Wilson's Arch* after its discoverer, which lies 180m N of the SW angle of the Haram platform. It rises 7.6m above the level of the present paving, and is 13.4m wide. The lower visible courses and spring of the arch are Herodian in date, the upper courses of smaller masonry are probably an Umayyad reconstruction.

Warren's Gate, or the *Gate of the Bath*. Warren supposed there was another gate similar to *Barclays Gate* (see below) further N along the Haram wall, because he discovered a passage piercing the W wall of the Temple in use in the 19C as a cistern. It is located just S of the *Bab al-Mathara (Gate of Ablution)* (see also the *Fountain of Qa'it Bay*, Rte 2B), at c 232m N of the SW angle of the Haram, and c 52m N of Wilson's Arch. It must have led out to the new section of the city enclosed by Herod the Great. The area is in the care of the Jewish Religious Authorities, and is usually accessible through a gate. A section of the wall with the largest Herodian stones yet discovered, c 13.5m and 14.5m in length, and occupying the height of three average courses of Herodian masonry, is visible in this area. The faces have projecting knobs, perhaps used to lift them into position. A further tunnel now leads N along the face of the Western Haram Wall and the S end of the Struthion Pool (see Rte 3) can also be seen.

The *complex of vaulted chambers* W of Wilson's Arch has not yet been properly studied and is still only partly cleared. As we leave Wilson's Arch one of the chambers at a lower level can be seen through the floor grilles, before we re-enter the complex of rooms and passages to the W. The most important is the so-called *Masonic Chamber*. It was explored by Warren in 1867, but discovered earlier and used secretly by Masons who connected it with Solomon's works in the adjacent temple. It lies c 26m W of Wilson's Arch, and can at present only be seen by looking down through a small opening in the S side of a dark narrow passage. The N–S axis of this chamber is skewed to the Haram wall, and Warren speculated that it was at least as old. It is a large rectangular vaulted chamber, 14m × 25.5m, the roof once supported by a central column, the broken shaft of which still stands at the centre of the room. The chamber is paved, and is built of square stones; at each corner is a pilaster with capitals, poorly preserved except at the NE angle. In the E wall a double entrance 2.25m high with decorated lintels and jambs leads E into other rooms. The vaults and passages to the N and W are those explored by Warren between 1867 and 1870, including the entrance to his 'Secret Passage', thought by Mujir al-Din (1495) to have connected the

Citadel to the Haram and to have been built by David. It is old, but probably Roman, Byzantine or later. The passage was traced to the W for some distance. On the way, the vaulted chambers supporting the causeway to the N can be seen; they show at least two building phases; that on the S is 7.16m wide and is the earlier (1C BC–AD?), that on the N is 6.4m wide, possibly dates to 8C– 11C and seems to carry the Mamluk aqueduct to the Haram. From the 1C BC water was brought by aqueduct from Solomon's Pools SW of Bethlehem to the Temple.

Returning to the plaza the visitor continues to view the Herodian remains.

The Western Wall or the **Wailing Wall. Since 1967 an expanse of the Herodian masonry 57m in length has been exposed; seven courses are now visible above the pavement, and a further 19 lie below to a depth of 21m. The fine yellow-grey stones with drafted edges are cut with great precison and set without mortar. The average height of the courses is 1m– 1.20m but the highest is 1.86m. Stones vary in length from 1m to 3m but many are longer; one stone near the SW corner of the Haram is nearly 12m long. Blocks weighing up to 100 tons were lifted 9m to 12m in this immense building project. The wall grades outward towards the base. The foundation courses have narrow drafted margins and rough central bosses which were not meant to be seen, and the upper ones a smoothly dressed flat boss and wider margin which makes the most of the fine colour and texture, to give an appearance of strength as well as beauty.

At the S end of the Western Wall part of the enormous stone lintel of *Barclay's Gate can be seen. Named after its discoverer (J.T. Barclay, British architect, 1855–57) it is c 82m N of the SW angle of the platform and at present is mostly hidden by a small prayer room used by Jewish women in the angle formed by the ramp leading up to the Moors' Gate. The lintel, a vast single stone, measures 7.5m × 2.1m, of which c 1m can be seen outside, and rather more inside the prayer room. The now blocked gate opening beneath it is 8.76m in height. The threshold, now missing, was probably at the 722.7m level, that of the Temple Court above at c 738m. According to Vincent, the pilastered enclosure which capped the platform began at the 741.5m level. Originally Barclay's Gate gave access from the stepped paved street to a passage and ramp leading up to the Temple Courts above (see also Rte 2G). This gate has been identified with the Kiponos Gate mentioned in the Misnah.

Most other remains in the Western Wall area are of later date. The upper 19 courses of the Western wall include four large courses perhaps of Roman or Umayyad date and 15 courses of smaller stones, parts at least of which belong to the Ottoman period repairs. The building with four rectangular windows above the NE corner of the plaza and the arch to the mens' prayer hall, is the Tankiziyya, an early 14C Islamic structure built on older foundations (Rte 3).

The paving of the plaza is post-1967 and the area against the wall itself is divided according to Jewish Orthodox requirements into separate men's and women's enclosures for prayers and the celebration of festivals. The area is very crowded at these times and is best avoided for sight-seeing from 15.00 hours on Fridays, all day on Saturdays and at the main religious festivals.

The southern end of the plaza is defined by a ramp left in the clearances of 1968 to allow access by the Moors' Gate into the Haram. A notice forbids entry to Jews: this is an Orthodox Jewish notice, for many Jews will not enter the Haram either for fear of treading on the site of the ancient Holy of Holies of the Temple (which was forbidden to all but the priests), or for fear of treading on the place where tradition holds the volume of the sacred law is buried. There is a fenced security check point near its lower end. To the S is the another archaeological zone.

*The Archaeological Zone against the SW and S wall of the Haram.

Set back within the SW corner of the Haram is the square shaft of the *al-Fakhriyya minaret* (Rte 2B). The upper structures at the SW angle of the Haram are of Crusader and later date, and include the **Islamic Museum** at the SW angle, with the *Fakhriyya Mosque* and courtyard (with trees) immediately N (Rte 2B and 2F).

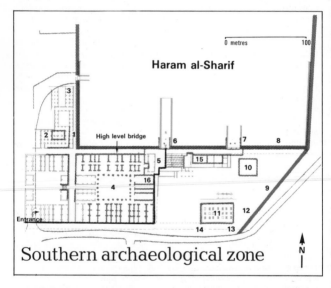

Haram al-Sharif

Southern archaeological zone

The archaeological area is entered just inside the Dung Gate and has been laid out with paths for tourist access. Remains of the Herodian and Umayyad periods are of particular interest here. Open daily 8.00–17.30; guided tour at 14.00; tours arranged at the Cardo Information Centre.

Taking first the path to the N, and looking above and to the right, at 12m N of the corner of the Haram are the springers and lower voussoirs (three courses only remain) of a huge arch jutting from the Herodian masonry called **˙Robinson's Arch** in 1835 after its American discoverer **(1)**. It has a span of c 12.40m. and a width of 15.50m. Until 1968 this arch was virtually at ground level and the visitor can judge the enormous quantity of debris that has been removed in the recent excavations (Mazar) by the different patina of the stone on the Haram wall above and below the former surface. It used to be thought (Warren) that another causeway, like the one at

Wilson's Arch, led across the Tyropoeon Valley from the Upper City to the W to the Royal Stoa of the Herodian Temple, but an alternative view following Josephus (Antiq. XV:410), that steps led up from the Lower City to the S, has been confirmed by the discovery of the *base of a single pier* **(2)** E of the arch from which a series of shorter piers carried the staircase to the S. These piers are visible opposite the arch. In the piers are four *Herodian shops* with flat lintels of fine drafted masonry and with small round relieving blocks above each doorway. The great paving slabs of the adjacent *Herodian road* were nearly a metre in length. Beneath the street lay a large partly rock-cut and partly stone-built drain. The Herodian masonry at the SW angle of the Haram is particularly well preserved, and contains one of the larger blocks known from the Temple platform, nearly 12m in length. Much fallen Herodian masonry was found in this area, including fragments of an Ionic T-framed doorway below Robinson's Arch, and the SW corner stone of the Herodian parapet which, according to its inscription, marked the spot where the trumpet (H. *shofar*) was blown to mark the beginning of the Sabbath. On the right a plastic screen on the Haram wall protects a Hebrew inscription, quoting Isaiah 66:14, which probably dates to the years 361–63 when for a short time the Jews hoped to restore the Temple.

Continuing to the N along the Haram wall, to the left are the remains of an *Umayyad paving*, and of a *Byzantine house* and a *bath house*. At the end, below the earth ramp, a view of the Herodian roadway can be obtained **(3)**.

Returning along the path, one can note two *horizontal channels* cut in the Haram masonry at and below the level of the base of Robinson's Arch, which were probably made in Umayyad times to carry water from the aqueduct to the newly built quarter S of the Haram. The masonry above the arch is a patchwork of various periods. At the SW angle itself four courses of probable Umayyad work survive above the Herodian. Above are areas which are probably Abbasid and Fatimid repairs, but most of the higher SW corner is Crusader work, with patches of Ayyubid, Mamluk and Ottoman work to the N. The other monumental walls adjacent to the SW angle of the Haram belong to the great Umayyad palace and hospices built in the 8C, described below.

History of the area south of the Haram. A complex history of occupation was revealed in the area adjacent to the south wall of the Haram. It is assumed to be part of the area within which Solomon built his palaces and House of the Forest of Lebanon, but few Iron Age structures have been found. It is the area described by Josephus as *Ophlas* or *Ophel*, and in Herodian times a monumental paved road and plaza with steps led along the S face of the Temple platform to two great gates which connected the Temple and the Lower City to the S.

After the Roman destruction the area was extensively quarried and not again occupied until the Byzantine period. From the mid-5C the S boundary of the city was at the S end of the Tyropoeon Valley and this was then again a properous part of the town. In the SW area opposite Robinson's Arch the large Byzantine bath house has been mentioned and a few-storied house just S of it had a cross carved on the lintel of the N door (Mazar). There may have been Byzantine hospices in this area (de Vaux). The buildings were damaged, possibly in the reign of Julian the Apostate (362–63) and certainly at the time of the Persian destruction (614) following which traces of Jewish occupation were found.

The whole area was completely re-developed in Umayyad times when a large complex of buildings was constructed adjacent to the Haram, perhaps by Walid I. It extended from at least the area of Robinson's Arch right round to the Triple Gate. Masonry from earlier buildings (including Herodian columns) was used in the work. Parts of six large buildings were uncovered, all rectangular structures with interior courts. It is recorded that the Umayyads restored the town walls and built a governor's palace or *Dar al-Imara*. The largest of these buildings lies adjacent to the western end of the S wall of the Haram, stretching from the SW corner all the way to the Double Gate, and most of the visible remains in this area belong to it. Most of these buildings were destroyed in the great earthquake of 747/8, but some occupation continued in Fatimid times in the 10C–11C. All these structures must be linked to the development of Jerusalem by the Umayyad Dynasty as a Muslim religious centre focussed on the shrine and mosque in the Haram. Thereafter the area was little used.

Visit to the area south of the Haram. The upper masonry of the W end of the S wall of the Haram was rebuilt on several occasions, by the Umayyads, by the Fatimid Caliph al-Zahir (c 1034) and by the Mamluk Sultan al-Mansur Qala'un (1280–90). Most of the masonry visible, including the cross-roads adjacent to the SW angle of the Haram, belongs to the Umayyad palace and hospices. The path leads E through the area of the **Umayyad palace (4)**, the remains of which cover the whole area in the angle between the present salient of the City wall and the Haram wall. The palace was 85m × 95m with long halls surrounding a colonnaded central court, two storeys high with the upper storey linked by a bridge to the Haram platform for direct access to the Aqsa Mosque. The palace entrances were in the centres of the E, N and W walls. Much of this building is visible, including the exterior walls, doorways and paving. Another building to the W was of similar plan, but very little is now visible. It may have been a hospice for wealthy pilgrims. To the S, the present S wall of the city (Ottoman, 16C, small stones) is built on top of the line of the S wall of the 8C Umayyad palace (large stones). Following the paved way towards the Umayyad E doorway, blocked by the foundations of the Ottoman city wall, it leads to a double-arched entry opened in the city wall during the recent excavations. Just to the N are the *structures* **(5)** built against the S end of the Aqsa Mosque. They have the appearance of a rather ruinous double tower, buttressed on the W side by two tall blind arches; the walls may have been built as a tower by the Templars in the 12C, and refurbished by Salah al-Din (inscription of 1191), perhaps also primarily as a tower. Within it the *Zawiya al-Khanthaniyya* was endowed at the same time. A room for the reader of the Friday sermon, the *Dar al-Khitaba* was located here in the 15C. The complex was already in a very ruinous state in the 19C. It is possible to go up this tower, and to walk around the city walls as far as the Dung Gate.

Pass through the opening in the city wall, round the corner of the tower to the left, and to the N is part of the blocked entrance of the **Double Gate (6)** (H. western *Hulda Gate (Misnah)*, A. *Abwab al-Akhmas*.) About three-quarters of this gate is hidden by the city wall built in front of it.

History. The gate was constructed by Herod the Great and formed one of the main approaches to the Temple from the Lower City. In front of it and the Triple Gate to the E was a paved street 6.4m wide, reached at this point by a flight of thirty monumental steps 65.5m wide with a plaza below to the S. The gate may well have been blocked in Roman times as the Temple area was then little used, and the ramp within may still have been filled with the rubble of the destruction of AD 70; it was cleared and rebuilt in the Umayyad period. It was blocked during Fatimid times (c 1033) and during the Crusader period when there seems to have been little occupation in the area S of the Haram, and it has remained blocked since that time.

Description. The gate, c 100m E of the SW angle of the Haram, was 12.8m wide with a thick pier dividing the entrance passage. The threshold is c 12m below the level of the Haram esplanade. The remaining E section of a decorative archivolt above the gate arch is

Umayyad. It contains relief acanthus rosettes reminiscent of carvings on the early wooden tie-beams of the Aqsa Mosque (especially tie-beam No. 8), and on the soffits of the tie-beams in the Justinian church at Bethlehem, all dating between the 6C and 8C. Above is a shallow relieving arch topped by a straight cornice with palmettes and dentils. The archivolt is set in front of, and partially obscures, the Herodian lintels, monoliths c 5.5m × 2m with simple drafted edges. The plan of the gate is closely paralleled by that of the Golden Gate (see below), and compares with probable double Umayyad gates on the W and N walls of the Haram. In the third course above the arch, under the end of the cornice, is a re-used *statue base* with inscription naming Hadrian (2C), which may have belonged to a statue placed in the temple area (TITO AE HADRIANO/ANTONINO AVGPIO/ PPPON-TIFAVGVR/DD). The later window in the blocking beneath the cornice gives on to the inner vestibule of the gate (Rte 2G).

Adjacent to the gate, the lowest course of masonry is the *Herodian master course*, 1.67m high and resting on two further courses of Herodian masonry set in the bedrock beneath the paving. The master course continues all the way to the SE angle of the Haram. The wall above is a patchwork of blocking and rebuilding. Much of the lower fine squarish stone courses may be Ummayad or earlier. The large *rectangular window* above to the right marks the floor level of the *Aqsa Mosque* and may be Crusader rebuilt, reconstructed in 1330–31 according to an inscription of al-Nasir Muhammad. The eight *buttresses* and *recesses* mark the aisles and arcades of the mosque; the central aisle being marked by the large window with round arch flanked by two smaller round arched windows with round windows between. These upper windows probably originate in the design of the third phase of the structural history of the Aqsa, probably 11C, but all the windows have been restored this century. The buttress at the E end is Ottoman, but the recess adjacent contains elements of much earlier work, in particular the lower windows, and may belong to the first period of the structural history of the Aqsa (Rte 2E).

The partially restored pavement, steps and broad plaza continue E towards the blocked **Triple Gate (7)**, (H. eastern *Hulda Gate*). This was a very large gate, c 15m wide, of which a fragment of the very large *Herodian jamb* with mouldings survives at ground level on the W side. This is the only Herodian fragment to survive *in situ* and the plan of the original gate is uncertain. Its history appears to be similar to that of the Double Gate. The extant triple arch is presumably that of the Umayyad reconstruction, blocked in the 11C. S of the gate are some re-erected marble columns found in the recent work.

Further E another blocked arch is visible in the S wall of the Haram, which is known as the **Single Gate (8)**. This, as is clear from the masonry around it, was not one of the Herodian gates, but was probably constructed as a postern gate in Crusader times and has been blocked since c 1187. It opens onto the sixth gallery of *Solomon's Stables* (Rte 2G). The arch is pointed, and the voussoirs begin at about the level of the surviving Herodian masonry. Beneath the level of this blocked gate the Herodian paved street, which descends eastwards from the area of the Triple Gate towards the edge of the Kidron Valley, was supported on a row of vaulted chambers. Indications of the burning of these vaults can be seen. From one of these chambers, 34m W of the SE angle of the Haram, a tunnel leads 21m N into the substructure of the Haram. It was discovered by Warren and Birtles in 1867 and recleared by Mazar after 1968. It is lined with fine Herodian masonry, is 1m wide, 3.5m high and ends at a doorway into a vault beneath Solomon's Stables that is now filled with debris. Further exploration could not be undertaken and the purpose of the passage is uncertain. The tunnel is not open to visitors.

Continuing E, windows (perhaps also of Crusader date or later) can be seen in the upper courses of smaller masonry, which allowed light and air to penetrate to the vaults beneath the Haram platform. Various repairs to the S wall of the Haram are noted, by al-Zahir in 1035 (whose inscription can be seen on two crenellations near the SE angle of the Haram wall), and by al-Nasir Muhammad (1294–1340), as well as by Sulaiman in 1537–41. Arriving at the SE angle of the Haram Wall the corner itself is traditionally identified with the *Pinnacle of the Temple* (Matt. 4:5, Luke 4:9). Here the level of the bedrock drops steeply to the Kidron valley and there is a fine view. The Herodian wall is founded on bedrock at 694.90m above sea level at this point and rises to support the Haram esplanade at 738m. 35 courses (c 40m) of magnificent Herodian masonry remain, c 14 above ground and 21 below until the clearances in the 1960's, but now more are exposed. Warren reckoned there were a maximum of 41 courses of masonry in the Herodian platform at this point, of which up to 26 would have showed above ground, the rest being foundations. Again some masonry is of great size, with the readily identifiable Herodian drafted edges.

The upper courses to the junction with the Byzantine city wall are visible **(9)**. The much smaller stones of the Byzantine wall abut the SE angle of the Haram and continue SW to enclose the Lower City. The Byzantine wall is probably that constructed by Eudocia in the 5C.

The large area SE of the Haram between the modern road above the Kidron Valley and the Old City Wall has all been cleared in the excavations by Mazar and others since 1968, and is enclosed within the southern archaeological zone. Just to the SE of the Triple Gate is a building **(10)** in which was found a staircase with carved stone balustrade. This may originally have been built as a palace for Queen Eudocia in the 5C, and later used as a monastery, described by the historian Theodosius in 530, to accommodate the 600 nuns of an enclosed order (Mazar), but the evidence is uncertain. A Byzantine street descends to the S where a large *Umayyad building* of the 8C **(11)** was excavated. Its rectangular plan is marked by massive piers. It is built over Iron Age remains, more of which can be seen to the E in a deep excavation **(12)**. These are the oldest features discovered in the area, dating to the 7C to 6C BC. They include part of a *tower, gate* and *storerooms* of unmortared stones which was built into the later Byzantine wall. To the S **(13)** is part of a building of the Herodian period, identified by Mazar with the Palace built by Queen Helena of Adiabene (see Rte 13), which is also doubtful. To the SW are more remains of Byzantine houses **(14)**. As one returns through the excavation area the principal remains visible are those of Herodian and Roman quarries, and washing places **(15)** which exist in some numbers between the stairways leading to the Double and Triple Gates and in the area to the S. Those coming to the Temple could wash before entering. Passing again through the entrance in the city wall, on the right steps descend to a preserved Byzantine house with *mosaic floor* **(16)**, from which it is possible to descend further to view a fine Herodian cistern.

It is necessary to return to the Dung Gate and walk round by the road to continue the tour along the outer E side of the Haram area.

The **East Wall of the Haram**. Most of this area lies within the Muslim cemetery and a special permit may be required to visit it. A good view can be obtained from the Mount of Olives opposite, especially with binoculars.

Standing at the SE angle of the Haram the Herodian platform seems to tower almost dizzily above one. To the left the debris was cleared by the Jordanian Department of Antiquities in 1965 to expose 13 courses of smoothly dressed small masonry with rubble fill, which abut the Herodian platform to the right. The wall to the left is that of the Byzantine city, built by Eudocia in the 5C. To the right the weathered courses of drafted Herodian masonry remain to within 7m of the top. Above and to the right there is much evidence for later repairs and rebuildings, including a window which gives onto the interior vaults. In Herod's original platform the interior was not a solid fill of rubble, but especially at this SE corner where the bedrock dropped away so steeply, the interior ground level was built up by as many as four tiers of vaults, of which *Solomon's Stables* were probably the second from the top.

Walking N, at c 20m the springers of another very large Herodian arch can be seen above. This is clearly a parallel feature to Robinson's Arch on the W side of the Temple, and probably supported another flight of monumental stairs leading up from the E or SE to an eastern entrance to the Herodian Royal Stoa. It also therefore implies that there was an outer line of defence wall to the E at this point. Warren during his explorations in 1867–68 certainly encountered sections of a rather massive wall 43.5m S of the Golden Gate, and 14m E of the Haram wall which was founded on bedrock. It ran N–S, was more than 1.5m wide of masonry with marginal drafts and projecting rough bosses. Built with mortar, the date is obscure. The Haram wall in this area shows very clearly the strong outward batter of the lower walls stepping down to the massive foundations which are set in a cutting in bedrock.

Just beyond the arch, at c 32m N of the SE angle of the Haram, is one of the still controversial features of the Haram platform, a straight joint continuing upwards for nearly half the present height of the wall. The later masonry to the left is certainly that of Herod the Great (from c 20 BC); the earlier masonry to the right has a different character, the blocks being within the smaller size range of the Herodian blocks, but differing in drafting and cutting, and in particular with a more projecting and rougher boss. Various explanations for this change have been suggested: that the wall here is part of the original Solomonic 10C BC construction (Laperrousaz); that it is Persian-style masonry and is part of the Zerubabbel post-exilic Temple platform of the 6C BC (Kenyon); that it forms part of the Seleucid fortress called the Akra built in the 2C BC (Tsafrir); that it forms simply a first phase of Herod the Great's building operations in the 1C BC (Avi-Yonah). None of these propositions has been proved, but the Persian or later dates are the most favoured. Warren, who first noted the seam in the 19C, was only able to trace the 'older' type of masonry for another 17m to the N and was inclined to see possible traces of Solomonic masonry in the central section of the E wall.

A path leads N from this point through the *Muslim cemetery* which lies adjacent to the whole length of the E wall of the Haram. Approximately 260m N along the wall is a small offset in the masonry by which is located the blocked *Bab al-Jana'iz*, the *Funeral Gate*, or *Bab al-Buraq*, the *Gate of Muhammad's steed*.

Nearly 40m further N is the **Golden Gate**, A. *Bab al-Dhahabi*, a double gate (also blocked) whose façade projects from the wall. The S entrance is called the Gate of Mercy, A. *Bab al-Rahma*; and the N entrance the Gate of Repentance, A. *Bab al-Tawba*; the central dividing pier is missing. (For the interior of the gate, see Rte 2B).

History. There are varied references to gates in the E wall of the Herodian and later platform and their location is often uncertain. In Herodian times and presumably deriving from the Persian period, *Shushan Habirah*, the *Gate of Susa the Capital*, lay in the E wall and was used by the priests during the Ceremony of the Red Heifer. This was a Jewish purification ritual, in which the High Priest led out a red heifer to sacrifice and burn on the Mount of Olives (Numbers 19:1–10; Talmud, Midd. 1:3). This E gate may also have been used in the Scapegoat Ritual performed annually on the eve of *Yom Kippur*, the Day of Atonement, when a goat symbolically laden with the sins of the community was driven out of the city to be killed in the wilderness to the E (Shekalim 4:2; Parah 3:6). The location of this Herodian gate is not known but two huge ancient interior jambs on the alignment of the Herodian wall suggest the Herodian gate may also have been on this site.

The present gate is cut through the wall at a height of 12.50m– 13m above the bedrock and the threshold is 6.50m below the interior level of the Haram. The date is uncertain: possibly mid-4C; perhaps built by Eudocia in the mid-5C to commemorate Peter's miraculous cure of the lame man at the Gate Beautiful (actually located to the W in the Herodian courts); a gate on the site is depicted on the Madaba Map in the mid-6C; it may have been built for the triumph of the Emperor Heraclius in 631; it could be Umayyad. Some elements of the decoration (the pilaster capitals supporting the archivolt) appear to be of late Roman style, probably re-used; much of the remainder suppports the attribution to the 7C–8C (the style of the relief work including the rosettes, the early form of joggled voussoirs on the S side of the structure inside the Haram). The plan is very similar to the Herodian double gates in the S wall, and the monolithic jambs visible in the interior are perhaps Herodian; the projecting façade implies a rebuilding at a later stage. It may not have been open regularly in the Byzantine or early Islamic period. In the time of the Crusaders (12C) it was opened twice a year for the solemn procession on Palm Sunday and on the Feast of the Exaltation of the Cross, and a Crusader chapel was located at the Porta Aurea. Since that time it has been blocked.

Traditions. The gate is the location of many Muslim and Jewish traditions: it is the gate by which the just will enter on the Day of Judgment, hence its popularity as a burial location. Many stories grew up around it from the 8C onwards when its name was confused with that of the Herodian 'Beautiful Gate', the Greek *horaia* beautiful, and Latin *aurea* gold. It is believed by many Christians that Jesus entered the city by this gate on Palm Sunday and that at the Second Coming he will again enter here. A Muslim tradition holds that a Christian conqueror will ride through the gate.

Description. The façade, c 18m wide, has a shallow double arch with elaborate archivolt supported at either end by pilasters with Corinthian capitals of late Roman or Byzantine style probably in re-use. The details are virtually identical with those on the interior façade of the gate. The central pier is missing . Narrow window slits are built in the false windows of the later blocking. Ornamental roundels and recessed panels of later date (16C) ornament the façade below the crenellations which extend all along the E side of the Haram platform. Muslim graves lie immediately adjacent to the entrance. 15.50m to the S of the gate is a blocked Crusader(?) postern, 1.40m high. Its flat lintel has a cross set in an elaborate nimbus.

At both sides of the gate large, rough, weathered masonry can be seen in the course at ground level. It has been suggested that parts of the original Solomonic E wall is to be seen here (Warren) and Josephus (Antiq. XX:219–22) narrates the events in the time of Agrippa II when work on the construction of the Herodian Temple had finally finished and 18,000 men were unemployed: 'so they persuaded him to rebuild the eastern cloisters. These cloisters belonged to the outer court, and were situated in a deep valley... and were built of square and very white stones.... This was the work of King Solomon, who first of all built the entire Temple. But King Agrippa, who had the care of the Temple committed to him by Claudius Caesar, considered that it is easy to demolish any building, but hard to build it up again, and that it was particularly hard to do it to those cloisters, which would require a considerable time and great sums of money'; so Agrippa wisely decided the unemployed could pave the streets of the city instead! Peter and the other disciples taught in Solomon's Portico after the Crucifixion (Acts 5:13).

The E wall of the Haram was restored in 961/2 by the Amir 'Ali b. Ikhshid, by al-Zahir in 1035 and by Sulaiman II in the 16C.

Continuing N towards the NE angle of the Haram the level of the bedrock again drops away and 77.7m N of the Gate it is 30.4m–38m below the surface. Warren showed that a deep valley originally ran through the NE area of the Haram towards the Kidron. He also noted a particular type of masonry in this part of the wall. The bosses of the stones are very rough and project as much as 0.3m– 0.6m. This type of masonry is found in the wall S of the NE tower, from the bedrock up to the present surface, a height of more than 38m; it is also found at the NW angle of the Haram. The upper NE corner of the Haram is marked by a change in masonry and by a tower-like projection. However, below ground level Warren recorded that the Herodian masonry of the Haram wall continues to the N and the tower does not extend to bedrock. Thus it is clear that the projecting tower was not part of the original plan, and the Birkat Isra'il was enclosed within the original Herodian plan. The section of wall N of the Birkat Isra'il to St. Stephens Gate is much more recent and stands on shallow foundations. To complete the tour the visitor continues on to **St. Stephen's Gate**.

B. Structures built into or against the inner face of the Haram wall

The inner face of the N wall of the Haram

At the NE corner is the *Bab al-Asbat, Gate of the Tribes*, in Crusader times the Gate of Paradise. Restored in 1816–17 but constructed of re-used Crusader masonry; gate and chamber form a small complex of pointed arches. To the W is the *North Riwaq*, a portico or arcaded ambulatory extending along most of the N wall of the Haram, formed from a magnificent row of pointed arches of smoothly dressed masonry built in various stages from the 10C to 1432 on the line of the earlier Herodian N wall of the Temple enclosure, and incorporating Umayyad, Fatimid and Ayyubid work. These arches are mostly walled in and provided with a modern window and door for use as classrooms. The frontage has several notable 13C–15C Mamluk buildings, mostly Muslim religious schools containing the tomb of the founder, with Ottoman additions. None of the buildings are open to visitors (some are now used as dwellings), but many of the Haram façades have characteristic Mamluk ornament.

Starting at the first pier W of the *Bab al-Asbat*, the first 11 piers are not later than 1345, but they contain no Crusader stones and may possibly be Ikhshidid (c 961–62) or Fatimid (11C) work. Built partly on the 11th pier is the base of the *al-Asbat* or *Isra'il Minaret*, built in 1367/8. Five steps lead to the portal in a pointed arched recess, which gives access to the roof of the portico. Above, a plinth with pyramidal buttresses has entrance on the E side to spiral stairs to the muezzins' gallery. The shaft has three storeys, with moulded string courses and incised friezes. The shaft may have been reconstructed in the Ottoman period, and the top was completely renewed after the earthquake of 1927. The founder's inscription is on the door lintel, which has red and cream joggled voussoirs, and a tympanum with four tiers of muqarnas (stalactite) vaulting.

Beyond the next three arcades to the W (which date before c 1397) is the small *Madrasa Ghadiriyya*, built in 1432 by the Amir Muhammad b. Dhulghadir (of a Turcoman Anatolian dynasty). Originally on two floors, the upper extended slightly to the N of the Haram wall; it hung out c 1.5m over the Pool of Isra'il and also extended over the four recessed arcades of the portico to the W. Most of this upper floor, which was the major part of the madrasa, has been destroyed. At the W end, above pier 18, there is one remaining blocked window with muqarnas ornament. On the ground floor, the recessed entrance portal, of red and cream masonry, with slightly pointed horseshoe arch, has the customary benches and founder's inscription, though the latter is mostly destroyed. The façade, now much neglected, has rectangular windows: one to the W and two to the E of the door, paired with slit windows above. The slits to the E have a larger trilobed window between them. Inside a vestibule and passage with three chambers survive.

The next group of structures which project S beyond pier 19 contains the *Karimiyya*, endowed in 1319 as a madrasa by Karim al-Din. This rather dull façade was perhaps originally a conversion of three porticoes on the Haram frontage into an assembly hall. The structures above are Ottoman. Much of the building lies to the N outside the Haram, with the entrance fronting onto the E side of the TARIQ BAB HITTA (Rte 3). Adjacent on the W side is the *Bab Hitta, Gate of Remission*, reconstructed in 1220 between piers 20 and 21. The gate and porch are part of a two-storey structure. The high, pointed arch with decorated cornice above gives on to a deeply shaded chamber with pointed domed ceiling, and contains some re-used Crusader masonry. It is closed by large wooden gates with a small wicket. It may have orginated as a double gate in the Umayyad period, with the second gate passage to the W now incorporated into the tomb chamber of the Awhadiyya (Burgoyne).

Bays 21–23 contain much re-used Crusader masonry, and date c 1295–98. Behind the blocked portico is the **Awhadiyya** (Rte 3), with the now inaccessible *Tomb of al-Awhad*, Superintendent of the Two Harams from 1295. The frontage is plain, though there was once a grilled window from the portico to the tomb chamber. **Bays 24–28** date from between c 1295 and 1345 and were perhaps built at the same time as the *Dawadariyya* which lies behind them and was completed in 1295 (see Rte 3). Above the blocked portico, at first floor level, is the façade of the *Basitiyya*. This madrasa or khanqah was endowed in 1431 by 'Abd al-Basit. It consists of several elements, which lack architectural cohesion. From the W (above pier 28) there is 1. a plain window and a blocked entrance portal with muqarnas arch of re-used masonry and benches at the sides, which was originally approached from the Haram by a staircase; 2. a triple line of rectangular windows with grilles which gave onto the main assembly room, with blind triple window above; 3. a double window recessed in a pointed arch with round oculus above, which uses unmatched Crusader marble columns, capitals and bases. A dome above was removed in the 19C; 4. two other small rectangular windows to the E.

Piers 29–38 are Ayyubid, constructed 1213/4, with later alterations. An inscription on pier 31 records the Ayyubid work. Between piers 30 and 31 is the *Bab al-'Atm, Gate of Darkness*, (also *Bab al-Malik Faisal* (of Iraq) or *Gate of King Feisal, Bab Sharaf al-Anbiya'* or *Gate of the Glory of the Prophets, Bab al-Dawadariyya* named for the building on the E). A high archway flanked by buttresses leads into a dark vaulted passage closed by wooden doors. It dates to 1213/14 but it has been suggested that the present gate is the W passage of an Umayyad triple gate like that at the S end of the Haram where the scale is smaller but the plan is similar. It has the same distinctive chamfering of the lower outer edge of the voussoirs, and the rear of the gate arch arranged so that the gate leaves could be folded flush with the piers (Burgoyne). Above the gate is the upper floor of the *Madrasa Aminiyya*, dating to 1329/30. It was built by Amin al-Mulk, a state official of Coptic origin in the time of al-Nasir Muhammad, who converted to Islam under Baybars II. This is now approached by an Ottoman outside staircase on the W side of the gate, built when the madrasa was converted to domestic use, and the W window was altered into a door. The original entrance and ground floor lie on the W side of TARIQ BAB AL-'ATM (Rte 3). The elaborate and symmetrical Haram frontage at first floor level has five windows; the middle three above the *Bab al-'Atm* have been recently restored. They have red and cream voussoirs supported on six marble columns with Crusader acanthus leaf capitals. The outer windows are set in recessed pointed arches. The high façade on the W is a later addition.

To the W is the *Madrasa Farisiyya* endowed in 1352/3 by Faris al-Din, a Mamluk official who was at one time governor of Gaza. It is built over the portico and entered by stairs under the portico that supports the Almalikiyya to the W. Most of the frontage was rebuilt in Ottoman times. Over piers 35 to 37 is the *Almalikiyya*, a madrasa endowed in 1340 by Almalik al-Jukandar, who started as a slave and rose to become a court official of al-Nasir Muhammad. He was the 'Bearer of the Polo Stick'. The madrasa has survived virtually unchanged, with an assembly hall overlooking the Haram and the founder's inscription which bears his blazon of polo sticks above the piers. New piers were built to support the structure, with buttresses continuing to the top of the façade, and a string course above the piers; at the top is a two-tiered muqarnas cornice. The intervening façade is recessed. Alternate courses of red and cream stone and three windows with round oculus above complete a façade whose symmetry is only marred by an extension beyond the W buttress. To the rear is an open courtyard with two tiers of cells and a tomb chamber.

Adjacent to the W is a fine complex marked by a long, symmetrical façade topped by three domes. This is the *Khanqah* or *Madrasa Is'irdiyya* which is built at first floor level over the portico, **piers 40** to **42** being constructed at the same time. It was built and endowed in 1359 for Majd al-Din al-Is'irdi, perhaps of a merchant family, who came from Siirt SW of Lake Van in Turkey. It was restored in 1927/8 with some modifications, when it became the *Aqsa Libary* (now in the *Ashrafiyya*, see below). The central feature in the façade is the curved salient of the back of the mihrab supported on muqarnas corbelling. The façade is an expanded version of the Almalikiyya, with four windows to the assembly room and a dome chamber at both ends. During the restorations various modifications were made to the windows, and the rectangular pediment above added. The E dome was then modified to match the W dome. The large double window of the W dome chamber contained Crusader columns, bases and acanthus capitals which were replaced with modern 'Islamic' muqarnas capitals and bulbous bases. The site is compressed against the rock scarp behind, and the interior of the building is divided into two sections by a massive E–W wall, 4m wide, which may be a surviving part of Herod the Great's Antonia fortress (Rte 3). The Mamluk builders had to cut through this to link the assembly room on the S with the court on the N. The court has two storeys of cells on three sides, approached by a spiral staircase in the NE corner. The façade of the court has pleasingly restrained decoration, with, from the top, a cornice with muqarnas band; a row of small keyhole ventilation windows; a row of rosette windows giving on to a line of upper cells; and a row of square windows to the lower cells which were approached from a rear corridor. On the S side of the court is an iwan, with a tomb, probably of the founder, on the W. The tomb chamber is finely decorated with a pointed horseshoe arch of black and white voussoirs supported by Crusader marble columns with un-matched capitals which are in excellent condition. There is a fine Mamluk iron grille protecting the chamber. Here the lower 2m of the wall appear to be of Herodian masonry with a section of the upper ornamental pilasters (as noted between the Ghawanima and Nazir Gates by Warren in the 19C). The court also contains a well.

At the W corner of the Is'irdiyya the portico ends and the Haram wall and rock scarp are set back to the N among trees. The sharp rise in the rock level is indicated by the scarp which may have been cut in Herodian times as the base for the Antonia fortress. Next to the Is'irdiyya the scarp is capped by the long two-storey 'Umariyya Boys' School built in 1923/4. Some Mamluk buildings were constructed here, but there is little of them to be seen now. A buttress against the W end of the Is'irdiyya is the last fragment of a portico which once contained the access to the *Subaybiyya*, a tomb and madrasa built before 1406 for 'Ala' al-Din 'Ali b. Nasir al-Din Muhammad, the governor of the fortress of Subayba (Castle of Nimrod above Banias). About 7.50m above the esplanade, and adjacent to the Is'irdiyya, is a blocked door and two windows of pink and cream masonry. The surviving lintel of the door and the left window are of mottled red granite; at either end of the door lintel are limestone blocks with cup and napkin blazons in lobed medallions. When the school was built above the ruins of the Subaybiyya, the interior became inaccessible. The N side may have included the ruined Mamluk doorway in the S frontage of the **Via Dolorosa** (Rte 3, Scala Sancta). Rising above the modern part of the school to the W is a cluster of buildings. These also have earlier foundations. In the highest domed building, the two top storeys are part of the Ottoman barracks. The third storey from the top is part of the *Jawuliyya*, a madrasa built for Sanjar al-Jawuli between 1315–20; its Haram frontage, of red and cream coursed masonry, has a row of five windows, the three central ones belong to the S iwan, and the outer ones to flanking rooms. All have been cut in a massive wall which probably belonged to the Antonia, like the wall in the Is'irdiyya to the E. To the W the *Madrasa Muhaddathiyya* was endowed in 1360 by a scholar from Ardabil. Part of a window with muqarnas decoration can be seen towards the W end of the complex.

Cut into the rock scarp c 8.9m above the explanade are several large sockets, 0.48m², which probably held the roof beams of the Herodian portico. Traces of porticoes of the Herodian, pre-Mamluk and Mamluk periods have all been found.

In the NW angle of the Haram is the *al-Ghawanima minaret* built 1298–99 by the superintendent of the. Two Harams in the time of Sultan al-Mansur Husam-al-Din Lajin. It takes its name from the nearby gate. This Syrian-type square tower minaret, the tallest and largest in the Haram, lends great character to the area, with six storeys rising well above the height of the enclosure wall. At the base blind arcades with columns and decorated stonework are surmounted by a muqarnas cornice; above, the upper storeys are approached from the E; each storey varies, and each is separated by moulded string courses. The second, fourth, fifth and sixth storeys all contain re-used Crusader columns, capitals and bases, either in the windows or in the corner nooks. At the sixth storey, the balcony level, Crusader capitals in the blind arcades on the W, N and E sides, though much battered, appear to depict two angels ministering to the seated figure of Jesus. It is thought that these capitals (and a fourth now in the Islamic Museum, Rte 2F) were brought from the nearby *Crusader Chapel of the Repose* ('*Umariyya School*, Rte 3) from which they were probably removed sometime after 1244. Above, an octagonal lantern is capped by a circular drum and a bulbous dome.

The inner W wall of the Haram

Just S of the NW angle of the Haram are steps up to the two pointed archways containing the *Bab al-Ghawanima*, a gate built 1307/8(?) and named after the Ghanim family, descendants of the man whom Salah al-Din appointed Shaikh of the Salihiyya Madrasa (Rte 3). The Crusader Gates of Grief were located here. To the S a group of two-and three-storey structures line the Haram wall, as far as the great **West Portico**. This has 69 piers supporting an open arcade constructed in various stages from 1307/8 to before 1483, which continues with few interruptions down most of the W side of the Haram, and is in itself a magnificent structure giving weight and dignity and an area of coolness to the court. The strong piers and simple cornice contain a splendid vista. The first six piers were constructed between 1345 and 1361, the first two incorporating much Crusader masonry. Standing over the first eight open bays with slightly pointed arches is the *Manjakiyya*, built as a madrasa by Sayf al-Din Manjak al-Yusufi in 1361 but possibly intended as his residence. He was a Mamluk official in the time of al-Nasir Muhammad, and had a chequered career, ending in Cairo, where he died in 1375. He was responsible for much building work in Cairo, Damascus and elsewhere. The endowments for this madrasa are listed in Safed, in and around Jerusalem and at Bait Safafa. The building now houses the Department of Pious Endowments and Islamic Affairs. The entrance is from the N side of the Tariq Bab al-Nazir (Rte 3). The Haram frontage contains a domed loggia with a fine double-arched window whose black and white voussoirs spring from three marble columns with re-used Crusader capitals and bases on the side columns; the central capital is a Mamluk copy(?). The columns themselves have unusual decoration. The round oculi above have reddish infills of later date. The remaining first-storey windows are rectangular, those at the S end give onto the prayer hall above the Bab al-Nazir. Above, at the second storey, is an unsightly Council Chamber built in 1935. The Mamluk façade is topped by a narrow cornice, and the central area is roofed by an octagonal drum with lights and a high cemented dome.

Continuing S, the *Bab al-Nazir, Gate of the Inspector* or *of the Watchman*, also *Bab al-Habs, Gate of the Prison* (from the prisons which were earlier located in the street outside) leads from the 8th arcade of the W portico. The original gate may be Umayyad but the voussoirs lack the characteristic chamfering; the restoration of the doors of the gate is noted, 1200; the portal was constructed in 1307–08. On **pier 9** of the portico, a beautiful inscription with fine calligraphy in a broad and ornate border records the building of the two bays S of the gate, that of the gate itself, and the one to the N in 1307/8. The moulding of the bay in front of the gate ends with a pair of pendant muqarnas stalactites and the dome in the portico is supported by a fine muqarnas transition zone. The same date is given to all the remaining bays to pier 16.

Piers 17 to **44** are relatively homogeneous, and being a part of the construction of the Bab al-Qattanin should date to 1336/7, though bays 23–29 around the Bab al-Hadid were rebuilt in 1928 after the earthquake of 1927, and bays 39–44 were affected by the building of the Ashrafiyya (see below).

Bab al-Hadid, the *Gate of Iron,* between piers 24 and 25, was restored on the same dimensions as an earlier gate in 1354–57 by the builder of the adjacent madrasa, and was thus sometimes called Bab Arghun. Behind the portico S of this gate various rooms have been employed during this century as the tombs of men honoured by burial close to the sanctuary. Immediately S of the gate is *al-Arghuniyya,* a madrasa and tomb completed in 1358 for the Amir Arghun al-Kamili, the viceroy of Syria, though possibly intended at first as a temporary residence for its owner. He was a court official, with the title of Master of the Robes, as indicated by the blazon on his inscription over the original entrance in Tariq Bab al-Hadid (Rte 3) which was blocked in 1931. The endowments for the madrasa included dues from near Krak des Chevaliers in Syria. The madrasa is cruciform in plan with a vestibule leading to a roofed court with iwans on E, W, and S The court is vaulted, with a closed octagonal oculus at the centre which probably once had a lantern dome. The tomb of the founder is placed in the NE corner chamber, with a window onto the first bay of the portico S of the gate. It has a cenotaph, with burial vault below. The S iwan has the mihrab, refurbished, with polychrome marble panels. The capital on the right is original, that on the left a restoration. There were five upper rooms intended as a dwelling in the original design. Some repairs and modifications were made to the building in 1571/2; rooms were built on the roof in the Ottoman period; and the court and iwans were refurbished in 1931 when the E iwan was employed as the tomb of King Husain ibn ʿAli who died in Amman in 1931. He was a leader in the cause of Arab Independence during and after World War I. The large cenotaph is covered by a gold-embroidered green brocade cloth made in 1946/7 in Cairo and can be seen through the ornate window in second bay of the Haram portico. The third bay contains the present entrance to the Arghuniyya.

To the S *al-Khatuniyya* is a madrasa begun in 1354 by Oghul Khatun, daughter of Shams al-Din Muhammad b. Sayf al-Din of Qazan (from Baghdad, perhaps from a Turkish or Mongol family), and completed in 1380. The original entrance to a large complex is from TARIK BAB AL-HADID (Rte 3). The Haram frontage is much altered. Originally it had a plain door into an assembly hall, and a grilled window into the tomb chamber. Now there is a new window and door, and the original tomb window is a door. This is now the only entrance to the tomb which contains two cenotaphs: on the S the smaller cenotaph is presumably that of the founder; on the N is the larger one of ʿAbd al-Hamid, a Hashemite Sharif. The pendentives and tympana of the wall arches of the tomb chamber originally had relief stucco decoration, which is not preserved. The dome collapsed in 1919–20 and has been badly rebuilt. The central window and the S door have elaborate funerary inscriptions relating to the five people buried in the assembly hall of the madrasa during this century, including the tomb of the Indian Muslim leader, Muhammad al-Hindi, friend and benefactor of the Arabs of Palestine. He was the first to be buried here in 1930. Also here are the tombs of Musa Kazim Pasha al-Husaini, Chairman of the Arab Higher Executive in Palestine and member of one of the great Palestinian families of Jerusalem, who died in 1933; and of his son, ʿAbd al-Qadir Musa Pasha who died in the battle at Qastal on 8 April 1948 in the Arab struggle for the preservation of Palestine. The assembly hall has much coursed red and cream masonry. Structures at first floor level above the portico were demolished in 1925; old photographs indicate there was a double window with coloured masonry.

Immediately S at **pier 32**, steps lead down to the *Bab al-Qattanin, Gate of the Cotton Merchants*, built in 1336–37 by the Amir Tankiz al-Nasiri for al-Nasir Muhammad as part of a new commercial complex (Rte 3, Suq al-Qattanin). It may well have been a new gate to the Haram, not standing on older foundations. The gate is set in a trefoil recess with cream and black voussoirs within a much larger recess with vast semi-dome. The semi-dome rests on five tiers of very fine stalactite corbelling, and has a pointed arch with red and cream voussoirs. The façade is capped by a stepped cornice. The gate itself has fine, carved wooden door panels.

Two bays S of the gate, between piers 34 and 35 is the *Bab al-Mathara, the Gate of Ablution*, which was open in Ayyubid times and restored 1267. The gate leads to the *Ablution Place*, the siqaya of al-Malik al-ʿAdil built in 1193. The rather plain archway leads to the ZUQAQ BAB AL-MATHARA. On the right is the *Ribat al-Zamani*, a late Mamluk pilgrim hospice built in 1476/7 by Ibn al-Zamin, who was a merchant and a favoured associate of Sultan Qaʾit Bay. The narrow site is squashed in behind the Suq al-Qattanin, the upper floors include three rooms taken from the S lodgings of the suq (Rte 3), and formerly extended over the Haram portico. Latterly the W side was used as the women's lavatory. The hospice has a tall entrance portal, with shallow trefoil arched recess with seven tiers of muqarnas work. Two courses above the door lintel is a joggled string course within a frame moulding. One course higher is the founder's inscription in a sunk panel. To the E of the portal is an elaborately decorated window with its original iron grille. There are four tiers of muqarnas work in the window recess. The work compares with that of the Ashrafiyya (see below), being late Mamluk with Cairene influences.

Opposite on the S side of the road is the entrance to the *ʿUthmaniyya* (see below). The decorated façade contains two windows to the tomb chamber and a flight of steps to the main portal which has red and cream masonry. It has elaborate detail in the ornamental voussoirs and string courses. Adjacent to the W is an annex of three storeys, of which the upper may date to 1656. These are built partly above the roof of the Ablution Place.

Reconstruction of the façade of al-Ashrafiyya (courtesy of A.G. Walls).

The *Ablution Place* at the end of the lane, though much altered, is the original water installation or siqaya built in 1193 by al-Malik al-'Adil. It has a cross-vaulted entrance bay with pointed arch with gadrooned voussoirs and brackets supported by elbow consoles. There were latrines for men and women on the S and N sides respectively of the Ablution Place, and on the W a bath house (Rte 3, Hammam al-Shifa'). The E wing of the Ablution Place now serves as a women's lavatory.

Returning to the Haram, behind and above piers 34 to 39 is the *'Uthmaniyya* a madrasa and tomb of Isfahan Shah Khatun, endowed in 1437, with original entrance on the S side of the ZUQAQ BAB AL-MATHARA. The founder is otherwise unknown, but perhaps came from Turkey and founded the madrasa for the study of religious law and for Sufi devotions. The lower storey has windows from the portico to the founder's tomb chamber (bay next to Bab al-Mathara) and to the assembly room (bay next to al-Ashrafiyya). The upper storey above the portico may once have extended to the N of the Bab al-Qattanin. At the S end of the upper storey is a window with red and cream jambs set in a recess with four tiers of muqarnas corbelling and a fluted conch. Of the six other windows the most elaborate is a large double window or loggia with pointed arches supported by three re-used marble columns. Above are roundels with interlocking radial voussoirs. All the rectangular windows have their original Mamluk iron grilles. Near the S end of the roof there remains one small pointed dome on an octagonal drum containing arches with gadrooned voussoirs (view from the Dome platform to E).

Jutting out from the portico to the S is the *'Ashrafiyya*, a madrasa built in 1482 by the Mamluk Sultan al-Ashraf Sayf-al-Din Qa'it Bay as a Shafi'i institution to house 60 Sufis and law students, it was by the 15C used for public enquiries. It suffered earthquake damage in 1496 and was being plundered for building stones by 1552. Its important upper storey became ruinous, but the ground floor assembly hall now houses the *Aqsa Mosque Library*. Though only part of this ruined school remains, in its original splendour it was called the third jewel of the Haram. The ornate decoration of its portal is a fine example of late Mamluk work.

The structure is the work of a Coptic architect following two previous attempts in the reign of Sultan Khushqadam in 1470–75 and 1480, which were demolished. The ground floor has an elaborate entrance porch of Cairene type with painted courses simulating coloured masonry. A cruciform panel with low relief strapwork with star patterns crowns the vault, with arabesque lozenges to the sides. On the N side is a bench and a grilled window which gives onto the assembly hall. It is set in a recess with muqarnas hood and has a lintel of interlocking stones, carved, with joggled pseudo-relieving arch above, and an oculus of carved voussoirs, coursed in red and cream stone. Amongst the elaborate decoration of corbelling and tympanum are three circular cartouches of Qa'it Bay. The doorway on the W has a trefoil-arched recess of red, black and cream masonry bedded in lead which would originally have outlined the stones in black (also a 15C Cairene technique). The decoration is very elaborate, with mouldings, carvings, and strapwork; six courses above the threshold is the founder's inscription. The lintel is of mottled grey granite. The original doors of walnut, inlaid with pine and bound by inscribed brass bands are now in the Islamic Museum. Muqarnas corner squinches support a shallow semi-dome, of limestone inlaid with patterns in red stone, a black substance and turquoise faience. The entrance leads into a lofty vestibule, and then to the assembly hall to the N. The assembly hall is built in three bays of the W portico, with three more built against them to the E. It is decorated with red and cream coursed masonry. The three windows in the E wall are recent restorations. The upper floor was more extensive, as it extended over the *Baladiyya* to the W (Rte 3). It consisted of terraces with cells and latrines at a high level around the screened Baladiyya court on the W side; but overlooking the Haram on the E and above the assembly hall was a notable madrasa, the ruined remains of which can be viewed from the Dome platform opposite. Only parts survive of the N, W and S walls of a room originally 10.5m high, with four iwans. The S iwan was the largest, with a mihrab originally inlaid with marble, porphyry and granite. A Koranic inscription (once gilded) runs round the walls above the windows. Originaly there was a loggia window on the E side, with marble columns, gilded capitals and tympana filled with polychrome glass set in plaster tracery. Mujir al-Din describes this madrasa: 'the floor is entirely paved with polychrome marble, and the walls are panelled in marble. The ceiling is of wood covered with gold leaf and azure; it is extremely well-built and beautiful and very high'.

Adjoining the S side of the Ashrafiyya is the W minaret of the Haram, the *Minaret of the Chain*, re-built in 1329–30 by the Amir Tankiz. The minaret may stand on the site of an earlier Umayyad minaret, and was damaged in an earthquake in 1496 or 1546. The upper part was probably rebuilt in Ottoman times, the Ottoman spire being removed in 1894 and replaced by an ashlar drum and dome. It was repaired in 1923/4. A traditional square Syrian tower of four storeys divided by string courses, the third storey is the most decorative, and has a recess with three tiers of muqarnas corbelling and nook shafts with re-used Crusader columns, capitals and bases.

To the S is the important double gate, with the closed *Bab al-Sakina*, or *Gate of the Ark* on the N and the *Bab al-Silsila, Gate of the Chain* on the S, built c 1200 (see Rte 2A). The gate is set down from the portico within a low pointed arch.

Piers 45 to **55** of the West Portico, S from the Bab al-Sakina, have been rebuilt and are not uniform. The second pier S of the gate, **pier 47**, had a re-used fragment of a Crusader gravestone built into its S face 'HIC JACET DROGO DE BUS...'. The upper storey of the *Tankiziyya* was built over this part of the portico in 1328/9 and an inscription indicates these piers were built in 1313/4. The Sufi madrasa and khanqah of the Amir Tankiz al-Nasiri is entered from the TARIQ BAB AL-SILSILA (Rte 3). The ground floor behind the Haram portico has four windows, and a blocked door which originally led to the madrasa above. The upper storey has been much altered, but includes a pair of arched windows, now partly blocked to take rectangular glazing, with black and white voussoirs supported by re-used columns, and elbow brackets from a central pier which replaces an original third column. The W portico continues; **Bays 56** to **67** are homogeneous, and date from between 1345 and 1483. The last two piers of the West Portico (of uncertain date between 1332 and 1483) contain the inner porch of the *Bab al-Maghariba*, the *Gate of the Moors*, 1314–15(?) which led out to the Moors Quarter and the Western Wall (Rte 2A).

The buildings to the S of the gate now house the Islamic Museum (Rte 2F) in Crusader and Ayyubid buildings, partly remodelled in 1871. Immediately S of the gate is a N-facing façade with two large pointed arched entrances, respectively the entrances to the

al-Maghariba mosque on the E and the *Fakhriyya mosque* on the W.
Neither is now used as a mosque. The entrance portals are mostly
constructed of re-used Crusader material, including the hood
moulds, and in the Maghariba entrance, elbow brackets supporting
the lintel. The Maghariba tympanum is now blocked, that of the
Fakhriyya partly open. The latter has a smaller pointed arch built
inside it, also of largely Crusader materials. Between the two is a late
Mamluk or Ottoman mihrab. The *al-Maghariba Mosque* was built in
a large Ayyubid vaulted hall c 1194, for the use of the Maghariba
community outside the adjacent Haram gate. The *Fakhriyya Mosque*
was the zawiya, khanqah or madrasa of Fakhr al-Din Muhammad,
Inspector of the Army in the time of al-Nasir Muhammad. He was a
devout Coptic Christian who considered suicide rather than conversion to Islam, but subsequently became a devout Muslim. It was built
before 1332 in the ruined remains of an Ayyubid vaulted hall and by
the 16C had become a Sufi khanqah. Its assembly hall was probably
located in the W end of the Crusader hall to the S. A local family, of
Abu al-Su'ud, a member of which was overseer of the mosque in
1556/7, gradually came to own and live in it until recent times, when
it was called the Dar Abu al-Su'ud, and was the centre of the Shafi'i
sect of which Abu al-Su'ud was mufti. The N entrance was still in use
early this century, but is now blocked. Inside it a vestibule led S to a
court with lodgings, and S to a second court in front of the mosque
itself. The latter is now entered from the S and is in use as the office of
the Islamic Museum. It is a columned hall, 8.10m × 8.3m, divided
into three aisles by vaults and piers. The piers and upper structure
were built in Ottoman times (c 1556?) when the original polychrome
and patterned marble floor appears to have been badly relaid. The
mihrab in the S wall is probably the Mamluk original. It has coloured
marble panels flanked by two Crusader columns still retaining their
capitals and bases; a loop and roundel at the top is inscribed 'for
Allah'. The doorway at the SE corner also has Crusader columns and
capitals in re-use and one stands on a bulbous Mamluk base.
Although the Fakhriyya is not accessible, it can be seen from the W
from the area S of the Western Wall. Passing the remodelled E façade
of the Maghariba mosque, now the Islamic Museum (Rte 2F) we
come to the *al-Fakhriyya minaret*, the SW minaret of the Haram, and
the smallest, built after 1345 but before 1496. It fell before 1546, was
rebuilt after 1672 and restored in 1923/4. Again a Syrian type square
tower with three storeys, it is built over the N wall of the Crusader
hall. The upper part, including the muqarnas corbelling, dates to
1923/4, but little is known of its original form.

The inner S and E walls of the Haram

With the exception of the Aqsa Mosque (Rte 2E) relatively few structures are built against the S and E walls. The S wall contains the façade of the S wing of the *Islamic Museum* and the *Womens Mosque* of the Aqsa, which are contained in a great Crusader hall built but probably not finished by the Templars probably in the 1160s. The façade has many 12C masons's marks, five windows and a fine Ayyubid doorway flanked by pairs of Crusader marble columns and capitals. For the Aqsa itself, see Rte 2E.

Approximately halfway between the Aqsa Mosque and the SE angle of the Haram is *the Mihrab Da'ud*, a large open-air mihrab rebuilt by al-Mansur Lajin between 1297–99. Paths and splendid views give a peaceful and serene quality to this part of the Haram, where gardens have been laid out. When accessible, the entrance to *Solomon's Stables* is in the SE angle (Rte 2G) and from here there is a good prospect of the Aksa Mosque, and a magnificent view from the *'Pinnacle of the Temple'* (p.94) over the Kidron Valley and the village of Silwan. Further N is one of the finest prospects of the Dome of the Rock, the Dome of the Chain and the E arcade.

About three-quarters of the distance along the E wall, one arrives at the inside of the blocked *Golden Gate or *Bab al-Dhahabi*. For its history, see Rte 2A. **Exterior:** lying 6.30m below the level of the present court the gate complex is set in a paved court. The double gate has two shallow round arches with floral relief ornament on the archivolt, similar to those on the outer E façade of the gate. Two free-standing lateral arches extend W from the corners of the gate hall. The N and S sides of the gate chamber have three engaged rectangular pilasters, and at the E end of the S wall is a round-arched lesser entrance. At the E end of the roof are two hemispherical cupolas on high drums which rest on the old pendentives. These were probably part of the Ayyubid Nasiriyya Zawiya above the Golden Gate which was rebuilt in 1214.

Interior (*not at present accessible*): a large hall, stone paved, with six domes supported on a central E–W axis by two free-standing monolithic marble columns with Byzantine Ionic capitals, and two wall piers with Corinthian capitals. The elaborate decoration includes pilasters (four on both N and S walls) with Corinthian style capitals which have been compared to 5C work. There is a carved cornice above. The decoration, incorporating some re-used elements, is thought variously to date between the 6C–8C. The interior door jambs are based on very large stones, respectively 3.40m and 4.50m high, which are aligned on the course of the original wall and could suggest the existence of an original Herodian gate.

Kursi Sulaiman or Solomon's Throne stands against the E wall of the Haram just to the N of the Golden Gate and is a rectangular structure with two shallow domes.

Its name derives from the Muslim story that when King Solomon died, it was necessary to conceal his death from the demons and thus avert the prophecy that his Temple would be destroyed and his kingdom disintegrate. The dead king was propped on his throne with his staff and not until that decayed and collapsed did the demons discover they had been released from his authority. The story is apparently old.

References are made to the Throne of Solomon in the 10C (Ibn 'Abd Rabbihi, c 913) and 15C (Suyuti, c 1470, and Mujir al-Din, 1496) but the building appears to date to c 1600 or later. It seems to be the same as that described by Evliya Chelebi in 1648–50. It is just possible that it was built by Sulaiman the Magnificent as part of his building program in Jerusalem, and in the course of time earlier traditions concerning Solomon accrued to it (Burgoyne). Alternatively the structure may have been rebuilt to the same pattern in the 19C, for various late 19C writers refer to it as a modern building. It contains a venerated cenotaph visited by Muslims at the Feast of Bairam. It is possible also that it preserves the tradition of Solomon's portico, which lay on the E side of the Temple and is referred to by Josephus (Antiq. XX:219–222).

Subterranean vaulting under this part of the esplanade, which also exists just N of the Dome platform and in the central N part of the esplanade (all recorded by Warren), may be part of the Herodian vaulted substructure (with later repairs). In this area the bedrock is at a great depth beneath the present surface. Continuing N one arrives at the *Bab al-Asbat* and completes the circuit of the inner Haram wall.

C.   Lesser shrines and structures within the Haram al-Sharif

These structures are numbered in sequence and shown on the accompanying map (p.82). Most are fountains, prayer platforms and mihrabs, summer pulpits or decorative structures and were pious donations for the use of the pilgrims and those who come to pray, teach and learn at the mosque and the sanctuary, added at various times since the Dome of the Rock was built. The fountains and cisterns are now mostly unused since piped water was brought to the Haram. Some of the cisterns are very old, perhaps originating in the time of the First Temple; many were in use in Herodian times when they were supplied by aqueducts, some from the pools SW of Bethlehem. The aqueduct system was repaired in Mamluk times and the present fountains are mostly of Mamluk and Ottoman date. The aqueduct system, though in a poor state of repair, was in use right to the end of the Ottoman period.

The north end of the esplanade

1. *Sabil al-Sultan Sulaiman,* the *Fountain of Sultan Sulaiman*, or *Sabil Bab al-'Atm* is located just inside the Gate of Darkness. One of the many fountains built in Jerusalem by Sultan Sulaiman II 'the Magnificent', it dates from 1537. Steps descend on the S side of a simple rectangular structure with an elaborately decorated arch containing a fountain in a recess with inscribed panels and stalactite ornament.
2. Directly S of the fountain is the *Pavilion of Sultan Mahmud II*, built in 1817–18. This is a square structure with heavy corner piers and large, open, pointed arches which support a low octagonal drum and a small steep dome.
3. To the W is *Qubbat Sulaiman* or *Solomon's Dome*, which may be a late 12C Crusader construction, modified by the Ayyubids c 1200. It is an elegant dome built over a jutting piece of bedrock, near the Bab

al-ʿAtm, around which many traditions have accumulated: one story is that Solomon prayed here when the Temple was completed. Names current in earlier years were the *Qubbat Sakfat Sakhra*, or *Dome of the Piece of the Rock*; and the 'Throne of Jesus'. Its likeness to the Chapel of the Ascension on the Mount of Olives, and to the Qubbat al-Miʿraj (see below) suggest it is Ayyubid work re-using Crusader material, perhaps from the destruction of the nearby buildings of the Augustinian convent. Standing on a prayer platform, the octagonal building with blocked pointed arch in each façade, has a tall circular drum with eight openings. Above them the hood moulding joins to form a continuous cornice, with another cornice at the top. Steps descend to the entrance on the N side, for the interior floor level is lower. If the archways were originally open, each may have been flanked by three columns with broad-leaved acanthus capitals, but this ornamentation is only certain for the outer two. The mihrab in the S wall is flanked by small columns and capitals, and was thought by Vincent to be an Ayyubid insertion, though others suggest it is original (Burgoyne). The building has a distinctive charm, and through its rather isolated position has an important landscape role in the Haram.

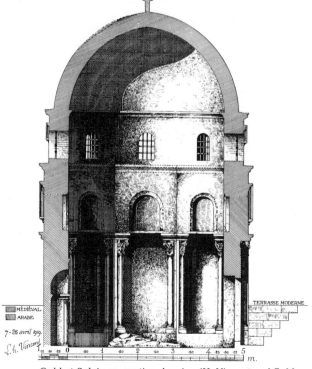

Qubbat Sulaiman, section drawing (H. Vincent and F.-M. Abel, Jérusalem Nouvelle, *Vol. II, pl. LXI.B: Gabalda, Paris, 1922).*

4. Just 10m NE of the Bab al-Nazir is the *Well of Ibrahim al-Rumi*, today called the fountain of *'Ala' al-Din al-Basiri* or *Sabil Basiri*, built 1435–36. This was a wellhouse for distributing water to the poor, but is now disused. The founder's inscription is on the S wall. The small square structure is built over a large, much older rock-cut cistern. It has a door on the E side, and water was distributed through pointed arched windows in the other three walls. The façade is capped by an ornamental cornice and is roofed by a shallow stone dome. The low profile of the dome is in keeping with its early date. It stands just in front of the Madrasa Manjakiyya (see Rte 2B). A raised prayer platform, the *Mastaba Basiri*, constructed 1400, is just to the SE. It has a rather heavy mihrab with a round arch flanked by columns and capped by a stepped cornice.

5. Just to the SW is the fountain of *Sabil al-Shaikh Budayr* built in 1740–41. This is a rather small, rectangular building with a high small dome, open round arched windows protected by metal grilles between the columns. It stands on a low plinth. It also has a raised prayer platform on the S side.

6. To the E, at the foot of the Dome platform steps, on the N side, is the *Sabil Sha'lan* built 1216–17, restored 1429 and again in 1627–28; with external mihrab dating to 1650–51. It is a rectangular structure with open arches. The dome over the angle of the L-shaped cistern room is one of the few early shallow stone domes remaining on fountains of a type once characteristic in Jerusalem.

West of the Dome Platform

7. The *Mihrab 'Ali Pasha*, is just NE of the Cotton Merchants' Gate, and was built in 1637–38.

8. The fountain of ***Sabil Qa'it Bay** is one of the most attractive small structures in the Haram, and is a typically late Mamluk structure with many Cairene influences. It was perhaps built as the final adjunct to the nearby *Madrasa Ashrafiyya* (also by Sultan Qa'it Bay) in 1482, restored in 1883 by 'Abd-al-Hamid II as the inscription records, and some repair work in this century. The inscription also refers to an earlier structure built by Sultan Inal (1453–61) which had a stone dome built over a well, nothing of which seems to remain. The fountain is located on the NW corner of a small open-air oratory (musalla) with a free-standing mihrab on the S. A large cistern beneath it may have been constructed in part of the ancient Herodian gate passage noted by Warren below the Bab al-Mathara. The overall height of the structure is 13.28m. The rectangular base has windows on the S, W and N sides which are covered by metal grilles which are at least partly Ottoman in date. The window ledges are supported by typically Mamluk brackets. The joggled decoration on the flat window lintels is not original and probably replaces strap work with a star pattern. The door lies on the E, placed to one side of an otherwise plain façade. Red and cream stone is employed, and highlights the relief arabesque and strap work. Each corner has an engaged column with some fine relief work, a Mamluk base and a stalactite capital. A fine calligraphic zone bordered with relief strap work runs right round the building and records the builder, its restorer, and verses from the Koran. Above, a transition zone with pyramidal buttresses converts the rectangular base to the round dome. This middle zone, with four arched lights, supports a tall stone dome with fine relief arabesques which give distinction to this charming fountain. Architecturally the structure seems to be patterned on contemporary funerary monuments in Cairo, but to have been influenced by local Jerusalem traditions and workmen. The interior (locked) has water troughs below the windows and cups were once chained to the windows. A well recess is located on the inner E wall. The window lintels are also ornate; above are muqarnas pendentives. On the S side, beneath the window, is a fountain trough which is perhaps made from a door-jamb of the Herodian Temple (Kane).

9. *Hujrat Bir al-Zait* is one of a range of rather domestic-looking buildings on either side of the stairs below the Dome platform. Those to the N of the stairs are of two storeys; this, just E of the fountain of Qa'it Bay, has one storey. Some of these structures are of Ottoman date.

10. *Sabil Bab al-Mahkama* and *Birka Ghaghanj* are an Ottoman fountain and pool dating to 1527. It is an octagonal structure with a leaded dome and a roofed verandah.

11. The *Mastabat al-Tin* just to the S is a rectangular raised prayer platform, built in 1760–61.

12. *Qubba Musa, Dome of Moses*, built in 1249–50 by al-Malik al-Salih Ayyub. This is a medium-sized dome just inside the Gate of the Chain with a mihrab on the S side of the prayer platform, used as a place where latecomers to the mosque can pray.

South of the Dome Platform

Just inside the Moor's Gate, near the former entrance to the Fakhriyya Mosque, is a small *Ottoman fountain*, the *Sabil Abu al-Su'ud*, named for the family who occupied the mosque for some centuries.

13. In the space between the Islamic Museum and the Aqsa Mosque is a small domed structure *Qubba Yusuf Agha (Dome of Yusuf Agha)*, built in 1681.

14. In the space between the Aqsa Mosque and the Dome Platform is the great ablutions fountain, *al-Kas*, the cup or fountain. Ritual ablution is an important preliminary to prayer at the mosque and the Haram needs a good supply of running water. Here a large stone basin is surrounded by a wrought metal screen, below which are taps and drains for washing. There are several reservoirs or cisterns under the platform to W, S and E of this fountain, some of which were originally fed by conduit and aqueduct from springs near Hebron, and Solomon's Pools near Bethlehem. The largest reservoir, named *al-Bahr, 'the Sea'* is SE of the fountain, and is 225m in circumference, 12m deep, with a capacity of 12,000 cubic metres. It is a very ancient rock-cut cistern, with a staircase descending into it and a roof suported by rock-cut pillars.

Another large cistern, the *Bir al-Waraqa* or *Well of the Leaf* lies to the S under the Aqsa Mosque. Its name derives from the charming story that one of the Caliph 'Umar's companions went down to recover the jar he had dropped while filling it at the cistern, and found at the bottom a gate leading into an orchard. He plucked a leaf to show to his friends when he emerged, and as it came from Paradise, it never faded.

The Platform of the Dome of the Rock
and lesser structures upon it

The **Dome Platform** is set 2.5m to 6m above the esplanade. A stretch
of the N side of the platform fell in 1868, when Warren noted it was
supported by a row of vaults with pointed 'Saracenic' arches. The
tops of the arches were 0.6m below the Dome esplanade, and the
arched vaults stood perhaps 6m high. The platform is surmounted by
eight flights of stairs, two on the N, three on the W, two on the S and
one on the E. The platform must date at least to the time of 'Abd al-
Malik when the Dome of the Rock was built. In the 10C and probably
earlier there were only six staircases; according to Nasir-i Khusraw
(1047) there was one each on the E and N, and two each on the W
and S sides. At the top of each flight is a graceful arcade, or *Qanatir*, a
'series of arches' (sometimes *mawazin* or 'scales', so-called from the
tradition that scales to weigh the souls of the dead will be suspended
from them on the Day of Judgement). These date mostly from the
10C to the 15C. There are 16 rooms, mostly on the N side of the
platform, which were used for the 'Servants of the Haram'. They
were built at various dates mostly from the 17C to recent times. They
have a mixture of marble and built stone columns; the local qualities
of their rather humbler architectural style add to the character and
charm of the Haram area.

15. *The North-east Qanatir (Mawazin Bab Hitta)* was constructed in
1326. Three stilted arches with gadrooned ornament are supported
on two columns and two piers. The columns and acanthus capitals
are in secondary use. Two inscriptions on the S face record the
building of the arcade and the paving of the terrace in the reign of al-
Nasir Muhammad. Cells flank either side of the arcade; the group on
the W being larger, with a portico at the front.

16. *The North Qanatir* is further W and was constructed in 1321. This
arcade replaced an earlier one perhaps destroyed by the Crusaders.
It has three arches on two re-used columns and two piers; the marble
columns, bases and capitals in Corinthian style are probably
Byzantine. There is a saw-tooth motif on the cornice above. An
inscription on the S façade records it was built in the reign of al-Nasir
Muhammad. These arches are also flanked by cells.

17. On the W side of the North Qanatir is the *Cell of Muhammad
Agha*, a domed structure with arcaded front, built in 1588.

18. *Qubbat al-Arwah, Dome of the Winds* (or *Spirits*), 16C(?) stands
on the left just to the W on a shallow plinth. It has eight marble
columns capped by unmatched capitals with dosserets of varied
heights. These support slightly pointed shallow arches with relief
rosettes; an octagonal drum topped by a cornice has a shallow stone
dome topped by a finial with crescent.

19. At the NW angle of the platform is the *North-west Qanatir* with
four arcades, rebuilt in 1376–77 and restored between 1519 and
1567. The steps are cut into the terrace. The arcade has inlaid red,
black and white roundels, and fine acanthus capitals on white
columns.

20. Standing above the S side of the NW stairs is the *Qubbat al-
Khadir* (16C?): a very small but elegant dome supported by six little
marble pillars and very mixed, rather plain capitals. It is named for
St. George or St. Elijah.

21. A short distance to the S is *Masjid al-Nabi* (1700/01), a roughly
square stone building with a new dome. It is rectangular, with two
windows to each side and a door on the E with inscription above. It is

associated with Shaikh al-Khalili from Hebron and also called *Qubbat al-Khalili*. It is now used for teaching.

22. Just to the SE is a tall domed, octagonal structure, the *Qubbat al-Mi'raj* or *Dome of the Ascension of the Prophet*, built 1200–01 (inscription above the door) to mark the spot where the Prophet prayed before he ascended to Paradise. There are similarities to the plans of Christian baptistries, and the remarkable series of (re-used?) capitals decorating the interior has led some to think it was originally the 12C Crusader baptistry, rebuilt or modified by the Ayyubids. Eight rebated arches with columns support a high leaded dome, topped by a small cupola. There is a mihrab in the S wall. The NE side was damaged in 1948 and repaired by King Abdullah of Jordan in 1951.

23. The small open dome to the SE is the *Qubbat al-Nabi* or *Dome of the Prophet* (or *Gabriel*), built in 1538–39 and restored in 1845. It is distinguished by its slender columns and leaded dome.

24. Almost opposite the W door of the Dome of the Rock is the *West Qanatir* built in 951–52 (builder's signature). 25 steps cut into the terrace lead up to four arches. Slender monolithic columns, three different capitals and high pointed arches combine with some elegance to decorate one of the main approaches to the Dome platform. The ends of the arcade are supported by rectangular piers.

25. At the end of the W side of the platform, the *South-west Qanatir* (or *Mawazin Bab al-Silsila*), built in 1472, has three arches similar in style to the Mamluk arcades on the N side. All the columns, capitals and bases are in re-use, and are probably all Byzantine. The central arch has red and cream voussoirs, the lateral arches are gadrooned. The inscription of the E face records its building by Sultan Qa'it Bay. The building abutting it to the N is Ottoman.

26. Occupying the W end of the S edge of the platform is the *Qubba Nahwiyya* or *Dome of Literature* or *Library*, built in 1207–08, originally as a Koran school but later used as a small school for literature and a library. The door is flanked by intricately knotted marble columns.

27. To the E between the library and the pulpit is *Qubba Yusuf* built in 1681. This is a tall, open, rectangular building, very decorative, with a tiny dome or cupola.

28. Immediately adjacent to the south Qanatir is the **Minbar of Burhan al-Din** or **'Summer Pulpit'**, added to and restored by 1388 by the Qadi Burhan al-Din, and again restored in 1843 by the Sultan 'Abd al-Majid. Until at least the end of the 17C prayers on Muslim feast days and prayers for rain were said from here. The original structure consisted of a hexagonal domed pavilion with trefoil arches and a relief fluted dome on an elaborate rectangular base with horseshoe arches, those on the N and S sides being blocked by later additions and abutments. Its purpose is uncertain, but it was built almost entirely of high quality Crusader marble sculpture, perhaps a former 12C ciborium, re-used soon after 1187. In 1345 it is noted as a dome (Qubbat al-Mizan, the Dome of the Balance) rather than a pulpit. By 1496 it was certainly in use as a pulpit; it may have been used as an occasional pulpit from the 13C, approached when needed by mobile wooden stairs. Burhan al-Din's work may have been to build the stone stair and balustrade. The 1843 work (recorded on a stele above the present entrance) blocked a columned rectangular opening beneath the upper section of the stairs with 19C Ottoman panelling. On the W side is a flat mihrab with marble panelling against the W abutment of the South Qanatir. It has a pointed arch on two re-used marble columns and is recorded by 1345. It is structurally later than the adjacent dome.

29. Adjacent is the *South Qanatir, Maqam al-Nabi*, 10C?. It has four arches supported on two piers and three monolithic columns, the two outer being of red granite, the inner of marble. On these rest sub-Corinthian capitals with, above, relief rosette roundels and pointed arches. 21 steps descend in the direction of the Aqsa Mosque.

30. Just over 30m to the E is the *South-east Qanatir, Maqam al-Ghuri* on which an inscription on the central spandrels, which may not be in situ, records that it was built in 1030; and another inscription on the N spandrel notes a restoration in 1211–12. It has three arches.

31. Perhaps more correctly regarded as an integral part of the Dome of the Rock, is the *small dome* which lies directly E of the E door of the Dome of the Rock, the *** Dome of the Chain**, A. *Qubbat al-Silsila.*

History. Built in 691–92 by ʿAbd al-Malik at the same time as the Dome of the Rock itself, and regarded by many as an architect's model for the main building, this dome was probably used as the treasury of the shrine (compare the treasury in the Umayyad Great Mosque in Damascus) and like the Dome of the Rock was probably also covered in polychrome glass mosaic. There are many theories about it, as it lies more or less at the exact centre of the Haram and the Herodian platform. It is possible therefore that it stands on the site of the Herodian (and Solomonic) altar of sacrifice with the Dome of the Rock to the W overlying the site of the Temple. If such traditions were still extant in the 7C at the time the site was selected, such sanctity would further have protected the contents of a treasure deposited there. Nasir-i Khusraw in 1047 notes a beautiful mihrab. In Crusader times it was the Chapel of St. James the Martyr (the Less) with Christian paintings. It was restored by the Muslims in 1199–1200 and remains of a probably early Ayyubid mihrab have been discovered beneath the later 13C work. It has undergone numerous alterations in the course of its 13 centuries and the current restoration work has involved stripping the whole surface.

Description. As in the Dome of the Rock, there are two concentric rows of columns, the outer 11 supporting the ambulatory roof and arcade with shallow round arches and the inner six supporting the hexagonal drum and the dome. The columns, of varied marbles, are monolithic, mostly re-used Byzantine, and are so placed that all 17 can be seen at one time from any angle. The capitals are of both basket and acanthus types. Some fragmentary mosaic remaining in the soffits of the outer ambulatory are Fatimid or just possibly Umayyad work. The exterior was coated with tiles in 1561–62 by Sulaiman II. The mihrab with pointed arch in the S side has marble decoration added in 1261–73 by Sultan Baybars, and the tiles there were added in 1760–61. The dome has a rather outward curve with a fluted knopf on top. It had a beautiful mosaic floor. The wooden ceiling of the ambulatory is coffered, and the wooden tie-beams between the columns are painted.

Traditions. The dome is also called the *Mahkamat Daʾud* or *David's Place of Judgment*; stories connected with it say that a chain was once stretched across the entrance or hung from the ceiling, either by Solomon or by God. If this was grasped by a liar a link fell, giving judgement on a witness.

32. The *East Qanatir* stands above the only stairs on the little used E side of the Dome platform, and may date to the 10C when a staircase is recorded here. Five arcades add a characteristically graceful sense of perspective to the view of the Dome of the Rock from the E. The columns are of light coloured marble, and have acanthus capitals of varied types.

D.   The Dome of the Rock

The * * **Dome of the Rock**, A. **Qubbat al-Sakhra**, formerly erroneously the Mosque of 'Umar, is the crown of the Haram al-Sharif, built in Byzantine-Syrian architectural style, with innovations marking it as one of the first great buildings of Islamic architecture. It is a shrine of gem-like beauty, once shining with the rich colours of gold and polychrome glass mosaic both inside and out. It was built by the fifth Umayyad caliph, 'Abd-al-Malik, and completed in 691–92. Its purpose was threefold: to recognise the sanctity of Jerusalem, and of the Rock associated with the Prophets on which it stood; to mark the consolidation of Islamic rule in Syria when Jerusalem, Damascus and other cities were rivalling Mecca as political and religious capitals; and to balance the great monuments of Byzantine Christianity which had already stood for centuries in the Holy City. The Prophet Muhammad at first prayed in the direction of the Holy City of Jerusalem, but following an inspiration the direction of prayer *(qibla)* was changed to Mecca. The prayer niche *(mihrab)* which later marked the direction of prayer in Jerusalem faces to the S. The Dome of the Rock is the third holiest place in Islam after the Ka'ba at Mecca and the Prophet's Mosque in Medina, and is the second most important place of pilgrimage. When political circumstances allow, thousands visit the shrine as part of a great annual pilgrimage to Mecca and Jerusalem.

The Dome of the Rock is located over the highest point of the rock on the SE ridge (c 743m above sea level), rather than centrally to the Haram enclosure, on a platform c 2.5m–6m high, which raises the structure to a dominant situation within the open court. The Dome is not a congregational mosque, but a shrine with ambulatories, intended as a place of pilgrimage and prayer. The empty spaces within reflect the iconoclast and monotheist traditions of Islam, enhanced by the beauty of the floral and geometric decoration which covers nearly the whole surface of the shrine.

The architects are unknown, but the Caliph could draw on many of the craftsmen and traditions of the world conquered by the armies of Islam. Greek- and Arab-speaking Christians, Jews and Persians may have been employed. Though the building belongs in the Syrian Byzantine tradition the result reflects a triumphant amalgamation of many elements. A later source recalls that 'Abd-al-Malik appointed two overseers, Yazid ibn Sallam and Raja'ibn Haiwa.

The building is of local stone, the lower walls decorated with marble veneer. The upper walls and drum, inside and out, were originally encrusted with gold and polychrome glass mosaics which were replaced and repaired at intervals, and eventually in the 16C the exterior mosaic work was replaced with Kashani tiles, which were renewed in 1958–62 during a complete structural renovation. The dome, constructed with an inner and outer vault of wood, covered in lead and originally gilded, rebuilt and repaired at various times, was replaced in 1961 by a lighter covering of gold coloured anodised aluminium. Over the centuries pious donations have seen to the continuous repair and refurbishment of this great and ancient shrine. Its plan has been copied elsewhere, for example in the Temple Church in London built by the Templars in the 12C. It is said to hold up to 3000 people.

History. Built by ´Abd-al-Malik in 691–92 on the site sacred to the Jewish, Christian and Muslim Holy Books, the Dome is revered for its associations with Mount Moriah, where Abraham offered Isaac as sacrifice, as the site of the threshing floor of Araunah the Jebusite purchased by David, where Solomon built his Temple and where the temples of Zerubbabel and Herod the Great had

Masonry hidden beneath the tiles of the Dome of the Rock (C. Clermont-Ganneau, Archaeological Researches in Palestine during the years 1873–1874, Vol. I, opposite p. 180: London, 1899).

stood. It is possible that the Herodian and Solomonic temples lay somewhat to the N of the present Dome of the Rock, on the same E–W axis as the present Golden Gate. This would presume very substantial quarrying of the whole rock surface in the Hadrianic period, which totally obliterated the original site: though plausible this theory would be very difficult to prove. However, if the earlier temples and altar were central to the Herodian enclosure, as seems likely, the present site is the more likely choice.

Following the Roman destruction of AD 70 the area was in ruins. These may have been cleared and levelled in the 2C when Roman statues were placed on the platform by Hadrian. No structure seems to have stood over the Rock itself between AD 70 and c 691 when the Umayyads started work, though already by

644 Muslims believed it was the site of Muhammad's miraculous Night Journey.

The design of the Dome of the Rock is based on Syrian-Byzantine traditions, and local craftsmen were employed to carry out the work. The building itself had contemporary parallels. The Constantinian Church of the Holy Sepulchre in Jerusalem had an immense dome of similar size over a rock in which the tomb of Christ was cut. The Chapel of the Ascension on the Mount of Olives in Jerusalem was an octagonal shrine protecting the footprints of Christ. A Byzantine octagonal church had been built over the site of St. Peter's House at Capernaum in Galilee. The great basilica church at Bethlehem, with external mosaics in Byzantine style, lay over the grotto of the Nativity. All these structures have reflections in the Dome of the Rock at Jerusalem, which is an octagonal building with a dome over a cave in a rock; but is also a shrine with two ambulatories which are reminiscent of the ceremonial circumambulation *(tawwaf)* of the Ka'ba at Mecca, which took place during the great annual pilgrimage.

The Dome of the Rock is the result of very precise geometrical design, with balanced and harmonious proportions which represent the first great period of Islamic architecture. It is said that the cost of construction was seven years' revenue from the province of Egypt, the money being placed in a model of the projected building (the Dome of the Chain) which was the Treasury of the Shrine. The last of the gold was sufficient for the gilding of the dome. In Umayyad days the cleaning of the shrine was done with water scented with attar of roses, musk and saffron; fragrant wood and incense were burnt on the Rock, and sweet-smelling oils were used in the many lamps.

Abbasid period. Al-Ma'mun (813–33) repaired the dome, altered 'Abd-al-Malik's founding inscription by putting in his own name but left his predecessor's date. He also left inscriptions on the lintels of the doors (831). Muhammad's footprints on the Rock are mentioned by Ya'qubi in 874. The mother of al-Muqtadir (908–32) presented doors of tannub wood from Indonesia to the shrine.

Fatimid period. The dome collapsed in part or completely, possibly due to an earthquake in 1016, and was rebuilt in 1022/3 by al-Zahir. At this time a marble balustrade was placed around the Rock, the floors were covered by silk carpets, and a great silver candelabrum was suspended above the Rock, which fell down c 1060.

Crusader period. A gold cross to mark its conversion to use as a Christian shrine was placed on the top of the Dome (depicted in the seal of Baldwin I) and an altar with steps in front was placed on the Rock. The building became the Crusaders' *Templum Domini*, the Temple of Our Lord, a prayer hall which was consecrated c 1142 and served by canons of the Augustinian order who had conventual buildings on the N side of the esplanade. Christian pilgrims began to remove bits of the holy Rock, which were sold as relics, so that the surface had to be paved with marble to preserve it, and a tall and beautiful wrought-iron screen was put up between the columns of the inner arcade. This was French work of the late 12C, and stretched half way up the columns. It remained in position until 1960, when it was removed to the Islamic Museum (Rte 2F). The Dome of the Chain outside the E door became the Chapel of St. James.

Ayyubid period. Following Salah al-Din's recapture of Jerusalem in 1187 the crescent was restored to the Dome, and the marble pavement and altar removed from the Rock. Salah al-Din restored the marble casing on the inner lower walls and piers and repaired the mosaics around the inside of the drum. Other rulers of this dynasty carried out repairs and pious works, and the wooden screen now around the Rock was installed by al-Malik al-'Aziz 'Imad al-Din in 1198/9.

Mamluk period. In 1270 Baybars I and in 1294/5 al-'Adil Zayn al-Din Kitbugha restored the mosaics on the outside walls. In 1318 al-Nasir Muhammad redecorated the inside of the dome, including the mosaics, and renewed the outer lead casing. In 1432 al-Ashraf Saif al-Din Barsbay endowed the shrine with land and property, the revenues of which were to be used for the upkeep of the building, which became the responsibility of the *Waqf* authority; a plaque recording this act was placed on the E wall of the shrine. In 1448 the dome was badly damaged by fire and repaired. In 1467/8 al-Ashraf Qa'it Bay gave four great doors sheathed with decorated copper (now in the Islamic Museum).

Ottoman period. In 1545–46 Sulaiman II replaced the mosaics on the exterior drum with coloured tiles, and not long after also on the upper walls of the octagon. Craftsmen were imported specially from Kashan (Persia) but may have made the actual tiles in Jerusalem. He also renewed six windows in the drum. He restored the N doorway in 1552, and the E and W doorways in 1566. In 1780 'Abd-al-Hamid I restored the W entrance. This Sultan brought craftsmen from made the actual tiles in Jerusalem. He also renewed six windows in the drum. He restored the N doorway in 1552, and the E and W doorways in 1566. In 1780 'Abd-al-Hamid I restored the W entrance. This Sultan brought craftsmen from Damascus to repair the tiles, and further work on them was done by Mahmud II in 1817–18 who again used craftsmen from Damascus but tiles of poorer quality and some different designs; at the same time he restored some of the external marble and built the porticoes of the S doorway. In 1853 Sultan 'Abd-al-Majid I repaired and strengthened the dome and redecorated the interior.

Not long after the Russian-Turkish treaty of 1856 non-Muslims were permitted to enter the Haram al-Sharif for the first time in centuries. From this time, and especially from the 1860s, drawings and photographs of the Dome began to appear: noteworthy are the publications of Comte Melchior de Vogüé (1864), Colonel C.W. Wilson (1880) and F. de Saulcy (1882) among others.

In 1874 Sultan 'Abd-al-'Aziz repaired the wooden ceilings and mosaics, releaded the dome, restored the marble paving on the floor, and the marble veneer around the piers and lower walls inside and out; he also repaired broken windows and placed a crystal chandelier inside the S entrance. He made repairs to the tiles, entirely replacing those on the W and SW sides, using rather poor quality Turkish tiles and introducing some different colours. In 1876 Sultan 'Abd-al-Hamid II carpeted the floor and hung a crystal chandelier over the Rock (which was removed to the Aqsa Mosque in 1951 and subsequently to the Islamic Museum). He also put the band of Kashan tiles bearing verses of Sura XXXVI from the Koran onto the upper part of the octagon walls, just below the parapet.

The British Mandate period. Tile-makers were brought from Kütahya in Turkey in 1919 to repair tiles on the Dome. In 1927 and 1936 Jerusalem was shaken by earthquakes, and during the 1930s it was clear that rising damp and decay were adversely affecting the structure. Repairs were started but hindered by the Second World War and the intensifying civil struggle. The Megaw Report on the interior mosaics in 1946 showed that they were in very poor condition. Some damage to the structure was sustained during the fighting in 1948. 22 windows on the NW side and part of the NW wall were damaged in mortar bombing

Jordanian period. In 1952 an appeal was launched by the Supreme Muslim Council for funds for the complete restoration of the shrine. The weight of the lead roof was exacerbating the damage to the structure and foundations caused by earthquake, penetration of water and age. £525,000 was donated by the Arab world and in 1956 work began under a Saudi Arabian contractor. The Egyptian Government also gave technical services then valued at £70,000; experts in mosaic restoration were brought from Italy, and the late King Muhammad of Morocco gave new carpets for the ambulatories. The foundations were strengthened with concrete, three pillars, two in the SE, and one on the N had to be replaced. The outer façade was completely refaced with tiles made specially at Kütahya in Turkey and with marble from Greece, and in 1961/2 the dome was completely resurfaced with a lightweight gold-coloured aluminium shell. The platform was repaved.

Since 1967 the Awqaf administration has continued the work of preservation of this holy place; many fragments of the old structure have been placed in the Islamic Museum.

Visit. The exterior. The base is a stone-built octagon c 53.75m in diameter, built of local limestone masonry in courses c 0.8m in height. Each exterior façade is c 20.59m in length. The base of the exterior wall forms a plinth, above which there are seven tall recessed panels or bays in each façade of the octagon. The lower wall is veneered with grey-veined white marble which was restored in 1958–62. The marble panels on the S and SW have red and black geometric inlay, that on the W has black only. The SW side also has a sundial. The other panels have mouldings. The original design of the Dome of the Rock also had polished marble covering on the lower walls. Some panels which survived in good condition were used to replace worn panels in the interior. In the centre of the SW and SE sides near floor level are rectangular windows protected by metal grilles.

The upper walls of the octagon are faced with predominantly blue, white, green, black and yellow tiles made in Kütahya in Turkey and

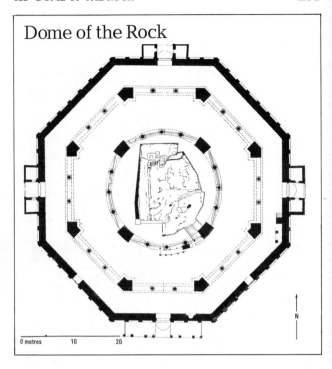

Dome of the Rock

0 metres   10   20

N

placed on the building in 1958–62, to much the same designs as those previously on the structure but with stronger colours. The patterns are mostly stylised floral motifs. They include the lily and lotus design, tulip patterns, other flowers and stars, and bands and borders of blue-glazed tiles. There are a number of fine panels of blue and white calligraphy which contain verses from the Koran; particularly to be noted is a band of tiles extending right round the façade just below the parapet which contains verses from Sura XXXVI, Ya Sin. This is a copy of the original placed by Sultan ʿAbd al-Hamid II in 1876. The first tiling dated to Sultan Sulaiman II in 1545–52. A selection of the older tiles removed in the restoration work has been preserved in the Islamic Museum. The upper walls of the octagon were covered with gold and polychrome glass mosaic before the 16C. A small area of the original mosaic was discovered within one of the window soffits earlier this century. The original mosaic designs showed mostly foliage and flowers and can be best understood after seeing some of the Umayyad work still preserved in the interior.

The eight sides each contain five windows, with a blind panel in the recess at either end. The outer faces of these 40 windows are covered by tiled grilles, with similar motifs to those of the adjacent walls, and contain small glazed areas which limit the amount of light penetrating to the interior through a wall 1.30m thick. These windows with their slightly pointed arches have been modified. In 691–92 they were built with round arches and probably had marble grilles of the type seen in the Great Mosque in Damascus. In the 16C

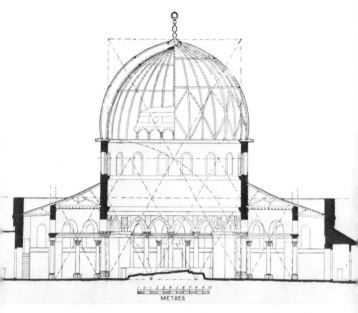

Section through the Dome of the Rock, from a drawing by E. Richmond (K.A.C. Cresswell, Early Muslim Architecture, Vol. I, Part 1, p. 70: Oxford, 1932–69).

when the exterior was tiled, the windows were given the then fashionable pointed arch, but the original round-arched masonry still exists beneath the tiling (see p.119). Six tiled (previously lead) spouts drain rainwater from the roof. The height of the façade, including the parapet, is 12.1m The parapet itself once had 13 small round-arched niches flanked by columns in each façade, covered with mosaic, but these were also hidden by the tiles in the 16C and only rediscovered in the restorations of 1873/4. The fragments of mosaic then uncovered were not the original ones but dated to a pre-Sulaiman restoration, probably that of Baybars in the 13C. In shades of yellow, red, brown, blue and green, the mosaic showed interlaced stars and rosettes.

Behind the parapet the roof of the ambulatories slopes up to the drum. The drum is circular, with four buttresses which rise from the interior piers, and has 16 tiled windows. The top of the drum has another fine inscribed band in blue and white which quotes the Koran, Sura XVII (the Night Journey). The drum was also originally covered with mosaics which were replaced with tiles by Sulaiman in 1545–46.

The dome itself, a wooden double dome of 1022, since 1961 surfaced with gold-coloured anodised aluminium, has also been restored several times since its original construction in 691/2. The original dome was a double wooden vault, with wool and hair insulation between the two vaults, and a gilded metal surface for which wool, felt and leather coverings were made to protect it in winter. That collapsed in 1016 and was rebuilt by al-Zahir in 1022 to much the same pattern. It is recorded that al-Nasir Muhammad renewed the lead casing in 1318; that it was repaired after a disastrous fire in 1448; and ʿAbd-al-Majid I strengthened and repaired the Dome in 1853. It is of fine proportions, notably wide and steeply rounded. At the top is a finial with a crescent. The latter is a modern replacement: two older ones can be seen in the Islamic Museum. The overall height of the building is 35.36m, not including the finial.

There are four doors or gates, with flat lintel and arched lunette above, oriented to the cardinal points of the compass and named for them. All the double leafed doors have been replaced in the recent restorations; the magnificent 15C ones should be seen in the Islamic Museum. It is not known what the original doors were like, but they had already been replaced by Umm al-Muqtadir (c 908–32). The doors are 4.35m high, 2.55m wide and have shallow tunnel vaulted tiled porches in front, which once possessed gable roofs. All the porches have been altered. Earlier this century the N, W and E doors had porches c 9m wide which contained small rooms on either side of the tunnel vault, which were clearly not original. The S porch was also partially enclosed until quite recently and differs from the others in now having an open porch supported on eight re-used monolithic columns with Corinthian capitals. The columns are variously of grey, green and red marble and porphyry. The porch ceiling is of coffered wood. It was originally built by Mahmud II in 1817. The arches and vaults are now decorated in blue and white tiles, and in the arcades above the lintels are excerpts from the Koran. The tunnel vault ceilings were originally covered in mosaic, which still remains above the *East Door, where it is perhaps a Fatimid replacement. It has rainbow coloured scallops and chequerboard patterns. Each lintel has a decorated metal plate on the soffit, with repoussé and studded relief work painted in gilt, black and green, mostly showing vine scrolls and leaves, grapes and acanthus, which probably date to the original structure and compare with the decoration on the tie-beams inside the first ambulatory.

The North door is the Bab al-Janna or Gate of Paradise. The West door, (Bab al-Gharb), has a shell-pattern stone grille on the lunette above it which is probably the original Ummayad work. The South door, marks the direction of prayer, the Bab al-Qibla and faces the Aqsa Mosque. The East door is also called the Gate of David (Bab Daʾud), or Gate of the Chain (Bab al-Silsila), because it leads to the Mahkamat Daʾud, David's Place of Judgment, which is the Dome of the Chain.

The interior. *Leave shoes, bags and cameras at the entrance.*

The visitor is first aware of the spacious dimness of the interior, with subdued light reflecting from half-seen golden ornament, before the eye is drawn upwards by the light from the less deeply set windows in the drum to the glories of the gold and red curving patterns in the dome. The partially screened but illuminated mysteries of the Rock, bare and quarried, but marking the ancient and long venerated point of contact between God and man, draw the visitor towards the central area beyond the ambulatories.

The Outer Ambulatory. On entry the visitor arrives in the outer ambulatory. The lower walls are veneered with grey-veined white marble with quartered panels cut to show symmetrical patterns of veining, an original scheme of decoration restored by Salah al-Din c 1189 with later renovations. On the lintels above the doors, and in a dado beneath the windows is a band of fine gilded work in black and gold at a height of 3.85m The inner grilles of the windows were installed by Sulaiman in 1528/9 as the inscriptions in the grilles themselves once recorded, but these have disappeared in the renovations of 1874 and subsequently. Generally what remains of the lower windows is 19C and later renovation. The lunette window over the W door has a stone grille which may be original. The window arches contain grey, red and black voussoirs.

The inner side of the outer ambulatory is defined by eight six-sided piers and 16 columns which support an octagonal arcade. The piers are veneered in grey-veined white marble with red and black inlays, also much restored from the time of Salah al-Din; there are fine marble panels with relief foliage designs and probable Umayyad origin set in the outer face of the pier of the SE side. The monolithic columns of red and green marble or porphyry are of varied height and origin, and mostly derive from the ruins of Roman and Byzantine Jerusalem. The unmatched and uneven bases are encased in marble boxes and collars which level the design. The capitals, in a variety of styles from Corinthian to Composite, are brightly gilded and one formerly showed a cross suggesting its original use had been in a Byzantine church. Above the capitals are grey-veined marble dosserets, which are of different thicknesses to bring the varied lengths of the columns to a uniform height. These support the arcades which are linked by ornate **•tie-beams**, a fine and original Umayyad feature, the design of which resembles a Corinthian architrave. These are iron and wood beams, encased in bronze sheathing, with marble casing on top, 0.64m deep. The undersides are 6m from the floor, painted black with green borders and with gilded relief work showing bunches of grapes, formalised vine, leaf and tendril designs, and studded bands in 16 different designs. The inner sides are equally ornate, with acanthus and other patterns in bands; the outer sides are plainer, with smaller gilded designs, and a projecting marble cornice above.

The wide and gently pointed **••arches** above are covered in gold and polychrome glass mosaic work, which, though much restored, date to the original structure of 691/2. The beautiful designs, with lavish rosette and floral patterns, are worked in shades of blue, green and predominantly gold, and the mosaic cubes themselves are set at projecting angles further to reflect and sparkle in the light. The spandrels each contain a vase with exotic flowers and acanthus-like leaves, which grow upwards, tree-like, and are ornamented with necklaces and pendants. In the half-spandrel adjacent to each pier the design expands downwards from a cornucopia. On the faces of the piers are acanthus plants with magnificent Byzantine jewellery; on the narrower flanks of the piers are either elaborate foliage designs or, on eight of the piers, much more naturalistic trees. On one is a wind-blown date palm laden with fruit with a stem encrusted with medallions and flanked by two little trees which has been compared with Byzantine mosaics from Ravenna. The Islamic concept of filling the field with decoration, and an Eastern delight in rich colour, of blue, indigo, gold and silver with added mother of pearl, gives this Syrian mosaic school a brilliance of its own. Olive or almond trees are also depicted. The leaves, green shaded with indigo, rest on gold stems, and gold and silver fruits, such as dates, olives, pomegranates, cherries, citrus and grapes are depicted. Shells, winged motifs and rosettes vary the patterns. The borders and soffits of the arches have more stylised rosette patterns and some splendid garlands.

At the top of the mosaic, both sides of the arcade contain the *founder's inscription* in a single line of Kufic script in gold on bluish-green mosaic, a full 240m in length, which runs right round the ambulatories and ends with the date 691/2 on the E end of the S outer face of the arcade. The name of 'Abd-al-Malik was inscribed on it; this was erased by al-Ma'mun (813–30), who inserted his own name instead, but the workman neglected to alter 'Abd-al-Malik's earlier date. The original inscription read (in part): 'This dome was built by the servant of God, 'Abd-al-Malik Ibn Marwan, the Prince of the Believers, in the year 72. May God accept it and be pleased with him. Amen.' Other sections of this inscription contain verses of the Koran which promulgate the Islamic rejection of Christianity and the Christian dogma of the Trinity. e.g. Sura IV, verses 169 'O you People of the Book, overstep not bounds in your religion, and of God speak only the truth. The Messiah, Jesus, son of Mary, is only a Messenger of God, and his Word, which he conveyed into Mary, and a Spirit proceeding from him. Believe therefore in God, and his prophets, and say not three. It will be better for you. God is only one God. Far be it from his glory that he should have a son.'

The octagonal arcade supports the roof of the outer ambulatory, the *ceiling* of which is of very fine gilded and painted plaster. The relief patterns, including arabesque and interlacing star patterns, medallions and intricately interwined foliage, are contained in rectangular and trapezoidal panels with multiple borders. Though much restored, this ceiling may date c 1318/19– 1327/8, from the reign of al-Nasir Muhammad. Some of the panels achieve great richness of design, gracefully relieved with light and harmonious colours, in which red, gold, green and blue predominate.

The E door, which leads to the Dome of the Chain, has on its S side an enclosed stairway (not open to the public) which gives access to the roof. A ladder up the outer E side of the drum gives onto a narrow platform with a small doorway leading to the interior gallery. Steps between the inner and outer vault previously led to a trap-door in the dome from which access to the crescent finial could be had.

Immediately E of the S door, set into the outer wall, is the mihrab which indicates the direction of prayer.

The Inner Ambulatory, which lies between the two arcades, has a more modern ceiling, also of wood with painted relief stucco designs, restored in 1780 and since, and inferior to those in the outer ambulatory. The design used to incorporate porcelain dishes set in the stucco.

The circular inner arcade is supported on four piers and 12 columns. The columns are of various sizes, of marble and porphyry, of various shades of grey, green and red. The bases are set at varying heights. The capitals, of Corinthian and Composite type, are older than the shrine, probably of Byzantine date, and heavily gilded. The arches rest directly on them, and are linked by narrow, undecorated tie-beams.

The arches, of grey-veined marble, have alternating black and white voussoirs, and alternate red and black panels inserted in the spandrels on the inner side. *The spandrels and arches* on the outer side however have also retained their original 7C mosaics. There is no inscription, and they appear to have survived in quite good order. This arcade, 1.1m in breadth, supports the drum itself.

Just opposite the S and door built against two columns of the inner arcade is a marble pulpit supported on ten pillars. It was given by al-Zahir Barquq in 1387.

• • **The Drum** is 20.44m in diameter and richly decorated. Directly above the arches is a decorative band with running spiral vine pattern in gold. It borders a great quarter-round moulding covered with designs and inscription in gold on a blue-green background. Above the moulding is a great panel of mosaic running right round the drum. Though re-done by al-Zahir, Salah al-Din, and al-Nasir Muhammad in 1027/8, 1189 and 1318 respectively, and again in 1853, 1874 and 1958–62, these magnificent mosaics appear to follow the original Umayyad designs faithfully. A great deal remains intact, as is indicated by the small rectangular inscription in the upper border, which records the restoration of the decoration of the dome by al-Zahir in 1027/8. The design on the *lower register* is uniform, with 16 panels having a total length of 64m and a height of 4m. The central motif of each panel is placed above each of the 16 columns and piers of the inner arcade, and depicts a bulbous vase encrusted with gems and mother-of-pearl, from which an acanthus plant springs. Within the spirals of the foliage are stems bearing leaves, fruit and grapes. Note that the vase above the NE pier is identical with those in the outer arcade. A cornice marks the upper border of this register of the mosaic.

The *upper register* contains 16 windows and 16 panels of mosaic. These have suffered far more from the passage of time but nonetheless retain much of the richness of the original Umayyad work. They were so badly decayed by 1946 that in the renovations of 1958–62 they had to be virtually remade. The preservation varied. Two panels on the SE, with geometric ornament, are complete replacements of Ottoman(?) date. Other panels have been considerably retouched, but five or six survived virtually intact. These show the original design of a pedimented vase covered with jewels, from which twine jewelled leaves; each panel and window has a rich border. The designs are picked out in many colours and in mother-of-pearl on a gold ground. The richness is enhanced by the borrowing of motifs from Byzantine imperial jewellery, such as diadems, breastplates and rosettes, symbolic of the conquest of the Byzantine lands by Islam.

The sixteen windows in the drum include six which date to the time of Sulaiman the Magnificent in the 16C, though Creswell thought some dated to al-Nasir Muhammad in the 14C; the rest are more recent restorations. They are made up of an inner window of plaster and coloured glass, an intermediate window of plaster and plain glass, and the outer window of pierced tiles.

Together, these two magnificent registers in the drum make up a total height of 9.40m and are surmounted by another great cornice.

• **The Dome.** The original of 691/2 fell in 1016, was rebuilt in 1022 according to inscriptions still on the ribs of the dome, restored in 1189, 1318, 1448, 1830 and 1874. The average diameter of 20.44m was clearly based on that of the dome of the Constantinian Church of the Holy Sepulchre which averages 20.46m. Its height at the apex is 35.30m. A painted wooden arcade marks the gallery at the base of the dome, which lies between the two wooden shells of which it is constructed, each of which contains 32 ribs which meet at a circular plate at the summit. Immediately above the gallery a strap work band of relief stucco links eight rectangular panels and eight medallions of beautiful calligraphy, which record the work of three restorers of the dome and its decoration. The first is that of Salah al-Din c 1189. His commemorative inscription reads: 'In the name of Allah, the Beneficent and Merciful God, Salah al-Din, our Ruler, Sultan and King, the Victorious Scholar, Just, Vigorous, son of Ayyub, may God rest his soul, ordered the renovation of the decoration of the Holy Dome in the year 586 H.'. Another panel records al-Nasir Muhammad: 'This dome was renovated and regilded, and the outer one leaded by order of our Lord, God's shadow on earth, Executor of His commands, Sultan Muhammad, son of the Victorious Martyred Qala'un, may God rest his soul, in the year 718 H' (1318). The third was by Mahmud II in 1818 who also releaded the outside of the dome. Other repaintings and repairs are listed e.g. by 'Adb-al-Majid I in 1853. The present much restored decoration is said to be based on that of al-Nasir Muhammad in 1318. The arabesques, which decrease in size as they move towards the apex subtly increasing the perspective of the height, are painted in gold, red and white on a green background over relief stucco. The effect is of great richness. Towards the centre, a circular inscribed band contains Koran, Sura II, verses 255 and 256 (in part): 'God! There is no God but He; the Living, the Eternal; nor slumber seizeth Him, nor sleep; His, whatsoever is in the Heavens and whatsoever is in the Earth!'

Suspended from the floral medallion at the apex is a heavy chain which once supported a chandelier.

'The Rock. At the centre of the building beneath the dome and encircled by the ambulatories lies the Holy Rock. It is surrounded by a very fine wooden screen with intricately carved and inlaid panels erected by the Ayyubid al-'Aziz 'Imad al-Din in 1199, according to its inscription. The Rock itself is 18m × 13m and projects c 1.50m above the present paving. At the SW angle of the Rock is a tall *rectangular shrine* with gilded grilles, topped by a small but elaborate cupola, which contains relics of the Prophet in a gilded reliquary, including a hair from his head. The base of the shrine is constructed of marble slabs carved with swags of foliage supported on tiny fluted and spiral marble columns through which the Rock can be seen. The marble base may be that of the gilded cupola resting on marble columns 'at the place of the Foot' that was constructed by the Crusaders to venerate what they believed to be the footprint of Christ, and which was recorded by the secretary of Salah al-Din. Here the visitor can touch the rock where Muslim tradition identifies the footprint of Muhammad. A medieval tradition recounts that the Rock tried to follow Muhammad as he ascended, leaving both the imprint of his foot at this point, and to the W the impression of the hand of Gabriel, who restrained the Rock which tried to follow the Prophet. At this place, in the 19C, was shown the Buckler of Hamza, uncle of the Prophet, a metal disc with relief decoration on one side, which was afterwards identified as a Chinese mirror of the 16C. The rock, cut for various purposes, still shows the traces of the Crusader reshaping.

At the SE angle of the Rock, adjacent to the SE pier, a fine marble entrance way of Crusader date leads to the cave beneath the Rock. A later pointed arch is supported by delicate composite capitals. These and the relief work are gilded. 16 new marble steps lead down to the cave below. The cave below is almost square, c 4.50m across and less than 2m high. Near the centre of the ceiling is a shaft less than 1m in diameter which has given rise to suggestions that the cave might have been cut nearly 4000 years ago as a shaft tomb (Gonen). The cave was certainly recut in Crusader times, and then used as a place of confession. Today there are *two small shrines* to Abraham and al-Khadir (Elijah) on the N and NW sides respectively. On either side of the steps are *prayer niches of David and Solomon*. That to the right as one descends (of Solomon) has a shallow but ornately decorated niche. Creswell has suggested that it may date to the time of ʿAbd-al-Malik, 691/2. The niche to the left as one descends has pairs of small twisted rope marble columns supporting a trefoil arch. The floor of the cave, of rather irregular bedrock but covered with rugs, has a shallow depression, c 0.2m deep, plugged by a marble slab. This was lifted by Parker in 1911 during illegal excavations and found to be just a depression and not to overlie a cistern or further cave as earlier proposed by de Vogüé.

Traditions. The cave has many traditions associated with it, some deriving from the 12C and 13C. A Muslim tradition holds that the Rock is the centre of the world, lying above the bottomless pit, with the waters of Paradise flowing beneath the cave; and that the Rock is supported on a palm tree growing out of the river of Paradise. Here too, the spirits of the dead can be heard awaiting Judgment Day, when the Kaʿba at Mecca will come to the Rock and God's throne will be planted on the Rock. The hollow in the floor of the cave is therefore called the *Well of Souls*, A. *Bir al-Arwah*. Abraham, Isaac, Jacob and Elijah are all associated with the cave, Muhammad prayed here, and from here was transported to Heaven on the back of his legendary steed, al-Buraq. The impression of Muhammad's head used to be shown on the ceiling of the cave. The Rock is said to have spoken at this time, and also to have greeted the Caliph ʿUmar after the conquest in 638.

In the Talmud the Rock lies at the centre of the world and covers the abyss in which the waters of the Flood rage. Abraham, Melchizedek and Isaac sacrificed or were almost sacrificed here; Jacob annointed the Rock. It is regarded in some traditions as the spot where the Ark of the Covenant stood; and some held that the Ark of the Covenant was concealed at the time of the destruction of Jerusalem in 587 BC and lies buried here still.

E. The Aqsa Mosque

The * *Aqsa Mosque**, A. *al-Masjid al-Aqsa al-Mubarak*, the *'Further-most' Blessed Mosque*, built against the S wall of the Haram, is the great congregational mosque of Muslim Jerusalem, the focus in particular of the Friday midday prayers and sermon, when the suqs of Jerusalem are full of people coming to the mosque. It is the ancient centre of Muslim worship, as opposed to the great pilgrimage shrine to the N on the higher platform, which from a distance appears to dominate the Aqsa. When the visitor comes nearer, the building can be better appreciated.

Whether the first mosque in Jerusalem, the mosque of ʿUmar, was built on or near this site shortly after 638 is not certain. The Christian pilgrim Arculf described a mosque in 680 which appears to have been on this site. Certainly a splendid mosque built by 715 by al-Walid is the basis of the structure visible today, though it has undergone considerable structural alterations in the course of the centuries. The mosque reached its maximum extent with 15 aisles in the 8C under the Abbasids. It was briefly the palace of the Crusader rulers of Jerusalem from 1099 and then the headquarters of the Knights Templar from 1118, both of whom also left their imprint on the building.

The present building, a great basilica consisting of seven aisles which are oriented to the S or qibla wall and Mecca, lies on the same axis as the Dome of the Rock and the great ablution fountain between the two. It has a magnificent façade with a portico of seven bays, rebuilt and extended between the Crusader period and the 15C, and a dome over the central nave in front of the mihrab. The dome has recently been covered with dark grey lead. The mosque contains interesting Fatimid mosaics, though the dome area is under restoration following the disastrous fire in 1969 which destroyed the pulpit of Salah al-Din. The S end of the building has extensions to E and W; that on the W is called the *Women's Mosque*, A. *Jami' al-Nisa* and that on the E contains three separate places of worship: *the Mosque of 'Umar, the Mosque of the Forty Martyrs*, and *the Mihrab of Zacharia*. The Aqsa is constructed of local limestone, is c 80m × 55m (including the porch), and has been the object of major restoration work in 1924–27 (just before the earthquake of 1927), 1938–43 and since, under the care of the Supreme Muslim Council. It can hold up to 5000 worshippers.

History. The early history of the Aqsa mosque is complex. The structural history (Hamilton, 1949) has been variously correlated with the limited historical evidence available. The question of where the first mosque in Jerusalem was built is not resolved. The name, al-Aqsa, was previously applied to the entire Haram area, and only in later centuries was it restricted to the mosque. Some say that the Caliph 'Umar, following his acceptance of the surrender of Jerusalem in 638, went to the site of the holy Rock, ordered the cleansing of the site and built the first mosque on or near the Rock itself. This is one reason why the Dome of the Rock was often called the Mosque of 'Umar by the Franks. Others think it was on or near the site of the present Islamic Museum (because of the ancient masonry and the traditions linking this area with the miraculous Night Journey of Muhammad). Another view, and perhaps this is more likely, is that 'Umar built the mosque in the S area of the present building, where the oldest parts of the present structure were preserved. Apart from the Double Gate with entrance passage beneath the mosque and parts of the platform itself, no traces of Herodian building have been discovered on the site. It is assumed that at least by the time of 'Umar (and probably in Roman and Byzantine times) the ruins of the Herodian Royal Stoa had been cleared, and the S wall of the Haram built up to near its present level, as the Herodian platform is the foundation of the mosque. The lowest visible repairs to the Herodian S wall are currently dated to the Umayyad period.

Phase 1 *of the structural history of the Aqsa.* The earliest mosque of which traces are preserved was of uncertain width, but was an aisled structure shorter than the present mosque, c 50.05m–51.45m in length and including much of the lower part of the present S wall. Its aisles varied from 4m to 6m in width. One of its N door sills was excavated below the floor of the present E aisle. Its floor, c 0.5m–0.8m lower than the present floor, was paved with pale grey marble. The character of the interior decoration is suggested by surviving fragments of marble revetment and painted plaster; mosaic tesserae are significantly absent. Until recently Arcades 1 and 3 to the E of the present dome, and arcade 1 W of the dome contained slender dark marble monolithic columns (0.5m in diameter) with Byzantine capitals on uniform Attic bases (total height 5m) which continued below the present floor level and aligned with pilasters in the original N and S walls. In 1948 these were the oldest extant parts of the structure, being re-used Byzantine spolia. There were also some fragments of wooden carving and 7C graffiti found re-used in the great tie-beams of the central aisle (see Islamic Museum, Rte 2F, and Rockefeller Museum, Rte 13). Creswell considered it unlikely that this structure had a dome because there were no adjacent piers to absorb the lateral thrust. Light pier bases (not columns) were found in the N end of the mosque. The court outside this mosque (under the present N end) was paved with white and pink *mizzi* flagstones with ornamental drain covers. A stylobate may have supported a porch 4m deep along the N façade. The cistern head of the older Bir al-Waraqa (which used to be visible in the mosque inside the N door of the second aisle from the E) was sited in this court.

Chronology of Aqsa 1. Hamilton proposed that this structure was Umayyad or earlier, but probably that built by Walid I in 715; alternatively it is identified as the original mosque built by 'Umar c 639–40 and is the structure described in a pejorative fashion by Arculf in 680 as a squarish and fairly roughly constructed building, partly of wood, in the ruins of the Herodian Royal Stoa. It is often assumed that this was a simple building, of an early hypostyle type attested elsewhere at this period, but which was, notably, large enough to hold up to 3000 people and served the Muslim community for about 70 years both before and after the construction of the Dome of the Rock in 691–92. The size of Aqsa 1 would suit a congregation of 3000, the figure given by Arculf for 'Umar's mosque, and it seems likely that the conqueror of Jerusalem would have availed himself of the skills of local craftsmen to build a first mosque befitting the new rulers of the city.

Phase 2 *of the structural history of the Aqsa.* The mosque was extended in length (12 small arcades) to the present N wall (internal measurements c 68m N–S). The present dome-bearing arches were built, and some of the arcades to the E of the dome (especially in arcade 2) were replaced with monolithic grey-veined marble columns with Byzantine basket capitals; the transverse arcades in the same area were supported on slender, square .masonry piers built alongside the monolithic columns, presumably to support the lateral thrust of a newly built dome; the same type of pier may have been employed further N for the aisles of the mosque. The floor level was nearly the same as at present. The N wall included the central section of the present N wall, with the three central N doors which still survive and are certainly 8C, probably Umayyad work, and are built of hard *mizzi* limestone. The arcades of the aisles sprang directly from this N wall, and the central aisle (11.40m) was wider than the subsidiary aisles. It is possible that parts of the S wall piers in the Mosque of 'Umar belong to this phase, otherwise the width of the mosque is unknown.

Chronology of Aqsa 2. Hamilton proposed that Aqsa 2 was the 15-aisled mosque rebuilt by the Abbasid Caliph al-Mahdi completed c 774, to which he attributes the wide central aisle and the first use of the great carved tie-beams over it. Alternatively this basilica-like structure was started by the Umayyad Caliph 'Abd-al-Malik (685–705) and completed by al-Walid I (705–15) in 709–15 (Raby). The extended length, the wide central aisle, narrower side aisles, the dome and the N dome-bearing arch, the three N doors, and the great cypress roof beams found re-used in the suceeding structural Phase 3 (which have inscriptions of the 7C and carving with stylistic links with Hellenistic work) are therefore Umayyad in date. This view would also agree with al-Muqaddasi (985) who noted that the dome of the Aqsa was Umayyad. Like the Dome of the Rock, it had mosaic decoration, for al-Walid had gilt glass tesserae brought from Constantinople. In the early years the main entrance to the mosque was by the Double Gate and the underpassages beneath the mosque, leading up from the Umayyad quarter to the S.

The doors of the Umayyad structure, whether in Aqsa 1 or 2, were covered in gold and silver.

Phase 3 *of the structural history of the Aqsa.* In a partial reconstruction of Phase 2, the whole structure between the dome and the N wall was demolished and rebuilt employing softer *malaki* limestone and mortar. Three central aisles, 52m long N of the dome, were carried on four rows of six columns, each supporting 7 arcades (each larger than the 12 they replaced) with slightly pointed, slightly stilted arches. The walls on these arcades supported the gable roof and contained a row of interior windows, with an additional upper row of cierestorey windows in the higher walls on either side of the central aisle. The arcades were supported on marble monolithic columns at the S end, at the N end on unbonded wall piers built against the older *mizzi* limestone N wall. This is the basis of the present layout of the mosque. The cylindrical columns were built of shaped blocks of masonry, with limestone bases and capitals all made as a set except for two at the N end of the central W nave. These masonry columns were 0.85m in diameter, the surfaces plastered and painted with marbling and diaper patterns to resemble marble columns. Three of them survived apparently in their original state (in a certainly pre-12C context) until the restorations of 1938–43. The arcades were braced by wooden tie-beams above the capitals. The central aisle was narrowed to c 10.68m, and abutted the older N dome-bearing arch. Great cypress beams 13m long formed the ceiling of the central aisle, which were re-used from the earlier structure when the aisle was wider. They had carved ornamental soffits or consoles at either end and more carving decorated the cross beams at the corners (see Islamic Museum, Rte 2F). Virtually the whole of this central area survived intact until 1938. Hamilton also dates the round windows in the S and N walls to this phase.

Chronology of Aqsa 3. It seems likely that this structure was the 15-aisled mosque built by the Abbasid caliphs al-Mansur and al-Mahdi between 754–85. The historical sequence in the Aqsa (from a text of 1351) indicates that parts of the mosque fell down in the earthquake of 747/8, which provides a reason for the demolition of the N aisles of Aqsa 2. Al-Mahdi said that the mosque was too narrow and too long, and ordered it to be re-made shorter and wider. The built columns would imply a period when money was short, and the marbling and diapering on the plastered columns compares to 8C work at Khirbat al-Mafjar. Some reconstruction took place c 758/9 when al-Mansur took the gold and silver from the Umayyad doors to pay for some of the repairs. The mosque was extended 771–80 (after another earthquake in 774 described by al-Muqaddasi) the work being credited to al-Mansur (754–75) and al-Mahdi (775–85). The mosque reached its greatest extent in this period. It consisted of 15 aisles, seven on either side of the central nave, with the central door at the N end, the Bab al-Nuhas al-a'zam plated with gilded brass. Of the seven other doors on either side, the central ones also had gilded plating. The mosque had 11 unadorned doors on the E side. In this mosque the older work still standing around the mihrab 'stood like a beauty spot'. Later a portico with marble pillars was built onto the N façade by 'Abd Allah ibn Tahir, the governor of Syria (820–22). The mosque had a gable roof and a great and beautiful lead-sheathed dome over the central aisle in front of the mihrab.

There was a great earthquake on 10 December 1033 which damaged the mosque. The Aqsa was restored c 1034–36 under the Fatimid Caliph al-Zahir (whose inscriptions mention work on the dome). The mosque was reduced in size to suit the increasing impoverishment and probable depopulation of the city. It was probably a five-aisled structure, as Nasir-i Khusraw in 1047 says it had five doors. The subterranean entrance passage from the S was blocked at this time, following the abandonment of the S quarter, and the main entrance to the Haram was thereafter from the W (see for example the Bab al-Silsila, Rte 2B). The glass mosaic on the N dome-bearing arch is dated by an inscription to al-Zahir (who had also restored the mosaics of the interior of the drum of the Dome of the Rock in 1027/8). Some of the earliest painting on the old tie-beams of the aisle arcades has also been credited to al-Zahir (see Islamic Museum, Rte 2F). According to an inscription just under the top cornice of the N façade, the upper part of the N façade above the porch, where the windows are slightly horseshoe-shaped, was (until 1948) probably the work of al-Mustansir c 1065.

The Haram area was an integral part of the Crusader town from 1099, and Godfrey of Bouillon, ruling with the title of 'Defender of the Holy Sepulchre', made the Aqsa his headquarters; it served briefly as a palace for his successor, Baldwin I, the first Crusader King of Jerusalem. He gave it to the Order of the Knights Templar which was founded in 1118, who in turn made it their headquarters (the *Palatium* or *Templum Salomonis*) and made various structural alterations and extensions to suit its new function. The mosque became a church topped by a cross, consisting of three aisles and a transept; the fine decorations remained undamaged; various annexes were constructed, including the great Templar Hall (now occupied by the Women's Mosque and the Islamic Museum); halls or tower were built out to the S over the Double Gate which remained blocked; a great triple portico was constructed in the area of the SE aisles with an open area to the N in the present NE aisles; the three central bays of the N porch were constructed between 1099 and 1187. Vaulted annexes running E of the N end of the building were contructed as baths and storehouses, and stood until demolished in 1943. Parts of the substructure served as stables, armoury or storerooms.

When Salah al-Din retook the city in 1187 he immediately restored the Aqsa to its previous function and form, removed the cross from the dome, refurbished the interior of the dome, and the floors and walls with marble and mosaics; he also made the mihrab with its mosaics. The earliest extant painted decoration of the wooden tie-beams of the central arcades may date to him or to al-Malik al-Mu'azzam. Salah al-Din also gave a beautiful pulpit of carved, inlaid and gilded cedar wood (which had been made for Nur al-Din Zangi in 1168, who had planned to install it in Jerusalem when he conquered the city). The exterior of the central bays of the N porch were rebuilt in 1217/8 by al-Malik al-Mu'azzam. He also rebuilt the central dome of the porch. The round window in the E wall above the Mihrab of Zacharia is thought to be 13C, perhaps added when a screen wall was built closing the Crusader portico.

Various works are recorded during the Mamluk period. Al-Mansur Sayf-al-

Din Qala'un (1280–90) replaced part of the ceiling in the SE part of building. Al-Nasir Muhammad (c 1328) made some repairs, including redecoration of the dome, and the restoration of some marble facing and some windows in the front wall. Al-Kamil Sha'ban I restored the mosque and doors in 1345, work which probably included the construction of the two outer W bays of the porch, the two doors and the N end of the two aisles behind that part of the porch. In 1350–51 al-Nasir Hasan probably built the two NE aisles and their doors as well as the two E bays of the porch, thus enlarging the mosque to seven aisles and to its present size. The work was carried out under the supervision of Faris al-Din, who also endowed a zawiya or madrasa *(al-Farisiyya)* in c 1352/3, probably in the NE Crusader annexes which still bore his name in 1862 (de Vogüé). His main madrasa lay above the N portico of the Haram (Rte 2B). Al-Ashraf Inal made many repairs in 1460 (mentioned by Mujir al-Din). Al-Ashraf Qa'it Bay built the crenellations and upper border of the façade in 1474 and made repairs c 1479. Al-Ashraf Qansuh al-Ghawri (1501–16) made general repairs.

Ottoman Period. Most of the masonry of Jami' al-Arba'in is Turkish (Hamilton). Sulaiman II made repairs in 1561. 'Uthman III replaced some wood and the lead of the dome in 1752. Mahmud II carried out extensive repairs to the mosque and dome in 1817. 'Abd-al-'Aziz installed stained glass windows in 1874. 'Abd-al-Hamid II (1876–1909) gave Persian carpets. A certain amount of painting and plastering of the interior seems to have preceded the visit of Kaiser William II of Germany in 1898, including some poor paintings by an Italian artist which covered the Fatimid mosaic on the N dome-bearing arch.

Later history. In 1924–27 the Supreme Muslim Council carried out major repairs to the Mosque, with the supervision of the Turkish architect Kemal al-Din. Three pillars beneath the mosque were strengthened with reinforced concrete. The eight pillars and four arches supporting the dome were replaced, as were the tie-beams. 30 new stained glass windows were installed. The painted plaster over the mosaic on the N dome-bearing arch was removed. All the work was faithful to previous designs and an inscription over the prayer niche records the repairs. In 1927 an earthquake damaged the mosque, followed by another in 1937, following which the E aisles were in a dangerous condition.

In 1938–42 the Supreme Muslim Council with the supervision of Mahmud Pasha Ahmad carried out major excavations and rebuilding, with the Department of Antiquities as observer (see R.W. Hamilton 'The Structural History of the Aqsa Mosque'. Oxford 1949). The work involved the demolition to the foundations of all the long walls and arcades of the mosque except for those of the two W aisles and the arcades flanking the dome. The reconstruction of the nave and E aisles followed, using monolithic marble columns imported from Italy, with locally carved capitals in Byzantine style; also the reconstruction of the upper part of the N wall of the mosque, and its complete internal refacing, including a partial reconstruction of the jambs and lintels of the central doors. The front five bays of the porch were restored, and the Crusader vaulted annexes to the E were torn down. At this time the roof was replaced with a steel structure. Much of the old plaster was stripped off, enabling a structural reassessment to be made, and repairs carried out. The E and central part of the floor was repaved. The decoration of the ceiling of the central aisle was the gift of King Farouk and the Egyptian government.

A number of bombs hit the mosque between July and December 1948, and repairs were carried out. In 1951 repairs ordered by King Abdullah of Jordan included the placing of a wooden partition between the Zacharia mihrab and the E aisles. Not long after, Abdullah was assassinated in the Haram on his way to the Aqsa. In 1967 an anodised aluminium silver-coloured outer shell replaced the old lead covering of the dome. On the 21st August 1969 Salah al-Din's minbar was destroyed by fire and the adjacent walls and ceilings of the mosque damaged. Extensive repairs including the making of a copy of the minbar are still under way. The old columns and much of the stonework in the SE section of the mosque have been replaced or refaced. The dome is newly re-covered in dark grey lead.

Visit. Though almost totally restored the mosque retains the plan and numerous details of its accumulated architectural history since the 7/8C.

The exterior. The mosque with its porch is essentially a large rectangular building aligned N–S, c 80m long and c 55m wide with extensions at the SE and the SW. It has a modern gable roof over the main aisle, modern flat roofs over the lateral aisles, with a recently

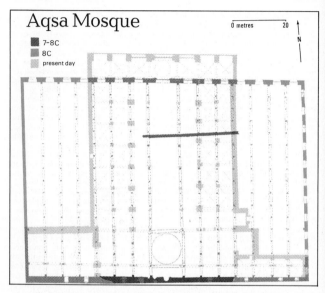

Aqsa Mosque

0 metres   20

N

- 7–8C
- 8C
- present day

re-covered 8C–11C dome over the space before the mihrab which is c 26.7m high, plus a crescent finial. The mosque is built of local limestone. The main N façade consists of a portico, with three pointed arches on either side of a larger central arch. The three central bays were originally constructed in the Crusader period and the central arch is somewhat Romanesque in style; the inner part of the central bays is still largely Crusader work, but the exterior and the porch dome were rebuilt in 1217/8. The two outer bays to E and W were constructed between 1345 and 1350, which is recorded in the inscriptions in the respective spandrels above the E and W piers. The central inscriptions, also set between small ornamental columns, record on the left al-Malik al-Mu'azzam's 1217/8 rebuilding of the porch mentioned above, and on the right. Sultan Qa'it Bay's contribution of the crenellations and upper border of the façade. Above the porch the wall was rebuilt in 1938–42; the three upper windows with slightly horseshoe-shaped arches date to 1065, probably the work of the Fatimid al-Mustansir, according to the inscription below the top cornice. To the rear of the porch, the bays match the seven rectangular doorways leading to the seven interior aisles. The *three central doors are notable, each set in a monumental moulded framework with flat lintels of joggled masonry, with very slightly pointed arches containing lunettes above; they are variously dated to the Umayyad or the Abbasid period. Stylistically and structurally they are certainly 8C, and probably Umayyad. The upper frame of the great central door is damaged, but the size of the opening is 6.85m × 4.8m and that of the smaller E door is 4.25m × 2.99m. The W door was restored in Crusader times, and again in 1938–43, the others survived better and were only partly renewed in 1938–43. The two outer pairs of doors to E and W with pointed arches above, like their respective porticoes, are probably 14C.

Just in front of the mosque and to the E of the main entrance are steps leading down to the subterranean Aqsa (Rte 2F). The W façade of the mosque fronting the courtyard has two rectangular windows and one door at a low level and 12 windows above. The E façade was completely rebuilt in 1938–42. There is one doorway in the E side, the *Gate of Elias*, A. *Bab Ilyas*, also rebuilt in 1938–43. Prior to the restoration it had a portal with gadrooned voussoirs, probably of Ayyubid date. The three structures which project eastwards at the S are respectively the *Mihrab of Zacharia*, the *Mosque of the Forty Martyrs*, and the *Mosque of 'Umar*. The rear of the Mihrab of Zacharia contains a rectangular window and round relieving arch; above is a 13C round window. The best views of the low drum and high dome of the Aqsa can be had from the SE corner of the Haram, or from the Mount of Olives.

The interior. Entrance by the main door, leaving shoes, bags and cameras outside. The restorations carried out this century, and the many windows, contribute to the sense of space and light in a vista of columns and rugs. The mosque contains 75 columns and 33 piers in addition to smaller ornamental columns in various places; there are 155 windows, of which 121 containing coloured glass are nearly all 20C replacements. The layout of the mosque developed between the 7C and the 14C, but almost all has been restored in the 20C.

The columns of the central nave and the two rows to the E are of Italian marble with limestone capitals in local Byzantine style. They were installed in 1938–43 and conform to the earlier plan. The central aisle is flanked by arcades with pointed arches; above each arch are three slightly pointed small arched openings each in turn paired with 21 clerestory windows to each side. The painted medallions at intervals along the upper wall name friends and relations of the Prophet, including 'Ali and 'Umar, in ornate calligraphy. The chandeliers and rugs are new. The carved and painted ceiling of the central nave, predominantly blue, white, gold and brown in geometrical and floral designs was given by Farouk I and the Egyptian Government in 1943. It replaces the massive wooden roofbeams whose carvings (7C or 8C) are now preserved in the Islamic Museum. The E aisles have a modern coffered ceiling, and first W aisle has a timber ceiling of no great antiquity, the other two aisles to the W have groined stone and plaster ceilings (14C). The tie-beams in the arcades, of gilded metal, are replacements of earlier wooden ones which had c 13C and later paintings (Islamic Museum).

In 1862 a large rectangular slab (with no existing inscription) lay in the centre of the central aisle level with the first N column of the arcade, and was noted by de Vogüé who thought it was a Crusader tombstone, which the Muslims identified as 'the Tomb of the Sons of Aaron'. It is also recorded as such in the Ordnance Survey by Wilson in 1865, who says it was protected by an iron railing. By the early 20C western guide and travel books were locating the graves of the murderers of Thomas Becket here. Thomas Becket was murdered in Canterbury Cathedral on 29 December 1170 by the knights de Traci, Fitz Urse, de Morville and Brito under debateable instructions from Henry II. According to Romuald of Salerno they were instructed by Pope Alexander III to go as penitents to Jerusalem and then to spend the rest of their lives in Montenegro (near Antioch in Syria) in miserable expiation. Herbert of Boehm says de Traci fell mortally ill en route in Italy, and made his confession to the Archbishop of Cosenza (and thus presumably died there). Roger of Howden, who went on crusade with Richard I, and probably came home in the convoy of Philip Augustus in August 1191 without visiting Jerusalem, says the murderers of Becket were buried before the door of the

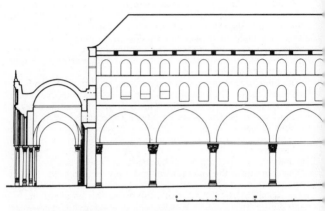

Section through the Aqsa Mosque (R.W. Hamilton, The Structural History of the Aqsa Mosque: *Oxford, 1949).*

Temple in Jerusalem (presumably Templum Domini, the Dome of the Rock, rather than Templum Salomonis, the Aqsa Mosque), with an inscription which read HIC JACENT MISERI QUI MARTYRIZAVERUNT BEATUM THOMAM ARCHIEPISCOPUM CANTUARIENSUM. John of Würzburg states that 'illustrious people were buried within the Haram in the vicinity of the Golden Gate' in Crusader times (which could be described as 'before the door of the Temple'). It seems unlikely that the murderers became Templars or merited burial within what was then the Templar's church. It is possible that the tradition (which apparently does not pre-date the 20C) is based partly on Roger of Howden's account of the burial, and partly on a confusion with the practice at the Church of the Holy Sepulchre where Crusader kings and knights were buried in the entrance to the church, in particular the 13C grave of Philip d'Aubigné who (Clermont-Ganneau noted in a publication of 1899) had an ancestor surnamed Brito. Other inscribed fragments of Crusader tomb stones have been found re-used in or near the Haram. Both the traditions, of the sons of Aaron (particularly Eleazar or al-ʿUzair) who are venerated by Muslims, and of the murderers of Beckett, may well have disappeared with the repaving of the mosque in 1938–42.

The dome and dome-bearing arches in front of the mihrab survive from Umayyad, Abbasid and Fatimid times. Although the eight pillars and piers supporting the dome were replaced in 1927, most of the work above is that of al-Zahir in 1034–36. In particular the *mosaics on the N face of the N dome-bearing arch, are of Fatimid date. They are dated by the double row of Kufic inscription at the top, which names al-Zahir. Elaborate acanthus and floral motifs expand upwards from the lower corner of the half-spandrel to the central window above the apex of the arch. Resemblances to the Umayyad

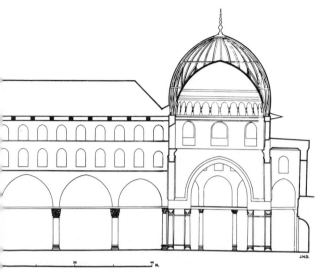

style are probably due to the use of the same workmen whom al-Zahir had employed in 1027/8 to restore the mosaics on the drum of the Dome of the Rock. The style here is much less flexible, and the attempt to fill the field of decoration less successful than in the Umayyad originals. *The dome itself, a double casing of wood and metal resting on a shallow drum, which has seven windows with stained glass, has been renovated on various occasions as its inscriptions record. Its interior apex is 23.5m above the floor. The mosaics on the drum were restored by Salah al-Din in 1189, and contain much gold and green in the designs of vases, trees, flowers, rosettes and leaves reminiscent of the probable Umayyad originals. There are also fine designs on the moulding and pendentives below.

Renovations to the dome were also made by al-Nasir Muhammad in 1327 and Mahmud II (1808–39) as the inscriptions in the panels of the dome record, in exactly the same way as these three rulers recorded their actions in the Dome of the Rock.

In the S wall of the mosque is the *mihrab or prayer niche of Salah al-Din. Six graceful small columns of variously coloured marble flank the niche, with mosaic in the upper part and marble casing below. The inscription, in gold mosaic reads: 'In the name of merciful and compassionate God, the restoration of this Sacred Mihrab and the entire restoration of the mosque was commanded by the servant of God and his agent Yusuf Ibn Ayyub Abu'l-Muzaffar, the Victorious King, Salah al-Din, when he conquered Jerusalem in the name of God in the year 583 H. He thanks God for this success and may God have mercy on him'. To the right until its destruction by fire in 1969 stood the beautiful inlaid cedar wood minbar or pulpit also presented to the mosque by Salah al-Din, which was one of the finest surviving wooden minbars of that period. Opposite this minbar is a *dikka*, or platform for the relayer of the prayers, supported on 14 slender columns with Crusader capitals, built against the NW pier supporting the dome, which is of later date and undergoing restoration. Immediately W of the destroyed minbar in the S wall are two small mihrabs, of Moses and of Jesus; the latter traditionally contained the footprint of Jesus said to have been brought here from the Chapel of the Ascension on the Mount of Olives in medieval times; to the right is a doorway leading S into the *Dar al-Khitaba* or room for the reader of the Friday sermon and other attendants of the mosque, which was built in the 15C in the earlier Crusader/Ayyubid tower (Rte 2A). Nearby two columns stand close together: tradition holds that if the faithful can pass between them they will see the houris of Paradise or, alternatively, may not enter Paradise if they cannot pass between them. The gap between the columns is much chipped and worn. The second aisles to E and W of the mihrab contain rectangular windows at floor level probably dating from the 12/14C.

To the W is the *Women's Mosque* A. *Jami' al-Nisa*, or the *White Mosque*, A. *al-Buq'a al-Baida'*. This is located in the E part of the great Templar Hall of the 12C. The W end can be seen in the Islamic Museum (Rte 2F). The E end of the hall was probably made into a mosque shortly after 1187 by Saladin.

The SE area of the Aqsa has a more complex history and has been almost totally restored recently. It contained the oldest preserved sections of the mosque, with Byzantine marble columns and capitals dating to the 7/8C. Restorations of some of these can be seen in the second E aisle. The slender piers adjacent are contemporary and supported the transverse arcades.

To the E and immediately adjacent to the S wall is the *Mosque of 'Umar* entered by an archway from the main mosque. It is 30m × 8m, constructed of limestone, with vaulted roof with pointed arches and three large and three small windows. The prayer niche, between the second and third piers of the S wall, has a twisted column on either side with richly and grotesquely carved capitals of Crusader date. Tradition says it marks the site of 'Umar's prayers in 638, and according to Mujir al-Din the building is a remnant of the mosque built by 'Umar in the 7C, hence its present name. Most of the fabric is Ottoman, but much of the exterior S wall is earlier and is perhaps Umayyad.

On the N side of the Mosque of 'Umar is the *Mosque of the Forty (Martyrs)* A. *Jami' al-Arba'in*. This is currently undergoing restoration; it is approached through trefoil arches with red and white voussoirs, and measures 9m × 8m. It contains two windows with coloured glass, the lower walls are cased in polychrome panelled marble, and verses from the Koran form a decorative dado on the walls above, in particular those describing Muhammad's Night Journey. The structure dates to the Crusader and Ayyubid periods.

On the N side of the Mosque of the Forty is the *Mihrab of Zacharia*, standing on the site where he is said to have been slain. The commemoration is perhaps of that Zechariah son of Berachiah (Matt. 23:35) who was killed in the time of the Persian Darius between the Temple and the altar, but confused with Zechariah, father of John the Baptist, whom tradition held to have been slain by Herod the Great because of the failure of the Massacre of the Innocents to kill John. This tradition is old, for according to the Bordeaux Pilgrim (333) within the ruined Temple enclosure was an altar in front of which was a marble slab with the blood of Zechariah. Nasir-i Khusraw (1047) mentions a mihrab of Zacharia, which might have been destroyed in the Crusader alterations. The S wall has a mihrab with an ornate marble trefoil arch decorated in high relief and supported by two pairs of small pillars with acanthus capitals. High in the E wall is a round window of the 13C, and below is a rectangular window which is flanked by a carved fluted column with acanthus capital on the N, and a squared marble box capped by a non-matching capital on the S. The lower walls have coloured marble facings. The piers on either side of the entrance are probably of the 7/8C but the rear wall is post-Crusader. North of this mihrab is the E door of the mosque, the *Gate of Elias*, rebuilt in 1938– 42. The E arcades were completely restored in 1938–43.

Returning to the main entrance, on the right of the door at the end of the second aisle from the E one used to be able to see the mouth of one of the great cisterns of the Haram area, the Bir al-Waraqa or Well of the Leaf (Rte 2C). As one leaves by the main door, it can be noted that the interior masonry of the 8C central doors was replaced in 1938–43.

F.   The Islamic Museum

The ****Islamic Museum** is located in 12C Crusader and Ayyubid buildings in the SW corner of the Haram platform, and was established in 1927. It contains a remarkable display, mainly of objects and architectural fragments of the Haram structures removed in the course of restorations which serve almost as much as the buildings themselves to illustrate the magnificence and antiquity of the sacred precinct. Admission charge. Hours of entry: Sun, Mon, Tue, Thu 10.00–12.30, 15.30–18.00; Wed 15.30–21.00; Sat 10.30–13.00; eve of Jewish holidays, 10.00–12.30; Fri and Jewish Holidays: closed.

The courtyard in front of the entrance contains many pieces of stone sculpture which have been collected from the buildings in and around the Haram. They include a variety of capitals, and a sarcophagus, probably of the 1C AD, which has had a varied history. It measures 2.02m long, 0.55m wide, and the front is decorated with five rosettes in relief; two wreaths, one with rosette, decorate the ends; the back is plain. It was discovered in the dismantling of a fountain which stood in front of the central W pier of the Bab al-Silsila/Bab al-Sakina in 1871. Clermont-Ganneau noted that it resembled another which had been in the nearby Tankiziyya Madrasa (Rte 3) and which was taken to the Louvre in 1866. A third in Tariq al-Wad may belong to the same group. These may have been brought from the Tombs of the Kings (Rte 13) by Sultan Qa'it Bay in 1482. Mujir al-Din says this Sultan had many fountains built, especially in the Haram.

The entrance and domed vestibule of the museum were built as part of a re-modelling of the E façade of the al-Maghariba mosque in 1871. To the left the first three sections of the museum are located in the S part of the mosque in part of an early Ayyubid hall with vaulted roof dating c 1194 (Rte 2B). At the S end is the remnant of the mihrab which has been cut through to provide access to the S part of the museum. Only the semi-dome at the top, and the flanking re-used Crusader marble columns and acanthus capitals remain. The mihrab itself was built in the blocking of the earlier W entrance to the Templar Hall. The display contains objects which illustrate the history of the Haram and Islamic Jerusalem: fine Korans (one 800 years old), documents, lamps including a fine example dating to the early Mamluk period, metal work and some textiles, including a beautiful multi-coloured robe found in the Baladiyya Madrasa near the Gate of the Chain.

Passing through the door we enter the *** *great Templar vaulted hall** built in the 1160s; it probably formed part of the monastic quarters of the Knights; after 1187 the E end was converted into the Women's Mosque of the Aqsa, and later the W end served as the assembly hall of the Fakhriyya madrasa (Rte 2B). Ten pointed vaults are supported by great central piers and wall piers in this half of the hall; the hall serves as a splendid display area for a remarkable collection of structural remains and objects of 7C and later date which have been removed from the buildings in the Haram in the course of various restorations, including fragments of the original mosaics from the Dome of the Rock.

The ***Great Doors of the Dome of the Rock** sheathed in ornamental copper plating, were presented by Sultan Qa'it Bay in 1467–68. Among the most impressive objects in the display, they were removed from the mosque in the recent restorations. The inscriptions at the top record the restorations of Sulaiman II between 1552 and 1566. Other objects on display include tiles of various periods from the 16C taken from the exterior of the Dome of the Rock; two great gilded finials from the top of the Dome, one removed in the restorations of 1899 and the other in 1961; and the crystal chandelier which was hung over the Rock by 'Abd al-Hamid II in 1876, removed to the Aqsa in 1951 before it came to the museum.

Perhaps the most important objects in the display are the fragments of the *** *great carved roof beams** from the central aisle of the Aqsa Mosque. Cut from cypress trunks and originally 13m in length, the beams had carved consoles and soffits. The beams were probably originally employed in the Umayyad Mosque (8C), were re-used in the Abbasid Mosque (later 8C) and remained in use until removed in 1948. The date of the earliest carving could be as early as the 7C or as late as the 11C, but 6/7C graffiti discovered on the beams, and the style of the carving, tend to support the earlier date. Their survival *in situ* into the 20C is remarkable. Some of the painted tie-beams from the arcades of the aisles are also preserved. The earliest painting apears to go back to the time of Salah al-Din or al-Malik al-Mu'azzam in the 12C–13C, some just possibly to al-Zahir in the 11C, but much is later.

The *marble balustrade* of Crusader workmanship which ornamented the mihrab in the Aqsa till the 19C is also in the Museum, as are some fine windows of the 16C and later. Some capitals of various periods are also on display including a white marble capital depicting two angels ministering to the seated figure of Jesus, thought to be the fourth of a set once decorating the Crusader Chapel of the Repose on the site of the 'Umariyya Boys' School (Rte 3). The other three still decorate the gallery of the al-Ghawanima minaret (Rte 2B). Dating c 1160 they are similar to Crusader sculptures found at Sebastiya (now in the museum in Istanbul) and Nazareth (in the Church of the Annunciation at Nazareth) which belong to a school of scuplture originating in the Bourges district of E central France (Folda).

G.   Subterranean Features

Subterranean features only accessible from within the Haram, are at present closed to visitors.

The Haram area as a whole appears to have about 34 cisterns incorporated in its substructure, many of which are ancient, some perhaps dating to the Herodian period or earlier (Tacitus, Hist. V:xii). The construction of the *Struthion Pool* at the NW corner of the Haram in 2C–1C BC appears to have cut an earlier channel feeding cisterns in the NW area of the Haram, and a conduit of the 8C(?) BC is said to lead S toward the temple from the northern Pool of Bethesda. Some Haram cisterns are rock-cut, others are built within the vaulting which supports the platform. Most are purpose-built to provide water for ritual ablution and cleansing within the Haram in the days when water was brought to the Haram by aqueduct. Piped water supplies have now largely superseded this need, and those cisterns still in use are mostly used for watering the gardens and cleaning. Some are very large, in particular the one called 'The Sea' with 12,000 cubic metres capacity (Rte 2C, no.14; Rte 2E for the 'Well of the Leaf'). Other cisterns nearer the Dome of the Rock may utilise rooms and passages once used by the Herodian priesthood.

Beneath the present Moors' Gate lies the blocked *Barclay's Gate*, a Herodian gate (Rte 2A). In the original Herodian plan, the low-level gate led into a level passage c 21m long running E under the Temple court to a chamber covered by a well-built dome; it then turned at right angles towards the S and rose at a gradient of 1 in 20 by a ramp or steps to the surface opposite Robinson's Arch (Warren and Wilson). A late Muslim legend claimed that Muhammad tethered his steed, al-Buraq, by the gate before visiting the Aqsa and ascending to Paradise. The gate was afterwards called *Bab al-Nabi*, the *Gate of the Prophet*. The inner gate passage was subsequently converted into cisterns and a subterranean mosque, called al-Buraq, now abandoned. Access to the mosque and the inside of Barclay's Gate is by special permission only.

The Subterranean Aqsa, A. *al-Aqsa Qadima*, the 'ancient' Aqsa. At present this is closed to tourist access, but interesting remains of Herodian and Umayyad times exist. A flight of steps just in front and to the E of the main entrance to the Aqsa Mosque, leads to a ramp which formed part of the original entrance way from the Double Gate in Herodian times. Unlike the ramp at Barclay's Gate, which turned at right angles, this was a straight sloping passage. The gate was refurbished and the ramp extended in the 7/8C and formed the main entrance to the Haram from the Umayyad Quarter to the S. It was probably blocked c 1033 in the time of al-Zahir.

Visit. A wide descending ramp running the whole length of the mosque above gives onto a square vestibule of Herodian masonry in which a massive white marble monolithic column, 1.25m in diameter with flat acanthus leaf capitals supports four arches and shallow, fluted pendentives capped by flat domes. To N and S semi-engaged columns of the same diameter are built into piers for lateral support, with another free-standing column in the double passage to the N. The ceiling has fine geometric and acanthus relief decoration of probable Herodian date, though Umayyad repairs are possible. The original Herodian double ramp only extended for c 58m from the S wall. In the 8C the W side was blocked with a heavy mass of masonry which forms a foundation for the mosque above, and the E ramp was extended to its present length of c 79m when the length of the mosque above was extended. The inclination of the ramp then also had to be adjusted, as the mouth of the ramp had to reach the surface further N. The inclination changes at the point of adjustment. The ramp runs through earth fill and is not connected to the vaults on either side. According to Wilson and Warren the 'Tomb of the Sons of Aaron' (according to Vincent the 'Tomb of Aaron') is identified by Muslims at a break in the W wall of the vestibule of the gate (cf. Rte 2E), with the 'Place of Elijah' opposite; the Well of the Leaf is near the N end of the ramp. Necessary structural repairs were made in 1926–27, and reinforced concrete inserted to support the mosque above.

*Solomon's Stables.** The whole SE angle of the Haram is supported by subterranean vaulting, part of which used to be accessible to tourists, though at present it is closed. The vaulting was first constructed by Herod the Great, and at the SE corner is estimated to have had four levels which raised the ground level from 694.90m above sea level to about the present level of the platform at 738m. Only the third level from the bottom at c 725.60m is accessible, and of that only the lower parts of the walls are possibly Herodian in date. The upper parts and arches were reconstructed in Crusader times. The 'stables' were actually used as stables in Crusader times, when the Aqsa above was called the *Palatium Salomonis* by the Templars. In Herodian times their use is unknown, but they may have been used for storage.

Visit. Not open at time of writing. Access is by the flight of stairs in the SE angle of the Haram. Beneath the entrance Muslim tradition locates the *Cradle of Jesus*, where it is said Mary and the infant Jesus rested before starting the journey to Egypt to escape from Herod. The shrine is constructed from a great block of stone, with a painted semi-dome supported by four marble pillars. Clermont-Ganneau suggested this was constructed from a Roman statue niche, with shell flutings, which once contained the small bronze cult statue from the Temple of Jupiter in Aelia Capitolina (which some authorities locate on the Temple platform). He noted two other niches nearby in the wall itself, which he suggested once contained the statues of Juno and Minerva. Others have suggested these are re-used Byzantine niches; it is possible that there was a Byzantine chapel here dedicated to St. James, and a Crusader one dedicated to St. Simeon. Arab tradition identifies the two subsidiary niches as the Mihrabs of Mary and Zacharia.

The area of the stables is impressive, approximately 500m², containing 88 pillars which divide the area into 13 N–S galleries. The piers are rectangular, the lower parts of drafted blocks of Herodian masonry. Many still show the rings by which the Crusaders tethered their horses. The arches and ceilings are of smaller Crusader blocks. At the S end of the sixth gallery from the E is the inner side of the blocked Single Gate, a postern and stable exit dating from Crusader times. The Herodian tunnel below the Single Gate leads into a lower level of the vaulting (Rte 2A). The 'Cradle of David' used to be pointed out near the Single Gate.

At the W side of the stables a door in the wall (now blocked) leads to another smaller galleried area with two rows of piers; to the S is the inner side of the blocked Herodian **Triple Gate**, where engaged columns suggest an inner vestibule similar to that at the Double

A view of Solomon's Stables (A. Duncan, The Noble Sanctuary, *p. 61: Longman, London, 1972).*

Gate, but here almost nothing is preserved and the plan of the Herodian gate is not known. On the exterior, the Gate has three semi-circular arches; on the interior they are elliptical and set so as to allow the folding back of the doors themselves, a feature which suggests they are Umayyad in date. Only a single exterior jamb of the Herodian period survives (Rte 2A). The gate passage to the N is 58.5m long, with the semi-circular arches of the vault supported by piers 1.19m wide and 3m apart. These piers do not seem to be original except for one engaged column about 18.3m from the S wall which only survives in its lowest course, but is similar to those at the gate. The sill of the gate is 11.58m below the level of the Haram (Warren and Wilson). The gate was probably blocked in the time of al-Zahir (c 1033) when the S quarter of the city was abandoned.

3   The Muslim Quarter

Introduction. Now the largest and most heavily populated quarter in the Old City, the Muslim Quarter occupies c 28 hectares (c 70 acres) and is the least known. The area contains the new suburb enclosed by Herod the Great in the 1C BC between the Gennath Gate and the Antonia, the Antonia itself, and the new quarter of Bezetha enclosed by Herod Agrippa in AD 41–44. The line of the present NE city walls does not seem to pre-date the 3–4C. The entire area was within the Christian Byzantine city. In Umayyad times the principal Muslim quarter lay to the S of the Haram but gates and repairs on the W and N sides of the Haram indicate activity in these quarters also; in Fatimid times the W side of the Haram became more important but there are also indications of increasing Muslim work along the N side of the Haram. Jews are noted as living in the NE quarter of the city in Fatimid times and it was then called the Jewish Quarter. It was taken over by the Christians during the 12C and the remains of several churches have been noted. These were mostly converted into Muslim schools and mosques under the Ayyubids and Mamluks, when the N side of the city was developed further and became part of

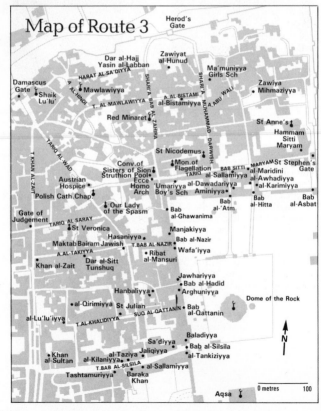

Map of Route 3

the Muslim Quarter. Several Ayyubid Muslim foundations are known in the areas N and W of the Haram. The areas adjacent to the Haram were developed particularly in Mamluk times for religious schools and tombs (although many of these are now also in domestic use). Along the route of the Via Dolorosa, especially from the 13C, Christian places of memorial developed into churches and hospices, many refurbished in the late 19C or early 20C. In Ottoman times the Antonia escarpment housed the seat of the Ottoman administration with the palace of the governor to the W. Shops, markets and caravanserais were located on the W side of the quarter, adjacent to the old suqs. Many of the present structures of the quarter incorporate older foundations and much exploration remains to be done. Despite early Ottoman refurbishment, the quarter has decayed since the 16C.

Visit. The area N of the Haram has numerous and varied places of interest, but very few of the Muslim monuments are open to visitors, being in private occupation. Because much of the decoration was lavished on the façade, especially the entrance, many are still well worth visiting. Entering the Old City by St. Stephen's Gate (Rte 1), immediately to the right inside the walls is an old **bath house**, the *Hammam Sitti Maryam*, still used in the 1980's. The bath house was fed by conduit from the pool outside the city walls, and was very popular with women. Many of the Arabic names for the monuments and the street in the vicinity of the gate are named after St. Mary because the gate led out to the tomb of the Virgin Mary (Rte 12). A **fountain**, the *Sabil Sitti Maryam* is also just by the gate, and is one of several built by Sulaiman II in 1537. The road to the N inside the walls leads past dwellings to the unoccupied NE corner of the city, which was used earlier this century for the cultivation of vegetables. On the left the road leads to the Haram Gate, the Bab al-Asbat (Rte 2). The area to the SW contains the filled-in *Birkat Isra'il* against the N wall of the Haram.

History. Herod the Great built this pool as an integral part of his monumental Temple complex in the late 1C BC. It was created to supply water to the Temple and lay within the city walls. It was a large rectangular pool, measuring 109.80m E–W, 38.40m N–S and was 12m in depth. The N wall of the Haram formed its S side; to the W a double tunnel beneath the surface was explored for 40m; on the E side an overflow channel led out through the Herodian city wall. The pool seems to have continued in use in Byzantine times. In c 1170 the Templars identified this pool with that of Bethesda (since excavated to the N, see below), and this identification was still accepted in the 19C. By then the Birkat Isra'il was out of use and almost filled with debris.

Continuing to the W along TARIQ BAB SITTI MARYAM, at c 45m on the right is the entrance to ***St. Anne's Church**, and the monastery of the White Fathers, with Greek Catholic seminary. The church is a fine 12C Crusader monument, converted into a Muslim school (the *Salahiyya Madrasa*) after 1187, and restored as a Christian church in the 19C. Its stark and fine simplicity make it one of the most peaceful places in Jerusalem. Excavations adjacent also contain the *Pools of Bethesda* (Latin, *Piscina Probatica*). Open daily 8.00–12.00, afternoons 14.00–18.00 in summer, 14.00–17.00 in winter.

History. The excavators propose that the earliest use of the site was for a reservoir or pool (the N pool) cut in the 8C BC which fed the First Jewish Temple to the S by channel. The pool was filled by rainwater collected on the slopes to N and W. The first recorded mention of the two pools is in the Seleucid period, the 'Great Pools', built by Simon the Just c 200 BC which were partly replaced by Herod the Great's Birkat Isra'il to the S, and then became known

The Birkat Isra'il from the east (C.W. Wilson, Picturesque
Palestine, *Vol. I, p. 66: Virtue and Co., London, 1880).*

also as the Sheep Pool. This was developed in Roman times as a healing pool,
where the sick, blind, lame and paralysed gathered to await a cure when the
waters were disturbed (90 BC–AD 70). It was the site of Jesus' miracle in
healing the crippled man (John 5:1–13).

By 135 it was associated with a temple or shrine of Serapis (Aesculapius), with
five colonnades. Origen (231–46) describes the five colonnades or porticoes as
being around the four sides, and the fifth across the central rock-cut division of
the pools. By the mid-5C a church 'at the Sheep Pool' or 'of the Paralysed Man'
had been built, and dedicated to St. Mary. This was built on the E side of the
pool, partly overhanging the central division of the pools. The birthplace of
Mary was also linked with Nazareth, but various details of her early life are
compatible with a birthplace in Jerusalem. St. Mary's is shown with its portico
on the Madaba map in the 6C. This church was probably destroyed by the
Persians in 614 and restored by Modestus soon after; some sort of church
remained in the 9C, when it is mentioned in the Commemoratorium as 'St. Mary
(where she was born at the Probatica) 5 (clergy) and 25 women dedicated to
God as anchoresses'. An Arab writer (Abu'l-Fida) says the Muslims had taken

over the church before the 12C, possibly after the attack of al-Hakim in 1016. By the end of the 11C only a very poor place known as St. Anne's still existed.

In the 12C it was associated with the birthplace of the Virgin Mary, and the House of St. Anne, her mother the wife of Joachim. Bethesda and A. *Bait Hanna* form a play on words meaning House of Grace. In the Crusader period a fine church was built on the present site, and also a chapel on the site of the earlier Byzantine church. These were part of a convent for Benedictine nuns, which was well endowed by Baldwin I who placed his wife, Arda (an Armenian princess) here in 1104. He then married Adelaide of Sicily. The convent endowments included the central great suq of Jerusalem (Rte 4). Joveta, the sister of Queen Melisande, was a novice here in 1130 before becoming head of the convent at Bethany (Rte 16). The church was extended later.

After Salah al-Din's conquest in 1187 the church was turned into a religious school (the Salahiyya Madrasa) for Shafi'ite Muslims, as the inscription of 1192 over the main door records. In 1699 it was still regarded by Christians as the house of Joachim and Anne, and although it was Muslim property, the Franciscans were allowed to say Mass there on the Feasts of the Immaculate Conception and the Nativity. The Muslims said it was haunted, and it began to be abandoned. In 1854 it was being used as a stable for the Turkish governor's horse soldiers. The church was granted to Napoleon III in 1856 by the Ottoman Sultan 'Abd al-Majid I in recognition of help rendered by France in the Crimea, by which time it had reached such a state of neglect that rubbish filled it nearly to the roof. Complete restoration followed in the 1860s, which amounted to a virtual rebuilding. The White Fathers and Mauss conducted excavations on the adjacent site in 1888–1900. The Museum of the White Fathers containing remains from the excavations and objects of biblical interest has suffered damage in recent years and is not at present open.

Visit. Passing through to the court (the *medieval cloister*), various fragments of masonry and sculpture discovered in the excavations are displayed. On the opposite side of the court is *St. Anne's Church*. This 12C building, in classic Romanesque style, has a fine entrance portal, with pointed arch and hood mouldings, in the tympanum of which the inscription of Salah al-Din (1192) records the establishment of the Salahiyya Madrasa. The archivolt and cornice are finely carved. The top window in the façade is the most ornate. It has gadrooned voussoirs supported by marble columns with acanthus capitals, and is capped by an elaborately carved archivolt. The church was extended by moving the façade W by 7m (straight joint in the N wall). The interior is a basilica with three naves, tall, dim and austere in style. The fine pointed vaulting is also restored. The crypt, to which stairs in the S aisle descend, contains chapels built in some of the caves of the earlier Roman temple. Despite the 19C restoration, the church is the finest example of Romanesque architecture in Jerusalem.

Outside the church, to the N, a noticeboard illustrates the discoveries relating to the *Bethesda Pools*. To the left parts of two very large, deep, rectangular rock-cuttings can be seen; originally stairs descended to the bottom. The N pool is said to date originally to the 8C BC; that on the S to the 3C BC. At the E end of the pools the remains of *caves* and *healing baths* of the Roman period can be seen, the foundations of the Byzantine church (a basilica with three apses which was partly built on vaulting at the E end of the pool), and a Crusader chapel.

Returning through the courtyard, in the wall on the right opposite the front of the church is a *12C niche*, which was installed here by Mauss at the time of the restoration of the dome of the Church of the Holy Sepulchre in 1867. It came from a chapel in an upper floor in the West Tower of the Church of the Holy Sepulchre, through which a view of the Tomb could be obtained from above the Rotunda gallery. Further along, a staircase with railing gives access to the SE corner of the southern pool; it is 13m deep.

St. Anne's Church (Middle East Archive, London).

Returning to the street and turning right, at c 80m is a crossroads; on the left the road leads to the Haram gate, the Bab Hitta. At the SW angle of the junction is the *Ribat al-Maridini*, a hospice built in 1361/2 for pilgrims from Mardin in modern SE Turkey. The frontage, on both TARIQ BAB HITTA, and TARIQ BAB SITTI MARYAM, is plain; the lower courses appear to belong to a pre-14C structure, and the upper storey is Ottoman. The entrance portal, on TARIQ BAB HITTA, is plain, with a pointed arched recess within which the door has been reduced in size. There is a relieving arch of joggled voussoirs, and space for an inscription in the tympanum. On the same frontage, the central window has a typical Mamluk iron grille; on the N frontage, with plain fenestration, a shop now occupies the W part.

To the S of the Maridini, just before arriving at the Bab Hitta, is the *al-Awhadiyya*, the tomb of al-Malik al-Awhad of 1298 (Rte 2B). The tomb (and possible hospice and madrasa) of the great-great nephew of Salah al-Din, who was Superintendent of the two Harams in Mamluk times, is now occupied as private dwellings. The E façade is the principal one, and has at the N end a fine entrance portal with re-used Crusader marble columns and capitals, and a cloister vault above with a blazon-like decorative hub. A few metres to the S is a blocked window to the courtyard, which has above it a carved panel of intricate Mamluk work. The blocked window to the tomb chamber is in the gate entrance. The façade has a cornice, and traces of Ayyubid and earlier walls in the lower courses.

The street ends at the Bab Hitta (Rte 2B), which has an outer porch of Ayyubid date; it contains some coursed drafted masonry, and a pointed dome. A re-used slab found in the gate had an inscription referring to the endowment of two (presumably nearby houses) for the accommodation of pilgrims from Diyarbakr (in modern SE Turkey) by the Amir Ibn Marwan Nasr al-Dawla (of the Marwanid dynasty) in 1053/4.

Opposite the Awhadiyya is al-Karimiyya (Rte 2B) a madrasa built in 1319. Karim was a Copt who became a great Mamluk state official (the Inspector of the Privy Purse in the time of al-Nasir Muhammad) and later converted to Islam. He was eventually disgraced, partly on an accusation of protecting Christians. He built a number of Muslim religious foundations in Cairo and Damascus. The simple entrance portal, with pointed arched recess and stone benches, contains a rectangular doorway with monolithic lintel and is now blocked. Most of the N end of the building behind is Ottoman.

Returning to the crossroads, continue to the left along TARIQ BAB SITTI MARYAM (or TARIQ AL-MUJAHIDIN). Beyond the shop in the W end of the Maridini hospice is a straight joint; to the W there is Crusader masonry in the lower courses, and Ottoman above. The wall from here to the corner forms the N frontage of the Sallamiyya Madrasa which is entered from the W frontage. At the E and W ends of this frontage are two blocked Crusader doorways. Continuing on to a vault spanning the road above the entrance to the TARIQ BAB AL-'ATM, on the right are the remains of a Syrian-type square tower minaret, the Mu'azzamiyya or al-Mujahidin Minaret. In 1865 a corbelled cornice still remained on the upper shaft. A marble plaque on the S face records the builder, al-Malik al-Qahir, in 1274/5. It served the Hanafi madrasa behind it, the Mu'azzamiyya Madrasa (later the Mujahidin Mosque) which was built by his father, the Ayyubid al-Malik al-Mu'azzam (endowed 1209, completed 1217/18). Its construction meant all four schools of Islamic law then had schools in Jerusalem. The minaret and the madrasa incorporated much re-used earlier rusticated masonry, and a slab with one of the Herodian inscriptions which banned non-Jews from entering the inner court of the Temple. It was found in the basement of the madrasa in 1871 by Clermont-Ganneau. The adjacent shop fronts are more recent. Just beyond on the left is the Tariq Bab al-'Atm which leads S to the Haram Gate of that name.

Turning S into TARIQ BAB AL-'ATM, mostly vaulted and thus gloomy, but containing some fine Mamluk portals which are well worth visiting. On the left are a row of *three fine Mamluk windows* with muqarnas hoods which give onto the assembly hall of the *al-Sallamiyya*, a madrasa built c 1338 by a merchant, al-Majd al-Sallami, who came from S of Mosul on the Tigris in modern Iraq. As well as mercantile activities, he was useful to Sultan al-Nasir Muhammad as a slave merchant and importer of Mamluks, and as a trusted diplomatic negotiator. The *main entrance* just to the S is very

The Minaret of the Mu'azzamiyya (the Mujahidin Mosque) in Tariq Bab Sitti Maryam (C.W. Wilson, Picturesque Palestine, *Vol. I, p. 30: Virtue and Co., London, 1880).*

fine Mamluk work. The portal, with benches set in a deep recess, has an unusual muqarnas canopy. The doorway, with red and cream coursed jambs, and a lintel with pseudo-voussoirs resting on three tiers of muqarnas work, still contains the original iron-plated double doors and heavy knockers. The balcony, above and to the S, supported on carved brackets and framed by mouldings, partly covered by later vaulting over the street, is a contemporary feature. This frontage has a number of parallels with Cairene work (Mosque of Almas, Cairo) unique in Jerusalem; it is suggested that it was the work of a team sent from Cairo (Burgoyne). The interior (not open) lacks these Egyptian features. It has a normal arrangement of vestibule and passage leading to a large open court, with 12 cells lining the N, E and S sides. The vaulted assembly hall lies to the NW The upper floors are largely Ottoman.

Adjacent to the S is the *al-Dawadariyya*, the khanqah built in 1295 by ʿAlam al-Din Sanjar al-Dawadari, a Mamluk Amir who served in turn under the Sultans Baybars, Qalaʾun, Khalil, Kitbugha, Lajin and al-Nasir Muhammad, from Aleppo and the N, to Damascus and Egypt in the S, took part in the assault on Acre in 1291, and finally died and was buried at Krak des Chevaliers in Syria in 1300. This is a large madrasa and khanqah which lies adjacent to the Haram N portico. Because of the gloomy vaulting it is hard to see the splendid entrance portal set in the plain façade. A red and cream coursed masonry recess containing benches has a doorway with monolithic lintel and joggled relieving arch; above the relieving arch the founder's inscription runs round all three sides of the recess. Above are three tiers of muqarnas work, and monolithic fluted cupolas. On the street side of these are two pointed trefoil arches, of which the central impost is suspended. The structure and decoration are complex, with parallels in Damascus, especially with the ʿAdiliyya Madrasa. The entrance opens directly into a large open court with cells on the W, N and E sides, and three larger ones on the S side. The cells have typical Mamluk pointed doorways, with slit windows to admit light and air from above. On the S side is the assembly hall, marked by a fine door and two flanking windows in shallow recesses. The entrance recess has a horseshoe arch. Red and cream coursed masonry, joggled relieving arches and rosettes in the tympana are all decorative features which add to the sense of importance. A cornice moulding marks the original height of the walls. This building was richly endowed as a Shafiʿi khanqah; it was converted to a school some time before 1914 (Madrasa al-Bakriyya).

The street ends at the Bab al-ʿAtm (Rte 2B); within the W end of the S wall of the Dawadariyya are two blocked archways which may be the two E passages of an Umayyad triple gate, with the present Bab al-ʿAtm in the W passage (Burgoyne). Opposite the Dawadariyya, on the W side, is the *Aminiyya*, a madrasa or khanqah founded in 1329/30 by Amin al-Malik, a state official of Coptic origin in the time of al-Nasir Muhammad who converted to Islam under Baybars II. The E frontage of this madrasa is obscured by buttresses and later vaulting; it has a plain doorway which contrasts with its ornate frontage onto the Haram (Rte 2B).

Returning to TARIQ BAB SITTI MARYAM, and turning left, at c 30m the Shariʿa Muhammad Darwish (also called the ʿAqabat Dair al-ʿAdas) on the right leads up to Herod's Gate. *A diversion for a walk through the Muslim quarter* to some monuments of which little can be seen may be made at this point, or the visitor can continue directly along the street to the Monastery of the Flagellation (see p.155).

Diversion. Ascending MUHAMMAD DARWISH ST, which is itself a fine example of a stepped and partly vaulted medieval street, at c 85m on the left a *medieval house* was noted as the Palace of Herod Antipas in a late tradition (see below, the Church of St. Nicodemus). For those really interested the second turning to the right (at c 130m) into a twisting lane (ʿAQABAT ABU WALI) leads E and then curves round to the S; take the second turning on the left and at c 30m on the right are the ruins of the *Mamluk Zawiya Mihmaziyya*, built before 1345. Returning to Muhammad Darwish St and continuing N, at c 180m on the right is the *Maʿmuniyya Girls' School*. It is on the site of a 12C Crusader church and cloister.

History. The Church of St. Mary Magdalene is said to have been built by the Copts (in the time of the Magistrate Makarios) c 819–30 (E. Moore). It was taken over in the 12C by the Syrian (Jacobite) church by agreement with the Latin Canons of the Church of the Holy Sepulchre, and is shown on 12C maps of Jerusalem. John of Würzburg (who visited Jerusalem in 1165) noted that it was inhabited by Syrian monks; it was visited by Michael, the Syrian Patriarch of Antioch, in 1166. It became a Muslim shrine after 1187, a madrasa endowed in 1197 by Faris al-Din Abu Saʿd Maʿmun, the treasurer of Salah al-Din. Later it fell into disrepair and in 1864 the large ruin still contained part of the porch, choir, side walls and two apses of the church and was occupied by a potter's workshop. Christian tradition then held it was the site of the house of Simon the Pharisee. Today the school stands on the site. The cloister attached to the church was revealed in recent work in the playground of the Maʿmuniyya school, and has been preserved (but is not visible) behind the walls of an underground shelter.

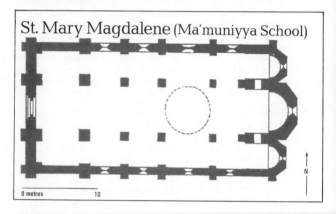

St. Mary Magdalene (Maʿmuniyya School)

0 metres 10

N

The road continues N to Herod's Gate (Rte 1); opposite it, on the S side an entrance leads to the *Zawiyat al-Hunud*, (or *Zawiyya Rifaʿiyya*, or of *al-Shaikh Farid Sakrakandj*), founded in the 13C(?), reconstructed in 1869/70 and in the possession of the Indian Muslims. We return c 25m to the S of the Maʿmuniyya School, to the street to the W, the ʿAqabat al-Bistami. Following it for c 60m, on the S side is the entrance to *al-Bistamiyya*, the zawiya of Shaikh ʿAbdallah, a sufi of the Bistamiyya order (Shafiʿi Muslim). It was established before 1369. The shaikh was born in Baghdad and buried in the Mamilla Cemetery (Rte 14). Mujir al-Din records he established his order in Jerusalem in the 'Easterners' Quarter', and this site is identified as the correct one, although there is no inscription. The modest portal is built of fine ashlar set into an older coursed rubble wall. There is an unusual cornice with protruding muqarnas decoration. The entrance now is nearly a metre below the present street level. The door is flanked by benches, and the door lintel rests on muqarnas shoulders. The interior, mostly now the private dwelling of the guardian, consists of a complex of rooms around a court, which belonged to various pre-existing structures bought in the 14C to form the zawiya, and are heterogeneous. At the SE corner of the court a horseshoe-arched recess flanked by rectangular windows contains the entrance to two large vaulted rooms, both with mihrabs. That to the E contains a fine old timber screen, beyond which is the larger of the two cenotaphs contained in the complex. The present guardians believe it to be the tomb of the 9C Abu Yazid al-Bistami, after whom the order is named, but who was buried in Persia. The cenotaph is more likely to be that of a later shaikh of the zawiya.

Continuing to the W along 'Aqabat al-Bistami, straight across into TARIQ AL-MAWLAWIYYA at the next crossroads, and taking the second turning to the right into 'AQABAT AL-HINDI we come almost immediately to the *Mawlawiyya Mosque* with minaret on the right. It is not open to visitors. It was a small Crusader church measuring c 13.9m x 6.5m. According to Pierotti (1864) the building had three aisles ending in semi-circular apses. Four plain piers supported a groined, vaulted roof with pointed arches. In 1865 traces of paintings of saints were visible under the whitewash on the walls (Wilson). The dedication is uncertain, perhaps to St. Agnes, for a church of St. Agnes is mentioned in the 12C as located somewhere in the then Jewish Quarter; alternative dedications are to St. Peter or St. John (E. Moore). It became a mosque after 1187. By the 16C(?) it was the Zawiya al-Mawlawiyya. The Mawlawis ('Dancing Dervishes') were established in Jerusalem well before the 17C; in 1864 only two occupied the convent adjacent to the mosque, which contained three tombs.

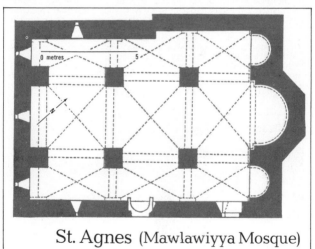

St. Agnes (Mawlawiyya Mosque)

If the road is followed N to the salient of the city walls, on the rocky crest of Bezetha above Solomon's Quarry (Rte 1) are the buildings established as orphanage and schools (later the Anna Spafford Memorial Hospital) by the American Colony (Rte 13). To the E other *medieval foundations* exist; the *Dar al-Hajj Yasin al-Labban* in the Harat al-Sa'diyya near Herod's Gate is recorded in Mandate archives as possessing a portal with gadrooned voussoirs, probably dating to the 12/14C. A twisted street leads W to the Damascus Gate. 10m SE of the gate is the modern Muslim Mosque of *Shaikh Lu'lu'*, which incorporates the Mamluk zawiya of Badr al-Din Lu'lu' Ghazi, endowed in 1373/4. It is marked by a 14C entrance portal, with deep pointed-arched recess with gadrooned voussoirs; the door has a monolithic lintel and rebuilt tympanum above. The interior (not open) has a vaulted tomb chamber on the S side of the entrance passage with an uninscribed cenotaph; and a court with the mosque on the E side. Most of the chambers around the court are Ottoman in date.

Now retrace your steps to the SHARI'A BAB AL-ZAHIRA, turn right and descend towards the Via Dolorosa. At c 40m on the right is the 'Red Minaret' *(manarat al-Hamra)* (16C?) and the restored mosque which was noted in 1865 by Sandrecski as a minaret with traces of red and cream masonry by a ruined mosque; and in 1896 by Schick as an isolated tower in a dangerous condition whose former mosque had fallen down.

Continuing to the third turning to the left brings us to HOSH BAKIR, a lane leading E along the N side of the Convent of the Flagellation, at the end of which is the **Greek Orthodox Church of St. Nicodemus**, on a site with numerous late medieval traditions.

History. The church is an old foundation, possibly originally Byzantine, but the suggested dedication to the Nativity of the Virgin Mary is unlikely in view of the location of that church at the Probatica Pools. It was investigated by Schick in 1896, who recorded a door at the end of the lane, leading by way of a passage and courts NE to a church on two levels, with additional underground vaults and cisterns: it appears to be a Crusader church standing on older foundations with medieval alterations. The lower level of the church had three apses, a broad plan, with a portico and court to the W; the upper level was approached by outside stairs from the court, and had a domed upper church. In medieval times it or a nearby house came to be associated with the palace of Herod Antipas to which Jesus was taken after his arrest at Gethsemane. Also in this area, in the 15C Felix Fabri visited the House of Simon the Pharisee who invited Jesus to eat with him (Luke 7:36) (see also above, Ma'muniyya School). Both stories are reflected in the name Dair Abu 'Adas (Convent of the Lentils, or Father of Lentils; Abu 'Adas is seen as a corruption of the name Antipas). In the 19C the church was linked with the Nativity of the Virgin. The church has been

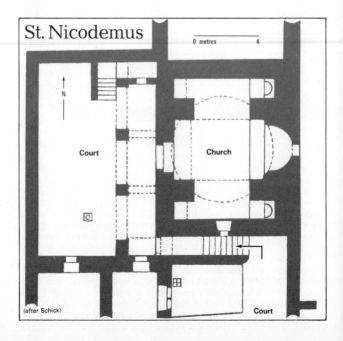

rebuilt and rededicated to St. Nicodemus, but an ancient pot is shown from which it is said the Patriarch Sophronius (7C) gave lentils to the poor.

Returning to the top of the lane, turn left to descend to the TARIQ BAB SITTI MARYAM, and turn left to rejoin the main route at the bottom of SHARI'A MUHAMMAD DARWISH. **End of diversion**.

Again continuing W along the TARIQ BAB SITTI MARYAM, a few metres from this point on the S side of the road, the frontage contains the right jamb of a *Mamluk doorway* in red and cream coursed masonry set within a moulded frame, with part of a joggled string course inlaid in black. This was the location in the 19C and early 20C of the **Second Station of the Cross**, the Scala Sancta of the Via Dolorosa of the Christians, believed to be the entrance to Pilate's Praetorium by which Jesus departed the Praetorium and outside which he took up the cross. Tradition links a staircase on this site with the 28 marble steps said to have been taken by St. Helena to Rome and installed in front of the Lateran Palace by Pope Sixtus VI in 1589. The doorway may have been the original N entrance of the Subaybiyya, the early 15C madrasa and tomb of a Mamluk official (Rte 2B) which became inaccessible when the Ottoman barracks and later the school were built on the Antonia.

On the S side of the street is the site of the **Antonia fortress** of Herod the Great, now occupied by the 'Umariyya Boys' School. On the N side is the Monastery of the Flagellation, and to the W the Convent of the Sisters of Sion. The history of this area is best treated as a whole.

History of the Antonia Fortress. The high rock peak NW of the Temple may be the location of the Hananel Tower rebuilt by Nehemiah (Neh. 3:1) which still had a garrison of 500 in Ptolemaic times. Antiochus IV Ephiphanes destroyed it in 167 BC. A new tower, of Baris, was rebuilt perhaps by Judas Maccabeus, but more likely by Hyrcanus I (134–104 BC). It was surrendered to Pompey in 63 BC, and to Herod in 37 BC who rebuilt it probably between 37 and 35 BC and named it Antonia in honour of his friend and patron Mark Anthony. Either Herod or his predecessors supplied it with water by cutting a stepped rectangular pool (the Struthion Pool) in the rock to the NW which was filled by rain water brought by aqueduct and channel from the slopes further to the NW. The fortress is described by Josephus (War V:238–45) as set on a precipitous rock, covered with flagstones both decorative and defensive, with a wall with four high corner towers enclosing a main tower. The Herodian N and W porticoes of the Temple were set against the rock scarp below to the S and could be entered from the fortress. The fortress was probably restricted to the top of the rock scarp, an area today c 120m × 45m. A wall, c 4m in width which runs E–W along the S edge of the scarp as far as the Is'irdiya Khanqah (Rte 2B), is the S wall of the Herodian fortress. The fortress was probably not the Praetorium at which Pontius Pilate condemned Jesus to death, more likely to have been at the old Herodian palace on the site of the present citadel.

After the expulsion of the Roman garrison from the Antonia in AD 66, it was occupied by the Jews during the First Jewish Revolt, and was one of the principal points of attack in the siege laid by Titus in AD 70. After capturing the Third and Second North Walls of the city (War V:302 and 331), Titus raised earthworks opposite the Antonia which were completed by mid-June and are described (War V:466): 'Of the first two, that at Antonia was thrown up by the V Legion over against the middle of the pool called Struthion (alternatively according to Maurer "in the middle of the pool"), the other by the XII Legion about 20 cubits away'. The defenders in the Antonia dug a mine right up to the wood and earth ramp, and destroyed it by fire. After building the siege wall around the city, Titus had the earthworks rebuilt. The second ramps were much larger and took 21 days to complete (War V:523; VI:5). The Jewish attack on them in mid-July failed, and Roman siege engines were brought up. At that point the wall of the Antonia collapsed into the mine dug for the first earthworks; and after a few delays, the Antonia was captured by the Romans on the 24 July; some of the Romans then got into the Temple precinct through the mine. Shortly after, the Antonia was razed (VI:43) to permit an easy approach for the final attack on the Temple itself. The description does not clarify the problem of the location of the Second and Third North Walls of the city, for it is apparent that Titus was already inside them and working against the Antonia.

In c 135 as part of the new Roman city, a magnificent pavement was laid over the Struthion pool, parts of which can be seen in the Convents of the Flagellation and the Sisters of Sion. It may be the site of a forum. It used to be thought that the triple gate of which the Ecce Homo Arch was the centre was first built as a triumphal arch in Hadrian's city (like the one that stood at the E side of the forum off the cardo, see Russian Mission in Exile, Rte 4); it has now been proposed that it was originally a city gate of the time of Herod Agrippa (AD 41–44) or earlier, like that at the Damascus Gate (the upper part of which was rebuilt by Hadrian).

Numerous late Christian traditions have grown up around this area, based on the supposition that the Antonia was the Praetorium of Pontius Pilate, where the events described in John 18:28–19:16 took place: the flogging and the condemnation of Jesus; and from which he was led out to be crucified. The pavement in particular has been associated with the tribunal and the mocking of Jesus by the Roman soldiers. Hence since the 13C the Via Dolorosa has started in this vicinity.

The Monastery of the Flagellation. Crusader churches of the Flagellation and Condemnation of Jesus were located here, and the traditions were particularly strong by the 14C when the Antonia escarpment above was inaccessible to Christians. Pilgrims in the 17C say the building was being used as a stable by the Ottoman Mustafa Bey c 1623–40. When he had a room for his harem built above it, the building collapsed at once (Roger, 1632). In 1719 it was being used by a Turkish weaver, but pilgrims were admitted on payment of a candle. The Franciscans were given the site by Ibrahim Pasha and restored and enlarged the chapel of the Flagellation in 1839. It was completely rebuilt in 1927–29 (architect Barluzzi). In 1901–03 they excavated the remains of a nearly square three-aisled medieval chapel in which four columns had supported the dome over the Roman pavement. This was later rebuilt as the Chapel of the Condemnation.

Visit. Entering the court, to the right is the *Chapel of the Flagellation*, a single-aisled chapel; a gold dome over the altar is decorated with the crown of thorns. The cloister contains various sculpted fragments found in excavations. On the W or left side of the court is the *Chapel of the Condemnation*. This early 20C chapel rebuilt on medieval foundations, with four central columns of pink marble, contains a section of the pavement of the 2C the larger part of which can be seen next door in the Convent of the Sisters of Sion. *Striated slabs* indicate the line of the Roman road. The Chapel is the **First Station of the Cross** in the Franciscan procession, marking the place where Pilate condemned Jesus. The **Second Station**, where Jesus took up the Cross, is in the entrance to the court.

The '**Umariyya Boys' School**, the site of the Antonia fortress, is approached by a flight of steps on the S side of the street almost opposite the entrance to the Monastery of the Flagellation. It also marks the First Station of the Cross. It is the site of the *Baris and Antonia fortresses* built by the Hasmoneans and Herod the Great respectively.

History. The Antonia was razed in AD 70 and most of the remains on the site are of a later date. The Byzantine tradition seems to have placed the Praetorium, and the Church of St. Sophia (of the Holy Wisdom, the House of Pilate) somewhere to the W or S towards the Tyropoeon Valley. It was destroyed by the Persians in 614, is mentioned in the 8C, but thereafter seems to have disappeared. The Crusaders found it difficult to locate the site of Pilate's House, but built a 'Chapel of the Repose' where Jesus spent the night after his arrest at this site. The site became inaccessible after 1187, and by the 13C the commemoration was at the Church of the Flagellation. The 12C Crusader Chapel of the Repose was converted into an Ayyubid tomb c 1200, and a Mamluk madrasa, the Jawuliyya, was built in 1315/20 adjacent to it. The complex was renovated in 1469 when the Jawuliyya seems first to have been converted into a government administrative headquarters. The Mamluk Governor of Jerusalem gave judgements from his seat in the iwan. The Ottoman governors seem to have retained the arrangement. Amico (1594–97) notes that the building was still being used as a praetorium, just as when Jesus was condemned to death. In 1835 in the time of Ibrahim Pasha, the complex was rebuilt as a barracks for the Ottoman garrison. In 1864 the former Chapel of the Repose was being used as a grain store for the artillery horses. In 1914 the Ottoman governor was still receiving visitors in the Jawuliyya. In 1923/4 the complex was converted to a school. The dome over the 13C tomb was demolished after the earthquake of 1927.

Excavations and studies: Clermont-Ganneau 1873–74; Vincent 1910–13, 1956; Benoit 1974; Burgoyne and Richards 1987.

Visit. Accessible out of school hours. On entering the courtyard of the school, opposite are the oldest remains in the complex which back onto the Haram. The lower rooms at the W end are pre-Mamluk vaulted structures. Towards the centre is a high arch which was originally the S *iwan of the Jawuliyya madrasa*, built by Sanjar al-Jawuli in 1315–20. He may have been a Kurd, from Diyarbakr in modern SE Turkey, and was a high Mamluk official. The iwan is flanked by two vaulted chambers, and all the recesses and windows at the back are cut through a massive 4m-wide pre-existing wall, probably that of the Herodian Antonia. The five Mamluk windows with coursed red and cream masonry can be viewed from the Haram (Rte 2B). From these windows one can gain a good idea of the way the Antonia fortress controlled the Temple area from above. Above the iwan arch, on the N side, are two heraldic blazons with two lines and a dot incised within a circle, probably those of the founder. The madrasa originally extended to the N with a court surrounded by cells on the W, N and E sides. It was entered from the N. All that part of the madrasa was destroyed in 1923/4.

Immediately W (or right) of the madrasa are the remains of the 12C *Chapel of the Repose* built c 1160 by the Templars on the site where it was thought Jesus rested in prison after his arrest in Gethsemane. The small chapel, like the Jawuliyya, is also built against the massive Herodian wall, with a curiously angled window cutting through the wall itself. On the N side were a vestibule and a domed chamber. The chapel vestibule was probably the original location of the four capitals showing angels ministering to Jesus which were re-used in the nearby al-Ghawanima minaret in the 13C. The domed chamber of the chapel was made into the tomb of an Ayyubid Amir, Shaikh Darbas al-Kurdi al-Hakkari c 1200. Several of the Kurdish tribe of the Hakkari fought with Salah al-Din. This large domed porch, with pointed-arched openings and drum, dome and cupola, was demolished after the earthquake of 1927, and only a modern low cenotaph now marks the Shaikh's grave. All the modern buildings on the E side belong to the school (1923/4). The rest of the structures around the complex are mainly Ottoman.

Returning to the street, continue to the next cross-roads and the visitors' entrance on the E side of the ***Convent of the Sisters of Sion**. This was founded as an orphanage and convent in 1857 and is now a hospice. The Convent contains a large part of the pavement or 'Lithostratos' laid over the Struthion Pool, and the N lateral arch of the Roman 'Ecce Homo' arch which can be seen in the street outside.

Excavations and studies: Pierotti (1851–64); Clermont-Ganneau

1873–74); Vincent (1954); Marie-Aline de Sion (1955); Maurer (1964); Benoit (1974); Blomme (1979). A visitor's centre and shop, and excellent tour route is provided. Open daily except Sunday 8.30–12.30, 14.00–1700.

The Struthion pool (the 'Sparrow Pool', or the Double Pool). This is a rock-cut water cistern with stepped edges, oriented NW–SE, 52m × 14m and c 4.5m–5.5m deep, with the floor stepping down towards the SE, and was originally an open tank or pool, cut in the 2/1C BC. A channel runs from the SW corner to the Temple area where it is cut by the Herodian wall. It was fed by channel from the Damascus gate area where rainwater was collected from the higher slopes. The pool was outside the Antonia, for Titus in AD 70 laid one of his siege ramps in the middle of the pool. The pool was roofed over in the 2C with impressive barrel vaults which add c 8m to the height of the cistern. What can be seen today is only a small part, c 27m × 5.9m, for the E half of the pool lies beyond the partition wall with round arches on the left of the viewing platform; the wall behind to the N is ancient, blocking off c 10m; and the wall at the far S end, with pointed vault, is modern and blocks off another c 13m. It was emptied of debris in 1934/5 and today is filled by ducts leading from the roof of the convent. (for S end, see p.88).

The Pavement, or *lithostraton* in Greek, *gabbatha* in Aramaic, is believed by some to be that pavement mentioned in John 19:13 where Pilate took his seat at the tribunal. The accepted date is later, c 135, the pavement being laid for a Hadrianic forum on the contemporary vaults over the Struthion pool below.

The pavement is c 48m N–S and 32m E–W; slabs of *mizzi ahmar* variously rectangular and square, often 1m in length and 30–35cm thick, have been laid on cement. The area of the street in the S part is striated to prevent horses slipping, but all the slabs are polished by long wear. Channels and drains led rainwater to the cistern below. Incised on the surface are various games, including one described as the 'King's Game' in which the winner lands on a sword. It is a game likely to have been played by soldiers, and it used to be held that the soldiers of the Praetorium might have played this game with those about to be executed. The pavement now lies c 2m beneath the present road.

The Ecce Homo Arch can be seen as we leave the convent. Tradition holds that it is the place outside the Praetorium to which Pilate led Jesus to show him to the Jews and said 'Behold the Man' (John 19:5). The central arch bridges the Tariq Bab Sitti Maryam and has since the 13C been part of the Christian Via Dolorosa. An inscription (medieval) on the W face reads TOLLE TOLLE CRUCIFIGE EUM. The N arch was revealed in 1851 during heavy rain when adjacent walls collapsed; it was later incorporated in the chapel of the Sisters of Sion and can be seen by entering a door off the TARIQ BAB SITTI MARYAM which leads into a vestibule at the W end of the chapel of the Sisters of Sion. The arch stands at the E end of the church. The S arch has been destroyed, but the footing was recorded in the Darvish al-Uzbakiyya building opposite. The Triple Arch has usually been attributed to Hadrian c 135 as a triumphal arch at his E forum, on the pavement on which it was said to stand, and which purpose it undoubtedly served in the 2C. A recent study (Blomme) has maintained that the sober if not severe style, the mouldings, the plan and proportions, which are closely paralleled by the Augustan gate at Aosta (and also those at Nîmes and Autun in France) indicate that it must have been built originally by Herod Agrippa I (AD 41–44) or earlier, and served as the E gate of the city. The footings are now said to extend beneath the pavement, and to pre-date it. The gate is c 19m wide, with the central arch being 5.20m wide and 6.25m high; the N lateral arch is 2.36m wide and 5.22m high. The mouldings can be seen on both sides of the arch. Barely legible Greek inscriptions discovered between the N and the central arches and above the main arch are of uncertain date, but must belong either to the 1C BC–AD or to the Byzantine period, for Hadrianic civic inscriptions are in Latin. The structures above the arch are later, belonging to the building on the S side of the road.

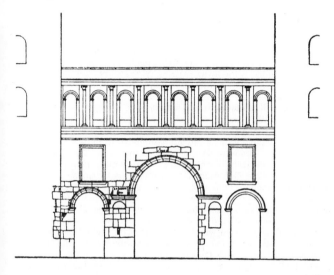

Reconstruction of the Ecce Homo Arch (Y. Blomme, Revue Biblique, 1979, p. 260, fig. 7).

Continuing W on the TARIQ BAB SITTI MARYAM walk down towards one of the main ancient streets of Jerusalem, the *Tariq al-Wad* (the *Valley Road*, following the Tyropoeon valley). On the N side before the junction is the *Austrian Hospice*, founded in 1863.

To the right the TARIQ AL-WAD ascends to the Damascus Gate (Rte 1); to the left it continues down the Tyropoeon Valley. Turning left, in the surface of the street some slabs of the *striated paved road* of the Roman-Byzantine city have been relaid after excavation some 3m below the present surface. This was one of the main porticoed streets of the city from the 2C–7C.

Immediately on our left is the *Polish Catholic Chapel* (usually closed), which marks the **Third Station of the Cross**, where Jesus fell. In the 19C this station was marked by a fallen column at the side of the street against the façade of the ruined 16C(?) bath house, the *Hammam al-Sultan.* Immediately S of it is the entrance to the *Armenian Catholic Patriarchate* and the *Church of Our Lady of the Spasm*, which marks the **Fourth Station of the Cross**, where Mary met Jesus.

History. In the 19C most of the ruins on this site were those of the Hammam al-Sultan. The E section of the ruins was used as a stable by the Pasha. In 1864 the one Armenian Catholic monk in Jerusalem purchased the land, as the traditional sites of the Third and Fourth Stations of the Cross. Excavations (Clermont-Ganneau, 1874) revealed mosaics 5.75m beneath the surface. The remains associated with the mosaics appeared to be those of a three-aisled Crusader cruciform church, possibly of the 13C. In the S apse was a patch of fine 5/6C mosaic, blackened by fire and depicting two sandals. The motif of two sandals is known elsewhere in Byzantine contexts which are not necessarily Christian or ecclesiatical, including almost identical mosaic sandals in a tomb near the Church of St. Peter in Gallicantu (Rte 8) and some in a bath house at Timgad in Tunisia. It is possible the site is that of a Byzantine bath house. Tradition holds these footprints mark those of Mary and the commemoration on the site seems to have started by at least the 13/14C; at the end of the 16C Amico locates the place where Jesus met his mother near this site. The modern church was built in 1881 on the older remains.

The streets which lead E and W off the TARIQ AL-WAD contain much of interest, in particular numerous Mamluk foundations. The first street to the left is the DARAJ AL-SARAY, leading to the *Haram Gate*, the *Bab al-Ghawanima* (Rte 2B) and the site of the *Old Saray* (palace of the governor). At c 80m on the left is the *Zawiyat al-Afghanistaniyya*, dating from 1630/31.

Follow the first turning to the right (or W) off the Tariq al-Wad, the TARIQ AL-ALAM or AL-SARAY, and continue the route of the Via Dolorosa. Immediately on the left is the modern **Fifth Station of the Cross**, where Simon of Cyrene took up the Cross. This station was previously located further S down Tariq al-Wad, at the site known as the *House of the Rich Man*. This (and the nearby *House of the Poor Man*) are dwellings built in the 14C. Continuing along Tariq al-Alam, at c 50m on the left is the *Zawiya Zahiriyya(?)* of the 15C(?). A little more than half-way up the hill, just beyond a turning to the left and where a vault covers the street, is, on the left, the *Church of the Holy Face and St. Veronica* which marks the **Sixth Station of the Cross**. The tradition that St. Veronica gave her handkerchief to the Lord and received it back with the imprint of his face goes back to the mid-14C. The story has varied much in the course of the centuries. In the 3C–4C it was believed that a drop of Jesus' blood fell from his head; in the 12C the story developed and included the handkerchief used to wipe his face. By the 13C the story included the imprint of his face on the handkerchief. The site seems to be associated with a Byzantine church, the 'House of Cosmas and Damian', the *Anarguri* or 'penniless'. Their birthplace is mentioned in the Commemoratorium in the early 9C and may be the same place as their 12C house (which was located between Golgotha and the present Church of the Spasm). The likelihood of the identification is increased by the finding of a damaged inscription on the site which mentions 'the holy A . . .' (plural), possibly the 'Anarguri'. The present church thus marks the site of an old church and a medieval tradition.

At the top of the street and at the NW angle of the junction with KHAN AL-ZAIT ST is the **Seventh Station of the Cross**, the *Porta Judicaria, Gate of Judgement*, where tradition holds that the sentence of death was posted. This station was included in the route of the Via Dolorosa in the 14C to prove to confused pilgrims that the place of Crucifixion and burial lay outside the city. (For the remainder of the Via Dolorosa, see Rte 4). Turning left, continue for c 55m along Khan al-Zait St and take the next left turning, into the 'AQABAT AL-TAKIYYA. In the SE angle of the junction lies the *Khan al-Zait*, a large vaulted hall with four aisles divided by two rows of four pillars. The pillars, with rather poor capitals, extend below the present floor level to the base of rock-cut cisterns. Probably originally a market, the khan was later a soap factory and the cisterns were used for storing olive oil. Shops line the W side, and a number of columns in the vicinity probably derive from the Roman-Byzantine cardo maximus.

Continuing down the ʿAqabat al-Takiyya, at c 110m on the right is one of the most important Mamluk monuments in Jerusalem, the **ʿDar al-Sitt Tunshuq**, a palace built by the Lady Tunshuq in 1388.

History. Little is known of this lady, who was living in Jerusalem by 1391/2 and is buried in her mausoleum opposite, for the building has no founder's inscription. It is possible that she was a Muzaffarid princess from the E, a refugee from the invasion of Timur. According to Mujir al-Din the street was called Market St before the palace was built. In 1552, Khassaki Sultan, the favourite wife of the Ottoman Sultan Sulaiman II established a charitable foundation in the complex, which included a Sufi convent, a soup kitchen for the poor, a caravanserai and stables. Because of its charitable function, 19C Christians regarded the place as the 4C Hospital of St. Helena. In the late 19C part of the building became the residence of the Ottoman governor (the new saray). In the 20C an orphanage for 150 boys was established here, the entrance to which is from the S.

The building is not open to visitors, but the façade is of interest. The main part consists of three portals. The central portal is the widest and least impressive. It has an unusual cinquefoil arch of red, black and cream masonry, and was intended as the entrance to the ground-floor stables. The tall W portal is now blocked, but is finely decorated. It has a moulded frame, red and cream masonry and a joggled string course. There is a rectangular window with inlaid star-pattern border above the door, which includes turquoise faience inlay. The inscription is from the Koran, Sura XV:46–55. This was the most important entrance, leading to a great reception hall and other chambers on an upper floor. The large circular window between the two doors gives onto the main hall. To the E is a third ornate portal, also blocked, which leads to an open yard. It is the most impressive entrance, with a deep recess, red and cream masonry framed by a red band and mouldings, with a joggled string course above the lintel. Above this are four tiers of muqarnas supporting a colourful semi-dome. Between these elements is an elaborate inlaid panel. Although a less important door, the decorative emphasis has been placed here to balance the ornate doorway of the mausoleum opposite. This is the only Mamluk palace known in Jerusalem.

The *Mausoleum of Sitt Tunshuq* opposite the E portal on the N side of the street was completed before 1398 when the lady died. It was converted to domestic use between 1720 and 1920, when a new doorway was cut on the W side of the original portal. The portal contains red, black and cream masonry and the doorway has a monolithic lintel with an undercut joggled string course. The inlaid strap-work in the tympanum compares with that on the palace opposite. The domed tomb chamber lies on the right side. It has a pair of windows with marble lintels, joggled relieving arches and marble inlay, with joggled string course above. The façade is capped by a parapet of finials. The dome, whose apex is 11.94m above the floor of the tomb chamber, is supported on a drum with 12 pointed-arched windows. The interior of the tomb chamber has a cenotaph on the floor and tomb beneath; a mihrab in the S wall has re-used Crusader capitals and a joggled pointed arch of rare marbles, with marble strapwork in the spandrels. The conch (and until 1935 other parts of the walls) has rare carved stucco work of probably eastern Islamic inspiration.

Adjacent to the E side of the E portal of the palace, a fourth portal, with an Ottoman trefoil arch, led to part of the Khassaki Sultan's charitable foundation. In the 1860s granaries, horse-turned flour-mills, ovens and kitchens in the complex still produced free food for the poor.

At the E end of the 'AQABAT TAKIYYA, on the S side, is the *Maktab Bairam Jawish*, or the *Madrasa Rasasiyya*, of 1540. This is an early Ottoman structure which retains many Mamluk features. It was built as a school and dwelling house by the Amir Bairam Jawish, and named 'Rasasiyya' because of the use of lead plates to bond the masonry. The façade has red and cream coursed masonry, with a central course of basalt. A compact façade set in a moulded frame surrounds a shallow portal recess. The doorway has a joggled relieving arch; the façade has three grilled windows. The central and most interesting feature is the pointed arch with chevron mouldings above, which is typical of the early Ottoman style in Jerusalem, especially that of Sulaiman II. The arch contains a fluted conch. The main room on the upper floor, now a classroom in the present school, was a mosque and contains a mihrab with polychrome panelling. The dome is set on muqarnas pendentives.

After crossing the Tariq al-Wad, follow the street leading ahead to the E, the TARIQ BAB AL-NAZIR or 'ALA' AL-DIN; note on the corner to the left the fountain built by Sulaiman II in 1537, the *Sabil Tariq Bab al-Nazir* or *Sabil al-Haram*. A heavy cornice surmounts the elaborate pointed arch, with corner columns with muqarnas capitals, and inner small columns with grotesquely twisted shafts. At c 50m on the left is the *Hasaniyya*, the Madrasa of Husam al-Din al-Hasan, of 1434. He was the Superintendent of the Two Harams and a governor of Jerusalem. The rooms are all at first floor level in a rather plain façade. Near the E end is a window which retains some of its original gadrooned voussoirs and gives onto the assembly hall of the madrasa, containing a very fine marble dado and mihrab (not open). Adjacent to the E but at ground floor level, is the entrance to the *Ribat of 'Ala' al-Din*, a hospice for poor pilgrims built 1267/8 by 'Ala' al-Din Aydughdi al-Basir, a Mamluk of the Ayyubid Sultan al-Salih Ayyub, and then of Baybars. He became blind, and took the office of Superintendent of the Two Harams under Baybars and Qala'un. By 1537 he was referred to as a wali (saint) and a shaikh. The building had a lively history, for in Ottoman times it was given as dwelling to the Sudanese Muslims who served as Haram guards. Later it became a prison for those who had been sentenced (hence the modern name Habs al-Dam, Prison of Blood), until the prison was moved to the Russian Compound (Rte 14) in Mandate times. It is now inhabited by the African community.

The façade is heterogeneous, including a doorway with an Ottoman lintel. On the E the rectangular window of the founder's tomb-chamber has its original iron grille. The interior (in private occupation) has a large open court with cells around the W, N and E sides and an assembly hall on the S which was converted into a mosque for the African community in 1971.

Adjacent to the E is the *Manjakiyya*, the madrasa (1361) of Manjak al-Yusufi an official of al-Nasir Muhammad who had a rather chequered career and died in Cairo in 1375. He did much building work in Cairo, Damascus and elswhere as well as this madrasa in Jerusalem. Built partly above the West Portico of the Haram (Rte 2B), the Manjakiyya had reached a ruinous state early in the 20C; it was reconstructed in 1921/2 and now houses the Awqaf Department of Endowments and Islamic Affairs, which is entered by a modern portal from the N side of the gate chamber of the Bab al-Nazir. The original entrance is adjacent to the W. It has corner columns with muqarnas capitals and three tiers of muqarnas corbelling supporting the dome above.

The outer porch of the Haram gate, *Bab al-Nazir*, has a semicircular frontal arch rebuilt c 1204 but with traces of earlier springing which may be Umayyad. The inscription on the wooden door indicates that it was renewed in c 1204. On the S side of the gate is the *Wafaʾiyya*, the zawiya of the Abuʾl-Wafa family, of 1380/1, much of which is possibly Ayyubid, a complex of probably pre-existing rooms bought by the family in the late 14C. The narrow frontage includes the shop in the outer gate porch, and the adajcent window and door. The upper part of the plain frontage is Ottoman.

Much of the S side of the street is occupied by the *Ribat al-Mansuri*, a pilgrim hospice built by the Sultan Qalaʾun in 1282/3 for poor Sufis and pilgrims. He also built a hospice and hospital in Hebron. Like the Ribat of ʿAlaʾ al-Din opposite, in Ottoman times the hospice housed the Sudanese Haram guards, then became a prison for those awaiting sentence (modern name Habs al-Ribat, the Prison Hospice). It also now houses the African community.

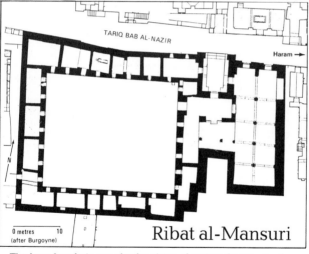

TARIQ BAB AL-NAZIR

Haram →

N

0 metres   10
(after Burgoyne)

Ribat al-Mansuri

The long façade is complex by virtue of various fragments of pre- and post-Mamluk stonework. Traces of earlier structures include the marble imposts of the main portal which may be re-used Crusader stones; towards the W end of the façade a change of alignment marked by a vertical cyma moulding may be part of a Crusader doorway (Burgoyne). Various sources refer to a Crusader church dedicated to St. Michael or to St. John the Evangelist (Pringle) in this area. According to Mujir al-Din a Byzantine church was occupied by two madrasas to the W of the hospice (the Yunusiyya and the Jarakisiyya). It seems likely that a Crusader church in the vicinity may have provided spolia for Ayyubid and Mamluk construction work. The Mamluk work includes two fine windows at the E end of the ground floor, which give onto the assembly hall. Above them is an unusual cornice with 20 table consoles (re-used Crusader work?) separated by fluted and scalloped conches. A wide pointed arch with red and cream voussoirs fronts the deep entrance porch which has benches and re-used Roman-Byzantine paving slabs. The founder's inscription is at the rear.

The W part of the façade has five plain windows. The upper façade contains later elements, most notable among which is an upper doorway to the right of the main entrance, once approached by lateral stairs. After the removal of the stairs it was converted into a window. The pointed arch with chevron ornament and a rosette in the tympanum is typical of the time of Sulaiman II, and probably dates to the mid-16C. The interior (not open) has a vestibule which leads on the E to a large hall with vaulting supported by an unusual row of four columns with early Mamluk(?) capitals. To the W is an exceptionally large open courtyard c 28m × 23m, with cells around the N, W and S sides. A cenotaph occupies a central cell on the N side.

Returning to the Tariq al-Wad, turn left to continue S. The next turning to the left is the twisting TARIQ BAB AL-HADID, which leads to the Haram gate of the same name. It contains six more monuments of the Mamluk period. At c 45m on the right at a junction of the lane leading S to the Suq al-Qattanin, the SW side is occupied by the entrance to the *Hanbaliyya*, the madrasa of Baidamur al-Khwarizmi, 1380. He was a Mamluk official who was several times imprisoned and finally arrested as implicated in a plot against Sultan Barquq. The complex, a spacious Mamluk complex with cells around a court with a fine iwan and mihrab is now occupied by small houses. The entrance portal, with a pointed-arched recess, has benches, and the doorway has a monolithic lintel with a flat relieving arch of red and black joggled voussoirs.

Continuing almost to the Bab al-Hadid, where the lane ends, the left side of the lane is occupied by two Mamluk *pilgrim hospices*. The largest frontage is that of the *Jawhariyya madrasa and ribat* built by Jawhar al-Qunuqbayi in 1440. He was an Abyssinian eunuch who rose to power under Sultan al-Ashraf Barsbay as Treasurer, then as Steward of the Royal Harem under al-Malik al-Zahir Jaqmaq. His hospice and school is built on two levels, the upper extending E over the adjoining hospice and the W portico and gate of the Haram. The lower façade, including the founder's inscription above the door, was damaged before 1914; the building was further damaged by subsidence due to tunnelling in the substructure in 1971 (the Jewish Religious area at the Wilson's Arch area, Rte 2A); and restored in 1982/3. It now houses the Department of Islamic Archaeology. The recessed entrance portal, with red and cream masonry framed by moulding, has two windows to the main hall on the right side. The most interesting parts of the remaining façade are those of the upper level to the E which contains three rectangular wndows; that on the E is plain, the central and W windows have roundels of carved chevron work above them; the central window also has three tiers of muqarnas work at the top; the W window has an incised diaper-work frame. The assembly hall of the madrasa above the Haram gate and portico has been demolished, but above the gate porch a blocked window remains, with a pointed arch with chevron voussoirs and its original iron grille. The intervening ground floor façade adjacent to the gate is that of the *Ribat Kurt*, built 1293/4 by Sayf al-Din Kurt, a brave soldier and a good Amir of Sultans Lajin and al-Nasir Muhammad, who died fighting the Mongols in 1299. The hospice is the oldest structure adjacent to the gate, and it may be that its foundation was the reason the gate was placed here. The gate (the Bab al-Hadid) and the twisted street, which is not on the alignment of the older city grid, may both belong to this period. The gate itself is first mentioned in the work of al-'Umari.

The S side of the street contains two other Mamluk foundations. Adjacent to the Haram is the *Arghuniyya, the madrasa and tomb of Arghun al-Kamili, a former governor of Damascus, who completed the building in 1358, when he also renewed the Bab al-Hadid (Rte 2B). He was a court official who became the Master of the Robes as is indicated by the blazon on his inscription. The façade is symmetrical except for the entrance doorway to the Khatuniyya on the right. It has coursed red and cream masonry framed by a moulding and contains a tall entrance portal flanked by windows. The portal, with pointed-arched recess and benches, has the founder's inscription running right round the recess with blazons showing a napkin in the middle of a shield with three fields. Above the lintel is a marble inlaid representation of a joggled relieving arch; and above, a frieze of joggling which extends around the façade. The windows on either side have the same delicate mouldings, and inlaid marble interlocking trefoils above. The E window, into the tomb chamber, has its original iron grille; the W window has been converted into a door. Features of the façade recall tombs in Damascus, and perhaps craftsmen were brought from there. The upper sections are part of Ottoman structures built on the roof. The original entrance to the interior court was blocked in 1931.

On the W side is the simple pointed-arched entry to the *Khatuniyya Madrasa* of 1354-1380 (Rte 2B). A long (14.45m) groin-vaulted passage leads to an open court enclosed by cells on S, N and W sides, with the larger chambers on the E side used for burials in the present century. The court has a decorated E façade, and some re-used Crusader elbow brackets in the N and S façades.

On the W of the Khatuniyya portal is the façade of the *Muzhiriyya Madrasa* built by Abu Bakr b. Muzhir in 1480/1, a Mamluk official perhaps of a family from Nablus; it was later used as a domestic residence and is now rather ruinous. It consists of a rather symmetrical arrangement of two storeys of rooms around an open court, with an iwan with red and cream voussoirs on the S side, and a well recess on the W wall with gadrooned voussoirs. The mihrab in the iwan has complex panelling and marble columns in the nook shafts with Mamluk bases and capitals. The upper floor originally extended to an elaborate assembly hall over the W portico of the Haram, which was demolished in 1925. The façade has a tall portal in a framed red and cream panel. The trefoil-arched recess has eight tiers of muqarnas corbelling; above the door lintel is a string course with black and yellow joggling. To either side above is an identical pair of double windows with pointed horseshoe arches divided by a marble shaft. Below on the E side a fine pair of rectangular windows with grilles have four tiers of muqarnas work above and greyish marble lintels. The relieving arches above the lintels have light arabesque tracery on alternate yellow stone voussoirs, also to be seen two courses above.

Returning to the Tariq al-Wad, turn left and continue S for c 65m, and on the left is the entrance to the *Suq al-Qattanin** or the **Market of the Cotton Merchants**. This is a splendid Mamluk bazaar

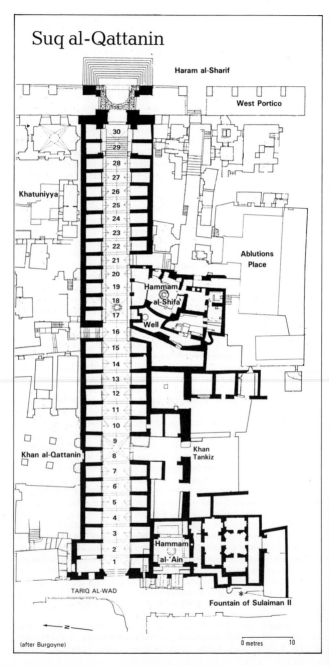

Suq al-Qattanin

Haram al-Sharif

West Portico

30
29
28
27
26
25
24
23
22
21
20
19
18
17
16
15
14
13
12
11
10
9
8
7
6
5
4
3
2
1

Khatuniyya

Ablutions Place

Hammam al-Shifa

Well

Khan al-Qattanin

Khan Tankiz

Hammam al-'Ain

TARIQ AL-WAD

Fountain of Sulaiman II

(after Burgoyne)

0 metres   10

completed in 1336/7, built by Tankiz al-Nasiri for the Sultan al-Nasir Muhammad. It was a rubbish dump by the 19C, repaired c 1890; the W end was restored in 1919, and extensively restored by the Awqaf in 1974. As well as a long covered market street with shops on either side and fine gates at both ends, there are living quarters above the shops, two bath houses and a caravanserai.

The W portal has a pointed-arched recess containing a flat lintel with seven interlocking voussoirs, with relieving arch and circular oculus in the tympanum. The four lower courses of masonry may be earlier Crusader work. It is a much less ornate gate than that at the E end (for which see Rte 2B). Inside, the covered street is 95m long, with vaulted roof and 30 pairs of side bays most of which contain shops on the ground floor and living or storage space above. The W end shows different construction to the E and may originally have been a Crusader market extended to the E by Tankiz. On the N exterior side, approached by stairs from bay 16, is a corridor providing access to the living accomodation. On the ground floor to the N of bays 6–10 is a vaulted hall which may have been part of a caravanserai (the Khan al-Qattanin) founded by Zaynab al-Khassakiyya, the wife of Sultan Inal (1453–61). To the NE is the Khatuniyya Madrasa (see above).

Steps at bay 29 lead up to the *elaborate gate* at the Haram end of the suq, which has two inscriptions on the W face of the original wooden doors.

There are numerous structures on the S side of the suq which are an integral part of the layout. Leading to the S off bay 21 is an entrance to the *Ablutions Place* of the Haram built by al-ʿAdil in 1193 (Rte 2B). The S side of the adjacent bays 20 to 17 contain the frontage (a blocked wide porch) of the *Hammam al-Shifaʾ*, a bath house built by 1330 with a curious alignment which may indicate it had an older predecessor. It is built on the traditional Roman-Byzantine bath house model, with the entrance leading to a changing room, and cold, warm and hot rooms served by a furnace or boiler. The bathing rooms are lit by domes with small glazed shafts. The main changing room has a marble floor, and a central octagonal oculus above a tank with a fountain made from a Byzantine basket capital which still retains its CHI-RHO monogram. In the NW of the bath house a well-shaft descends through accumulated debris for 26m to a water source, with a rock-cut passage to a deeper pool. This rather poor and bad-tasting source of water was investigated in the 19C. The water seeps from a subterranean source in the Tyropoeon valley.

A broad arch at the S side of bays 8–9 leads to the *Khan Tankiz*, a caravanserai. In the early 20C the khan contained a flour mill, and was a farm in the 1960s. It is now very ruinous. A wide passage flanked by four bays (shops) leads to the doorway, which is 2.7m wide with a monolithic lintel and a relieving arch containing three very large stones. The founder's inscription is carved on the keystone of the relieving arch, on the lintel and on the corbels which support it. The blazon of Tankiz is carved on the lintel and the corbels, showing a cup on a circular field. Inside little remains of the original squarish court off which opened cell-like rooms. There may have been an upper storey.

Immediately adjacent to bays 1–3 at the W end is the *Hammam al-ʿAin*, built by 1330.

Leaving the suq, turn left and the bath house entrance is in the Tariq al-Wad. In 1812 it was reported to be in a ruinous condition; it was restored by the Department of Islamic Archaeology in 1984. A fairly modern porch and steps lead down to the changing room roofed by a dome on pendentives. It also has a central tank with fountain, and raised alcoves around the walls for changing. It was originally paved with coloured marble, only a small fragment of which survives in a W subsidiary room of the warm room. A large tank in the SW of the bath house served the fountain built against the outer wall of the bath house, the *Sabil Tariq al-Wad*, built by Sulaiman II in 1536. This can be seen on the left about 20m S of the bath house entrance. A pointed-arched recess with archivolt supported by built columns and acanthus-style capitals has three tiers of muqarnas corbelling in the semi-dome, and the founder's inscription beneath. An ancient sarcophagus with three roundels, probably dating to the 1C AD, has been employed as the water trough.

Almost opposite the entrance to the Suq al-Qattanin, 'AQABAT AL-KHALIDIYYA leads W. At c 20m on the right a blacksmith's workshop occupies a well-preserved *Crusader church*, uncertainly identified as that of St. Julian (mentioned in a document of 1177) (Bahat and Solar) or possibly of St. John the Evangelist (Becker). A three-aisled basilica with three apses, it has two rows of three piers, all with cornice mouldings. These, with wall pilasters, support the groined-vaulted roof. The N and central apses are preserved, and contain windows. The central apse has a rectangular exterior chevet. The floor may have been 2m lower than the present surface. Much of the S, N and W walls has been rebuilt. The interior dimensions are 14.80m × 10.50m, and the plan is similar to those of St. Mary of the Latins and St. Mary Minor in the Muristan (Rte 4). Continuing to the W, passing a turning to the right, and at c 120m a turning to the left, we arrive at the TARIQ AL-QIRIMI (HAKKARI ST). In the angle on the left is the *Madrasa al-Lu'lu'iyya*.

The *Madrasa al-Lu'lu'iyya* was founded in 1373/4 by Badr al-Din Lu'lu' Ghazi, a freedman of Sultan al-Ashraf (whose zawiya is now a mosque adjacent to the Damascus Gate, see above). The façade, now disrupted by the addition of modern buttresses, occupies approximately the SW quarter of the street. It had a rather fine if severe frontage, with both the upper and lower storeys defined by cornices. The ground floor has two entrances. The S portal (now altered, and containing a shop) leads to a long vaulted range of rooms which may once have been an extension of al-Khalidiyya St and connected with the main bazaar which is only 26m beyond to the W. This part of the building, and the lower three courses of the façade, are older than the madrasa. The upper courses of flat rusticated masonry in the façade may be constructed with re-used stones. The main portal, with simple pointed-arched recess, has red and cream voussoirs and employs re-used marble imposts. The doorway within has red and cream coursed masonry, and a window in the tympanum above. It leads to a roofed madrasa with four iwans. The upper storey of the complex extends over both the madrasa and the S vaulted rooms, and contains a fine reception hall with two sets of windows above the two ground floor entrance doors. The hall may have formed part of the residence of the founder. In 1854 the madrasa was called the 'German Inn'. The lower floor was restored in 1983 and the upper floor is a private dwelling.

Adjacent on the N is the *Madrasa Badriyya*, an Ayyubid foundation of 1213/14, built by Badr al-Din Muhammad al-Hakkari for the Shafi'i sect. A plain entrance leads to an open court.

Continuing N just beyond the Badriyya and on the opposite side of the road is the *Zawiya al-Qirimiyya*. It was built before 1386 by an

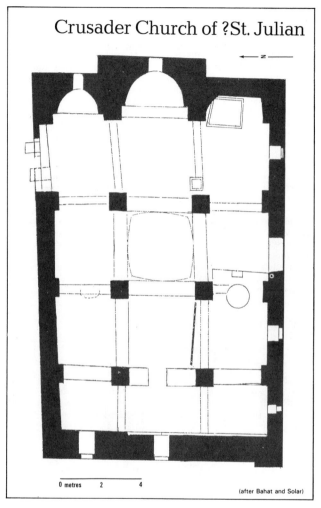

Crusader Church of ?St. Julian

0 metres 2 4

(after Bahat and Solar)

amir who was a disciple of the ascetic Shafi'i Shaikh Shams al-Din
Muhammad al-Qirimi (1321–86) who, with some of his descendants,
was buried here. The frontage has been much rebuilt and buttressed.
The shallow entrance recess with pointed horseshoe arch has a door
of red and cream masonry with carved borders; above the lintel are
joggled voussoirs with a simple but attractive pattern and a small
window in the tympanum. The hall inside has now been converted
into a mosque; partitioned off on the N side is the founder's tomb
chamber which is lit by two grilled windows from the street.

Returning down the street past the Lu'lu'iyya, turn left and take the
turning on the right which leads S to the TARIQ BAB AL-SILSILA; turn
right into this main street and walk almost to the main bazaar. At

c 55m on the right an entrance leads into the *Khan al-Sultan or al-Wakala**, a Crusader caravanserai restored in 1386/7 by Sultan Barquq, the revenues from which then went to the upkeep of the Haram. This is a remarkably preserved dependency of the great bazaars to the W, which illustrates further the role of Jerusalem as a prosperous medieval commercial centre under the earlier Mamluks. It was a place to which merchants brought goods for retail distribution, and was probably intended in particular for valuable goods, to serve as a bonded warehouse where taxes would be levied (perhaps a system established by Frederick II, c 1229). It provided lodgings for merchants and pilgrims on the upper floor, stabling for animals, and storage space for goods on the ground floor. The stable was used for donkeys until recently, and the complex now contains small industrial workshops.

Visit. The entrance passage leads past shops and to the left a covered market street, which are at least as early as the Crusader period. On the N side it leads to a market hall, an almost intact Crusader edifice with splendid corbelled cornices. Two tiers of cells on either side are reached by galleries. In the middle of the W side is the entrance to the stable. To the N is a courtyard complex added by Barquq. Some of the cells on the E and central W sides are Mamluk, but most of the remainder are later additions. Original staircases in the SW and SE corners led up to the upper floor, parts of which are Ottoman. The inscription on the N wall records a fountain of 1763/4 which no longer exists.

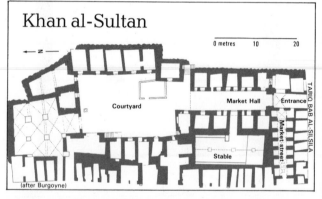

Khan al-Sultan

Courtyard

Market Hall   Entrance

TARIQ BAB AL-SILSILA

Market street

Stable

(after Burgoyne)

Leaving the Khan al-Sultan, turn left and begin a walk down the full length of the **Tariq Bab al-Silsila**. This is one of the main streets of the city, which is partly founded on the great Hasmonean/Herodian/Mamluk vaulted causeway or bridge which crossed the deep Tyropoeon valley, and linked the Upper City to the Temple Platform. It was one of the principal cross streets of the Hadrianic city, the Street of the Temple in Crusader times, and remains one of the main links between the E and W sides of the town.

The street is partly vaulted. At c 110m on the SE corner of the first turning to the right (A. *Harat Maydan* or H. *Misgav Ladakh St*), is the Mamluk **Tashtamuriyya**, established by Sayf al-Din Tashtamur in 1382/3. At the peak of his career he was the First Secretary of State of Sultan Sha'ban (1370–77), but later was permitted to resign and live in Jerusalem, where he built this combined residence, tomb and religious school with charitable adjuncts, cultivated his interest in religious sciences, poetry and music, died, and was buried in the tomb chamber on the ground floor. The SW corner of the three-storey building abuts the slope of the Upper City and utilises some pre-existing structures on the E side. The main façade on Tariq Bab al-Silsila has an elaborate portal in a frame just W of centre. It has a trefoil recess with muqarnas hood; below is a joggled string course, and a doorway set in red and cream coursed masonry flanked by benches. To the right is the façade of the large domed tomb chamber. Here two fine rectangular windows with iron grilles, fine marble mosaic paving on the sills, and monolithic lintels beneath the founder's inscription set in a panel bordered by joggled motifs, are also enclosed within a moulding. The decoration of the windows is designed to draw attention to them as the site of readings from the Koran. Inside the tomb chamber are two cenotaphs, probably those of the founder and his son. There is a mihrab in the S wall; and a fine door with the original decorative bronze knockers leads from the vestibule on the E side.

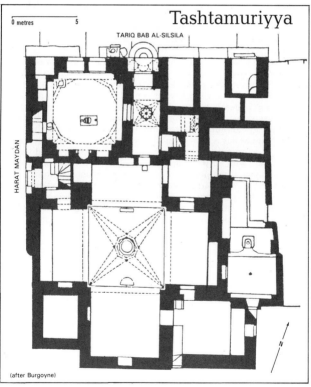

Tashtamuriyya

0 metres 5

TARIQ BAB AL-SILSILA

HARAT MAYDAN

N

(after Burgoyne)

At the W end of the façade is a fountain, and above it a room built partly on projecting brackets which was intended as a place for the care and teaching of orphans. Behind the tomb chamber on the ground floor is a vaulted madrasa with four iwans, which was entered both from the main door and from the W frontage on Harat Maydan. The E side of the frontage contains three shops on the ground floor, possibly part of a pre-existing market. The reception hall and roof court were built on the top floor (entered from N and W and extending on vaults over the Tariq Bab al-Silsila), and residential quarters occupied the middle floor. The latter were probably entered from the E where the remains of a tall portal (one red and cream coursed masonry jamb) in the 'Aqabat Abu Madyan 8m to the E may have led into this part of the residence. Seen from this side, a window at the middle level with gadrooned voussoirs may have been that of Tashtamur's own room, with a fine view towards the Haram. The lowest parts of the E wall appear to belong to pre-existing structures. Parts of the building are in private occupation. Also in the 'AQABAT ABU MADYAN on the W side above the steps leading down to the Wailing Wall is the site of the *Wali Abu Madyan* of 1852/3. Abu Madyan was a Muslim theologican who built a zawiya in Jerusalem but died in Morocco.

Opposite the Tashtamuriyya are the remains of *Crusader vaulted market halls* containing limestone columns with simple capitals. The upper storey is probably Ottoman, and a wooden oriel window obscures an arch with gadrooned voussoirs. On the E side of the halls, dating to sometime after 1352, is *al-Kilaniyya*, the tomb of Jamal al-Din Pahlavan (who came from Gilan in the Caspian area). The tomb complex, though not the tomb chamber itself, was remodelled for domestic use and became a family sinecure in the 18C. The original plan contains a pair of domed tomb chambers on either side of the portal: that on the E with central cenotaph and probably a burial vault beneath, presumably being that of the founder but there is no inscription. It also contains re-used Crusader thick-leaved acanthus capitals and columns flanking a recess in the E wall. The W tomb chamber has a burial vault beneath it. To the N a central open court had a pre-existing (probably Crusader) barrel-vaulted hall on the NW side with a reception hall above. The symmetrical façade of the Kilaniyya is topped by a rectangular pediment and cavetto moulding. The recessed entrance portal has a three-tiered muqarnas hood, with a set of three windows above. To either side are pairs of rectangular windows (those on the E are blocked) set in moulded frames. The windows and door have an undercut relieving course above the lintels, and blank panels above were perhaps originally intended for an inscription. Above each is a single window with muqarnas hood, and each of the three units of the façade is topped by a dome. The original iron-plated wooden doors remain, as do the original grilles and shutters on the W windows.

Still on the N side of the street, and to the E of the Kilaniyya, is *al-Taziy ya*, the memorial madrasa (Koran school) of Sayf al-Din Taz, c 1361. He was a Mamluk official (Cup-bearer) of the Sultan al-Nasir Muhammad, whose career ended miserably: after being blinded, he died and was buried in Damascus. It has a modest façade, with a large rectangular window with red and cream masonry, grille, and monolithic lintel with a dedicatory inscription which includes the founder's blazon of a cup in a circular shield at either end. There is joggled panelling above. On the upper floor is a typical Ottoman oriel timber window set in the Mamluk façade with small Mamluk windows on either side. The building, bounded by pre-existing structures, has an unusual layout, with two tomb chambers on the ground floor entered from a corridor along the E side; the remaining chambers to the N and on the upper floor seem to have been residential, including a private bath house. It was probably occupied by the descendants of Taz. Much of the upper floor is 18C Ottoman. The ground floor tomb chambers now contain a shop with raised floor level.

Opposite the Taziyya, on the S side of the street at the corner with 'AQABAT ABU MADYAN, is the *Turba (Tomb) of Baraka Khan*, built between 1265 and 1280, extended in 1390 and now the Khalidi Library. Only the façade remains, the interior having been almost completely rebuilt in the 19C. Its principal feature is a remarkable early Mamluk doorway built in Romanesque style. Baraka Khan was one of the four chiefs of the Khwarizmian bands invading Syria and Palestine in the 1230–40s, whose power ended in a battle S of Homs in 1246, following which it was said Baraka Khan's head was displayed on the citadel gate at Aleppo. The tomb was built some-time after his death by a member of his family. He was married to a half-sister of an Ayyubid Sultan, his daughter married the Mamluk Sultan Baybars I and a grandson became Sultan al-Sa'id Nasir al-Din Baraka. A son of Baraka Khan died in Damascus in 1279, and his body was transferred to Jerusalem in 1280 and buried here with his father.

The building has a complex history. The lowest projecting courses may be part of the vaults of the 8C–11C reconstruction of the causeway/aqueduct. The three tallest pointed blocked arches visible in the E part of the façade may be the remains of early 13C Crusader shops, bought in the later 13C by the family of Baraka Khan. At this stage the fine door to a tomb chamber on the W end was added. It has outer gadrooned voussoirs and an inner chevron-decorated arch; this was once supported on re-used Crusader elbow consoles and capitals. The hoodmoulds and imposts appear to be Mamluk. The doorway was converted into a window to the present library by 1920. In 1390 extensive alterations were made, the high Crusader arches were blocked, and a typical Mamluk doorway and window were constructed inside them. The portal has a pointed horseshoe arch, and had imitation gadrooned decoration to copy the door to the W. The door jambs are of red and cream masonry. A niche on the right side contains a drinking trough and it also was gadrooned. The window in the arcade to the W is very ornate, with red and cream masonry; the lintel has an inscription and two blazons (perhaps the tribal badge of the family) with polychrome marble veneer above. The inscription in the tympanum recording the burial of Baraka Khan is not *in situ*, and above is an oculus. In the mid-19C the building contained a school on the E side and on the W a ruined mosque (Jami' al-Magharibi al-Qadim, or the Old Mosque of the Moors). Almost the entire interior was rebuilt in the late 19C by the Khalidi family, and the Khalidi library of some 12,000 books and manuscripts was created here in 1900, with a reading room on the W side of a courtyard.

A few metres further E is the *Dar al-Qur'an al-Sallamiyya*, the Koran School of Siraj al-Din 'Umar al-Sallami, endowed in 1360, in a 13C building. A single barrel-vaulted chamber was blocked in the 13C, leaving a small window. A later door was added to the right. It became a Koran school in 1360, and has been a waqf of the Khalidi family since 1788/9. The upper two storeys are later additions; the stairs across the frontage were added in 1811 and replaced in 1983. The ground floor was used c 1836 for the burial of a Shaikh al-Khalidi.

Opposite, on the N side of the street and on the W side of the steps (DARAJ AL-'AIN or the AQUEDUCT STEPS) descending to the Tariq al-Wad is the *Tomb of Baybars al-Jaliq*, the *Jaliqiyya* dating to 1307. He was a Mamluk of the Ayyubid Sultan al-Malik al-Salih Ayyub, one of the 'men of the wardrobe', who was an amir under Baybars, fought against the Mongols in the battle of Homs in 1281 and died outside Ramla. The building consists of a domed tomb chamber at the corner, with an antechamber to the N originally entered from the Daraj al-'Ain (now blocked).

The Jaliqiyya stands on earlier foundations which rest on the vaults of the ancient bridge. On the spandrel of the E arch of the S façade is an inscription recording Sultan Qa'it Bay's restoration of the Haram aqueduct which ran across the bridge. The vaults supporting the bridge were cleared in 1977 to form the underpass which connects the Tariq al-Wad to the Wailing Wall (Rte 2A). The S façade of the Jaliqiyya has a window giving onto the tomb chamber, with inscription above. The chamber contains a cenotaph of the founder(?), and another smaller one of an unknown person. The upper storey is Ottoman. The E façade shows at least three periods of masonry, and has another window to the tomb chamber and the blocked original entrance. Somewhere on the W side of the Jaliqiyya was a Dar al-Hadith, a Tradition School, founded in 1268 by Amir Sharaf al-Din al-Hakkari, son of the founder of the Ayyubid Badriyya Madrasa in the centre of the city (see above).

Continuing E towards the Bab al-Silsila, at c 45m on the left is the *Turba of Turkan Khatun*, of 1352/3, another lady about whom little is known, but perhaps again of eastern Islamic origin. The tomb contains two chambers, that on the street being the original tomb but when the room was employed for domestic uses the cenotaph was moved to the N. The façade is elaborately carved. The window jambs are of alternate blocks of red and cream masonry, but the rest of the masonry is plain limestone. Above each of the window lintels is a large elaborately carved stone, with slight undercutting to relieve pressure on the lintel. The carving has a pattern of stars and palmettes. Another recessed carved panel sits above each window, and a smaller one on the central pier. A later parapet obscures the dome, which is set on an octagonal drum with eight pointed recesses, four containing windows. The interior of the tomb chamber also has panels of low relief carving in the tympana. The original entrance was on the W side. When it was blocked, the W window was converted into a door.

At c 35m further E we arrive at the little courtyard before the Bab al-Silsila. On the entrance corner on the N side is *al-Sa'diyya*, the tomb of Sa'd al-Din Mas'ud, Chamberlain in Damascus in the time of al-Nasir Muhammad. It was endowed in 1311. The modern name is the Dar al-Khalidi. It has a tomb chamber on the E with two windows with grilles, a vaulted hall on the W, and an entrance between them with an early muqarnas portal. The doorway is set in red and brownish coursed masonry. Above the door is a frieze of inlaid strapwork, in which the inlay seems to be of mortar coloured red with crushed pottery, and black with charcoal.

Entering the little square, against the E wall of the Sa'diyya is an ornate Ottoman fountain *(Sabil Bab al-Silsila)* installed by Sulaiman II in 1537. On the N side of the square, and extending over the Sa'diyya, is the *Ribat al-Nisa*, a Women's Hospice endowed in 1330, which was founded by the Amir Tankiz. It has a high trefoil-arched portal recess, and is now a shop. On the E side of the square is the

Columns at the Bab al-Sakina, south side (courtesy of Kay Prag).

important double gate, the *Bab al-Sakina* and *Bab al-Silsila* (Rte 2A).

Tucked away in the N wall of the outer porch is the entrance to the *Baladiyya*, the funerary madrasa of Manklibugha al-Ahmadi, c 1380. It is now partly incorporated in the Aqsa Library, and partly privately occupied. The present small door is not the original entrance to the complex, which lay c 3.23m to the N. The inscription (not *in situ*) above the door records the mausoleum of Manklibugha, but he may not be buried here. Another inscription higher up over three windows is that recording the first building stage of the Ashrafiyya in

1470 (Rte 2B). The interior of the Baladiyya has a large open court with four iwans built on deep cruciform foundations recently explored in the excavations N of Wilson's arch (Rte 2A). These may have been built specially for the Baladiyya on a site N of the ancient bridge. A Crusader church of St. Giles may have stood on the site, and it has also been proposed that the foundations were intended for it. The sculpture still ornamenting the gate could have come from such a church.

On the S side of the gate is one of the most important of the buildings of medieval Jerusalem, **al-Tankiziyya**, the madrasa and khanqah of Tankiz al-Nasiri, of 1328/9.

History. The Tankiziyya is built on the earlier substructures associated with the ancient bridge beneath it, of Herodian, Roman, Umayyad and later date. Tankiz was a Mamluk slave who rose to prominence under al-Nasir Muhammad, became the governor of Damascus in 1312, and effective ruler of all Syria until he fell from power in 1340, was imprisoned and put to death in Alexandria. He was eventually buried in Damascus in 1343. He is known to have carried out various works in Damascus and Jerusalem (see above, Suq al-Qattanin). The building was used as a tribunal in the time of Sultan Qa'it Bay, becoming the regular seat of the Qadi in 1483. Probably during the 19C it became a law court (al-Mahkama), continuing to be used as such during the early years of the Mandate period, and then became the residence of the head of the Supreme Muslim Council, Amin al-Husaini. Restorations were carried out in the 1920s. Since 1967 it has been an Israeli army post. Various traditions have clung to this area over the centuries. The ancient Council Chamber of the Sanhedrin (Jewish religious court) was located somewhere in the vicinity. It may have been this recollection which led to the location of the Byzantine Church of the Holy Wisdom, or St. Sophia, on the site of the Praetorium, (linked with the condemnation of Jesus by the Jewish High Priests and elders of the Sanhedrin) on an unidentified site in the Tyropoeon valley between the 4C and the 6C. The tradition had disappeared by the 12C, and eventually in medieval times the Praetorium was identified with the site of the Antonia (see above). Whether such traditions influenced the choice of the Tankiziyya as a law court is unclear, and latterly it has been suggested that the site of the Byzantine 'Praetorium' lay at the Palatial Building excavated beneath the Yeshivat HaKotel (Rte 7).

Only the façades of the Tankiziyya can be viewed, for the building is not open to visitors. The main feature of the façade is the portal which abuts the Ayyubid outer arch of the Bab al-Silsila. The portal has three tiers of muqarnas work in a deep recess, supporting a pointed semi-dome with chevron fluting. The doorway has a monolithic lintel, with joggled inlay above. The founder's inscription runs right round the recess in the course above, and contains three depictions of the founder's blazon, a chalice on a circular field, one above the door, the others on either side of the recess. Above is another joggled course. The portal has close parallels with that of the mosque built by Tankiz in Damascus. The four shops to the W (or right) of the entrance are part of the original endowment. The interior has three storeys, the upper ones approached by a stairway within the vestibule, with the principal rooms of the Khanqah over the Haram portico (Rte 2B).

The ground floor interior contains a cruciform madrasa with four iwans, with central octagonal oculus. Under the oculus in the court is an octagonal stone basin with fountain, in former times supplied from the aqueduct. A fragment of the original marble paving survives in the S iwan and the mihrab has marble panelling probably laid by Syrian craftsmen. The mihrab contains two Crusader columns and capitals, and Damascus glass mosaic in the conch. The finely decorated interior also originally contained a marble dado. A splendid enamelled glass lamp inscribed 'madrasa of Tankiz' is now in the Islamic Museum (Rte 2F). The S elevation of the building, resting on large, heavily bossed Crusader masonry in the lower courses, and containing four rectangular windows which give onto the ground floor, can be seen from the plaza at the Western Wall (Rte 2A).

The visitor can return through the city either to the Damascus or Jaffa Gates, or exit to the S by the Dung Gate.

4   The Christian Quarter

Introduction. The NW quarter of the Old City is occupied by various of the Christian communities, excluding the Armenians who have their own quarter to the SW (Rte 6). It occupies c 18 hectares (c 45 acres). The Christian community expanded during the Byzantine and Crusader periods, but was greatly reduced in 1187 when the Latin Christians either paid ransom to leave, or went into slavery; a small community remained, mainly Orthodox and Jacobite, in the vicinity of the Church of the Holy Sepulchre and a few other Christian monuments. Today the quarter is bounded on the E by KHAN AL-ZAIT ST (on the line of the Byzantine cardo maximus) and on the S by DAVID ST (the old decumanus). This area was probably not part of the city until the time of Aelia Capitolina (135) when Hadrian built the forum here.

The principal points of interest are the **Church of the Holy Sepulchre**, the **suqs**, the **Pool of the Patriarch's Bath**, the **Church of St. John the Baptist** and the **Muristan**. Much of the quarter is occupied by patriarchates, schools, churches, hospices and convents belonging to the various Greek and Latin communities. DAVID ST and CHRISTIAN QUARTER ST are the main shopping streets for tourists and specialise in local embroidery, glass, pottery, antiquities and copies of antiquities. The food-selling areas are along the main streets between the Christian and Muslim Quarters: KHAN AL-ZAIT ST with mixed goods, fruit and vegetables, confectionery, spices, nuts and herbs; and the three great central bazaars where meat, hardware, metal and textiles are sold, and which are in large part Crusader markets standing over the Byzantine cardo maximus. A walk in these suqs is one of the best introductions to the city and its people. Country people also bring their produce to sell along the streets from the Damascus Gate to the Muristan. Nearly always crowded, the shallow stepped streets, graded for pedestrians and for loaded baggage animals, are partly roofed to protect people and goods from the hot sun and winter rain. Even narrower and often steeper streets lead away from them to the dwelling houses.

Visit. Entering the Old City by the Jaffa Gate, **the Tourist Information Centre** is located a few metres inside on the left. Information about places of interest, bus services, maps, and current events is available. Various tours start from this point. On the right is the Citadel (Rte 5). Information on times of services at the various churches can be had from the **Christian Information Centre** opposite the Jaffa Gate, in Armenian Patriarchate Rd. Continuing straight ahead to the beginning of David St, on the left is the *Petra Hostel*, from the roof of which the best view of the *'**Pool of the Patriarch's Bath** (A. *Birkat Hammam al-Batrak*) can usually be obtained for a small payment. Also called the **Pool of Hezekiah**, this large pool (nearly 72m × 44m and c 7m deep) is entirely surrounded by buildings fronting on to the steets around.

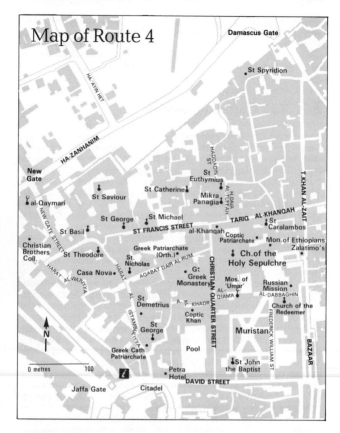

Map of Route 4

History. The original date of the pool has not been properly established though tradition ascribes it to Hezekiah. Quarries of the 7C BC existed in this area, and it is possible that a rain-fed pool existed from that time, just N of the line of the 8C–7C city wall. It could also be part of a Hasmonean or Herodian quarry or water storage system. It is probably the pool Josephus (War V:468) calls the Amygdalon or Tower Pool, where Titus built siege ramps in AD 70. It was probably connected with the Upper Aqueduct from Solomon's Pools, constructed by the Tenth Roman Legion to provide water for the Legionary camp in Jerusalem after AD 70. Thereafter the pool was in virtually continuous use. Charters of 1137 and 1167 indicate that the pool then belonged to the Latin Patriarch, whose palace lay adjacent to the Church of the Holy Sepulchre. The water was used by him and the occupants of neighbouring houses, who paid him for the water. Salah al-Din transferred these rights to the mosque which he founded in the Patriarch's palace after 1187. In more recent times it was fed by a channel from the Mamilla Pool to the W (Rte 14), and the waters were used for the bath house to the E in Christian Quarter St. The pool now contains water only after rain when it is a splendid sight; at other times it is unsightly due to the rubbish which almost fills it.

Visit. Viewed from above the pool has changed little in appearance since the 19C. The large slightly irregular rectangle is surrounded by houses. The N side is occupied by the plain two-storey façade of the *Coptic Khan* (see below) behind which rise the truncated bell tower and the grey dome of the *Church of the Holy Sepulchre*, one of the few places from which a good prospect of these structures can be obtained. On the E is a range of domed buildings characteristic of Jerusalem with rooms jutting out over the pool. Above them is a fine view over the E side of the Old City, with the tower of the *Church of the Redeemer* to the NE, and to the E, in the foreground the silver dome of the Church of St. John the Baptist (see below), in the distance the golden Dome of the Rock (Rte 2) and the Mount of Olives.

Continuing down David St with its many small shops, turn left into CHRISTIAN QUARTER ST and almost immediately on the right is the entrance to the little courtyard containing the Greek Orthodox ***Church of St. John the Baptist or Prodromos, the Forerunner**, and adjacent monastery.

History. St. John Baptist was beheaded at Machaerus in Transjordan by order of Herod Antipas (Mark 6:28); his followers were permitted to remove his body for burial, which traditionally took place at Samaria-Sebastiya. The tomb was pillaged by pagans in 362, but some relics were rescued and sent to various other cities, including Jerusalem (a 4C monastery on the Mount of Olives). Another story says the head was sent to the palace of Herod Antipas in Jerusalem. There is no 4C tradition of a church of St. John the Baptist in Jerusalem, but the presence of the relics may account for the construction of a church on this spot in the 5C, most likely in the time of Eudocia c 450–60 (other churches dedicated to John the Baptist had already been built in the late 4C in Constantinople, Alexandria, Damascus and Emesa). The existence of such a church is noted by John Rufus c 500. The present crypt and foundations date to the 5C and the door on the S side, and the old cisterns, suggest there may have been a monastery attached. It was destroyed, and many Christians massacred,

12C reliquary found in the Church of St. John the Baptist (H. Vincent and F.-M. Abel, Jérusalem Nouvelle, Vol. II, pl. LXVI: Gabalda, Paris, 1922).

in the Persian attack of 614. It was rebuilt by St. John Almoner (Eleimon), Patriarch of Alexandria, who is particularly commemorated for the aid he rendered to the Christian community of Jerusalem after the Persian devastations. The church was rebuilt by the Italian merchant community from Amalfi in the 11C (for the complexities of the various chapels and churches built by the Italians, see below, the Muristan).

The crypt of the present church seems to have been been filled with debris and largely abandoned in 1187, after which the upper storey only (the present church) remained in use. By 1347 according to the pilgrim Poggibonsi there was a tradition that this church was the site of the house, not of Zechariah the father of St. John the Baptist, but of Zebedee, father of St. John the Evangelist. In 1483 Felix Fabri notes there was a mosque near the Church of the House of Zebedee, and in 1596 Amico relates that the upper church of Prodromos was a mosque. However it certainly came back into Greek ownership at this period, if not earlier, and in 1660 a large hospice for Christian pilgrims was built adjacent. In 1674 Nau rejected a Latin claim that the church had been dedicated to St. John the Evangelist.

The crypt was cleared out in the 19C and a splendid reliquary (now in the Greek Orthodox Treasury of the Church of the Holy Sepulchre) was discovered hidden in the masonry of the altar. Formed from a large piece of rock crystal in the shape of a mitre it was bound with gilded copper bands with filigree work and set with semi-precious stones. It contained a wooden panel encrusted with relics on both faces; these included a fragment of the True Cross; relics of St. Peter and St. John the Baptist, of almost all the apostles and some other saints, and of King Oswald, a 7C king of the Anglo-Saxons. The latter relic led Clermont-Ganneau to infer that the reliquary had been intended for use in Britain, but had to be hidden hastily in 1187. It is a splendid testimony to the importance of relics to the medieval pilgrim. The excavations revealed various decorative architectural fragments of Byzantine and Crusader origin.

Visit. A pleasant small courtyard with trees and with a balcony at an upper level greets the visitor. If the church is locked, it is necessary to find the priest. The façade has a small modern belfry, and various fragments of re-used frieze and pilaster built into it. Faint inscriptions can be seen on the façade and belfry. The present church is of the 11C with renovations, and is a trefoil shape with three apses built to N, E and S of a central square (5.56m) where four pillars or piers support the dome. The drum contains eight windows; the exterior of the high dome is painted silver. The plan is based on the 5C church, which is partly visible in the crypt, lying c 6.50m below the modern road level. The approach to it is from the S, whence steps descend to the narthex. In the crypt the central area is roofed by groined vaulting, and the side apses have been much rebuilt. The wrought-iron grille over the altar may be 12C. The exterior E side of the church may be seen from the central square in the Muristan, including the modern window cut in the upper wall of the E apse.

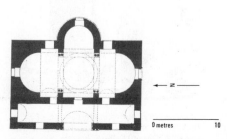

0 metres   10

St. John the Baptist

Continuing along Christian Quarter St, 90m to the N on the right a covered street, the QANTARAT AL-QIAMA, leads down to the Church of the Holy Sepulchre. Descending the steps, past shops selling candles, incense, olivewood and pictures as suitable mementos of a visit to the holy places, immediately ahead is the entrance to the '*Mosque of 'Umar*', originally the *Mosque of Afdal 'Ali*, in Ottoman times of 'Umar b. al-Khattab. This is a place of prayer for Muslims rather than a tourist site, but the history of the mosque is of interest. It was built in 1193 by Afdal 'Ali, the son of Salah al-Din, on the NW corner of the property of the Knights of St. John. The popular name derives from the story that in 638 the Caliph 'Umar went outside the Church of the Holy Sepulchre to pray: in fact he went to the entrance portico at the E end of the church and a 10/11C mosque later marked that site, which Christians were forbidden to enter. The present 'Mosque of 'Umar' was built following the capture of the city by Salah al-Din in 1187 on the S side of the Church of the Holy Sepulchre, where the entrance then lay.

The outer entrance to the mosque was rebuilt between 1839 and 1861. On the E side of the courtyard is a tall minaret re-built before 1465 (and possibly earlier, before 1417–18). This has a Syrian-type square tower with shaft divided by mouldings into three storeys. The base contains much Crusader masonry, some of which may be *in situ* remains of the 12C *Hospital of the Knights*. The first storey has slit windows set in pointed horseshoe arches with Koranic inscriptions on the tympana. Above the one on the S side is a sundial. The second storey has windows on all four sides, those to E and W being paired. Above the muezzin's gallery an octagonal lantern supports a small round drum and dome.

Continuing past the mosque, a sharp left and right turn brings the visitor to the courtyard of the Church of the Holy Sepulchre.

**The Church of the Holy Sepulchre is the focal point for the Orthodox, Latin and Protestant branches of the Christian church. It is located on the traditional sites of the Crucifixion, burial and Resurrection of Christ. First dedicated in 335, it has had a dramatic and continuous history, illustration of which is preserved in the fabric of the present building. Despite its great dome, the building is hardly distinguishable architecturally in the massed buildings of the city around it. Divided ownership and diverse use by the many sects, and the continuous stream of services, pilgrims and tourists make this a difficult building for the hasty visitor to appreciate. It is however, a church which greatly rewards time given to it. Deeply imbued with the weight of its own history, and above all by the faith of the millions of pilgrims who have prayed at and venerated this site for more than 16 centuries, the church is one of the great monuments of Jerusalem despite the loss of many of its ancient glories. A major restoration of the church was carried out from 1959, which, in removing partitions and other accretions which had grown up in the course of years as well as performing vital structural repairs, restored much of the church as a coherent monument of the 12C.

History. Archaeological investigations have shown that this site was outside the city until the Roman Aelia Capitolina was built in the 2C. The location is c 230m N of the line of the First North Wall of the city, and perhaps 120m W of the line of the Second North Wall, the route of which is, however, uncertain. The earliest remains found beneath the church seem to be quarrying and tombs of the 8C–6C BC and the 1C AD on a rocky hillside rising to the W, on which 2C buildings of Aelia Capitolina were built. It is therefore possible that it could have been the *Place of the Skull (Golgotha)* used c AD 30 for the Crucifixion and burial of

Jesus as described in the Gospels (Matt. 27:32–3; 28:11; John 19:17, 41–42), when Joseph of Arimathea gave his nearby tomb for the burial. All the closest companions and followers of Jesus saw the site in a garden close outside the city, and there is thus the basis for the development of a positive tradition. This lends weight to the early (4C) tradition which maintained that the first Christians immediately following the death of Jesus venerated the site of his tomb on this spot. The tradition is said to have been sufficiently strong to survive the turbulent events which intervened, perhaps partly due to a continuous succession of bishops in Jerusalem from St. James the Less (who was martyred in AD 62). These events included the departure of the Christian population to Pella c AD 66 and the destruction of Jerusalem in AD 70. The Temple of Venus was built over the site by Hadrian in 135. Following the departure of the Romans in 324 and inclusion of Palestine within the Eastern Roman Empire the tradition provided sufficient basis for the Roman temple to be torn down in 326 in the search for the tomb buried underneath its podium. The description of the search and the successful outcome are given by Bishop Eusebius of Caesarea in his Life of Constantine (c 337–40). The rock-cut tomb was found where the tradition had dictated in 326/7 by Bishop Makarios of Jerusalem, the direct episcopal successor of St. James the Less.

Constantine gave orders for the building of a great church, and the basilica or Martyrium at Golgotha was dedicated on 17 September 335. It is thought that the great Rotunda of Constantine (the Anastasis, or Church of the Resurrection) over the tomb itself took longer to complete and was not finished until sometime after 340. A great deal of rock had to be quarried and levelled, to leave the tomb standing free of its original hillside. At first the tomb was covered by a small columned structure in a court surrounded by porticoes. Eusebius does not record the story that Queen Helena, the mother of Constantine, discovered the fragments of the True Cross in a cistern adjacent to the rock of the Crucifixion. This tradition is first mentioned c 351.

The Church of Constantine. This was much the largest church to stand on the site and its plan has been restored from fragments still·existing in the present structure and in adjoining buildings. It consisted of two main elements, the *Basilica of Constantine*, then also called the Martyrium or place of witness, marking the site of the Crucifixion, and the *Rotunda* over the tomb which was called the Anastasis or Resurrection. Between and around the two main buildings were courts and subsidiary buildings. Descriptions of the church and its services have survived in the accounts of the Pilgrim of Bordeaux (333) and Egeria (384).

The basilica itself was entered from the E from the cardo maximus by a propylaeum with three doorways. This led to a large, slightly irregular atrium with porticoes and exedra; thence by three or five doors to the basilica itself which was oriented W towards the tomb. It was a five-aisled church, the central aisle being the widest (perhaps 13.50m). The lateral aisles contained an upper and lower gallery, supported by large columns in the front row (height estimated as 4.80m at the lower level, 3.62m at the higher level) with square pillars in the back row. The height of the roof of the central aisle was perhaps 22m with clerestorey windows. The apse at the W end is described as having twelve columns capped by great silver urns. According to Eusebius, the exterior was covered with fine polished stone, the interior with many-coloured marble. The basilica had a lead roof, and inside the coffered ceiling was covered with brilliant gold which sparkled and 'which, like some great ocean, covered the whole basilica with its endless swell'.

The N and E walls of the basilica, and the S wall of the atrium may be re-used elements of Hadrian's civic basilica (Coüasnon) or of the Temple of Venus.

Access to the great porticoed court to the W was by doorways at the head of the lateral naves. The W side of the great court was formed by the façade of the great church of the **Anastasis** over the tomb of Christ. The dome of the Rotunda had a diameter of 20.44m–48m (Harvey, 1934). The depiction of the Constantinian buildings on the mosaic in the apse of St. Pudenziana at Rome shows a rather low dome, presumably built of wood with a lead covering. It was supported by columns, with a semi-circular ambulatory on the W with a diameter of 35m. The semi-circular back wall contained three apses oriented N, W and S. The Anastasis was set in walled courts lined by monastic cells on the N, W, and S sides. Inside, the dome was supported by 12 columns and eight piers, the latter set in pairs at the cardinal points. The columns, including the bases and capitals, had a height of 10.50m, were tall and slender and gave a sense of lightness as well as providing more space for circulation than heavy piers would allow. The tomb itself was beneath the dome, on the central axis

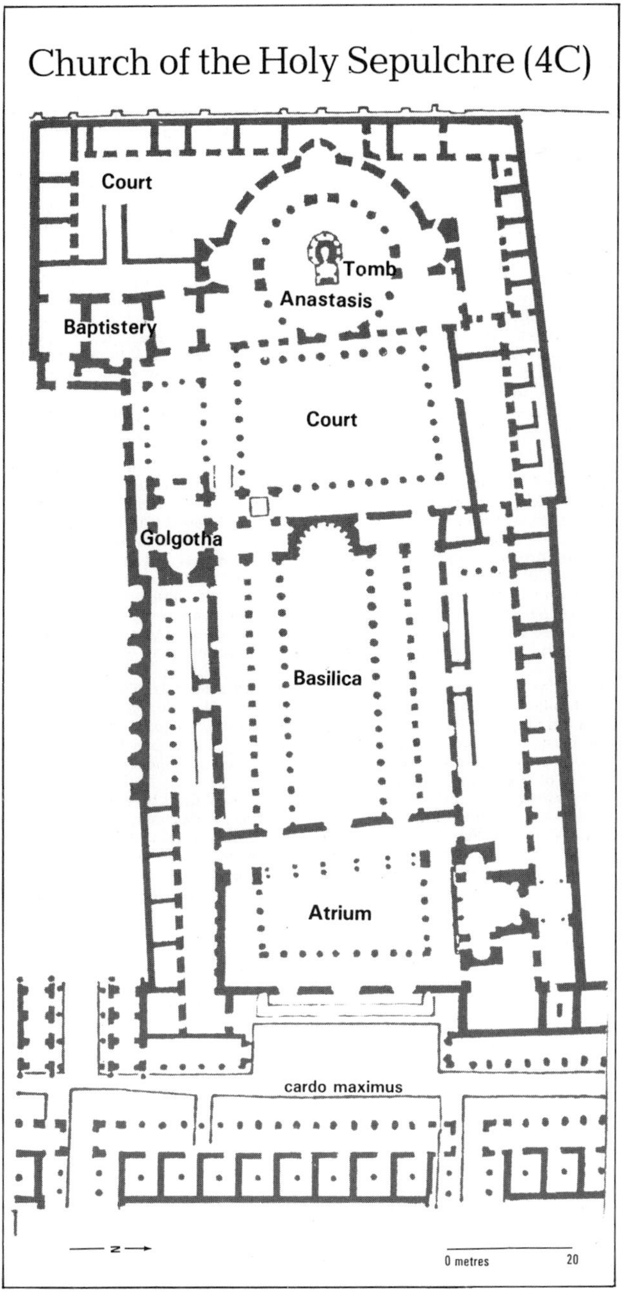

Church of the Holy Sepulchre (4C)

Court

Tomb
Anastasis

Baptistery

Court

Golgotha

Basilica

Atrium

cardo maximus

0 metres 20

but slightly N of centre. The Rotunda was not on the same alignment as the basilica, which was offset to the S and aligned on Golgotha. Egeria describes the liturgy celebrated in the Anastasis in 384, and how the Bishop went inside a screen to enter the cave tomb to pray. The Stone moved by the Angels from in front of the tomb is mentioned by 348; the Tomb itself was adorned with columns and its had roof decorated with gold and silver. Daily prayers at night, morning, noon, afternoon and evening were said in the Anastasis. Egeria describes also the decoration, of mosaic, gold, jewels, and silk with gold stripes for curtains and hangings; at night candles and great glass lanterns gave bright illumination.

The Anastasis has parallels with Roman mausolea (e.g. the Mausoleum of Constantia at Rome which is smaller) but the greater use of wood and more slender columns employed here must have created a greater sense of light and spaciousness. It was intended as a monument to the glory and triumph of the Resurrection rather than a memorial to the dead.

To the S of the Constantinian complex lay a *court and the baptistery*. On the site of Calvary, where today the almost vertical pillar of rock rises 4.75m from the surrounding quarried bedrock, the remains are less certain. Egeria refers to a Cross, and to services conducted both before and behind it. The chapel behind the Cross seems to have been part of the Martyrium, at the W end of the S aisle. The Church of Golgotha may have been built after the restoration by Modestus in the 7C.

Fire damaged some areas near the Rotunda early in its history, and the original wooden floors were replaced by vaulting, perhaps in the time of Justinian.

On 6 May 614 the Sassanian army reached Jerusalem, seized the fragments of the True Cross, slaughtered many of the monks and burnt the church. The roof, decorations and furnishings were destroyed. Repairs were carried out by Modestus, Abbot of St. Theodosius in the Judaean desert (Rte 17), whose work is still commemorated by the Orthodox church. The church described by the pilgrim Arculf in 680 is the Constantinian church as restored by Modestus, with a church of St. Mary to the SE of the Anastasis, and the Church of Golgotha built on the site of the Crucifixion. Arculf says that in his time the Stone moved by the Angels had been split into two unequal parts, and squared into altars.

The Emperor Heraclius retrieved and returned the fragments of the True Cross on 21 March 631, but as the threat to the E Byzantine empire increased, he removed them to Constantinople in 633.

On the surrender of Jerusalem to the Arab armies in 638, the Patriarch Sophronius led the Caliph 'Umar on a tour of the Holy Sepulchre and when it was time for prayers invited the Caliph to pray in the church. 'Umar declined because his followers would otherwise take the church as a Muslim place of prayer, and the treaty of surrender had guaranteed the sanctity of the Christian places of worship in the city.

An earthquake, probably that of 808, loosened the timbers of Modestus' repairs and more work was carried out. In c 815 the Patriarch Thomas appears to have restored the dome of the Anastasis; from the description he rebuilt it as a wooden cone. At about the same time Charlemagne was responsible for the construction of the nearby Church of St. Mary of the Latins (see below).

Eutychius records that the Muslims in the 10C had become more aggressive, and in 938 had rioted, burned the S doors and half the portico, and devastated Golgotha and the Anastasis. They took part of the entrance to the Holy Sepulchre and built a mosque to mark the site of 'Umar's prayers. An inscribed stone (probably of al-Hakim or al-Zahir in the early 11C) forbidding entrance to Christians was found in 1897 in the SE area of the basilica, which may derive from this mosque. In another riot in 965 Muslims and Jews set fire to the doors and woodwork, and not long after the Rotunda roof was replaced.

On 18 October 1009 on the orders of the Fatimid Caliph al-Hakim, the church and the tomb were destroyed in an act of anti-Christian fanaticism. The work, described by the Arab chronicler Yahya, was devastating. The basilica was left a complete ruin; the tomb of Christ itself, though cut in the bedrock, was demolished with pickaxes and virtually obliterated. The Rotunda proved more resistant, and although the columns and superstructure were overthrown, much of the lower exterior wall survived in the ruins.

Restoration was permitted following the Peace Treaty of 1030, made between the Byzantine Romanus III Agyros and the Fatimid al-Zahir, the son of al-Hakim, but first delays and then the earthquake of 1033 inhibited the work. In 1042 in the reign of Constantine Monomachos money at last arrived from the Imperial Treasury in Constantinople and by 1048 the Rotunda was rebuilt but the Basilica of Constantine remained in ruins.

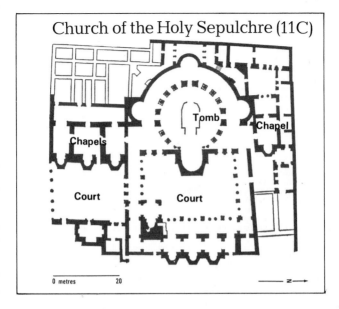

Church of the Holy Sepulchre (11C)

Tomb

Chapel

Chapels

Court

Court

0 metres   20

N →

The Church of Constantine Monomachos in 1048 was restricted to the area of the Rotunda, and the adjacent courts and chapels. The Rotunda was reconstructed on the lower wall and design of the previous Constantinian Anastasis. The columns were cut in half and re-erected to only half their original height. They thus had rather clumsy proportions, with large rough capitals, and supported slightly pointed arches and an upper gallery instead of the original flat architrave. Some fine Umayyad carving was re-used in this work. The dome was reconstructed as a timber cone. A large apse with a great arch was built out on the E side. A small rectangular edifice with cupola was erected to mark the site of the tomb destroyed by al-Hakim. The *Chapel of St. Mary* on the N side of the church is of this date. In the SE corner of the court the *Chapel of Adam* backed onto Golgotha. An upper storey was added to the porticoes around the court. The *Chapel of Melchizedek* (above Golgotha), which had escaped the destruction by al-Hakim, was incorporated into this upper storey. Three chapels replaced the former baptistery on the W side of the forecourt, and their 11C apses still project into the present forecourt. The principal entrance to the church was from the forecourt S of the Rotunda as it is today.

The Church on Golgotha was said to contain relics of the True Cross; and also a cup, variously thought to have been used at the Last Supper, or that from which Jesus drank the vinegar and gall; other relics included the sponge, the reed and the lance connected with the Crucifixion.

Barely 50 years later the Latin Christians from the West captured Jerusalem, and on the 50th anniversary of this event, 15 July 1149, a rebuilt and restored **Crusader church** was dedicated. This church with little alteration forms the structure that we see today. It used the Rotunda with its 11C form almost intact, but the 11C E apse was demolished and the church again extended over the W end of the Constantinian basilica. Here they built a new church in the style of the Romanesque galleried churches of contemporary France, whose altar and apses were placed to the E and which was entered from the W through the great arch (the Arch of the Emperor Monomachos) which had supported the 11C apse. However, despite building in this European style, the Crusaders' work was made to harmonise with the pre-existing buildings. Thus they built on the same two levels as previously, and also used pointed arches. Part of the double portico over the entrance from the S forecourt was demolished, and a new façade with the same proportions and alignment as previously was constructed in 12C style. The present façade is this work and leads into what seems to be a typical transept of a 12C Romanesque church. Two Crusader kings were buried in the church. Later, c 1170, a bell tower of five storeys was built adjacent to the W end of the façade and over one of the chapels.

Under the terms of the treaty of 1187 Salah al-Din spared the church, though he took off the cross, broke the bells and locked the doors. A Sufi convent occupied the Latin Patriarch's palace. The Orthodox and Jacobite Christians were allowed to remain in the city. The Latins were expelled until 1192, when two priests and two deacons were allowed to return and pilgrim access was restored. Despite Byzantine pressure to restore to the Orthodox the sole rights they had enjoyed under the Fatimids, Salah al-Din refused to allow any one sect to control the church. Following the treaty of 1229, when Jerusalem was restored to the Franks, Frederick II of Germany crowned himself in the church. In 1244 the Khwarizmian Turks sacked the church, massacring the Christians inside, broke the 11C marble slab over the Tomb, and pillaged the Crusader royal tombs in the Chapel of Adam. The Stone of the Angels was again broken, and a fragment retrieved by the Armenians and taken to their church at the House of Caiaphas (Rte 8).

In the 14C Greeks, Latins, Georgians, Armenians, Jacobites, Copts and Ethiopians all had rights in the church, and to avoid dissent the keys to the main doors were held by Muslims. The Franciscans, who returned to Palestine in 1335, had probably gained a foothold in the church by 1345. In the 15C the edicule over the Tomb was in their hands. The Armenians had by then been supplanted by the Georgians on Calvary and the Jacobites owned the Chapel of Helena. The earthquake of 1545 did some damage to the belfry. In 1555 the edicule was rebuilt. Conditions in the 15C and 16C were difficult, and tension grew between the communities in the church. Territorially the Greek and Armenian Orthodox were the most successful. In 1644 the Georgians left, unable to pay the Ottoman taxes; the Ethiopians met the same difficulties, sold much of their property to the Copts to meet their debts and retreated to the ruined cloister. For a short period the Copts left, and on their return in the 16C the Sultan gave them the ruins of the cloister of the Latin Canons where they built the present convent and church. In 1632 Sandys described the Easter ceremony of the Holy Fire as 'fitting better the solemnities of Bacchus'. By 1685 the Georgians had left Jerusalem, crippled by debt and declining numbers; most of their churches and convents were taken over by the Greeks. By 1699 only the Greeks, Latins and Armenians could afford to pay the Ottoman taxes and still said mass in the church.

Repairs to the Dome of the Holy Sepulchre were carried out in 1719 by the Greeks and Latins (Ladoire) in which work the Armenians had hoped to join (Rte 6); the height of the bell tower, by now rather unsafe, was also reduced. The Armenians got the Chapel of Helena from the Jacobites, and laid a new floor there.

On 12 October 1808 fire broke out in one of the chapels of the Rotunda and spread through the whole building. The Rotunda in particular was badly damaged, seven of the ten surviving 4C/11C columns disintegrated and two-thirds of the building collapsed including most of the W end of the cathedral. Numerous problems and intrigues arose over the restoration, in the course of which the Greek Orthodox secured rights over more of the church, as also did the Armenian Orthodox, who contributed substantially to the cost of repairs. In the restoration, the Greek architect Komnenos rebuilt much of the complex and encased the pillars of the Rotunda and the Choir in rubble pillars faced with stone. The structure over the site of the tomb was replaced with the present ugly building with heavy dome. Also at this time the tombs of Godfrey of Bouillon and Baldwin I, which had stood as monuments of the Latin Kingdom of Jerusalem just inside the entrance to the Chapel of Adam, were removed by the Greeks, as were other Crusader tombs near the Stone of Unction.

Curzon gave an account of horrific scenes in the Rotunda which occurred during the Easter ceremony of the Miracle of the Holy Fire in 1834. 17,000 pilgrims were estimated to be in the city, of whom a good number were in the Sepulchre for the ceremony. The crowds and numbers of candles were such that the smoke rolled in great volumes out of the aperture at the top of the dome. Hysterical frenzy was followed by a panic to get out and it was estimated that 300 were crushed to death in the struggle.

A restoration to the dome was carried out in 1867/8 at the joint expense of France and Russia. Other work was done on the W tower (Mauss).

In 1927 an earthquake shook the building and the 12C dome over the crossing in the Greek cathedral had to be taken down and reconstructed; the S façade was encased in steel scaffolding and buttresses, which remained until the recent restorations.

In 1959 a plan for repair and restoration was at last agreed by the various communities now owning parts of the structure, and implemented in the following years.

Various excavations have been made in the church: Wilson (1863), Corbo (from 1960), Ekonomopoulos (1968), the Armenian Patriarchate, Broshi and Bahat (1970, 1975–76, 1977–80). Detailed studies were published by Coüasnon in 1972, and by Corbo in 1983.

Visit. The church is open from 4.00 to 19.00. *Visitors of both sexes should not wear shorts or sleeveless garments.* A list of the times and dates of the services and the principal ceremonies during the Easter period and at other times is usually available from the Christian Information Centre, in Armenian Patriarch Road, opposite the Citadel.

The forecourt or **Parvis (1)**, c 25m × 17m, has the remains of an arcade constructed in the 11/12C near the S end. The entrance to the church is on the N side of the court; the *Crusader façade con-structed before 1149 is the most prominent feature. A double arcade with frieze at both ground and first-storey level are each surmounted by a cornice. The upper cornice is re-used 2C Roman work; the lower cornice is a 12C copy. The pointed arches are of typical Romanesque-Gothic type with gadrooned voussoirs. A hoodmould of finely carved rosettes surmounts the gadrooned arches of the portals. The entrance doors (the right entrance was blocked after 1187) are flanked by rebated marble triple columns with capitals and imposts carved in floral designs which support flat restored lintels. The carved originals were removed to the Rockefeller Museum following the 1927 earth-quake (Rte 13). These are of very fine late 12C workmanship deriving from a contemporary French school. The left lintel shows scenes in the life of Christ prior to his Crucifixion; the right lintel in rather different classical style shows human and animal figures within arabesques of foliage, fruit and flowers. The left tympanum shows the impression of the mosaic which once adorned it. A pair of less pointed upper windows above and to the E of the dome over the Chapel of the Franks belong to the 11C façade.

Just in front of the central columned jamb beneath boards, is the *tomb of Philip d'Aubigny*, an English Crusader who died 1236. He was one of the councillors of King John at the time of Magna Carta, Governor of the Channel Islands and Tutor to Henry III. He made several pilgrimages to the Holy Land, including one in 1222 when he travelled by Damietta and Acre. The tomb has a trapezoid slab with bevelled edges, with a three-line epitaph in 13C lettering: HIC IACET PHILIPPVS DE AVBINGNI CVIVS ANIMA REQVIESCAT IN PACE. AMEN. Beneath are his arms, four fusils in fess on a shield. The tomb was preserved under a bench, and discovered during its removal in 1867. Above the façade the dome over the crossing can be seen, which was reconstructed after the earthquake of 1927. The modillions on the drum have characteristic 12C carving.

The W wall of the Parvis contains the rectilinear chevets of the 11C chapels built on the site of the Constantinian baptistery. They belong to the Greek Orthodox community. The S chapel **(2)** is that of *St. James the Less*, the brother of Christ; the central chapel **(3)** was originally the *Chapel of the Trinity*, later of the *Forty Martyrs*, and was used for marriages and baptisms; and the N chapel **(4)** is

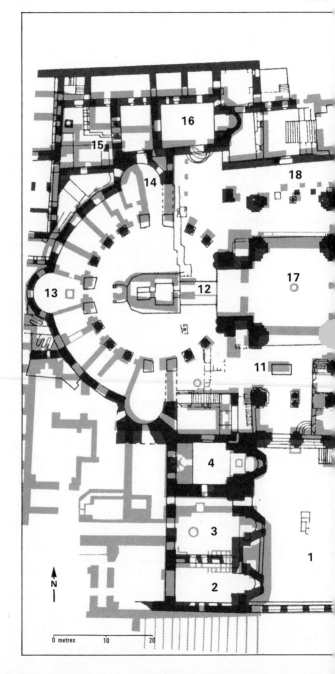

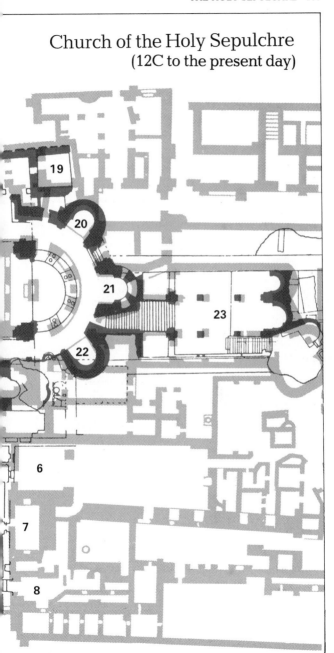

Church of the Holy Sepulchre
(12C to the present day)

dedicated to *St. John the Baptist* but has also been associated with the Monastery of the Trinity where formerly the Patriarchs of Jerusalem were buried. The Crusader bell tower above it was built c 1170 by Joudain. It had five storeys, but the height was reduced by nearly half in 1719. That it was subsequent to the original design of the façade is indicated by the destroyed symmetry of the main façade, including a blocked window above and to the W of the entrance, which can just be seen.

The E wall of the Parvis has, adjacent to the church, a small domed structure which was once the 12C Crusader entrance to the Church on Calvary, afterwards converted to the ***Chapel of the Franks (5)**. Now it has the Greek *Chapel of St. Mary of Egypt* (below) and the Latin *Chapel of the Agony of the Virgin* (above); both are closed. The former marks the spot where the 6C ikon of the Theotokos prevented Mary the Egyptian from entering the church. The latter can be seen through a window from the Chapels on Calvary.

The area in the vicinity of Calvary was particularly richly decorated by the Crusaders. Externally, the small marble columns and ornamental carving of cornice and window arches are well preserved. The 12C door has a fine carved relief tympanum with twined foliage and bunches of grapes; the 12C capitals have acanthus leaves and volutes, and the imposts have foliage. There is a frieze of birds in a vine over the window and an agreeable pair of confronted lions at the SE corner of the cornice. The other buildings with entrances in the E wall of the Parvis are first the Coptic *Chapel of St. Michael* **(6)**, with a painting of St. Michael weighing souls; from this a staircase leads to the *Chapel of the Ethiopians* and the *Coptic convent* to the NE; the next entrance to the S leads to the Armenian *Chapel of St. James* **(7)**; and near the SE corner of the court, the Greek *Monastery of Abraham* **(8)** from which access is obtained to various churches in the upper storey, including the *Church of Abraham* where tradition locates the sacrifice of Isaac on Mount Moriah. At various periods, traditions originally linked with Mount Moriah (Rte 2), including the sacrifice of Isaac, and the Tomb of the Skull or Adam's tomb seem to have shifted to the vicinity of Golgotha. This shift seems to have been due to comparisons drawn between the church and the Temple in the early 4C. Below ground level is the old *Chapel of the Apostles*, discovered in c 1669. It has a fine iconastasis. The huge vaulted cistern under the monastery is thought to date to the Hadrianic period.

As one enters the Church of the Holy Sepulchre it is as well to remember that the entire structure is divided between six sects of the Christian church: principally the Latin Catholics, Greek Orthodox and Armenian Orthodox, to a lesser extent the Jacobites (Syrians), Copts and Ethiopians all of whom guard their rights to various parts of the building jealously.

We enter the S transept of the 12C church, truncated at a short distance by the restored wall of the present Greek cathedral. To the left of the entrance was formerly the high bench or diwan where the hereditary Muslim doorkeeper sat. He held the keys of the church to prevent disputes arising among the various Christian sects. The steep stairs to the right behind the blocked E doorway (early 13C) lead up to **Calvary** or **Golgotha**, meaning the place of the skull, the traditional site of the Crucifixion of Christ and the two thieves, and associated also with the burial place of Adam. At the top of the stairs are two chapels. On the S is first the Latin *Chapel of the Nailing to the Cross* **(9)**, with a 12C mosaic depicting the Ascension on the ceiling. The other mosaics are modern. Here, at the **Tenth and Eleventh Stations of the Cross**, Jesus was disrobed and nailed to the Cross. Through a window in the S wall the *Chapel of the Agony of the Virgin* **(5)** can be seen. On the N side is the Greek *Chapel of the Exaltation or Raising of the Cross* **(10)** which marks the **Twelfth Station of the Cross**. The slot cut for the cross is shown in the E apse as are also those of the two thieves. The top of the rock, here nearly 4m² and 4.75m above the adjacent quarried surface, can be touched under the altar of the Greek chapel and also seen through glass in the Chapel of Adam below.

The site has been venerated as that of the Crucifixion since the 4C, and a church has existed probably since the 7C. It was incorporated in the lateral aisle of the Crusader church and the present four arches probably form part of the older ciborium, though the chapels were enlarged in 1810. Between the two chapels is the Latin 'Stabat altar' the **Thirteenth Station** where Mary received the body on its removal from the Cross. Above is the *Chapel of Melchizedek*. The doors on the N side lead out to the gallery of the cathedral, and to the entrance to the Greek refectory.

After descending the steps, beneath Calvary is the *Chapel of Adam*. The chapel of the Skull (of Adam) was located here against the face of the rock of Golgotha in the original 4C Constantinian layout, for it was early associated with the tradition which said that Adam was buried at Golgotha (Origen, 185–253). Part of Calvary can be seen under glass in this chapel, with a fault in the rock said to have been caused by an earthquake which occurred at the time of the Crucifixion, but probably an original flaw which caused the workmen to abandon this section of the old quarry. Near the entrance were the tombs of Godfrey of Bouillon and Baldwin I, the two first Crusader rulers, but they and a third tomb disappeared during the repairs of 1810. The tombs had already been disturbed during the invasion of the Khwarizmian Turks in 1244.

Just beyond the entrance to the chapel is the *Stone of Unction* **(11)** where tradition holds the body of Jesus was anointed by Nicodemus after being taken down from the Cross (John 19:38–40). This low slab of limestone replaced a 12C slab destroyed in 1808. The location and ownership of the slab has varied in the course of the centuries, and now the many lamps over it are variously owned by Armenians, Copts, Greeks and Latins. Three more Crusader tombs once existed near the wall of the Catholicon. A short distance to the SW near the foot of the steps up to the Armenian Chapel is the traditional place from which the women watched the annointing.

Continuing to the left, past the end of the restored wall of the Greek Catholicon one comes straight to the partly restored remains of the devastated **•Rotunda** or **Anastasis (12)**, the *Church of the Resurrection* built by Constantine, and under it, the site of the **Tomb of Christ**. Only slightly displaced, the present piers and columns mark the location of the original 12 columns and eight pillars of the 4C Rotunda. Two marble columns on the NE side, which were the top and bottom halves of one Constantinian column re-used in the 11C, survived the fire of 1808. The present two columns date to the recent restorations and are exact copies. They permit one to visualise the scale of the original Constantinian Rotunda. The Rotunda is heavily buttressed following damage in the earthquake of 1927; the present dome is a replacement following the fire of 1808 and restorations of 1867/8. It is now a double dome with iron ribs and cross bracing. The outer dome is lead-lined, the inner lined with tin and painted. There is a glazed metal screen covering the aperture at the apex. The diameter of the dome is 20.44m–48m and the height is c 34m. The external diameter of the base of the Rotunda is 36.52m.

Now walled in by the partitions of storerooms, the ambulatory behind the columns is divided by cross vaulting into two storeys. The rear wall, though not visible within the church, is still largely 4C and preserved to a height of 11m, to just below the level of the original cornice. The 4C exedras to N, W and S survive. The S exedra is not accessible. The *Syrian Chapel (13)** is located in the W exedra. Through a hole in the masonry on the S side of the chapel entrance can be had to a dark, rock-cut tomb typical of the 1C BC/AD, part of which was cut away when the rock around the Tomb of Christ was removed in the 4C. A 16C tradition located the tombs of Joseph of Arimathea and Nicodemus here. The antechamber of the original tomb may have lain to the E, and the tomb chamber may have contained ten *kokhim* or burial places with an ossuary in the floor; the ossuary and several *kokhim* are still visible. This tomb and a tomb on the S side of Calvary, perhaps one under the Coptic Monastery, reinforce the evidence that the Tomb of Christ was part of a cemetery outside the walls in the 1C BC/AD. A staircase led up from the antechamber of the Syrian Chapel to the Armenian section of the gallery above (not accessible). Above this W end of the church is a square tower (not accessible); the chamber above the Syrian chapel gave access to Christian St, and a 12C door led to the gallery of the Rotunda. The chamber above, called the 'Room of the Patriarchs', and another above again, belong now to the Khanqah Mosque (see below). An intervening chapel on the E, with a niche giving a view of the Holy Sepulchre from above the gallery of the Rotunda, was taken down in the work of 1867/8.

Most of the N exedra of Constantine can also be seen **(14)**. A later passage cut through the 4C wall leads to a small court **(15)** with a deep cistern to the NW. Other 4C Constantinian fragments survive in this area, including parts of the original passage from the N to the W court, and some of the cells which existed against the N wall of the court, each having a door with flat lintel and shallow relieving arch, and a small window. Some of these sections are not accessible.

The site of the Tomb and Resurrection of Christ (12) is covered by an ugly small chapel dating to 1810. The original tomb venerated in the 4C was demolished on the orders of al-Hakim in 1009. That was certainly the tomb, probably of 1C BC/AD date, discovered by Makarios in 326 and which tradition then held was that of Jesus, in which he was laid on the eve of the Sabbath and from which he rose on the Easter Sunday morning. There is a possibility but no certainty that this was the tomb of Christ, but its importance lies more in the faith, prayers and veneration surrounding it than in any material remains. The original tomb, with candles on it, was set sideways under an arch according to Arculf c 680. The present apsidal marble structure, (c 8m × 5.5m) conforms in general layout to the earlier edicule, and is approached from the E. It contains two tiny chambers and is served by the Greeks, Latins, Armenians and Copts. Within is first the *Chapel of the Angels* (c 3.4m × 3m). In the centre is the small altar formed from part of the large stone said to have been rolled away from the mouth of the tomb by the Angels. In the wall by the entrance steps ascend to the roof. A low door gives entry to the *Chapel of the Holy Sepulchre* (c 2m × 1.8m) which is the **Fourteenth Station of the Cross**. Inside the door of the marble lined chamber is an inscription naming Komnenos, the Greek architect of the restorations of 1810. Three bas reliefs in white marble represent the Resurrection; a marble bench covered with a marble slab, cracked in the 13C, lies against the N wall. It marks the empty burial place of Christ.

At the rear of the edifice of the tomb is the *Coptic chapel* which is said to preserve a tiny rock-cut remnant of the original tomb which survived al-Hakim's destruction in 1009. A fragment of cut and polished granite is shown which is not part of the original tomb cut in the limestone.

To the N of the Rotunda is the *Chapel of St. Mary* **(16)** where legend relates that Christ appeared to Mary, his mother, after the Resurrection. Built in the 11C it was only a little altered by the Crusaders in the 12C, when it was approached from the street to the W by an impressive entrance portal with gadrooned voussoirs resting on fine acanthus capitals (see Christian Quarter St below). It is now the most important Franciscan chapel. To the right of the entrance, a relic said to be a fragment of the *Column of the Scourging* is displayed. To the N is the *Franciscan Convent*. To the E is the *Latin Sacristy* where sword, spurs and cross said to be those of Godfrey of Bouillon were preserved. These formed part of the investiture regalia of the Order of the Holy Sepulchre, an order with Crusader origins conferred on illustrious pilgrims in later centuries. Here steps led up to the Latin parts of the galleries.

Returning towards the Tomb, opposite it to the E is the great arch—**The Arch of the Emperor**—which was constructed by Monomachos in the 11C to support his new apse. Short twin columns were built up with heavy bases and capitals which contained re-used Umayyad elements. Monogramed capitals of Justinian formed great imposts to support the springing of the arch. The apse itself was removed by the Crusaders in the 12C, who employed the arch as entrance to their new church. The 12C W piers are built adjacent to the great arch. Through the arch we enter the *Greek Catholicon* **(17)**, which occupies the central aisle of the Crusader church. It is separated from the Crusader side aisles by later partition walls, once necessary as supports but since the recent restorations no longer functional apart from their capacity to bear ornament. An early tradition associated the Centre of the World with the site of the Crucifixion and Resurrection, and by the 10C it was marked by an omphalos, now located in the W end of the cathedral. Most of the Catholicon lies over the Constantinian and 11C courtyard; the remnants of the 4C apse (which was at the W end of the Constantinian basilica facing towards the tomb) were uncovered a few years ago partly under the S side of the present choir. The present Greek semicircular choir contains two episcopal thrones, that on the N for the Patriarch of Antioch, that on the S for the Patriarch of Jerusalem.

The 12C Crusader church can be seen both inside and outside the Catholicon. Completed by 1149 it consisted of a nave and side aisles, with ambulatory and semicircular apse facing towards the E. It was much restored from 1959. It has the character of a Romanesque-transitional Gothic galleried church, with vaulted upper galleries over the side aisles. The use of vaults on ogival transept crossings was also imported from the W. The pointed arches are characteristic, but much of the sculpture has an Eastern character as also does the cupola resting on drum resting on pendentives over the transept crossing. Five Umayyad capitals were re-used in the N transept and the crossing. Other fragments of masonry which were probably found in the ruins of the Constantinian structure were also re-used in the 12C. Parts of the 12C structure were merged with those of the 11C and this can be seen by returning through the great arch and walking round to the right to the N aisle **(18)**. Here the massive piers and columns of the 12C cathedral and the narrow round arches of the portico in the 11C courtyard or 'Holy Garden' sit side by side. The latter are called the 'Seven Arches of the Virgin' and contain a remarkable jumble of re-used and restored elements including Byzantine basket capitals at the W end.

At the E end of the N aisle is the chapel called the *Prison of Christ* **(19)**, which according to 12C tradition housed Jesus and the two thieves before the Crucifixion. Epiphanius the Monk mentions the Prison of Christ in the 8C. The chapel probably originated as a liturgical station where the Passion and Death of Christ were commemorated, and later an 11C chapel in the Monomachos courtyard was incorporated into the 12C church. A 15C story notes the footprints of Jesus in an altar to the right of the entrance.

Continuing into the ambulatory or retro-choir of the Crusader church there are three chapels located in the three apses in the outer wall probably also remodelled from the 11C court. The NE chapel is the Greek *Chapel of St. Longinus* **(20)**. A 5C tradition claims he was the Roman soldier who pierced Jesus' side with a spear (John 19:34). He was blind in one eye, but on being cured by the water and blood which spurted forth, he repented and was converted. The central E apse contains the Armenian *Chapel of the Parting of the Raiment* **(21)**. The third chapel in the SE apse is the Greek *Chapel of the Derision* or *the Crowning with Thorns* **(22)**. A relic, the *Column of Derision*, stands near the centre but may not be of particular antiquity.

Between the two first chapels is an ornate 12C doorway which led to the Canons' Monastery. Between the two last chapels 29 steps lead down to the large ***Chapel of St. Helena (23)**, (c 20m × 13m), which is 5.3m below the level of the church. It is the Armenian *Chapel of St. Krikor (Gregory)*. Many crosses have been carved on the walls by medieval pilgrims. The chapel consists of three aisles and two apses. The N and S walls are probably the foundations of the lateral naves of the Constantinian church (they are aligned on Golgotha) and it is thought the crypt did not exist in the 4C. It was built by the Crusaders in the early 12C, when older monolithic columns were re-used to support the dome. The pointed vaulting dates to the 12C. There was a tradition that the columns shed tears, attributed by some to the marble sweating in subterranean humidity. The N apse is dedicated to the Penitent Thief, and S to the Empress Helena. A seat in the SE corner is said to have been occupied by the Empress during the search she instituted for the True Cross, a story first mentioned in c 351. Thirteen more steps descend in the SE corner to the later *Chapel of the Invention or Finding of the Cross* which was discovered in a cave. The Greeks have the right side, the Latins the left of the chapel. A life-sized statue of Helena holding the cross has been placed here. The chapel is c 7.3m², 5.3m high and is part of a larger cave walled off in antiquity. A section of the larger cave to the N was investigated in the 1970s (Armenian Patriarchate, Broshi and Barkay) and after clearance is now the Armenian *Chapel of St. Vartan and the Armenian Martyrs* (9.8m × 10.3m). The whole underground cutting (c 25m long and 6.5m to 13m in height) is part of a *malaki* cave-quarry of probably the 8C–6C BC, with many similarities to Solomon's Quarries (Rte 1). The ceiling consists of a harder stratum of *mizzi* limestone. Quantities of Iron Age sherds were recovered, and remnants of walls built by Hadrian in the 2C. One of these contains a re-used stone, perhaps of the 1C BC, with a drawing of a merchant ship and inscription DOMINE IVIMVS, 'Lord we shall go'. The Hadrianic walls were cut by those of Constantine, and rectangular cisterns to N and S of the Chapel of St. Helena may also be of Constantinian date because they are on the same alignment as the 4C walls. These may be the Constantinian cisterns mentioned by the Bordeaux Pilgrim in 333. Another deep cistern lies to the N under the Coptic Monastery, which is also called the *Cistern of St. Helena*; it is also probably of some antiquity (see below). At least 12 cisterns are known under the Church of the Holy Sepulchre.

Returning to the main church and continuing along the S Crusader aisle, we pass on the left a flight of steps up to Calvary, and further on to the left arrive again at the main entrance.

Other fragments of the Constantinian Holy Sepulchre can be seen in adjoining buildings (see below, the Russian Mission in Exile and Zalatimo's shop).

The modern route of the Via Dolorosa and the Stations of the Cross
(summary).

The original route depends on the location of the site of the Praetorium, which tradition locates at the '*Umariyya School* on the site of the Antonia fortress to the E, but which is more likely to have been on the site of the present *Citadel* to the W. The beginnings of this act of pious remembrance are described by Egeria in c 384 when it began at the place of Jesus' arrest at the foot of the Mount of Olives, and a proceeded with hymns through the E gate of the city to Calvary, arriving by dawn on Good Friday. The pious rite became very popular in the 13C, when it started at the House of Pilate and the Chapel of the Flagellation. The present locations are largely those established by the 17C. The buildings at each station are of various periods, all later than the time of Christ. The pilgrim route is regularly performed and starts near the W end of the TARIQ BAB SITTI MARYAM, at the 'Umariyya School (Rte 3), crosses the centre of the Old City and ends at the Holy Sepulchre. The Franciscan pilgrims' procession starts from the Chapel of the Flagellation every Friday at 15.00.

Station 1, the Praetorium where Christ was condemned, at the 'Umariyya School on the site of the Antonia Fortress or at the Chapel of the Flagellation.

Station 2, in the entrance to the Monastery of the Flagellation (Franciscan); formerly in the street, where the 'Scala Sancta' marked the place outside the Praetorium where Jesus took up the Cross. The route then passes the Ecce Homo Arch.

Station 3, where Christ fell, just opposite the Austrian Hospice at the junction with the Tariq al-Wad at the Polish Catholic Church.

Station 4, just down the Tariq al-Wad on the left, at the Armenian Catholic Church of the Spasm, where Christ met the Virgin Mary. Before taking the next turning to the right the House of the Rich Man can be seen, built over the road to the S. Next to it was the House of the Poor Man, both part of the tradition from the 14C, and where the 5th Station used to be located.

Station 5, at the first turning to the right into Tariq al-Saray, on the left, where Jesus fell for the second time and Simon of Cyrene took up the Cross. A modern chapel.

Station 6, continuing up the hill, to the Church of the Holy Face and St. Veronica, mid-way up on the left. Since the 13C tradition located this as the place where St. Veronica offered her handkerchief to Jesus, and received it back with the imprint of his face.

Station 7, at the top of the ascent at the intersection with Khan al-Zait St, is the Porta Judicaria. This station, at which legend relates the decree of death was posted on the city gate, was introduced in the 13C to prove that the Holy Sepulchre was outside the city in the time of Jesus.

Station 8 at the Monastery of St. Caralambos, where Christ addressed the women who accompanied him: 'Daughters of Jerusalem, weep not for me'. This is marked by a plaque on the left of the street up the hill opposite. This station has moved quite often. Return to the suq, turn right and continue a short distance to steps ascending to the left. Continue along the street to the W to . . .

Station 9, at the entrance to the Coptic Convent, where Christ fell for the third time. In the 13C this station was located in the Parvis.

Stations 10, 11, 12 and **13** are on Calvary in the Church of the Holy Sepulchre (see above).

Station 14, is at the Tomb.

Leaving the Parvis by the small doorway at the SE corner one enters the HARAT AL-DABBAGHIN. At c 70m on the left is the **Russian Mission in Exile**, once the Alexandrovsky Hospice of the Russian Palestine Society, built following the visit of the Grand Duke Sergei Alexandrovitch in 1881 (see Rte 14, Russian Compound). Open Mon–Thu 9.00–15.00.

Remains of archaeological interest were discovered and preserved during the construction of the present building. Excavations were carried out by Wilson in 1865, by Clermont-Ganneau in 1874, in 1882, by Antonin in 1883, and by Guthe and Schick in 1885. The rather destroyed fragments are carefully preserved in the basement. They include complex fragments of buildings of Hadrianic Jerusalem re-used in the time of Constantine (see the plan of Constantine's Church of the Holy Sepulchre, above).

Descending the stairs **(1)**, on the right **(2)** is a *column* of the time of Constantine Monomachos (1048) with a plain cushioned capital and cross carved on the shaft. It was constructed on the site of the triple-arched E entrance to the principal forum of Hadrian (AD 135), of which a part of the N bay is preserved **(3)**. Two *Corinthian capitals* survive, with acanthus leaves surmounted by two birds flanking a knot. The higher capital to the left is still *in situ*; the one to the right has been incorporated into the later Byzantine arch. Descend through the arch and turn left, on the left the sill **(4)** at the top of another flight of stairs marks the level of the Hadrianic podium or of the Constaninian S cloister. In front are the remains of the walls of the *Hadrianic basilica* or *temple platform* **(5)** which were re-used by Constantine for the Church of the Holy Sepulchre. The entrance **(6)** may have been part of the Hadrianic arch, but was employed in the Constantinian lay-out as an entrance to the S cloister; tradition holds that it is the entrance by which Jesus was led out of the city on the way to his crucifixion. On the right are the remains of two shattered and blackened columns **(7)** which derive from the portico of the Hadrianic and Constaninian cardo maximus. Remains of others have been noted nearby. To the left are the remains of the *S entrance* **(8)** *to the basilica* of the Holy Sepulchre cut in the Roman wall by Constantine; the remains of the *principal entrance* **(9)** exist in a shop to the N (see below, Zalatimo's Sweetshop). Constantine had the Roman wall veneered with marble, and the pitting in its surface is

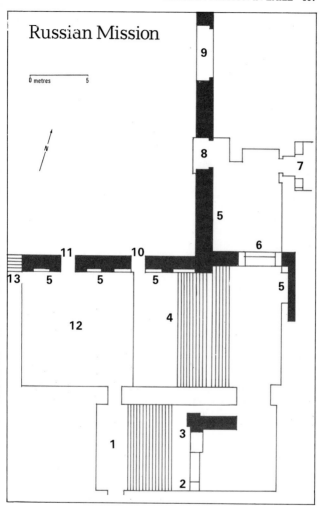

Russian Mission

0 metres — 5

N

due to this. Two other doors on the S side **(10** and **11)** may also have
been cut by Constantine as entrances from the S cloister to the atrium
of the basilica. At the top of the stairs is a modern chapel **(12)**; just
above floor level on the N side drafted Roman masonry is visible.
Through the doorway **(11)** is a small *museum* which displays objects
found in the excavations. The 11C inscription prohibiting non-
Muslims entrance to the Mosque of 'Umar built at the entrance to the
Church of the Holy Sepulchre was found in these excavations. To the
left of the museum entrance is a *medieval archway* which led to the
Canons' Cloister **(13)**.

Leaving the Russian Mission, continue to the end of Harat al-
Dabbaghin, and turn left into KHAN AL-ZAIT ST. At c 50m on the left,

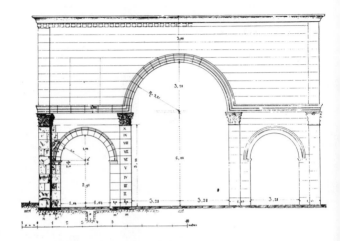

Reconstruction of Hadrian's Arch in the West Forum of Aelia Capitolina (H. Vincent and F.-M. Abel, Jérusalem Nouvelle, Vol. II, fascicles I and II, p. 31, fig. 13: Gabalda, Paris, 1914).

tucked into the angle beyond the steps, is *Zalatimo's Sweet Shop*. Permission may be sought from the owner to visit a storeroom containing the massive remnants of the *4C central doorway* between the propylaea and E atrium of the Constantinian basilica (better preserved than the S doorway seen in the Russian Mission). The wall in which it was inserted is probably also part of the Hadrianic Basilica (135). This central door still stands nearly 4m high.

Ascending the adjacent steps brings the visitor to various other remains associated with the Church of the Holy Sepulchre. At the top of the steps, continue along the 'AQABAT DAIR AL-SULTAN, pass the small doorway into the courtyard, turn left and continue to the end of the lane. A blocked doorway to the right used to lead to a deep flight of 43 steps descending to the old *'Cistern of St. Helena'*, of uncertain date; straight ahead is the entrance to the *Coptic Patriarchate*, with the *Queen Helen Coptic church* on the right. In the 16C the Sultan gave the Copts the ruins of the 12C Latin cloister, where they built the bishop's house, a hospice for pilgrims, and a church (now restored); the complex is thus called locally the Dair al-Sultan. The column shaft to the left of the entrance marks the **Ninth Station of the Cross**. The entrance on the left side of the passage leads to the **Ethiopian Monastery** on the roof above the Chapel of St. Helena. Through heavy Ottoman taxation and debt the Ethiopian community lost their ownership to various parts of the Church of the Holy Sepulchre (the Chapel of St. Mary the Egyptian, of St. Michael and of the Apostles in the Parvis were taken over by the Copts in the 16C and 17C) and now occupy small cells built in the ruins of the 12C Canon's Cloister, over the ruined aisles of the 4C basilica. Despite the poverty it is a very peaceful and attractive place. The central dome in the court is that of the Chapel of St. Helena. On the W is the E end of the Greek cathedral. In the ruined S and W walls are the remains of the 12C arcades with numerous fragments of carving, including elbow brackets from which the arcades spring, and carved voussoirs. Just S of the cathedral the back of the *Chapel of Melchizedek* above Calvary can be seen; and on the S of the cloister are parts of the 12C refectory. A door in the SW corner leads down to the **Chapel of the Ethiopians**, and then to the **Coptic Chapel of St. Michael**, from which it is possible to exit to the Parvis.

Retracing our steps either through the little door in the SE corner of the Parvis, or back through Khan al-Zait St and Harat al-Dabbaghin, this time look to the S and to the area of the **Muristan**, which occupies the whole block S of the Church of the Holy Sepulchre, and was the location of the headquarters of the Crusader Knights of St. John, the Hospitallers. The area has an interesting history, but few remains survived the major redevelopment carried out at the end of the 19C. The modern name is derived from the Persian word for hospital and dates from the 13C. It now contains on the E the German Evangelical Church; in the centre the New Bazaar; on the N side a Greek monastery and a Muslim mosque (see above); and on the SW the Church of St. John the Baptist (see above).

History. Excavations (Warren and Wilson, 1867; Kenyon, 1961–63; Lux, 1970–71) have shown that the area was quarried in the 7C BC and was presumably outside the town until the time of Hadrian (2C) when a great fill was employed to level the surface prior to the building of Aelia Capitolina. Some 2C and Byzantine remains were uncovered. A hospice built by Pope Gregory I in 603 is recorded. At the beginning of the 9C, in the time of the Abbasid Caliph Harun al-Rashid, the Emperor Charlemagne built a church and hospice for pilgrims here, which was served by the Benedictine order. It was visited by Bernard the Monk in 870, who describes the hospice standing beside the Church of St. Mary, with its library, and endowment of land in the Valley of Jehoshaphat. It was destroyed in the persecution by al-Hakim in 1009.

The merchants of Amalfi, established in Jerusalem in the 11C, received from the Fatimid Caliph some land in this area; probably between 1036 and 1070 they built a monastery in honour of St. Mary, perhaps on the older ruins, served by an abbot and monks from Italy. This church was called St. Mary of the Latins (St. Mary Major) and was almost certainly on the NE corner of the area. A daughter convent adjacent (probably that near the centre of the Muristan) was built by 1080 for women pilgrims, first called St. Mary Magdalene, later St. Mary Minor. They also founded c 1170 a hospital and church for poor and sick pilgrims dedicated to St. John (Almoner, according to William of Tyre) but it is not clear whether this was a separate foundation from the ancient church of St. John Baptist in the SW corner of the area. At an early date both dedications appear to exist. A 12C tradition held that Zechariah, the father of St. John the Baptist, had governed the hospital in its earliest days. By 1099 there were at least three Benedictine foundations S of the church of the Holy Sepulchre, St. Mary of the Latins with its hospice; St. Mary Minor and its hospice for women; the church of St. John Baptist, and the hospital for sick pilgrims, perhaps with another chapel dedicated to St. John Almoner. The administrator of the hospital, dependant on the Abbot of St. Mary's, was Gerard, who remained in the city during the Frankish siege of 1099. After the capture of the city the hospital received generous gifts from Godfrey of Bouillon and in particular from Baldwin I, and became independent of the Benedictine Order by 1113. By this time the Order of the Knights of St. John and the Hospital in Jerusalem was an international organisation governed from Jerusalem. Gerard died in 1120 and was succeeded by Raymond du Puy, under whom the Order developed its characteristic form and Augustine rule. He was noted for his piety, but was also an able politician and negotiator. By the time of his death (c 1158–60) the Order had received many gifts, eventually becoming one of the richest of the medieval orders, and had begun to take on a military role which almost overshadowed its primary charitable purpose.

A Papal Bull of 1154 made the order independent of the local church, responsible directly to the Pope. Stupid quarrels developed in this invidious situation; the Hospitallers rang the bells of the Hospital during the Patriarch's sermons, and actually fired flights of arrows into the Church of the Holy Sepulchre which were collected and hung up in Calvary by the angry Patriarch. At the same time, the hospital's treatment of the sick was in advance of anything in the contemporary west, and had undoubtedly derived benefit from Arab medicine and practice from the 11C onward.

The buildings of the hospice and hospital of St. John were enlarged and beautified in the 1150s; 400 knights lodged there in 1163. The hospital itself, if the remains excavated in the SE area belong to it (where the largest and most numerous cisterns are located), was over 70m long, 36.5m wide, with arches nearly 5.5m high. John of Würzburg in the 1170s says there were 2000 patients of both sexes in the hospital at the time, including gynaecological cases; it was so busy that 50 dead were removed in one night (see Aceldama, Rte 15), and were immediately replaced by new patients. They were looked after by four doctors and four surgeons, with nine sergeants to each ward; the records of the quantities of food and bedding required show this account was probably not exaggerated. In 1179 there were at least 900 in the hospital and a few days later 750 wounded were admitted after the Battle of Montgisard.

The Order was involved in formulating the terms of surrender to Salah al-Din in 1187, and with the Latin Patriarch, the Knights are accused of ungenerous treatment of the poorer Latin Christians whose ransoms were not paid and who were sold into slavery. Ten Hospitallers were allowed to stay in Jerusalem for one year to look after the sick, but the Order was dispossessed of the church and the hospital. The spire of St. Mary Major was thrown down, the church turned into a mosque, and the adjacent hospice into a Shafi'ite College; in 1192/3 the NW part of the property was given to Salah al-Din's son who built a mosque; and a hospital was established in 1216 in the old hospital by Salah al-Din's nephew, Shihab al-Din. When pilgrimage recommenced, Latin pilgrims lodged outside the city in the Asnerie (Rte 13), but Frederick II stayed in the palace or hospice of the Knights opposite the Holy Sepulchre when he crowned himself king in the Church of the Holy Sepulchre on 18 March 1229. In 1336 a Latin nun was in charge of a hospice in the Muristan; and in 1347 Niccolo da Poggibonsi recorded a hospice 'above John Baptist'; in 1384 a hospice close to the Church of the Holy Sepulchre may have been under the care of the Franciscans. Nompar de Caumont stayed there in 1418–20, and was made a Knight of the Holy Sepulchre by the Franciscan Custos. In 1483 Felix Fabri described a hospice in a large vaulted building, which was squalid and ruinous, in a part of the ancient hospital which looked like a monastic refectory. It contained 400 pilgrims, but could have held 1000. Not long after it was so dirty, and the pilgrims so pestered by the local inhabitants, that they had begun to seek accommodation elsewhere. By c 1524 it seems to have been abandoned. In 1537–41 some of the ruins were quarried for the building of the city walls. The Greek Orthodox built a hospice in the SW c 1660. Le Bruyn could still see the ruins of the 'House of the Knights of Malta' in 1674. Later the site fell into further decay, and in 1868 was mostly ploughland.

In 1869, on the visit of the Crown Prince Frederick William of Prussia, the Sultan gave Prussia and the modern Order of the Knights of St. John the E half of the Muristan. In the NE corner the German Protestant Church of the Redeemer (Erlöserkirche) was built, and consecrated on 31 October 1898 in the presence of the Emperor William II and the Empress Augusta Victoria (the daughter of Queen Victoria of England). This is built on the site of the church which was probably that of St. Mary of the Latins, and follows its plan closely. On the S side the old cloisters and refectory were preserved. In the SE part is some land belonging to the Order of St. John. The W side belongs to the Greek Orthodox Patriarchate, with new bazaar, the Church of St. John the Baptist and the monastery of Gethsemane. The Mosque of 'Umar is located at the NW corner.

Visit. The Church of the Redeemer and tower. Open Sat–Thu 9.00–13.00, 14.00–17.00, Fri 9.00–13.00. The original scuplture on the N door (the principal Benedictine entrance) on Harat al-Dabbaghin has been carefully restored in the late 19C building. The main series of reliefs on the arch depict battered and mostly headless figures of the months, which were named but are now very difficult to distinguish. The series begins at the bottom left with January and is capped by the sun (a half-figure with disc above the head) and moon (a female with crescent) at top centre between June and July. The most easily discerned figure is August, a thresher. The full series included February, a man pruning a tree; April, a seated figure; May, a kneeling man cultivating; July, a reaper; August, a thresher; September, a grape gatherer; October, a man with a cask; November, a standing woman. Above, a frieze of rosettes and modillions with grotesque faces support a cornice. The lively figural art is reminiscent of the sculptures on the nearby façade of the Church of the Holy Sepulchre. Heraldic shields occupy the corners.

The modern entrance is from the W in FREDERICK WILLIAM ST. The church is built on the lines of the earlier Church of St. Mary of the Latins (11C–12C, converted to a mosque by Salah al-Din after 1187) and was consecrated in 1898. The belfry at the SW corner is the highest tower in the vicinity and from it a fine prospect of the Old City may be had. By previous arrangment only it is possible to visit the deep excavations under the church (Lux, 1970–71), the foundations of which are placed on bedrock nearly 14m below. The remains of a 7C BC quarry, and a wall of the Hadrianic period were discovered. The entrance is from the cloister. On the S side of the church and entered by the door to the Evangelical Hospice in Frederick William St, are the *cloisters and refectory* belonging to the 12C hospice, but altered when the buildings were converted to use as a Muslim law school in the 13C–14C. The cloisters, with two storeys surrounding a square court, have the refectory on the S side. On the W is an Ayyubid staircase moved from the N side to its present site during the reconstructions in 1898.

To the S of this complex is land belonging to the Knights of St. John of Jerusalem, where excavations were carried out by Kenyon in 1961–63. Clearance at the end of the 19C was so drastic that only the foundations of the massive medieval piers were discovered (perhaps part of the hospital itself). On the opposite side of Frederick William St is the *New Bazaar* built in 1901 and belonging to the Greek Patriarchate: its elaborate diagonal layout and central fountain has a strong 19C European orientalising character. It stands over the site of the 11/12C Church of St. Mary Minor, a church with three aisles and three apses which was uncovered briefly during the construction of the bazaar. The Greek *Church of St. John the Baptist* lies to the SW (see above), the Greek *Convent of Gethsemane* to the N (said to be on the site of the residence of the Grand Master of the Knights of St. John). The convent was built in the 19C. It requires considerable imagination to visualise the area as the well-built and busy 12C headquarters of a great hospital and military order.

Continuing to the S end of Frederick William St, and turning left onto DAVID ST brings one down to the **main bazaar** or great covered markets of Jerusalem. Daunting in their dimness, size and the massed quantity of goods in small shops, they epitomise the market of an oriental town. They are made up of three parallel streets interconnected by small alleys. They were Crusader streets, built over the Roman and Byzantine cardo maximus at the heart of the city. On the W is the *Suq al-Lahhamin*, or *Street of the Meat Sellers*, in Crusader times the vegetable market. In the centre is the *Suq al-'Attarin*, the *Street of the Spice Sellers*: in the 12C it was the covered market for the drapers and was the property of St. Anne's Church (Rte 3). Some of the shops, set in arched recesses covered by vaults with pointed arches, still have the monogram 'SA' incised in the masonry. When St. Anne's was converted into a mosque and school by Salah al-Din after 1187, he endowed it with this property. The streets on either side were then endowments of the Aqsa Mosque. On the E is the *Suq al-Khawajat, Street of the Merchants*, in Crusader times called Malcuisinat St. In the 12C at the N and S ends

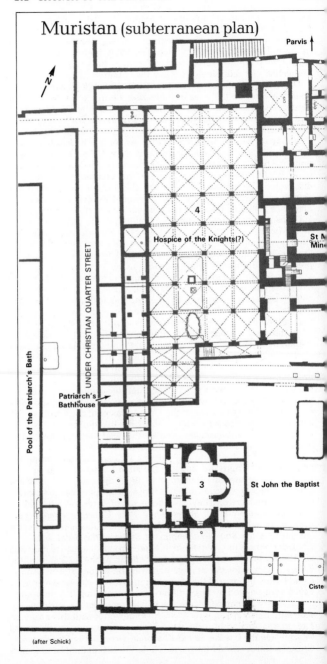

Muristan (subterranean plan)

Parvis ↑

N

4

Hospice of the Knights(?)

St M
Min

UNDER CHRISTIAN QUARTER STREET

Pool of the Patriarch's Bath

Patriarch's
Bathhouse

3

St John the Baptist

Ciste

(after Schick)

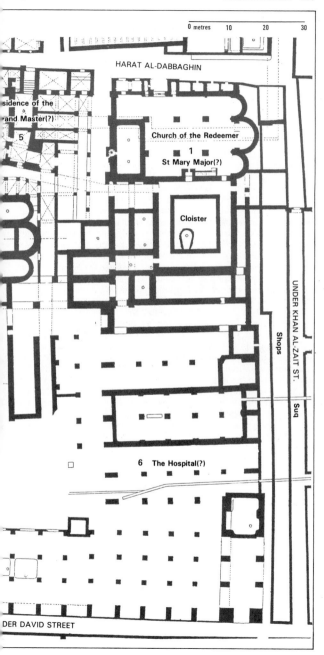

HARAT AL-DABBAGHIN

sidence of the
and Master(?)

5

Church of the Redeemer

1

St Mary Major(?)

Cloister

Shops

UNDER KHAN AL-ZAIT ST.

Suq

6   The Hospital(?)

DER DAVID STREET

of the markets, the streets running to the E contained that other
necessary adjunct to a busy market, the shops of the money
changers; that of the Syrians lay to the N, and that of the Franks to
the S (in the modern TARIQ BAB AL-SILSILA). Nearby were at least two
caravanserais, the *Khan al-Zait* and the *Khan al-Sultan*. The
atmosphere of these markets can have changed relatively little in the
last 2000 years. A short stroll southwards brings one into the
excavated section of the Byzantine cardo maximus (Rte 7). It is
possible to savour the contrast between the living entity and the
preserved monument, both contributing important images to the
historical picture of Jerusalem.

At this point the visitor can continue N from the bazaar to the
DAMASCUS GATE, or return up DAVID ST to the Jaffa Gate having
seen the principal monuments of the Christian Quarter. Alternatively
a walk through the more distant streets of the quarter can be taken.
For the latter, return up David St and just beyond the Petra Hostel
turn right into the HARAT AL-ISTAMBULIYYA, opposite the corner of
the citadel. Under the building on the opposite side of the street and
following the same line as the street, a wall was uncovered during
rebuilding earlier this century which is proposed by some as the
Second or *Third North Wall* of the Roman period, but is probably
Byzantine. It starts from the NE corner of the Citadel opposite. About
35m up the street on the left a covered passage leads into a little
circular crossing. A lamp at the centre is placed on a column with
Latin inscription dating to the beginning of the 3C. It reads: M(ARCO)
IUNIO MAXIMO LEG(ATO) AUG(USTORUM) LEG(IONIS) X FR(ETENSIS)—
ANTONINIANAE—C. DOM(ITIUS) SERG(IUS) STR(ATOR) EIUS. It honors a
prefect of Judaea and was erected by one of his staff. Another
inscription of the Tenth Legion with the names of Vespasian and
Titus was found in the excavations S of the Haram.

Returning to the street, opposite to the left is the *Greek Catholic
Patriarchate*; go directly opposite into MUEZZIN ST which twists its
way past first, on the left, the *Coptic Monastery of St. George* or *Mar
Jirias*. It is a convent and hospice with an old, dark church, in which
(according to Schick in 1896) the insane were cured by the healing
powers of St. George. 12C Crusader maps mark the *Church of St.
George infunda* probably on this site; a Church of St. George served
by two clergy is mentioned in the 9C Commemoratorium (see also St.
Demetrius, below). Continuing a further 70m, into 'AQABAT AL-
KHADR (ST. GEORGE ST) the **Coptic Khan** is on the right. The Khan
was built by the Copts in 1836/7 on the site of a sesame oil mill and
garden with olive trees, with voluntary Coptic labour at a cost of
500,000 piastres, for use by the Coptic pilgrims from Egypt. Its rear
wall overlooks the Pool of the Patriarch's Bath. It is variously
occupied by workshops and rather dingy.

Opposite the Khan is the rebuilt Greek Orthodox *Monastery of the
Most Holy Virgin, Megale Panagia*, 'the Great All-Holy', known as
the *Dair al-Banat*, or *Nunnery*, a 12C church and once possibly the
site of the *Church of the Spoudaioi*. The latter was built by the
Patriarch Elias in c 494 for the society of monks who had attached
themselves to the Church of the Anastasis and at first lived near the
Tower of David. It contained a Church of the Mother of God. The
street then debouches on to CHRISTIAN QUARTER ST just before the
turning to the Church of the Holy Sepulchre. Continuing to the left
up Christian Quarter St, past numerous shops, one can note 2C–7C
paving stones with ridges polished by long use, which were discovered several metres below the present street level during recent

relaying of the drains in the Christian Quarter. Part of a fine gadrooned archway can be seen on the right. It was a Crusader entrance to the Church of St. Mary on the N side of the Rotunda of the Church of the Holy Sepulchre.

At 90m on the left 'AQABAT DAIR AL-RUM leads to the entrance of the **Great Greek Monastery**, a very large Orthodox complex mentioned in c 1400 as the Monastery of St. Thecla, to whom the main 12C church is dedicated. The monastery is probably older, and is a labyrinth of houses and courts, steps and lanes extending to join the Church of the Holy Sepulchre on the E. The chapel of Constantine abuts the Rotunda. Another chapel is dedicated to St. Helena. It has a large library, including manuscripts of 10C date. On the opposite (N) side of this street is the **Greek Orthodox Patriarchate**.

The Greek Orthodox are an important and ancient Christian community in Jerusalem: in 1922 it was estimated that there were nearly 33,000 in Palestine, of whom 6000 lived in Jerusalem. The problems arising from a mostly Greek-born and Greek-speaking clergy with a largely locally born and Arabic-speaking congregation caused some resentment in the 19C and early 20C; the Patriarch is one of the four Orthodox Patriarchs of the East. *The Patriarchate Museum* contains sarcophagi from Herod's Family Tomb (Rte 14). Next door on the W is the Greek Orthodox *Church of St. Nicolas*, acquired by the Greeks when the Georgians left in 1685. It stands on 12C foundations.

Returning to Christian Quarter St, and continuing to its N end, on the right in AL-KHANQAH ST, is the **al-Khanqah Mosque**, the Salahiyya Khanqah. Built in c 1120 as the palace of the Latin Patriarch in Crusader Jerusalem (it lies just NW of the Church of the Holy Sepulchre), the property was confiscated after the Latins left in 1187 and was endowed by Salah al-Din as a khanqah (convent for Sufi mystics) in 1189. The assembly hall with mihrab was restored in 1341, and the minaret and portal were constructed before 1417–18. The minaret is almost identical to that of the Mosque of 'Umar (see p.181). It is built on the E side of the entrance to the mosque, a square tower with four storeys, and gallery, lantern, drum and dome above. The octagonal lantern has an arch with gadrooned voussoirs in each face. The mosque and imam's house were damaged in 1719–20 during the restoration of the Dome of the Holy Sepulchre, when some Byzantine mosaics were also destroyed. Enlart recorded that a Byzantine chapel (perhaps that of St. Chariton) complete but for the apse was destroyed in building work on this site in 1928.

One can now continue down St. Francis St towards KHAN AL-ZAIT ST, passing the Greek Orthodox *Monastery of St. Caralambos* with the **Eighth Station of the Cross**, and turn left for the Damascus Gate; or to complete the walk through the Christian Quarter, there are numerous small churches with long histories along St. Francis St and up towards the NW corner of the Old City and the tour can continue to the New or the Jaffa Gate.

Opposite the Khanqah Mosque a street to the N. (HARAT DAIR AL-TUFFAH) contains, to the left, the Greek Orthodox *Mikra Panagia 'Little St. Mary'*, or *Saidnaya (St. Anne)*, a 12C church with hospice for women; adjacent to the N is the Greek Orthodox *Church of St. Euthymius*. The present church of St. Euthymius (formerly the Byzantine church of St. Sergius according to E. Moore, rebuilt by John the Almoner after the destruction of 614) existed in the 12C. Following the street W onto HADDADIN ST, one can either walk NE towards the Damascus Gate to the Greek Orthodox *Monastery of St.*

Spyridion (formerly St. Serapeon) in the salient of the city wall to the W of the Gate; or go SW on Haddadin St to the Greek Orthodox *Church of St. Catherine*; a 12C church on this site was acquired from the Georgians in 1685. Little of the Crusader structure seems to have survived. Continuing S from the latter church, one regains St. Francis St (formerly the Street of the Franks). Turning right, at c 20m on the left just beyond the vaulting over the street is an *inscription* (which may not be *in situ*) which records the repair of a mosque, the Masjid Mansuri (1287–88) and its endowment in the reign of Sultan Qala'un. The existence of this mosque is confirmed in a court register of 1661, when it is referred to as the 'Jami' Qala'un'. At c 50m on the right is the *Church of St. Michael*, and next that of *St. George*, both acquired by the Greek Orthodox from the Serbs in 1623. St. George is probably a Byzantine foundation, also recorded in the 12C. At the next angle of the road on the right is the large establishment of the *Friars Minor* or *Order of St. Francis* and the *Custodia Terrae Sanctae* with the *Church of St. Saviour* and monastery.

History. The Franciscans returned to Jerusalem in 1335 and were granted the right of custodianship of the Christian Holy Places for the Latins. They settled at first on Mount Zion (Rte 8). Boniface of Ragusa who was the Franciscan *custos* after 1555, bought the 12/13C Church of St. John the Theologian from the Georgians in 1559, and called it St. Saviour. The Franciscans received permission from the Ottoman Government to repair the church c 1652, but rumours that it was being fortified in collusion with the Franks (the Muslims continued to fear another Crusade) caused trouble among the Muslim population and the church was attacked. In the 19C the church was small, with four pillars supporting a low vaulted roof with a dome in front of the high altar. It was inadequate for the large congregation. The monastic complex was fortress-like, and contained cisterns, gardens, courts, stables, cellars, storehouses for food, wood and charcoal, horse-mills, ovens, forges, carpenters shops, turners, cobblers, candlers, dispensary and printing press, as well as monks' cells, infirmary, library and treasury. The present church on the site is modern with a large square 19C tower and spire.

Following the road to the right towards New Gate, at a short distance a cul-de-sac to the right leads to the Greek Orthodox *Church of St. Basil*. The church is noted in the 12C and the 16C, and was acquired by the Greeks from the Georgians in 1685. Little of the older structure survives.

New Gate St leads N to the New Gate. A small early Ottoman mosque *Masjid al-Qaymari* is adjacent to the city wall, and in the NW angle of the walls is *Christian Brothers College* (for both of which, see Rte 1). Continuing by one of the various streets running to the S, on HARAT AL-WARIYYA is the *Latin Patriarchate and Seminary* begun in 1859, adjacent to the W wall of the Old City. To the E, on ISTAM-BULIYYA ST, is the Spanish hospice, the *Casa Nova*. Just N of the Casa Nova is the small Greek Orthodox *Church of St. Theodore* on two levels; a 6C church probably on this site is mentioned by Cyril of Scythopolis. South of the Casa Nova, on the E of the street and now part of the Greek School, is the *Chapel of St. Demetrius*, a church mentioned in the 14C. It is said to stand on Byzantine foundations, and has a dome supported by four piers. Its relationship to the nearby Coptic church of St. George is unclear. As we return in the direction of the Citadel and the Jaffa Gate, we pass through the area which was the Grain Market in Crusader times.

5 The Citadel

Introduction. The *Citadel of Jerusalem, A. *al-Qal'a*, stands on the S side of the Jaffa Gate on one of the highest points of the Old City overlooking the steep-sided Valley of Hinnom to the W and a minor transverse valley to the N which was filled in probably in the 2C. The site was strategically located against attack from both inside and outside the city. Herod the Great built three great towers over earlier foundations to defend his adjacent palace, which became the basis of citadels at later periods. Probably the site of the Praetorium at which Jesus was condemned to death, and the scene of a massacre of the Roman garrison by the Jews during the First Revolt, the Citadel was called the Tower of David in Crusader times and was restored by both Mamluk and Ottoman rulers. It is now the Museum of the History of Jerusalem.

History. The earliest remains recovered in archaeological excavations on the site are of 7C BC date when the area was quarried for stone for the city walls. The area appears to have been outside the city then though there was a considerable build-up of 7C BC debris. The earliest defensive wall (which formed the NW angle of the city) has been dated to the Early Hellenistic period by Johns (1934–48), to the Hasmonean period by Amiran and Eitan (1968–69) and by Bahat and Broshi (1971), and to the period of Herod the Great by Tushingham (excavations to the S in the Armenian Garden 1962–67) and may date to the reign of the Hasmonean John Hyrcanus (134–104 BC). All agree with the evidence of Josephus (War V:161–176) that Herod the Great constructed three great towers on the site, which he named after Phasael his brother, Hippicus his friend and Mariamne his wife. Immediately abutting the towers to the S Herod the Great built his palace, which is also described by Josephus (War V:177–183) as notable for its large rooms and porticoes, its fine groves, dovecotes and streams of water. The excavations have shown that this was constructed on a podium which raised the ground level by 3–4m and covered most of the area from the citadel S to the present S wall of the Old City, being perhaps 300–350m in length. Very little of the palace remains, apart from a few wall stubs on top of the podium, and some fragments of painted wall plaster.

The palace continued to be used following the death of Herod the Great, first by his successors, then by the Roman prefects and procurators on official visits from the capital at Caesarea and it seems likely that this was the Praetorium in which Jesus was condemned by Pontius Pilate c AD 30. The palace was attacked and one of its towers was mined by the insurgents in the course of the First Jewish Revolt in AD 66 (Josephus, War II:431–56). The Roman garrison took refuge in the Herodian towers, but were treacherously slaughtered by the Jews after agreeing to surrender. After the revolt the area was used for the camp of the Tenth Legion (of which very few traces remain though the towers were preserved and presumably used as part of the fortifications of the Roman camp), and very little else survives until the Crusader period, although at least one of the Herodian towers must have continued to stand and there is some evidence to suggest there was an Umayyad palace on the site. The Fatimid garrison made its last stand in the Citadel in the face of the Crusader onslaught in 1099 and from it negotiated their surrender. It was rebuilt on its present line by the Crusaders. The Turres David was a major landmark of the Crusader town, built on the great tower base usually identified with the Phasael tower of Herod, but possibly that of Hippicus. The association with David is a late tradition. The Crusader king Baldwin II chose the site as his palace (the *curia regis*) in 1118. Queen Melisande was besieged in this palace-citadel in 1152 by her son Baldwin III. Parts of the palace, including two vaulted ground-floor storage chambers, 17m long, have been found c 125m S of the Citadel. Great rock-cut cisterns were found beneath them (Bahat and Broshi).

The citadel continued to be used, restored and added to in the Islamic period. The Ayyubids added a tower, the Mamluks under al-Nasir Muhammad in 1310–11 built extensively and added a mosque. The mosque was a 'Friday Mosque' to allow the soldiers to attend Friday prayers without leaving the Citadel unguarded, and is the only mosque built in the Mamluk period known in the city. The Ottoman rulers also restored the Citadel, in particular Sulaiman

II in 1531–32, who also added a minaret. The barracks of the Turkish garrison adjoined the citadel to the S. Allenby proclaimed the liberation of the city from the steps in front of the entrance in 1917. The Citadel was a police post and barracks until 1967, and has now been restored as a museum.

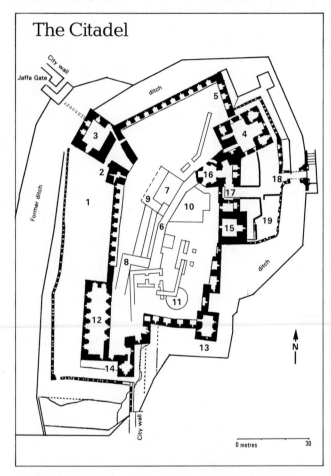

The Citadel

Visit. The Museum of the History of Jerusalem is open daily 8.30–16.00 in winter, 8.30–17.00 in summer; Friday 8.30–14.00; admission charged. It is entered from just outside the Jaffa Gate where the road lies over the filled-in dry ditch which once surrounded the medieval Citadel. The visitor enters the outer *barbican of Sulaiman II*, which is paved **(1)**. Ahead is the Mamluk wall of the inner citadel. The fine machicolations of the *NW tower* **(3)** and the *tower on the SW* are also Mamluk. Below the SW tower were Crusader stables and a postern. To the right the continuation of the rampart walk to the S with entrance below the minaret; and to the left the ticket office and the *inner gate of Sulaiman II* **(2)**. Inside, the visitor can first ascend the

NW gate tower, to the *small museum* **(3)**. This contains a reconstruction of the three towers of Herod the Great, and a display on the mechanics of contemporary Roman warfare, with reconstructed ballista machines, and the original lead ballistae they fired; other weapons such as arrows and the butts of spears are shown. Objects from the citadel excavations include roof tiles of the Tenth Roman Legion, pottery and drain pipes; and Ottoman coffee cups and tobacco pipes of the 16C–17C. In the adjacent tower is a model of the Old City, with an audio-visual aid to the location of many monuments in the city.

It is possible to walk round the citadel ramparts and then to descend to the interior to view the remains of the older citadel. A numbered series of descriptive panels provides a detailed guide for the visitor. In a beautifully designed garden with lawns and some interesting plants, including papyrus and cactus, the remains of the *Hasmonean and Herodian wall and towers* can be seen lying right across the centre of the present citadel.

To the E the solid base of the great **tower of Herod the Great (4)** rises direct from the grass. Very large stones with flat dressed edges and low but rough bosses are characteristic of his work. The preserved top of the Herodian work in the tower is 21.4m × 17.10m, and wider at the base (22.60m × 18.30m) with eight courses remaining which are founded on bedrock. The preserved height is 18.95m. It is usually identified with Herod's Phasael Tower for which the dimensions given by Josephus are closest, but there are also grounds for suggesting it is the tower of Hippicus, with those of Phasael and Mariamne yet undiscovered to the E. The smaller masonry in the upper tower is the work of al-Nasir Muhammad in the 14C.

Abutting the tower on the N side is the remnant of a *city wall of the Byzantine period* **(5)**, thought by some to be part of the Third North Wall of the period of Herod Agrippa. The present citadel wall is built above it. A jumble of masonry of different periods lies across the centre of the court. The *Hasmonean wall with two towers* **(6, 7, 8)** lies to the W of the Herodian tower. The Hasmonean masonry is typically of smaller blocks, with wide drafted edges and low pecked bosses. The Hasmonean city wall was up to 5.40m in width, and Herod the Great increased the size of the *central tower* **(9)** and thickened the wall to c 8.00m. On the S side of the wall and towers, excavations which descended nearly 11m beneath the surface of the courtyard showed rooms abutting the Hasmonean wall **(10)**. These remains were covered by the construction of the podium for Herod the Great's palace, 3m–4m high, retained by a network of walls on a different alignment. On the podium a few low fragments of house walls were preserved from the destructions in AD 66–70. Other additions were made to these defences in the 1C AD and in the Byzantine and medieval periods.

At the S end of the court is a wall with attached *round tower* **(11)** in the style of the Umayyads, with fragments of stone window grilles. It could be part of an 8C Umayyad palace in the citadel. The Crusaders constructed a castle straddling the old Jewish wall on the present lines, which was first refurbished with the addition of a tower by al-Malik al-ʿAdil I in 1213–14 and then dismantled a few years later by al-Malik al-Muʿazzam.

Continuing to the SW area of the citadel the Mamluk and Ottoman work on the citadel can be admired. The citadel gained its present appearance under the Mamluk al-Nasir Muhammad in 1310–11. He built the *mosque* in the SW corner (12) above a Crusader vaulted hall which had a postern gate at its NW corner (now blocked) and entrance at the SE corner. He also built the *SE tower* (13) and the upper part of the *Herodian tower* (4). A general restoration was made in 1531–32 by Sulaiman II. The inscription over the minbar in the mosque records his repair of the mosque, and the adjacent *minaret* (14) was probably built at this time and restored in 1655. Passing the SE tower the visitor arrives at the complex which includes the E tower, adjacent E gate complex, and the NE tower founded on the base of the great tower of Herod. The *E tower* (15) is probably Mamluk, built over Crusader foundations. The excavations in the court can be seen from above at this point.

Entering by the fine 14C *Mamluk hexagonal chamber* (16) which has a display of the history of the walls of Jerusalem, the visitor should proceed up to the *viewing point on the roof of the restored NE tower (4) whence a splendid prospect over the Old City may be obtained. The **Model Room** in one of the upper storeys contains a display of Jerusalem people and costumes.

A *book shop* is located just inside the fine *Crusader and Ottoman entrance gate*. Here (17) a 12C complex of guard room with benches, inner gate with a right-angled turn and portcullis leads to the entrance built by the Crusaders and restored by the Mamluks (1310–11). The iron-plated doors are Ottoman. The *outer barbican* (18) was built by the Ottoman Sulaiman II over part of the Crusader gate system. His inscriptions can be seen on the outer gate, at the *open-air mosque* (19) S of the bridge and on the N side of the bridge itself. Allenby proclaimed the conquest of Jerusalem from the outer steps on 11 December 1917.

6   The Armenian Quarter

Introduction. The Armenian Quarter occupies c 10.5 hectares (26 acres) of the SW part of the Old City. It is divided by Armenian Quarter Road, with a relatively empty plot, the 'Armenian Garden', on the W, and the densely built up convent and residential section on the E. Just outside the city walls to the S are the Armenian Church of the Holy Saviour and the Armenian cemetery (Rte 8). The N and E fringes of the quarter are occupied by other groups, including Anglican Protestant Christians, Syrian and Greek Orthodox Christians, Muslims and Jews (for the latter, see Rte 7).

History. The Armenian Christians come from the areas of modern SE Turkey and NW Iran which were occupied in ancient times by the Kingdom of Urartu. Armenian merchants and mercenaries are mentioned in Palestine in the Roman period; their kingdom was early converted to Christianity and pilgrims came to Jerusalem as early as the beginning of the 4C. By the 7C an Armenian doctor named Haratoun listed 70 Armenian convents in Jerusalem, mostly founded during the Patriarchate of St. Gregory the Illuminator, of which few traces remain apart from the Armenian mosaic not far from the Damascus Gate (Rte 13) and another found on the Mount of Olives (Rte 12). These suffered during the Persian and Islamic invasions of the 7C and the list of establishments was reduced to 15.

Nearly half the Armenian population of the Araxes Valley and Van migrated SW to the mid-Euphrates, Taurus and Cilician areas in the 11C due to pressure from the Seljuq Turks, and by c 1077 were establishing small states there. They profited by the scramble for territory among the Byzantines, Turks and Crusaders to establish the Kingdom of Armenia c 1098 which endured until

1375 in Cilicia. Baldwin became Count of Armenian Edessa in 1098, before succeeding Godfrey as ruler of Jerusalem in 1099. Revival of their fortunes in Jerusalem began in the 12C when the Armenians bought the Church of St. James from the Georgians (also Orthodox Christians, from the Caucasus area of modern Russia). Some expansion is recorded in the 14C; and the 17C and mid-18C were also prosperous periods for the Armenians, when they extended their rights in the Church of the Holy Sepulchre. The Armenian Patriarch in Jerusalem was linked by close cultural and hierarchical ties with the Patriarchs in Constantinople and Etchmiadzin and most higher clerical appointments were filled by Armenians born in the north.

In 1880 Wilson described the Armenians as few in number, but a thriving community occupying one of the pleasanter quarters of Jerusalem, with a seminary and educated clergy; the convent of St. James was the largest and richest in the Old City. The grim massacres of Armenians in the north by the Turks at the beginning of the 20C had their reflections in the attitudes of the community and some survivors came to Jerusalem. The convent retains many of the splendours of the past despite impoverishment and emigration. The population is now about 2000, and Jerusalem is a religious centre for some five million Armenians dispersed world-wide.

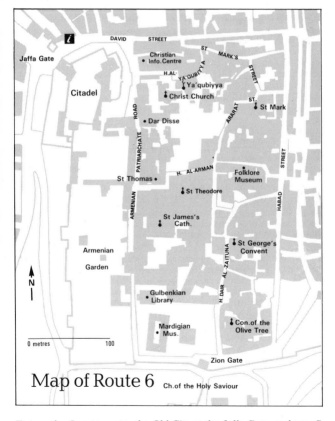

Map of Route 6 Ch.of the Holy Saviour

To tour the Quarter, enter the Old City at the Jaffa Gate, and turn S along Armenian Patriarchate Road. Passing the Christian Information Centre on the left, where times of services etc. can be obtained, a turning to the left almost directly opposite the entrance to the Citadel

(Rte 5) leads to the *Anglican Christ Church* and hospice which is principally of interest for the history of the Protestant Christians in Jerusalem. In 1841 on the iniative of Frederick William IV of Prussia a joint English/Prussian bishopric in Jerusalem was established and endowed, partly under the impulse of historical piety and missionary intentions, partly to relieve and support distressed Oriental Christians. Bishop Alexander was consecrated at Lambeth Palace, London, on 7 November 1841; he arrived in Jerusalem in 1842. A firman granted by the Ottoman government for the building of Christ Church was obtained on 10 September 1845. Bishop Gobat succeeded (1846–79) and the church was opened in 1849; Bishop Barclay followed (1879–81). The church was the centre for the London Society for Promoting Christianity among the Jews (founded 1820) and the Church Missionary Society (from 1851). The various missionary organisations built schools and hospitals to the W and S of the Old City (Bishop Gobat's School; the Protestant Cemetery; Rte 8). The Prussian/Anglican partnership was dissolved in 1887. (See also St. George's Cathedral, Rte 13, and the Church of the Redeemer, Rte 4).

Immediately behind Christ Church, to the NE and approached by HARAT AL-YA'QUBIYYA opposite the Citadel, is the small Muslim shrine called the **Ya'qubiyya**. Originally this was the Byzantine church dedicated to St. James Intercisus (or St. James the Cut-up) who was a Persian martyred under Varahran V in 422. It is sometimes also identified as the Church of St. James the Less. The present building is largely of 12C date with some later alterations.

History. It may originally have been the site of the monastery founded by Peter the Iberian after his arrival in Jerusalem c 430, to whom were brought the relics of the Persian James. Later, either before or after Peter left Jerusalem, taking the relics with him to Behnasa in Egypt, it became the Church of St. James. A church of St. James with one clergyman is listed in the 9C Commemoratorium. It was mentioned by John Zosime in 956–86; there was a small Crusader church of the same dedication, but after the expulsion of the Latin Christians in 1187 it was little mentioned; in the Haram Documents of 1394 it is called the Zawiya of Shaikh Ya'qub al-'Ajami (James the Foreigner) and is mentioned as such in 1495 by Mujir al-Din, but became delapidated thereafter. At one time it was used as a prayer hall for the soldiers garrisoning the Citadel, and at the time of the Crimean War it was used as a barracks.

The W end of the mosque has a large pointed 12C arch partly blocked by a smaller portal. Inside, a nave narrowing at the choir has 12C masonry, a cavetto cornice and pointed vaults to the windows and blocked apse. A mihrab is built in the S wall.

A diversion to the NE part of the Quarter should be made to visit the Syrian **Church of St. Mark**. Continue to the end of Harat al-Ya'qubiyya, turn right into HARAT AL-RISHA (ST. MARK'S ST) and right into ARARAT ST. This is a Syrian Orthodox or Jacobite (also called Assyrian) convent, on the traditional site of the 'House of Mark'. The church is 12C on older foundations and is linked with a number of traditions. The Jacobites (or Monophysites) practice an eastern form of Orthodox Christianity which became separated from the mainstream of Orthodoxy at the Council of Chalcedon in 451 after a theological definition of the nature of Christ. The ancient Syriac language is still employed in the liturgy of this church.

History. Mark, author of the second and probably the oldest Gospel, is often identified with John Mark, son of Mary of Jerusalem, who had a large house. Tradition links the Last Supper, the site of Pentecost and the place to which

Peter went on his release from prison by the Angel (Acts 12:12) with this house (see also Rte 8). The church is also believed to be the place where the Virgin Mary was baptised. A Byzantine church is mentioned from the 4C. The present church has a portal and interior vaults of the 12C but the builders are uncertain. The Jacobites fled to Egypt before the Crusader capture of Jerusalem in 1099, and their properties were granted to Gauffier, a Frankish knight. He in turn was captured in Egypt in 1103, and believed dead. The Jacobites were given back their property and there was a problem when Gauffier returned in 1137. A settlement allowing the Jacobites to retain their property was reached only after the intervention of Queen Melisande. It has been suggested that the Crusaders rebuilt the church in the 12C, and it reverted to the Jacobites when the Latins departed in 1187. The convent became the seat of the Syrian bishops in the 15C, and numerous rebuilds are noted in the 18C–20C.

Visit. Open daily 9.00–12.00, 15.00–17.00 except Sun and holidays.

The *12C entrance portal*, of the convent with gadrooned voussoirs in a pointed arch, leads to a much restored court. The church opposite is largely 12C with a fine old stone font against the S wall in which the Virgin Mary is said to have been baptised. Above it is a portrait of the Virgin, said to have been painted by St. Luke, which is probably Byzantine in origin. An inscription said to date from the 6C is located on the W pillar inside the entrance. The wall to the left of the altar has a fine variety of blue-on-white *Kütahya tiles* identical to some in the Armenian Convent of St. James (see below). Elia, who did so much work in the Armenian convent between 1726–37, also records that he worked on this Syrian church and presumably also installed the tiles.

A twisting route along HARAT AL-ARMAN through the area behind Christ Church can be followed SW to the remnant of the probable Byzantine and Crusader *Church of St. Thomas*, which lies on the N side of the lane just before reaching ARMENIAN PATRIARCHATE RD, just opposite the SE corner of the old citadel barracks. The building, as planned by Schick in 1896, had an entrance vestibule on the W and blocked earlier entrance on the S, which contained a mihrab. It had a single apse and a narrow choir with small chambers on either side. It is 12C on older foundations. A 16C tradition located the appearance of Christ to St. Thomas here. In 1632 Sandys noted the entrances were blocked because of a Muslim superstition; in 1652 it was believed that if a Muslim or a Jew entered they would die, and thus the door was shut in case they should enter unknowingly. In 1674 Le Bruyn says it was a mosque. By the 1960s it was a ruin with a few remnants, including a cornice, and remnants of a chevet, which attested its Crusader origins.

Continuing to Armenian Patriarchate Rd, and turning right, for about 75m to a point opposite the NE corner of the Citadel barracks, on the E side of the road is the *Dar Disse* or shrine of Shaikh al-Disse. The site has been identified (E. Moore) with that of the chapel and hospice of St. Saba, which was also sometimes called the Church of the Three Marys where Christ appeared to them as they returned from the empty Tomb. St. Saba (Rte 17) founded two hospices near the Citadel in the 6C which were still used as late as the 12C when the Church of St. Saba was marked on the Cambrai map. This building became the dwelling of the Muslim Disse family, with tomb, by the time of Felix Fabri (1483). In 1674 Le Bruyn noted it belonged to the Muslims.

Now return S along Armenian Patriarchate Rd, passing beneath a vaulted section, to arrive (on the left) at the entrance to the Armenian Convent of St. James.

Armenian Convent of St. James

Introduction. **The Armenian Convent of St. James** lies on the E side of Armenian Patriarchate Rd. It is a complex built at different times on various levels, entered by a single gate through a high 18C wall. As well as the Cathedral of St. James it contains two other churches, the residence of the Patriarch, accommodation for monks, nuns and pilgrims, a refectory, seminary, library, museum, printing press, administration buildings, school, dwellings and shops. The entrance, closed at night, lies between two vaulted sections of the road and leads into a *vestibule* **(1)**. A double-angled entry leads to the *courtyard* **(2)** of the **Cathedral of St. James**. Except by previous appointment with the Patriarchate, only the cathedral is open to visitors, and then only during the afternoon service (Mon to Fri at 15.00, Sat and Sun at 14.30).

History. The church is dedicated to St. James the Great, the son of Zebedee, one of the first of the apostles. He was beheaded by order of Herod Agrippa I in AD 44 during a time of persecution of Christians, when Peter also was arrested (Acts 12:1–3). The site of his tomb was located in Jerusalem by the 4C; but various later confusions included the 6C–7C legend that he preached in Spain, where his body was discovered at Compostella in the 9C. There is no evidence that the present church of St. James is earlier than the 11C–12C, but the chapel building on the NW side is older and may have been the 5/6C martyrium of St. Minas. That was built by the Lady Bassa, friend of the Byzantine Empress Eudocia, who came on pilgrimage in 438 and endowed a church and nunnery, of which an Armenian named Andrew was made abbot. These foundations undoubtedly were affected by the Persian invasion of 614.

After the sack of Jerusalem in 1071 by the Seljuq Turks, the Georgian Christians were permitted to build a church and monastery on the site which was dedicated to St. James the Great (between 1072 and 1088); that building forms the central part of the present cathedral. The Georgians became impoverished in the 12C and the Armenians bought the church from them. The earliest Armenian inscription is dated 1151; another mentions Abraham, Patriarch of Jerusalem who died in 1192. Other inscriptions date to the 13C and 14C.

The Armenians made some alterations including the rededication of the chapel on the NW side to St. Sargis as well as St. Minas. Later the E end of the cathedral was extended and two more chapels were built above the altar, dedicated to St. Peter and St. Paul. The principal relic however was the head of St. James the Great; the rest of the body was reputed to be in the church of St. James at Compostella, and other relics in Constantinople. Contacts with the Spanish church were at times close, and included Spanish subsidies in the 15C. Marie, the widow of Constantine XI, and his aunt, withdrew to the convent in Jerusalem, died and were buried in the church in the 15C. Le Bruyn (1681) is the first to mention the tomb of Makarios (the Bishop of Jerusalem in the time of Constantine) in the church.

The main entrance was originally on the S side where the 12C doorway is still in use. An arcade along the exterior S wall was blocked, either in 1651 or 1670, to create the Etchmiadzin Chapel. The work was done either by Philip, Catholicos of Etchmiadzin in Armenia, while on a pilgrimage to Jerusalem (who was also responsible for repaving the floor of the cathedral), or by Eliazar, previously Patriarch of Constantinople, then of Jerusalem, who claimed that communications with his superior in Etchmiadzin were too difficult, and had himself proclaimed supreme Patriarch in his own Chapel of Etchmiadzin in 1670.

The Patriarchal throne was donated in 1680. The convent prospered in the 17C, receiving many gifts from pilgrims. Through the mismanagement of the appointed agents sent from Constantinople to control the finances of the convent in Jerusalem, the convent fell into serious debt by the beginning of the 18C. The debts were repaid by the efforts of two Armenians from Bitlis; John the Patriarch in Constantinople; and Gregory the Chainbearer, appointed Patriarch of Jerusalem in 1719. He gained his soubriquet by begging with a chain around his neck in the doorway of the Church of the Holy Mother of God in Constantinople for three years, until the debts (variously described as 400 or 800 purses of gold) were repaid.

The financial problems of the Armenians in Jerusalem were pressing at this time, for not only was the Convent of St. James in debt, but repairs to the Church of the Holy Sepulchre were urgently needed, and support for this cause was also sought amongst the Armenians in the north. Permits from the Ottoman government to restore the Dome of the Holy Sepulchre were granted in 1718–19 and the Armenians were very desirous of joining with the Greeks and Latins in the task. Fine tiles for the Church of the Holy Sepulchre were made and donated by Armenians at Kütahya in Turkey, but for some reason were not used in the repairs. Gregory arrived in Jerusalem in 1721, paid off the debts and initiated another period of Armenian prosperity. He built the wall around the convent; the altar of the Holy Cross in the Cathedral; repaired the Church of the Holy Archangels; and in 1727 he repaired St. James and added many of the decorations—gold and silver ornaments, gold-spun brocades, precious stones and pearls. Fine pottery and the pictorial tiles from Kütahya made for the Church of the Holy Sepulchre were placed in various parts of the convent, probably between 1727 and 1737. Nearly 10,000 fine blue-on-white tiles, mostly from Kûtahya, were placed in the various churches and chapels at various times and form an unparalleled collection (Carswell and Dowsett). Among many interesting objects, the treasury contains sceptres of ancient kings, a staff made from a single large piece of amber and a fragment of the True Cross in a jewelled casket.

Visit. Visitors are only admitted during the afternoon services, and not to the chapels on the N side of the church, where the treasury of the convent is located.

The *small court* **(2)** contains a 19C fountain; there are Armenian inscriptions on the W wall, the earliest of which dates to 1151; others refer to Abraham, Patriarch of Jerusalem who died 1192; and Bishop Vartan of Kars (died 1238). In the porch are the wooden bars which were struck like gongs in Turkish times when the use of church bells was prohibited.

Inside the church is very dim except during festivals on fine days when sunlight from the high windows and the lights of all the lamps create a dazzling amd memorable reflection on the rich vestments, ornaments, tiles and other treasures of the cathedral. Maundrell (1697) describes the 'rich mitres, embroider'd copes, crosses both silver and gold, crowns, chalices and other church utensils without number . . . the tortoise-shell and mother-of-pearl are so exquisitely intermingled and inlaid in each other that the work far exceeds the materials . . .' which are still so vivid today.

The **church (3)** has a wide nave and narrow lateral aisles, separated by four squared piers supporting vaulting and a dome. There are three apses to the E with raised altar platforms. The original 12C entrance is in the S wall, the present W entrance dates to the 17C. The marble floor, with inlaid geometric patterns (1651), is usually covered with rugs. The lower piers and walls of the church and those of all the adjacent chapels are tiled mainly in blue-on-white 18C Kütahya tiles with floral and geometric abstract designs. The middle zones of the walls and piers are covered with paintings of saints on canvas mostly of 18C and later date, some of which hide earlier frescoes; the piers have medieval pilaster capitals which belong to the cruciform piers that exist under the 18C tiling. On the W face of the SE pillar is an *unusual 12C capital* with kneeling lambs amongst foliage. The low dome, with unusual design deriving from 10C Georgian and Armenian churches, rests on a tall arcaded drum with six lights and 18 blind arcades. The space beneath the vaults is hung with ornaments and lamps making a glittering image of the heavens, and with massive chandeliers. To the left on entry (in the NW corner) is a *hidden staircase* in the W wall **(4)** which ascends to chapels at the upper level to the N notably the *Chapel of the Apostles* **[5]**. It has a raised altar, marble floor and tiles, some of which are concealed by cupboards built against the S wall.

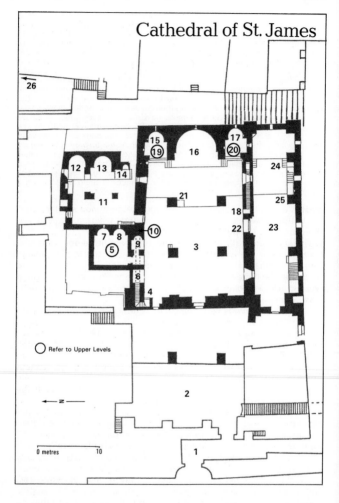

Cathedral of St. James

Close to the W end of the N wall of the church is the small 12C *Chapel of St. Makarios* **(6)**, Bishop of Jerusalem from 311/12 to c 334. It has some Chinese porcelain tiles set into the Kütahya tiles above the altar, and an 18C inlaid wooden door. Adjacent to it is the entrance to the oldest part of the cathedral, containing the *altars of St. Minas* **(7)** and *St. Sargis* **(8)**. Between them is the *altar of St. Haratoun*. There are many lamps and hanging ornaments. The next entry is to the most important shrine, the small 12C *Chapel of St. James the Great* **(9)** on the reputed site of his beheading. A piece of red marble with a circular cavity lies beneath the altar. The chapel also contains Chinese porcelain as well as 18C Kütahya tiles. In the vaulting above is the little chapel dedicated to *St. Nishan* **[10]**.

Further E is the entrance to the **Church of St. Stephen (11)**, the sacristy and baptistery of the Cathedral, with two central piers and three raised altars in apses at the E end dedicated respectively to *St. Cyril*, Bishop of Jerusalem from c 351 **(12)**, to *St. Stephen* **(13)** and to *St. Gregory the Illuminator* **(14)**. The font in the NE corner has on the wall above it the chain worn by the Patriarch Gregory in 1719–21. This church is also tiled with predominantly blue-on-white tiles. In the cathedral itself, the NE apse contains an altar dedicated to *St. John the Baptist* **(15)**, the inscribed *main apse* **(16)** and the SE altar dedicated to the *Virgin Mary* **(17)**. The S wall contains another *hidden staircase* **(18)** leading to the chapels of *St. Paul* **[19]** and *St. Peter* **[20]** above the main lateral apses. These are also tiled, predominantly with blue-on-white tiles. The entrance to the staircase has a fine carved wooden door inscribed and dated 1355/6, but remodelled for its present situation. Note the fine egg-shaped hanging ornaments in the church, usually painted in green and yellow on a white ground, sometimes with the winged heads of angels.

Adjacent to the NE pier are *two patriarchal thrones* **(21)**. That next to the pier was donated in 1680, and is inlaid with tortoise-shell and ivory in Turkish style. It is said to be the patriarchal throne of St. James the Less, of the family of Jesus and first Bishop of Jerusalem, martyred c 65/6 at the instigation of the Sadducees. The smaller patriarchal throne to its right is more commonly used, the other being reserved for important occasions.

The doorway **(22)** near the centre of the S wall was the original entrance to the church in the 12C and leads to the ***Etchmiadzin Chapel (23)**. The S side of the doorway has a pointed arch with gadrooned voussoirs (cf. the 12C entrance to the Church of the Holy Sepulchre and the Syrian Convent of St. Mark), and small marble rebated columns. The vaulting in the chapel is supported by 12C elbow brackets. The chapel, built in 1651 or 1670 by blocking in an earlier portico, is long and narrow and contains the *Altar of Sinai* **(24)** at the top of five steps near the SE corner. This contains stones from Mount Sinai, Mount Tabor and the place of baptism at Jordan for the consolation of pilgrims who failed to reach these more distant places. The most notable features in the chapel are the delightful and colourful series of pictorial tiles which ornament the N wall on either side of the door, and a section of the S wall **(25)**.

The vertical rows of tiles on the N and S walls located beneath capitals were installed by the monk Elia in 1727–37; the horizontal bands by the entrance on the N wall were collected from various places in the convent and placed in position in the mid-20C. Originally made in Kütahya in Turkey in 1718–19 for repairs to the Church of the Holy Sepulchre, they formed sets of scenes (at least 165, of which 52 survive) from the Old and New Testaments which were linked by a description in Armenian on their lower borders. Those for the Old Testament have uncial characters; for the New Testament, cursive; but they are not installed in sequence. There was also a more varied set, which included pictures of saints. The inscriptions mention the names of at least 52 Armenians in Kütahya who donated the tiles, as well as the name of the painter. They are part of a tradition reaching back to the 15C in Turkey, and bear comparison with tiles in the Armenian Church at New Julfa in Isfahan (Iran). The scenes are drawn in brownish black on a white ground with painting in blue, green and yellow, with added red dots in the background. The edicule of the Holy Sepulchre is depicted on one. They are placed among blue-on-white tiles of more abstract design, among which are also interspersed a few Italian majolica tiles.

In 1835 a women's gallery was built at the W end of the church, entered by a staircase from the Etchmiadzin Chapel.

Two other churches lie within the convent walls. The small *Church of St. Theodore* lies just NE of the cathedral. Entrance is by a tiled porch on the S side containing altars of St. Thaddaeus and St. Sanduxt, with another door on the W. The interior is a single vaulted nave with a raised altar platform. There is a tiny sacristy to the NE in the Chapel of St. John the Baptist. In the SE side of the apse is a tiny chapel of St. Mercurius. The walls are covered in mostly blue-on-white Kütahya tiles installed in the 18C. Tradition says the church was built in memory of Theodore, son of Hethum I, who died fighting the Mamluks in 1266. Since 1897 the church has been used as a manuscript library. It contains one of the largest collections of Armenian manuscripts in the world with 4000 items, second to that of Erevan which has 10,000. The collection includes some documents in Syriac, Coptic, Ethiopic, Arabic and Turkish. The oldest manuscripts are Gospels of the 11C, which were not written in Jerusalem. The oldest manuscript actually written in Jerusalem (in the Church of the Holy Archangels) dates to 1316.

The larger *church and convent of the Holy Archangels* lies at a distance to the SE of the cathedral, in the SE corner of the convent, just E of the Mardigian Museum (see below) from which it can also be approached. Since the 14C the church has been venerated as the site of the *House of Annas*, to whom Jesus was taken after his arrest (John 18:12–24) before being sent bound to the House of the High Priest Caiaphas, the son-in-law of Annas (see House of Caiaphas, Rte 8). It is also called (since the 15C) the **Convent of the Olive Tree**, A. *Dair al-Zaituna*, as an olive tree in the courtyard is said to mark the site of the scourging of Jesus. A stone in the exterior NE corner of the church is reputed to be one of those that would shout aloud if the disciples kept silent (Luke 19:40). The church has a large narthex at the W end, with entrances to N and S, and contains the *Chapel of the Flagellation* in the NE angle. The church itself, similar in plan to St. James, has four piers dividing a wide central nave from narrow lateral aisles, with three raised altars in apses at the E end. The lateral altars are also dedicated to John the Baptist and the Virgin Mary. To the left of the entrance is the *Chapel of the First Prison of Christ* which has an inlaid wooden screen. The main tiling scheme is 18C in uniform blue-on-white, with some polychrome tiles and a few Italian majolica tiles in the W wall.

A chapel at the SE angle of the complex is dedicated to *St. Hrip'sime*. It has a carved wooden door inscribed with its date of 1649. Porcelain hanging ornaments, with white ground painted with six winged angels in yellow, blue and green within blackish brown outlines, inscribed in memory of pilgrims in 1739, hang above the main altar and the main nave. The church also contains fine incense holders. The church probably dates to the second half of the 13C, but a church of the same name is mentioned before the 8C. An inscription on the N wall mentions a restoration in 1377; another inscription is dated 1362. The Patriarch Gregory repaired the convent after 1721 and added the altar of Hrip'sime.

The *Refectory* N of the entrance to the convent (not accessible), is on vaulting over Armenian Patriarchate Rd, and was built in 1741 by Gregory Vardapet. The floor is paved with polished slabs of *mizzi*

Church of the Holy Archangels
(Dair al-Zaituni)

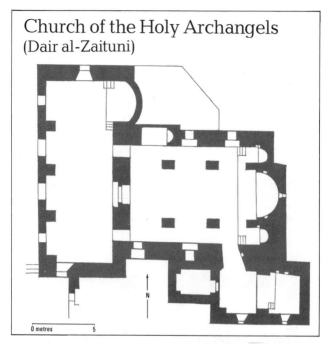

0 metres   5

ahmar, the lower walls are tiled with fine blue-on-white Kütahya tiles of the 18C, though with considerable later patching.

Leaving the Armenian convent and continuing along Armenian Patriarchate Rd, note that the area behind the wall and buildings to the right is called the **Armenian Garden**. It contains various buildings of the Armenian community, including a new seminary, a prospect of the Ottoman wall, and was the site of archaeological excavations in 1961–67 (Kenyon and Tushingham) of which nothing can be seen.

History. The earliest remains in this extreme SW corner of the Old City were sherds, evidence of quarrying and some minor walls of the 8C–7C BC. This area lay outside the Iron Age walls of the town. The line of the Hasmonean city walls was not traced at this point. The earliest visible city walls were those of Herod the Great (1C BC) when Herod's palace occupied the area immediately S of the Citadel, and the podium on which it was built extended to the present S wall of the Old City. Only a few fragments of the palace, including some pieces of painted wall plaster, survived the destruction of AD 70. The camp of the Tenth Roman Legion was located here from AD 70 to late in the 3C but very few traces apart from stamped tiles survived. A Roman gate in the al-Basura area at the extreme NE corner of the Armenian Quarter at the entrance to al-Dawa'iyya St was noted by Pierotti, measured by Warren and discussed by Vincent as perhaps a gate at the NE corner of the camp of the Tenth Legion in the time of Hadrian. The most notable surviving monument in the Armenian Garden belonged to the Byzantine period, when the remnant of an apse and a fine mosaic depicting a rabbit or hare and a quadruped beneath a tree were unearthed. The building may have been a triple-apsed basilica, and the inscription on the mosaic could uncertainly be translated to identify it as a church built by the Lady Bassa in the 5C. She may have built the nearby martyrium of St. Minas (see St. James, above), and also a nunnery, and it is possible that this church might have been attached to it. The mosaic is now in the Mardigian Museum (see below). Parts of the 12C Crusader royal palace have been discovered at the N end of the Armenian Garden area (Broshi).

The area was within the Byzantine and Crusader city walls, but the next notable building probably dates to the period of Salah al-Din, or perhaps al-Malik al-Mu'azzam (1187 or after 1212) when a khan or like building existed, probably from c 1212–1219/27. It had a rather short history, as al-Mu'azzam is recorded as dismantling at least the upper part of the adjacent city walls in 1219. It did however have another period of use c 1375–1400 in the Mamluk period. It was around that time that the garden was bought by the Armenians. The Armenian archives show that the Patriarchate owned property in the garden as early as 1336–37, when there was a large building or khan frequented by people from Hebron. In 1533–34 houses and gardens were destroyed by the Armenians to make a large rectangular garden. The ownership was confirmed in 1566 and 1579 by the Ottoman government, by which time the area must have been a pleasant spot, with the city walls rebuilt by Sulaiman II in 1537–41 enclosing it just as they do today, but then planted with olives and other trees.

Just beyond the second vaulted section of Armenian Patriarchate Rd is the entrance to the **Mardigian Museum** which occupies an old Armenian seminary (built 1843). Open Mon–Sat 10.00–17.00, the museum has two floors with objects, manuscripts and books illus-

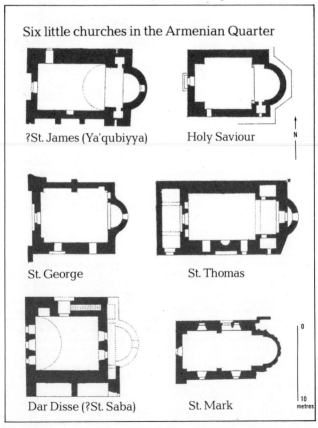

Six little churches in the Armenian Quarter

?St. James (Ya'qubiyya)   Holy Saviour

St. George   St. Thomas

Dar Disse (?St. Saba)   St. Mark

0

10 metres

trating the history and culture of the Armenians and the community in Jerusalem. The adjacent *Gulbenkian Library*, built in 1929, is open Mon–Fri 15.30–18.00 for printed books, magazines and newspapers relevant to Armenia.

The *Church of the Holy Saviour* and the *Armenian cemetery* (Rte 8) lie just outside the Zion Gate and the tour of the Armenian Quarter can be completed by walking out through the Zion Gate to this church and then round the outside of the city walls to the Jaffa Gate; or simply by returning along Armenian Patriarchate Rd to the starting point. Alternatively a visit can be made to the E side of the convent to the site of a *Greek Orthodox Monastery* and *Crusader Church of St. George*, on HARAT DAIR AL-ZAITUNA on the N side of the Armenian Convent of the Olive Tree.

7 The Jewish Quarter

Introduction. Between the 16C and 19C the S central area (c 9 hectares or 22 acres) of the Old City became known as the Jewish Quarter. Prior to that date, from the destruction of AD 70, the areas of Jewish settlement were less well defined and sometimes non-existent. In the Late Roman period Jews were forbidden to live in the city, and the S area was occupied by the camp of the Tenth Legion. There is sparse evidence for Jewish occupation in the Byzantine period. In the Fatimid period the Jewish population was located in the NE quarter of the Old City but it was massacred or expelled in 1099 and re-settlement was again proscribed in the early Crusader period. The wretched conditions of the few Jews then living in the town are described by Moses ben Nachmanides who settled in the city in 1267. A small community developed in the present quarter and he is credited with building the first medieval synagogue. By the 16C pilgrimage and prayer at the Wailing Wall was a strong tradition and in the Ottoman archives of 1525/6 a total of 199 Jewish households are listed in the Old City. By the end of the 17C there were thought to be 300 Jewish families in the city, of whom nearly a quarter were scholars and rabbis.

During Ottoman times taxes were heavy for Jews as well as for Christians. In c 1880 the Jewish population of Jerusalem was estimated at c 9000 in three principal divisions, the Sephardi (Spanish) Jews who had been established in Jerusalem since the end of the 15C; the Ashkenazi (European) Jews, a group of whom arrived c 1700, mainly from Germany, Austria, Poland, Hungary and Russia and which included the Hassidim or 'pious' Jews; and the Karaites, a separate and long established small community rejecting the authority of the Misnah and the Talmud.

From c 1860 attempts were made by wealthy Jews in Europe (Montefiore, Rothschild and others) to improve conditions in the Jewish community by establishing hospitals, schools and accommodation for immigrants. Various proposals were made to buy the area in front of the Wailing Wall, but these were aborted by disputes among the local Jewish community. Friction increased from 1929 as tension between the Jewish and Muslim communities in Palestine grew, and culminated in the abandonment of the quarter during the fighting of 1948, when the Old City lay to the E of the eventual armistice line. The quarter was badly damaged and then occupied by Arab refugees until 1967.

Following the June War in 1967 the quarter was taken over by Israel and in addition the houses and mosque in the Moors' Quarter on the E side were annexed and demolished. Since then excavation, restoration and rebuilding on a tremendous scale has taken place during the 1970s, followed by the settlement of immigrant Jews during the 1980s.

The great open area before the Wailing Wall, renamed the Western Wall, has become the focus of Jewish religious and national ceremonies and celebrations. Climbing up the steps linking the new plaza and the Jewish Quarter the contrasts are great: between old masonry and traditional, but neglected buildings, and modern structures of concrete with local stone facings, including Jewish religious schools, shops for tourists, artists' centres and apartment blocks interspersed with pleasant small open plazas and childrens' play

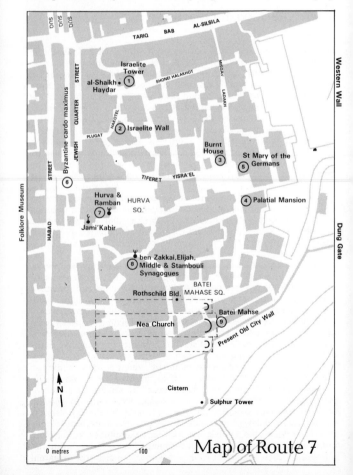

Map of Route 7

areas. The latter, in a modern idiom, do most to preserve the character of the city.

The central part of the quarter was the most ruinous after 1948 and much rebuilding is taking place there; restoration to preserve the previous character is taking place in the NE area. The modern quality and wealth of the quarter distinguishes it from the rest of the city, and as so often in Jerusalem, it is the contrasts the visitor will find which reward exploration. Archaeological excavation prior to building has uncovered numerous remains of interest, and it is no longer possible to say, as guide books written earlier this century recorded, that there is nothing of interest to be seen in the Jewish quarter.

Visit. The quarter can be variously approached; the following tour attempts to provide a route with some historical perspective. See map p.222.

Entering the Old City by the Jaffa Gate and descending DAVID ST, pass the Christian Quarter and the suqs (Rte 4) to the STREET OF THE CHAIN and take the first turning to the right into the Jewish Quarter and PLUGAT HAKOTEL ST. At its junction with SHONEI HALAKHOT ST several flights of steps lead down beneath the street to the remains of the *Israelite Tower and Hasmonean defences (1 on the map). These impressive remains are carefully preserved and beautifully displayed and explained beneath the modern buildings. A massive tower, with walls over 4m thick, still standing 8m high, is dated to the 7C BC. It may have been built by Manasseh, and be part of a gate tower in the Israelite city wall. Against the corner, amid signs of burning, arrowheads were found which probably date to the Babylonian sack of Jerusalem in 586 BC. Following this destruction the area was abandoned until the 2C BC when another city wall was built (the First North Wall of Josephus). A Hasmonean tower and city wall, which abuts and partly incorporates the earlier Israelite one, has dressed stones with broad drafted edges. Its continuation can be seen beneath the cardo maximus to the W (see **6**).

On the N side of Shonei Halakhot are the ruins of the *Zawiyat al-Shaikh Haydar* a small Muslim shrine with a plain tomb built c 1275–76 for the Shaikh and the Haydariyya Sufis. Another zawiya, of 'Alam al-Din, lay c 50m to the E.

Immediately S in Plugat HaKotel St c 40m of another *Israelite city wall* (**2** on the map) can be viewed in an open cutting. Known as the 'Broad Wall', it is 7m in width, and between 2 and 7 courses survive to a maximum height of 3.3m. These are only the foundations of a city wall, built of large partly hewn stones laid without mortar, perhaps by Hezekiah in the late 8C BC. It is earlier than the Israelite tower **(1)**, and on a different alignment.

For historical coherence the visitor should next see the remains of the *Burnt House (3 on the map) although this means a longer route. It lies near the E edge of the Jewish quarter and is reached by continuing S on Plugat HaKotel St, turning E on TIFERET ISRAEL ST nearly to the junction with Misgav Ladakh St. The exhibition is on the left in the basement of the new 'Arches House'. Open 9.00–17.00 daily except Friday 9.00–13.00. Admission charged. Audio-visual presentation in a number of languages.

The Burnt House is part of a complex excavated in 1970 (Avigad) which was destroyed in the Roman sack of Jerusalem in AD 70. The building may have belonged to the wealthy but oppressive priestly family of Kathros, and is particularly interesting for the fine collection

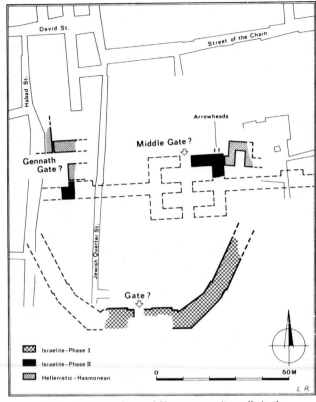

Plan of the Israelite and Hasmonean city walls in the Jewish Quarter, with a conjectural reconstruction of an Israelite gate (N. Avigad, Discovering Jerusalem, *p. 50, fig. 30: Oxford, 1984).*

of furniture and everyday objects illustrating the life of a well-to-do Jewish family in the 1C AD. The house and its contents are displayed just as they were when the fire destroyed them. The exhibition includes several display cases with objects, the remains of the house (mostly *in situ*), built with plastered blocks of the soft *nari* limestone.

Continuing to MISGAV LADAKH ST (A. *Harat Maydan*), and turning right, pass the top of the steps leading down to the Western Wall and under the Yeshivat HaKotel on the left the exhibition of another building destroyed in AD 70 is in preparation. This building, called the **Palatial Mansion* **(4)** lies on the E edge of the Western Hill overlooking the Temple and the Lower City. Its floor level is some 7m below that of the present street level. Covering an area of c 600m² is a series of rooms around a central court, on two, perhaps originally three, levels. The central court is paved, with cisterns beneath it. To the W, the best preserved wing of the building contained living and guest quarters. Here there are two rows of rooms, constructed of rough ashlars, surviving to ceiling height at 3m with the sockets of

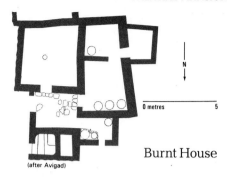

Burnt House

(after Avigad)

cypress ceiling beams preserved. Traces of fresco on the plastered walls survived in all rooms. The entrance room to the W wing has a damaged *mosaic floor*: the mosaic has fret and guilloche patterns in the borders, pomegranate motifs in the corners, and possibly a rosette at the damaged centre. The room to the S has frescoed plaster in red and yellow panels on the S wall surviving to a height of 2.5m. The painting shows windows, cornice and acroteria. To the N is a very large reception hall, 6.5m × 11m, decorated in stucco panels imitating ashlar masonry. Moulded fragments found in the debris had fallen from the ceiling. This type of decoration is paralleled in the 1C BC in Asia Minor and Italy. An earlier phase of plastering was painted rather than moulded, with a very attractive floral frieze. The SW room off this hall contained an architectural fresco dating to an early phase of its decoration.

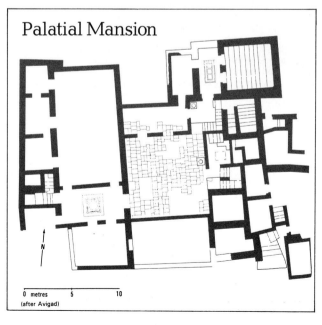

Palatial Mansion

0 metres 5 10

(after Avigad)

The *E wing* of the building was less well preserved. A small bathroom with a mosaic with rosette motif was located near the centre. Stairs descended on the S to the service area at a lower level, where there was a rock-cut corridor, with two doorways and steps descending to a large pool with a barrel-vaulted roof. On the N other steps led down to a small court and mosaic, and another very large stepped immersion bath with two entrances and a barrel-vaulted roof. A little of the fine furniture of the house survived, amongst which were small stone tables, some very expensive glass ware and delicate painted ceramic bowls. Despite the strong Hellenistic influence, the wealth shown in the furnishing and the number of immersion baths have led the excavator (Avigad) to propose that this was the house of one of the High Priests of Jerusalem. An alternative view (Pixner) proposes that the earlier phase of the building was the Hasmonean and early Herodian (37–23 BC) palace, and was later the site of the Byzantine (4C–7C) Church of St. Sophia, the Church of the Holy Wisdom, where Jesus' condemnation at the Praetorium was commemorated. No traces of this Byzantine church have been uncovered on the site; alternative but vague traditions link the church with the site of the Tankiziyya (Rte 3).

Returning to Misgav Ladakh St on the N side of the steps which descend to the Western Wall, is the ruin of **St. Mary of the Germans (5)**. This is a carefully preserved ruin which is combined as a monument and garden on several levels. A notice on the W wall and a plan on an interior wall give the history of this building. It was the 12C Crusader church, hospice and hospital of the German Knights of the Hospitallers Order, established in 1128 to serve the German-speaking pilgrims coming to Jerusalem. This area was part of the German quarter of the Crusader town, when Misgav Ladakh was called the Street of the Germans. In 1190 the German Knights established a separate military order, the Teutonic Knights. In the later 13C the buildings were partly destroyed by the Mamluks and subsequently used for other purposes. Part of the complex was in use as a stable in 1967. A programme of excavation and conservation was undertaken in 1968. Entering by the main W door of the church on Misgav Ladakh St, opposite is the restored remnant of *three apses*. On the left a doorway gave onto the hospice, and on the right another doorway led to the hospital at a lower level, which is now mainly occupied by a small garden. A view of the exterior E wall of the church may be had from the garden. Another *Crusader church* belonging to the German community was discovered a few years ago in the Jewish Quarter and is partly preserved in the second floor of a private house. This was identified as the *Church of St. Thomas des Allemands*. The upper parts of two columns with rather plain capitals were preserved.

Recrossing the Jewish Quarter to the W, brings one to the STREET OF THE JEWS or Jewish Quarter St. Under this street and Habad St which runs parallel to the W is the older *****Byzantine cardo maximus (6)** the scene of much excavation and restoration. Some 180m of this street were traced, approximately 2.5m below the modern ground surface. It was probably built by Justinian (527–65) and formed the monumental S extension of the cardo maximus of the Roman Aelia Capitolina built in the 2C. It led to the Nea Gate inside which Justinian built the Nea Church (see **9** on map).

The Byzantine cardo maximus was a monumental porticoed street, c 22.5m wide, bordered on the W by a wall and on the E by an arcade resting on square pillars. The road itself was 12m wide. The columns

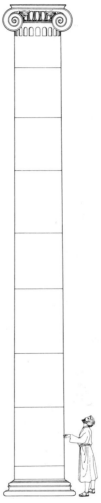

Reconstructed column found in excavations in the Jewish Quarter (N. Avigad, Discovering Jerusalem, p. 163, fig. 180: Oxford, 1984).

of the portico were monolithic, and stood on bases of Attic type which were not uniform in size; the Byzantine capitals were of Corinthian type; the total height of columns was c 5m. In the S section traces of small shops can be seen, which were cut back into the rock face on the W side behind the portico; one arch is preserved.

Continuing through the tunnel to the N under the new buildings further sections of the cardo maximus are preserved, mostly on the W side. Excellent explanations and reconstruction drawings of the remains are displayed. Continuing N deep shafts with glazed covers permit a view of sections of the deeply buried city walls of earlier periods. Two sections are said to be the W continuation of the *Hasmonean wall* (2C–1C BC) and one the W continuation of the 7C BC *Israelite wall* seen on Plugat HaKotel St (**1** on the map). The depth of these shafts gives a clear idea of the amount of debris built up over the centuries in this part of Jerusalem. Much of this deposit derives from the sack of Jerusalem in AD 70, which was followed by massive levelling operations for Aelia Capitolina in the 2C. No better testimony to the turmoil of the various sackings of Jerusalem can be given than the sight of the battered walls of the cardo maximus itself. At the N end of the cardo maximus are the beginnings of the great suqs (Rte 4) which overlie the Roman-Byzantine cardo maximus to the N.

On the W side of the central section of HABAD ST in the flanks of the Armenian quarter is the section known as the 'Ari Quarter' where much rebuilding is in progress. Around the old Or-Hayyim synagogue and the courtyard called Bet Weingarten are a number of refurbished buildings, containing the *Folklore Museum* of the Jewish Quarter opened in 1975. The restored *Old Yishuv Court*, house and synagogue in use by the Sephardi and Ashkenazi communities from the mid 18C to 1948 is at 6 Rehov Or-HaHayyim. Other exhibits illustrate contemporary life in the Old City. Open Sun to Thu 9.00–16.00, except the eves of holidays. Admission charged.

Just E of the preserved S end of the cardo maximus in a small plaza is a complex of *synagogues and a mosque* **(7)**. The **Hurva and Ramban synagogues** are complex and poorly preserved remains which stand on the ruins of the Crusader Church of St. Martin. A copy of the letter written by the scholar Moses ben Nachman (called the Ramban or Nachmanides) in 1267 is displayed here. He describes the miserable conditions of the city of the time, the presence of two Jews in a population of 2000, and how he converted a ruin into a synagogue. The Torah scrolls were brought from Nablus: they had been removed for safe-keeping in 1244 at the time of the Khwarizmian invasion. The new synagogue provided for the needs of the tiny community and for Jewish pilgrims to Jerusalem. The ruins appear to show a two-aisled hall which was converted into a synagogue towards the end of the 14C. The synagogue collapsed after heavy rain in 1474; a dispute that followed led to its demolition, and the dispute was only resolved by the intervention of Sultan Qa'it Bay. The synagogue was rebuilt by 1523 when it was said to be the only synagogue in Jerusalem. It was closed by order of the Turkish governor of Jerusalem in 1586. A group of Ashkenazi Jews settled in Jerusalem in 1700 but their project to buy land and build a synagogue foundered on internal dissent, debt and the death of their rabbi (Judah he-Hasid), and the land and partly-built synagogue were siezed for non-payment. This, the Hurva or 'Ruin', was returned to the Ashkenazi community by Ibrahim Pasha in 1836. A large quadrangular synagogue with central dome was at last completed c 1856, was destroyed in 1948 and its restoration begun in 1977.

Close by the Ramban is the small mosque and minaret of Sidi 'Umar or the *Jami' Kabir*, built before 1473–74. The original name of the mosque is unknown but has also been associated with the ruins of the Crusader Church of St. Martin because of the columns inside. According to Mujir al-Din (1495) the mosque was renewed after 1397. The minaret is a square tower of Syrian type, with octagonal muezzin's gallery. The upper part is typical of 15C minarets in Jerusalem. The mosque was damaged in 1967, and repaired in 1974.

To the SE is a complex of four synagogues **(8)** covering approximately 800m² which has undergone extensive restoration. These are the **ben Zakkai, the Elijah, the Middle and the Stambouli Synagogues**.

History. The synagogues are the focus of the Sephardi community, who built the complex with limited funding over an extended period following their ejection from Spain under Ferdinand and Isabella at the end of the 15C. The earliest, the ben Zakkai synagogue, was built c 1606–10 at a time when the Sephardi community was the largest of the Jewish communities in Jerusalem, and named in honour of Yohanan ben Zakkai (a rabbi in AD 70, a moderate horrified by the hideous strife among the insurgents in the First Revolt, who escaped to the Roman camp. He led the council of rabbis at Jamnia, which defined the conservation and interpretation of the Law following the destruction of the Temple). The building was extended by a study and meeting hall on the NW side in c 1625 which was also converted to a synagogue c 1702 and named for Elijah. Probably between 1702 and 1720, certainly by 1837, a courtyard on the NE side of the ben Zakkai was converted into the Middle Synagogue. Repairs were carried out in 1835. By c 1857 the large Stambouli synagogue was built on the NE side of the complex.

The complex grew rather haphazardly over the centuries, without adhering strictly to any particular architectural concepts. There is no imposing façade; the floor level is below the modern street level. Built of stone, mostly in secondary use, with plastered interiors, the ben Zakkai and Middle synagogues are long halls with cross vaulting; the Elijah and Stambouli buildings have the traditional cross on a square pattern. The seating was, as in all Sephardi synagogues, around a high bimah at the centre of the hall. The Arks of the Law (double in the ben Zakkai) were in the E wall, but those in the Elijah and Stambouli were pushed rather to the NE corner by the position of the door. The women's galleries were placed where space permitted. Abandoned in 1948, the structures survived virtually intact, though lacking all wood work and furnishings and in a damp condition, until restoration began after 1967.

Visit. Open 9.00–16.00, except Friday 9.00–14.00 and Saturday during services. The four synagogues have been restored and entirely refurnished. Some original details, like the upper windows in the ben Zakkai, have been altered. On some walls the masonry has been exposed rather than replastered. The bimah used for the reading of the Torah, has been lowered from six steps to one to make space for a larger congregation. The doors are designed by various modern artists; the Arks in the Elijah and Stambouli Synagogues are Italian of 15C or 16C date, recently donated.

To the NE on TIFERET ISRAEL ST is the site of the *Tiferet Israel*, or *Glory of Israel*, also called the *Nisan Bak*. It was the principal synagogue of the Hassidic Jews, completed in 1865 and destroyed in 1948. Opposite was the *Court of the Karaites*, a sect which rejects the authority of the Talmud. The ruins of 1948 were removed in the 1970s.

At the S end of the Jewish Quarter is a large complex of buildings around a paved plaza, with the *Batei Mahse* **(9)** on the S side. It was built in 1862 to house poor immigrant Jews from Europe. The *Rothschild Building* is on the W side. To the SW is a large open area which has been extensively excavated since 1968. In 1865 this area between the Burj al-Kibrit and the Zion Gate contained on the W some lepers' houses and a cattle market; to the N the synagogue of the Jews of Warsaw and the nearby site of a slaughter house; to the E the Jewish 'Poor House'; in the centre were some open fields (Sandreczki). The most important structure discovered in the recent excavations and which underlies much of this area, though little can be seen, is the **Nea** or **New Church of Justinian**.

History. The 'New Church of St. Mary, Mother of God' was built by the
Emperor Justinian and dedicated in 543. This, the largest basilica known in
Palestine, was built, like the S extension of the cardo maximus, as part of a fine
new layout for the Mount Zion area which became so important to the
Christians of the Byzantine and Crusader periods. The church was famous for
its size and magnificence, but before the recent excavations (Avigad, 1970–77;
Ben Dov 1975; 1982) it was only known from Procopius and other literary
sources and from the Madaba map which indicated its probable location. Its
actual location was lost. In 1970 parts of·its foundation were identified in the
courtyard of the Batei Mahse; parts were probably also uncovered in 1862
during the construction of the Batei Mahse. Other fragments identified in the
years to 1982 have led to a complete reconstruction of the plan.

Its length, including the narthex, was 116m, internal dimensions were 100m
× 52m, with two aisles and a central nave, and three apses facing E. Parts of
both lateral apses have been uncovered. The threshold between the narthex
and the S aisle was 5.4m wide. The interior was flagged with marble. The W
wall was aligned on the cardo and had two huge columns before the entrance. It
was surrounded by porticoes on all but the E side. As well as the church, the
complex included a hospital, a hostel (Rte 1), a monastery and a library, none of
which have been identified. Literary sources record that the site was too narrow
for the planned complex. The N side, going down to bedrock, has foundations in
a fill 8m deep, but massive vaults had to be built up at the SE corner, where
supporting walls 7.6m high extended the site. This wall had a series of vaulted
openings with relieving arches. Little of the superstructure (built of alternating
courses of stone and brick) of the church remains, but part of the NE apse, the
tremendous cistern in the vaults to the S, and the external SE corner which
extends below the Ottoman city wall into the adjacent garden (Rte 1) can still be
seen.

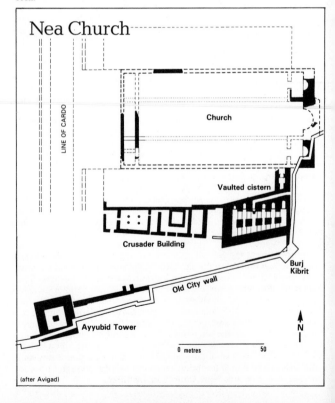

Nea Church

LINE OF CARDO

Church

Vaulted cistern

Crusader Building

Burj
Kibrit

Old City wall

Ayyubid Tower

N

0 metres   50

(after Avigad)

Visit. The NE apse of the church is preserved below the Batei Mahse. Open, 9.00–17.00 daily. In the courtyard of the Batei Mahse (with back to the Rothschild Building) take the steps descending to the right, turn left at the bottom, and descend by more steps to an entrance with grille.

The courtyard of the Batei Mahse contains sculpted fragments, including a huge Attic base and Ionic capital found in a Herodian or Hasmonean context in excavations further N in the Jewish Quarter (Avigad). They were not found *in situ* and what building they decorated is unknown. Much of the 5C cistern is visible adjacent to the small open-air theatre recently built inside the Burj Kibrit to the S. The cistern was 10m in depth and was explored by various antiquarians in the 19C. It is built of compacted rubble faced with strong pinkish plaster. There are six interlinked chambers oriented N/S with niches in the N face. The complex measures 9.5–17m × 33m and is supported by pillars 3.5–5m square. It was entered from the NE corner by a stepped passage, also plastered and vaulted, which leads into the cisterns at the third vault from the W. Opposite the entrance and 8m above the floor, a moulded plaster inscription in Greek on a panel 1.58m long records that it was the work of Justinian carried out by Constantinus, Priest and Abbot 'in the thirteenth (year of the) indiction', after the dedication of the church itself. Part of the SE corner of the church can be seen 50m to the NE outside the next angle of the city wall (Rte 1).

The area N of the Batei Mahse along the E flanks and steep slopes of the Jewish Quarter has been extensively rebuilt with two yeshivas (centres for religious study) just above the Dung Gate (the Poret Yosef Yeshiva on the lower road, and the Yeshivat Hakotel above). The effect of the rebuilding, which includes the Nebenzahl House with its five storeys E of the Batei Mahse, has been to create a new skyline on the ridge of the western hill which towers with stark modern lines over the Western Wall and the Haram.

The visitor may complete the tour by descending to the Plaza and the Western Wall (Rte 1) or simply return by the cardo maximus and David St to the Jaffa Gate.

8   Mount Zion

Introduction. The area now called **Mount Zion** lies outside the Ottoman city walls on a plateau at the S end of the Upper City. It was enclosed within the Byzantine city walls, and in the 4C was identified by Christians with the location of the Last Supper, with Jesus' imprisonment in the House of Caiaphas, with the Descent of the Holy Spirit at Pentecost and with the site of the earliest Christian church. The name Zion given to this area was due to a confusion of traditions. Located here today in a late medieval complex are the Tomb of David, the Room of the Last Supper, the Armenian Church of St. Saviour on the traditional site of the House of Caiaphas and the Church of the Dormition where the Virgin Mary fell asleep. Most of these medieval buildings overlie and incorporate fragments of earlier structures.

Mount Zion can be approached by road and a car park from the E just below the Zion Gate; from within the Old City by the Zion Gate; or by paths and road from the W. Bus 38.

Excavations were carried out by Warren (1869) at the British Cemetery; Modsley (1871–75) at the site of Bishop Gobat's school; Bliss and Dickie (1894–97) at the city walls to the S; Germer-Durrand (from 1899) at St. Peter in Gallicantu; Pinkerfield (1949) at David's Tomb; Kenyon (1961–67) on the W slopes of the Tyropoeon valley; Broshi (1971) in the Armenian courtyard.

History. The name Zion is of uncertain etymology, perhaps related to the H. *sayon*, 'dry place', or A. *sahwa*, 'mountainous ridge'. Mount Zion is mentioned in poetic parallelism with the heights of Zaphon, the northern mountain of the Canaanite Baal in Ps. 48:2. It is first referred to in the Old Testament in II Sam. 5:6–10 and I Chr. 11:4–9 as the stronghold of Jerusalem on the SE ridge captured by David (Rte 10). Later the name achieved a poetic equivalence with the Temple, and with the city of Jerusalem as a religious capital. The concepts of Zion as the heavenly Jerusalem and as a holy mountain where the Messiah would appear were also deep-rooted. The Davidic and the Christian traditions became confused especially as remembrance of the real location of the ruined city of David on the SE ridge was lost, and the name Zion was attached to the SW hill by Christians by the 4C. They believed this was the place of the house with upper room in which the Last Supper was held at the time of Passover (Mark 14:15); of the house of Caiaphas the High Priest where Jesus was taken after his arrest at Gethsemane and Peter denied him three times (Mark 14:53–72); and of the house in which the disciples gathered at the time of Pentecost or the Descent of the Holy Ghost (Acts 2:1). Here also was the house of Mary, the mother of John surnamed Mark, where Peter came after his miraculous release from prison (Acts 12:12) and here, by the 5C, the tradition that the Virgin Mary died in the House of John was located. In the 4C Mount Zion was also associated with James the Less, the brother of the Lord and first Bishop of Jerusalem, thus the place of his patriarchal throne. From this tradition grew the title 'Mother of all the Churches' for the great church on Zion.

The earliest defensive walls around the plateau are probably of 2C BC and survived to AD 70. This area was therefore part of the walled city in the time of Jesus. The New Testament gives no indication of the location of the venerated places, thus the Byzantine Christian locations are plausible but uncertain. The 4C Byzantine city wall enclosed this upper part of Zion, but not the Tyropoeon Valley below. According to the Bordeaux Pilgrim in 333, inside the walls at Zion was the site of the palace of David and one remaining synagogue. Outside the walls on the E were the ruins of the House of Caiaphas. The first Church of the Apostles was built by Bishop Maximus between 336 and 349. According to Egeria in 384 the church was at the site of Pentecost, but she makes no reference to the chamber of the Last Supper. It was, says Epiphanius of Salamis (c 374–94) 'the Church of God, a small building, on the place where the disciples on their return from the Mount of Olives, after the Saviour's Ascension, assembled in an upper chamber' in a part of Mount Zion which had escaped destruction in AD 70. He also records that a synagogue building (one of seven originally located here) had survived to the time of Constantine. He implies that this synagogue was another building, which had disappeared by his time. Not long after, between 397 and 417 the church was rebuilt by Bishop John II of Jerusalem. In the mid-5C it was called Holy Zion, the Mother of all the Churches.

After 450 Eudocia (who extended the wall of the city to enclose the Tyropoeon valley) built a new Church of the Visitation of the Holy Spirit at Pentecost and one dedicated to St. Peter on the site of the House of Caiaphas. These churches are shown on the 6C Madaba Map. By the 6C the Upper Chamber of the Last Supper had been identified with the Upper Room of Pentecost. It is probable that by the 6C a monastery marked the site where Peter went outside the House of Caiaphas and wept.

The churches were destroyed in the Persian sack of 614. The plan given by Arculf in 680 is presumably of the building restored by Modestus after 614. Arculf notes it was large and the Commemoratorium in the early 9C records it was marginally larger (at 39 × 26 dexteri) than the Church of the Nativity at Bethlehem and was served by 17 presbyters and clergy. Arculf describes a broad room building with similarities to the much smaller rectangular building we visit today, with entrance near the corner in one of the long walls. It had the place of the Last Supper in the opposite corner, and of Pentecost in the corner opposite to the right; the place where the Virgin Mary died was commemorated in the further corner of the long entrance wall; in the centre was the column of the Flagellation; and outside the short wall adjacent to the door was a rectangular projection marked as the Stone of the Flagellation. Traditions concerning Mary's death in the House of John on Mount Zion seem to date from the 5C and in 451 Jerusalem was decreed to be the location of this tradition, and not the rival Ephesus in Turkey.

The tradition of the Tomb of David appears to be a late one. Apart from the 4C mention by the Bordeaux Pilgrim and later references to a Palace of David on Mount Zion, and a rather uncertain reference to a mihrab of David in the time of the Caliph 'Umar, al-Mas'udi (943) refers to the tomb of David at Gethsemane; the first Christian reference to a tomb of David on Mount Zion occurs in the 11C. In 965 (according to Yahya) the Muslims attacked and set fire to the church on Mount Zion as well as the Holy Sepulchre. The area was in ruins when the Crusaders took the city in 1099.

Although the site was outside the city walls in the 12C, the Crusaders lavished much care on it. They refurbished the holy sites, and built the Monastery and Church of St. Mary on Mount Zion, which were served by the Augustinian order. This 12C church was also large, perhaps 54.8m × 27.40m with three aisles. It had a crenellated roof, towers and other defensive features because of its situation outside the walls. The Abbot of Mount Zion owed 150 sergeants in service to the crown, a rating or ranking that can be compared to that of the Patriarch and Chapter of the Holy Sepulchre who owed 500 each. The church was on two levels, the upper containing the room of the Last Supper, and in the lower level tradition began to locate David's tomb. Not far away was the Church of the House of Caiaphas.

Following the capture of Jerusalem, in 1192 Salah al-Din rebuilt the city wall to enclose Mount Zion. Local Christians seem to have taken over the service of the church and convent, which may have been affected by al-Malik al-Mu'azzam's dismantling of the defences in 1219. Work on the restoration ceased in 1244, after which it was a ruin. The chamber of the Dormition and the double chapel of the Cenacle were still frequented by pilgrims, albeit with difficulty. Pilgrims (Perdiccas, Pépin) in the 13C and early 14C mention the Tomb of David near the lower chapel, and the tombs of the Kings of Judah in an adjacent rubble-filled crypt. In 1335 and 1337 the Franciscans managed to negotiate the purchase of some land on the S side of the Cenacle (the Upper Room of the Last Supper); by c 1342 they had a hospice serving the members of monastic orders; and by 1346 they had obtained the Cenacle, Pentecost, and the place of Christ's appearance to Thomas. The Hall of the Last Supper was restored with modifications to the 12C building. The Sisters of St. Mary of Mount Zion had a hospice with 200 beds for female pilgrims in a convent on the site of the Dormition by the 1350s which was under the supervision of the Franciscans by 1373. The Franciscans built a cloister against the S side of the Cenacle in c 1377. Jews and Muslims became convinced of the authenticity of the Tomb of David in the lower storey, and disputed the Christian right to it. After several attacks on the place in 1368–72 the Muslims succeeded in gaining rights over the tomb and by c 1450 had built a mosque in the lower storey with a marble cenotaph which destroyed the altars and paintings there. They blocked it off from the rest of the building and prohibited access. The custodianship was placed in the care of a Muslim family. The Franciscans were permitted to rebuild the church, but were expelled from it also in 1523 (decree of Sulaiman II) and his inscription of 1524 in the E wall of the mosque at the Tomb of David forbade access. The Franciscans were finally expelled from their convent also in 1551 under the pretext that they were armed and constituted a threat to the defence of the city and the nearby city walls which had been recently rebuilt by Sulaiman. From the mid-16C only very limited access to any part of the complex was permitted to Christians and Jews.

There has been little alteration to the building since that date, mainly the addition in the mid-16C of a superior cenotaph, a leaded dome and a minaret. The area around was used extensively for Christian burial. Near the Ottoman City wall are the cemeteries of the Latins, Armenians and Greeks; the Protestant Cemetery lower down near Bishop Gobat's School dates from 1870. The Dormition was built from 1898. The Muslims were unable to retain their rights in 1948, and the Tomb of David is now a major Jewish shrine surrounded by a number of Jewish religious schools and prayer rooms. There is access also to the Cenacle in the upper storey.

Visit. The principal complex containing the Tomb of David and the Room of the Last Supper can be approached from various directions. Arriving on foot from the Zion Gate, the visitor approaches down a lane on the E side of the Armenian **Church of the Holy Saviour** which tradition holds to be on the site of the House of the High Priest Caiaphas, where Jesus was imprisoned and Peter denied him three

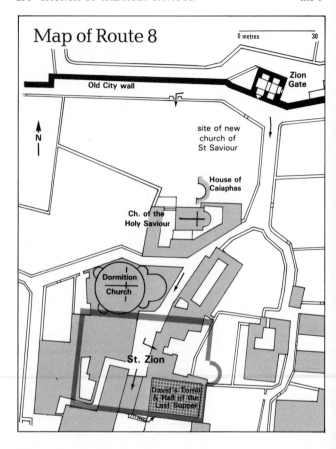

times. The true location of the House of Caiaphas is quite uncertain but this may be the 5C site of the church built by Eudocia.

History. The remains of houses of the 1C BC were excavated in the N part of the property. Mosaics and an apse of the 5C were excavated on the S side of the church in 1899, and a Byzantine street and houses with mosaics were found on the N side in 1971–72. Parts of the enclosure wall of the 12C Monastery of St. Mary were also found on the N side of the church which was destroyed by the Khwarizmians in 1244. The present church probably dates from the 12C; it was acquired by the Armenians in the 14C. In the 15C the community was poor and thought to sell the site, but c 1480 a wealthy Armenian pilgrim rebuilt the church and a cloister. It is mentioned by Borrely (1668) and Nau (1674). From 1948 to 1967 the church lay on the armistice line and was used as a gun emplacement by Israel. The interior was badly damaged, with most of the fittings and many of the wall tiles and paintings destroyed. A new, much larger church on the N side of the older one is under construction.

Visit. The entrance to the complex is from the N. The new church occupies the NE of a large courtyard. At the SE the older church is a simple vaulted structure (c 14m × 8m). The narrow W door with window above leads to a single nave narrowed at narthex and choir, with raised altar in the apse. The apse originally had a single window, now blocked. Groined vaulting supports the roof. At the SE corner is the tiny *Chapel of the Second Prison of Christ* (for the First Prison, see Rte 6, House of Annas). At the SW corner is the sacristy. The lower walls of the church have blue-on-white 18C Turkish tiles. The chief relic in the altar of the church is a fragment of the *Stone of the Angels* removed from the Church of the Holy Sepulchre after the sack by the Khwarizmian Turks in 1244 (Rte 4). Outside are the cells of the monastery, and the quadrangle containing the tombs of the Armenian Patriarchs who were buried here up to 1948. The earliest extant gravestone in the cemetery is of a monk who died in 1636.

Next on the right is the *Dormition Church*, the *Dormitio Sanctae Mariae*, the place where Mary fell asleep or died. Closed between 13.00 and 15.00. The land was presented by William II of Prussia to the German Catholic Society of the Holy Land in 1898; the Church of the Virgin was built 1901–10 in Romanesque style, architect H. Renard. It is a landmark on the S side of the city with its great circular tower with conical roof and four tall turrets. The interior is lavishly decorated with mosaics on floor, walls and dome, which depict mainly the prophets and apostles. The Byzantinesque Madonna and Child on the ceiling was constructed in 1939. The crypt contains the *Chapel of the Dormition*, with statue of the sleeping Mary and dome mosaic of Christ receiving her soul. Various remains were uncovered during the laying of the foundations, including part of the W wall of the great Byzantine Mother of Churches and the entrance of the 12C church of St. Mary of Mount Zion. The tall tower of the *Dormition Abbey* to the SW, setting back in stages from a rectangular base to a balcony and elongated dome with clock, is also a landmark dating to the early 20C.

Opposite the Dormition, to the E and S, is the large complex of *medieval vaulted passages and buildings* called until 1948 *al-Nabi Da'ud*, the Prophet David, which contains at its centre the 12C building restored in the 14C which incorporates earlier remains, in which are located David's Tomb (below) and the Hall of the Last Supper (above). This is a rectangular two-storey building with battlements, topped by a dome over the tomb at the NE angle and small 16C cylindrical minaret at the SW angle.

On the left of the lane is the entrance to the **'Hall of the Last Supper**, the **Coenaculum** or **Cenacle**. Enter by a pointed-arched entrance with chevron and fret design (16C), ascend the stairs immediately to the left in the courtyard of what was an old pilgrim hospice, then an Ottoman house and leads now to a Jewish yeshiva. Follow an open passage around to the left at first floor level and enter the rectangular hall.

The hall (internal dimensions c 15.05m × 9.75m) was probably constructed in the 12C and restored in the Gothic style by Latin architects brought in by the Franciscans in the 14C, on the traditional site of the Last Supper of Jesus and the disciples in an Upper Room before the Crucifixion, and the site of Pentecost (the descent of the Holy Spirit to the disciples after the Resurrection). Two free-standing columns (that at the E is granite), and a third against the W wall support the roof. Originally the altar and choir lay to the E but were destroyed in the building of the dome over the Tomb of David in the lower storey. The capitals are of varied type (mainly 12C and Gothic) and from them springs fine groined vaulting. Traces of *14C painted heraldry* remain on the wall just inside to the right of the door. A sculpted mihrab was added in the S wall (16C). In the SW corner steps (no entry) descend to the antechamber of the Tomb of David. Previously the Franciscan entrance from the upper level of the cloister was located in this corner. A dome above the stairs is supported on little marble columns with a noteworthy small capital depicting pelicans pecking their parent's breast, with feet resting on grotesque heads. The pelican is a symbol of charity in Christian art; the popular fallacy that the parent bird restored its young to life with its own blood made it a symbol of parental devotion. Attractive but damaged *Ottoman coloured glass windows* can be seen in the S wall. Retracing our steps, a good view of the Dormition can be obtained from the open passage, and as the descent of the courtyard staircase is made, note the star, bird and other designs in relief (16/17C?) re-used on the wall above to the S.

Medieval capital in the Hall of the Last Supper (courtesy of Kay Prag).

Returning to the lane, turn left and go up a few steps and through the high 16C pointed arch with gadrooned archivolt; on the right is now the Jewish *Diaspora Yeshiva* and 'King David's Psalm and Prayer Room'. Turn left into a passage and the 14C Franciscan cloister leading to the **Tomb of David**. Open winter: Sun–Thu 8.00–17.00, Fri 8.00–13.00; summer: Sun–Thu 8.00–18.00, Fri 8.00–14.00; Sat and Holy Days 8.00–18.00. *Men should cover their heads.*

Variously claimed as the site of a 1C/4C AD synagogue, and that of a 4C church, the site is certainly not that of the Tomb of David, who was buried in his city on the SE hill (Rte 10). The Tomb of David was first located on this site in the 11C. It was a Christian shrine commemorating the Last Supper, Pentecost and the death of the Virgin Mary from the 4C to the 15C when it was taken by the Muslims as the shrine of the Tomb of David, and then by the Jews in the war in 1948, in whose custody it has been since. We enter at the SW corner a hall (c 22.75m × 9.75m) which was part of the 12C *Lower Church of St. Mary* which was blocked off in the 15C and modified for use as a mosque. The larger W part forms a low, rectangular antechamber with piers and vaulting; the E wall has fine tiles (18C?), which frame the two square doorways leading to the second ante-chamber and the tomb. The older tiles, with floral designs in blue, green and red, are patched with green and black geometric tiles of the same make used in 19C–20C repairs to the Dome of the Rock. The same mixture of tiles is employed on the mihrab of the S wall of the second antechamber and on the E half of the screen wall before the tomb. The mihrab was probably first inserted c 1452. Three small windows in the E wall light the chamber.

The screen wall contains three square-framed doors and windows which give onto the very large cloth-draped cenotaph venerated as the Tomb of David, which probably dates to the 16C. Behind it is a N-oriented niche in blackened and ruined masonry which is prob-ably of 4C date (Pinkerfield) and may be part of the first church. The argument that this is part of an earlier synagogue incorporated in the 4C church depends on the orientation of the niche. Early synagogues were oriented towards the Temple in Jerusalem. This niche is thus correctly oriented to the N as in a synagogue constructed S of Jerusalem. The niche is also unlikely to be the apse of the 4C church, which should face towards the E (unless, like the Martyrium of Constantine, it was oriented on the Tomb of Christ). It has been reconstructed by Wilkinson as a niche in the exterior S side of an inscribed E oriented apse of the 4/5C church. The burning on the wall may be attributed to the sack of the church by the Persians in 614 or by the Muslims in 965.

The visitor may return from here to the lane and continue to the S for the view, and to visit the Protestant Cemetery; or turn left through the 14C Franciscan cloister and a garden (adjacent to which is now housed the modern *Chamber of Martyrs*, a memorial including gas ovens to the Jews who died under the Nazi regime), and from there turn left to the car park, and descend to the E to visit the Church of St. Peter in Gallicantu (see below).

Bishop Gobat's School and the Protestant cemetery are located low on the SW flanks of Mount Zion, S of the Institute for Holy Land Studies, and can be approached by steps descending to the W of the open ground S of the Tomb of David. Ring for admission.

The School was a boys' school built by Bishop Gobat (1846–79) during the period of the Joint Protestant Bishopric. The Church Missionary Society ran the school. A rectangular scarp was dis-covered when the school was under construction, which formed the base of a tower on the city wall probably of the 2C BC.

The Protestant cemetery (since 1869/70) lies to the SE. At the far end of the cemetery the remains of excavations on the line of the Herodian, Byzantine and medieval city walls can be seen. Near the centre of the cemetery is the grave of the great British archaeologist, Sir W.M. Flinders Petrie, who, after a distinguished career in Egypt, in 1928, turned his attention to the excavation of sites in Palestine, including Jemmeh, Ajjul and Fara. He died in Jerusalem in 1948. His work was significant in advancing archaeological technique, but he had a mathematical and logical genius for assessing his finds, as well as immense energy. He found at Luxor in Egypt the Stele of Merenptah, c 1230 BC which mentions the 'people Israel' for the first time in an historical document. He remarked 'This stele will be better known in the world than anything else I have found'. Also buried here is Leslie Starkey, who was the British excavator of Lachish in the 1930s, murdered on the Hebron road in 1937; and C.S. Fisher, the American excavator of Beth Shan (1921–23) and Megiddo (from 1925).

On the E flank of Mount Zion is the modern church of St. Peter in Gallicantu (St. Peter at the place where the cock crew). It was built by the Augustin Assumptionist Fathers, and stands on older remains. The site is held to be that of the House of Caiaphas where Jesus was taken after his arrest, and outside which Peter wept bitterly after denying his Lord three times before the cock crew (Matt. 26:75). Open daily except Sun 8.30– 12.00, 14.00–17.00. Guided tours and explanations can be obtained. Small shop. Approached from the road around Mount Zion which leads to the Dung Gate. Bus 1, 38.

History. The early history of this place is conjectural. The archaeological and textual evidence indicate that the remains in the vicinity date to the 1C AD and later. The site was probably outside the walls at the time of the Crucifixion and is therefore unlikely to be the site of the house of the High Priest Caiaphas. In 333 the Bordeaux Pilgrim saw the ruins of the House of Caiaphas on the E slope of Zion outside the then walls. There appears to have been no church here in the 4C, when no dedication to St. Peter is mentioned, perhaps because this site was outside the walls. The House of Caiaphas and Peter's Denial of Christ seems to have been localised to the N of the Cenacle by the 5C–6C and continued to be venerated there. There may have been another church at this site marking St. Peter's Repentance (Vincent and Abel). There are fragmentary remains which could be those of an early 6C Armenian monastery with Byzantine mosaics and sculpture over a deep cistern-like cave. These might be linked to a 9C mention of a Greek church of St. Peter 'where the glorious apostle wept' which was served by five priests according to the Commemoratorium. That church seems to have survived the difficulties of the 11C and was important in the 12C when almost all pilgrims visited the 'Church of St. Peter in Gallicantu' which was down from the House of Caiaphas towards the Pool of Siloam. It passed into Armenian hands c 1165 but was in ruins by 1323. Records of pilgrims still visiting a cave exist thereafter, but by the mid-15C there seems to have been no trace surviving. The excavation of the ruins on the Assumptionist Fathers' property in the early 20C by Germer-Durand revealed complex and fragmentary remains of mosaic, walls, steps and street,tombs and rock-cuttings, some of which are preserved in, under and beside the church.

Visit. The church, built in 1928–32, is cruciform in plan, with four large and four small apses, an inlaid stone floor, a coloured glass cross in the dome and contemporary mosaics on the walls. On the E side is a terrace with a fine view over the SE hill with the ancient city of David, and over the excavations in the garden revealing an old stepped street, probably Byzantine, which led from the lower city on the E hill up to the new city on the W hill. It is suggested that it may be part of route along which Jesus was taken from Gethsemane to the House of Caiaphas. The church is built on different levels to accomodate the ancient scarp and rock-cuttings. Taking the inside stairs to the left of the entrance to the church, descend to the crypt where there is a chapel; from here a view of the rectangular mouth of an ancient cistern may be had, on which ancient crosses are carved. A pair of high windows are cut into the upper part. Nearby are various fragments of mosaic. Modern steps lead down into the cistern itself. On the wall of the cistern to the right of the steps is a blurred image of a figure with outstretched arms which is also ancient and said to show the crucified Christ. On the wall opposite three red crosses are painted. This site is venerated as the site of Jesus' imprisonment in the house of the High Priest Caiaphas on the night before his Crucifixion (Luke 22:54–65).

The visitor should return to the road above, and either return in the direction of the Zion Gate and the Old City, or descend towards the E to the Dung Gate and the Tyropoeon Valley (Rte 9).

9 The Tyropoeon Valley

The road leading down the **Tyropoeon (Cheesemakers') Valley** leaves the ring road S of the walls of the Old City approximately 130m E of the Dung Gate. Bus 45 from the Damascus Gate Bus Station.

Although little is visible in this area much archaeological work has been carried out. Under the present car park entrance to the right, Kenyon (1961–67, Site M) discovered traces of a Solomonic casemate wall and houses of the Byzantine period. Approximately 45m S of the car-park, under the line of the modern road, Crowfoot (1927) discovered a city gateway which may have served the W side of the Iron Age and Hasmonean city. It is sometimes identified with the Valley Gate at which Uzziah built towers (II Chr. 26:9) and which Nehemiah repaired (Neh. 2:13, 15). There are extensive remains of Herodian and Byzantine paved streets and buildings and a medieval quarter in this area.

The floor of the valley to the W of the road is under many metres of debris, and was once very much deeper and steeper. In the 1C AD and the Byzantine periods the street plan included a large drainage system which is preserved right down to the Kidron valley. Though no ancient remains are visible, the road forms a good point for observing the position of the ancient city on the SE ridge to the left, and that of the later, upper city on the western hill to the right. Above to the right, is the Church of St. Peter in Gallicantu (Rte 8). The modern road descends very steeply to the Kidron. At c 300m the road moves W of the rock scarp which marks the assumed line of the early defences, and follows the line of the 1C AD paved street and drain system.

Towards the lower end of the Tyropoeon Valley, at c 450m, the low minaret of a small mosque on the left side of the road marks the site of the **Pool of Siloam**, (Latin, *Siloë*; A. *Silwan*). The mosque is a rectangular stone building with a court and minaret in the NW corner. It was first built by the Silwan villagers on the debris of the underlying Byzantine church in 1894–97 during the excavations of Bliss and Dickie. Below the mosque a passage to the left leads to the modern pool of Siloam.

History. No trace of the pool or covered cistern originally constructed by Hezekiah in the late 8C BC has been found; this may have been the pool referred to by Isaiah (Isaiah 22:9–11) as the pool between the two walls, and referred to elsewhere as the Upper Pool. It was fed by Hezekiah's Tunnel from the Gihon spring (Rte 10), and was part of a defensive water system built in the face of the Assyrian invasion by Sennacherib in 701 BC. The contemporary inscription recording the cutting of the tunnel was discovered a short distance inside the S end of the tunnel in 1880 and was removed to the museum in Constantinople, where it can still be seen.

The water from the pool was used by Jews for purification ceremonies,

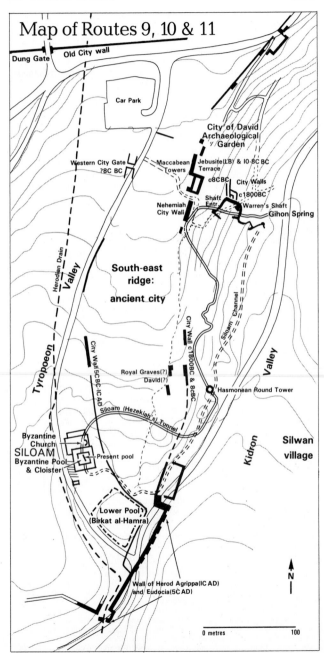

Map of Routes 9, 10 & 11

possibly under the belief that it was the actual spring of the City of David. It is referred to in the Mishnah (Parah. 3:2) for one ceremony, and was also used during the Feast of Tabernacles (Sukkah 4:9). The pool still existed in Jesus' time and was the location of the miracle which cured the man blind from birth (John 9:1–12). Possibly it was the site of the Shrine of the Four Nymphs built by Hadrian in the 2C, and some of the masonry used in the Byzantine pool may be Roman in origin (Wilkinson). Certainly changes in the stepped approach to the pool seem to indicate a Byzantine alteration to a pre-existing plan (Kenyon). There seems also to have been a Roman bath-house at the bottom of the Tyropoeon Valley which would fit with a fairly extensive use of the pool and its waters in Roman times.

The Byzantine Pool of Siloam was nearly square (c 22.8m × 21.6m), was rock-cut on its N and W sides, and probably had an arcade on all four sides. It was approached by a flight of steps descending round the W and S sides to a paved

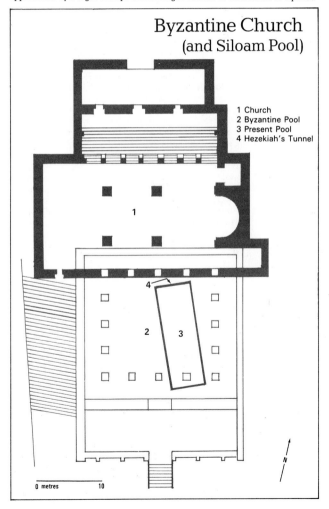

Byzantine Church
(and Siloam Pool)

1 Church
2 Byzantine Pool
3 Present Pool
4 Hezekiah's Tunnel

1

4

2   3

0 metres   10

N

and columned court 1.75m above the level of the pool. A rock-cut tunnel on the S side took the overflow from the pool. A Byzantine church overhung the N arcade of the pool, and appears to have had three aisles with an interior length of c 30.4m. A mosaic with simple geometric pattern was uncovered (Warren, 1867; Guthe, 1880; Bliss and Dickie, 1894–97). This was probably the church commemorating Jesus' miracle built by Eudocia in the mid-5C which was described by the Piacenza Pilgrim c 570.

Visit. The pool lies deep in a narrow stone lined pit c 18m × 5m, occupying only the central part of the earlier pool. It receives the water from Hezekiah's tunnel (Rte 10) under an arch at its N end, with an overflow channel at the S. During the building of the mosque the upper part of the N wall of the Byzantine pool was exposed, including a moulded course which is still visible and may have originated in the Roman period.

Continuing to the bottom of the Tyropoeon valley, the overflow channel from the pool is exposed in the rock-scarp at the S end of the SE ridge. It was originally a hidden tunnel, the end of which utilised the S end of the earlier Kidron channel or Siloam Channel (Rte 10) and led into the Lower Pool (also called the Old Pool, possibly the King's Pool and the Pool of Shelah or the aqueduct), today the *Birkat al-Hamra'*. This ancient pool may well have existed in the 10C BC. It is now a garden in a walled enclosure in the angle of the Tyropoeon and Kidron Roads. The fertile gardens, which belong to the village of Silwan opposite, were undoubtedly used in the Late Bronze Age and early Iron Age and since at least the 8C BC and probably earlier were irrigated with the waters of the Gihon spring.

Fragments of city walls of various periods can be seen blocking the mouth of the Tyropoeon valley: some belong to the Byzantine period and the 1C AD, some have been dated to the 1C BC or even earlier (see History). The walls on top of the S end of the scarp have been investigated, but nothing earlier than the Byzantine period could be identified with certainty.

Variations on Rte 10, 11 or 15 can be followed from this point, and Buses 43, 44 and 45 return to the Damascus Gate Bus Station.

10   The Ancient City on the South-east Ridge

Introduction. The south-east ridge of Jerusalem is the site of the ancient city, occupied from c 4000 BC more or less continuously until the present day, though outside the city walls since about the 11C. The extent and nature of the occupation has been summarised in the History essay pp.16–42. Very few remains of the ancient city are visible except in the Archaeological Garden of the City of David and in the vicinity of the spring Gihon.

The City of David Archaeological Garden. Open daily 9.00–17.00. The main access route is by a footpath from the road S of the Haram; another footpath leads E opposite the car-park entrance near the top of the road down the Tyropoeon valley. These paths continue as steps down the steep slope to Warren's Shaft and the Gihon Spring in the Kidron valley. Extensive excavations by Warren (1867), Parker (1909–11), Macalister (1923–25), Crowfoot (1927), Kenyon (1961–67) and Shiloh (1978–85) have taken place on the crest and slope of the ridge above the spring.

Approaching the site from the N note the steep sides of the Kidron valley, and the village of Silwan opposite. The Silwan area was used as a burial ground in the Iron Age. Inside the archaeological zone each feature is identified by a numbered panel.

The *5C city wall* **(1)** is at the crest of the slope. It was built by Nehemiah and was re-used in Hasmonean times. Two Hasmonean towers abut it. The larger *S tower* **(2)** is c 17.4m × 5.5m and the smaller *N tower* **(3)** is c 5.5m × 1.2m. They are constructed of roughly coursed masonry with massive, dressed corner stones. The foundations of the larger tower still stand to a height of 9.85m. The earlier city walls lay further down the slope.

The archaeological evidence in this area shows that c 1800 BC the houses were built on the natural slopes and terraces but in the 14C–13C BC a stone podium was built up to widen the flat area at the top. This was done by building stone compartments on the first terrace of the slope which can be seen most clearly at the NE foot of the *S Hasmonean tower* **(8)**. These compartments were filled with stone rubble, and built up the level to a height of at least 10m above the bedrock. Above this very impressive podium the citadel of the Jebusites was built, but no trace of it has been recovered. It was this citadel which was captured by David early in the 10C BC. During the reigns of David and Solomon the podium was extensively repaired and faced with large stones (perhaps the Millo of II Sam. 5:9). This *massive stone ramp* **(4)** which is visible from the top down to the first natural terrace of the slope is the most impressive feature of the site today and dates mostly to the 10C–9C BC.

In the 7C BC terraces were cut into this ramp, and houses built on them. One of these, now called the *'House of Ahiel'* **(5)**, has been preserved under a roof on a platform supported by iron girders. These houses are about a third of the way up the slope, and typically for Israelite houses have monolithic stone pillars as parts of the walls and roof supports. Some notable finds were made in the destruction debris of these houses, which were set on fire by the Babylonians in 586 BC. As well as pottery of the period, a fine set of stamped clay seals (from the *'House of the Bullae'*) **(7)** and some ostraka were recovered, with wood carvings and other small objects, especially in the *'Burnt Room'* **(6)**. One house contained a lavatory. Much of the rubble which overlay the excavation zone is debris of the Babylonian destruction in 586 BC, and erosion debris following the destructions in the Roman and Byzantine periods.

Leaving the Archaeological Garden by the S gate, and descending further down the slope, the visitor arrives at the entrance to *•**Warren's Shaft***. Open daily 9.00–17.00. Admission charged.

This impressive shaft and tunnel were part of the early water system of Jerusalem by which the inhabitants had safe access from the town to the Gihon spring in the Kidron valley below. It was discovered and entered by Warren and Birtles in 1867, cleared by Parker in 1909–11, and again cleaned and systematically examined by Shiloh (1978–85), who dates its creation to the 10C–9C BC; it continued to be used into Roman times. The water system has been made accessible by inserting metal stairways, but the descent includes 82 steps and some steep areas.

Description. Either in the Late Bronze Age or the Early Iron Age a natural fissure to the W of the Gihon spring was enlarged and employed as part of a protected tunnel and shaft system of access to the water. The entrance to this system was located inside the Iron Age city wall, and indeed inside the walls of the 18C BC, which were built on the slopes below. Today it is entered through an Ottoman building, with a small exhibition of finds, and a recently built tunnel.

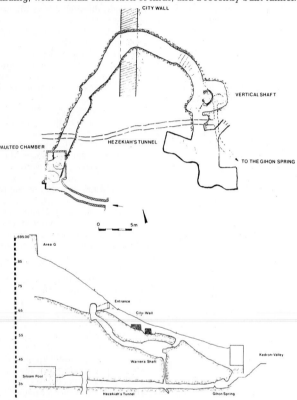

Plan and section of Warren's Shaft, Gihon Spring and the entrance to Hezekiah's Tunnel (Y. Shiloh, Excavations at the City of David, QEDEM: 19, 1984).

The system consists of several sections: **(a)** The first section is a tunnel with rubble walls and pitched corbel roof. **(b)** A very steep section in which the top part is Roman and is built with a barrel-vaulted ashlar roof. At the bottom of the first flight of steps the rock-cut entrance of the earlier Iron Age tunnel is reached. The original steps are very worn, and descend steeply for 8m. Chisel marks are visible on the walls. **(c)** The passage then widens to a system of double steps leading to a platform; and then becomes rather smooth and much less steep for 28m curving down to a natural cave, the outer entrance of which was blocked in antiquity. An additional natural shaft which does not give access to water is also located here. **(d)** A natural vertical shaft in the karst limestone, oval in section, which descends 12.30m, forming a natural line of defence against any intruder but up which water could be hauled in buckets from **(e)** an enlarged natural fissure extending 22m E to the spring which allowed the spring water to flow to the base of the shaft. The water is not visible from the top of the shaft. To obtain water in this way must have been an arduous task given the steepness, poor lighting and bad surface. Warren originally explored the system by climbing up the shaft.

Climbing again to the entrance, and returning to the path, the visitor can then descend to the floor of the Kidron. On the left is the **8C BC City Wall**, still standing to a height of over 3m in some parts, and overlying a small fragment of the **Middle Bronze Age City Wall (18C BC)** which is just below to the E. The latter, of massive roughly cut masonry, is 2m wide. Both the Iron Age and the Middle Bronze Age walls may be part of towers adjacent to the water gate of the city, giving access from the town to the spring below. Note the strategic placing of these walls, which control the valley floor and the entrance to the spring, and enclose the entrance to the water system above. The walls higher on the slope are modern retaining walls.

Descending the path and turning right to the S side of a school constructed in the early 20C the visitor arrives at the entrance to the spring. (Alternatively Bus 45 serves this area).

The **Gihon Spring** (from H. 'to gush forth', A. *'Ain Umm al-Daraj*, the Spring of the Mother of Steps, the Virgin's Fountain or Well) was the sole good water source for ancient Jerusalem and the reason for the location of the early city on the SE ridge. It gushes forth strongly but intermittently once or twice a day in the dry season, more frequently after a wet winter. It is first mentioned in the Old Testament as the site at which Zadok the priest and Nathan the prophet anointed Solomon king (I Kings 1:33, 38, 45). Its vulnerable location low in the valley of the Kidron below and outside the city; its intermittent flow and its associated natural karst fissures and caves have resulted in a complex history for the use of the spring.

History. Presumably the earliest inhabitants of the town above brought containers to the spring to fill and carry back to their houses, but how soon the intermittent flow was canalised and stored in pools for irrigation of the valley floor to the S, and for other purposes, is not known. It seems likely that there would have been a gate and defended path above the spring in the Middle and Late Bronze Ages. Warren's Shaft was the earliest of the defended water systems connected with the spring. A second water system is also dated by Shiloh to the 10C–9C BC but could also have been in use earlier. The Siloam Channel led the waters of the spring through a rock-hewn and built channel/ tunnel down the W side of the Kidron Valley to the Silwan area. Its waters could be utilised through sluice-like apertures to irrigate the gardens on the valley floor and any excess could be held in reservoirs at the bottom of the Tyropoeon Valley (see Lower Pool, Rte 9). The channel was also used for collecting rainwater run-off from the slopes of the ridge above.

At the end of the 8C BC. Hezekiah built a third water system, the famous Siloam or Hezekiah's Tunnel which largely replaced the Siloam Channel and still functions today. This also starts at the Gihon Spring, is 533m in length and pursues a very irregular course beneath the SE ridge to the Siloam Pool in the lower Tyropoeon Valley. The gradient is very slight; the height of the rock-cut tunnel is generally about 2m, though towards the S end it reaches 5m, presumably the result of adjusting the gradient downwards. Its sinuous course is variously attributed to (a) inadequate ancient surveying methods; (b) avoidance of hard bands of rock and employment of natural fissures; and (c) an attempt to avoid the burial places of the kings, which some scholars (Weill) locate towards the S end of the SE ridge (see below). The attribution of this tunnel to Hezekiah is generally accepted (II Kings 20:20; II Chr. 32:30) and agrees with the evidence of the inscription found near the S end of the tunnel in 1880, which is now in the Museum in Istanbul. The inscription tells us that the tunnel was cut from both ends, and of the excitement when the two groups finally met about 300m from the S end where there is an especially hectic twist in the tunnel's course. Some assume that as Hezekiah was bringing the waters of the spring within the protection of the walls, therefore the lower Tyropoeon valley where the Pool of Siloam is located was within the line of the walls at that time. Others (Kenyon) think that the valley was not yet enclosed, but that Hezekiah's storage pool was a hidden underground reservoir just outside the W wall of the city. The tunnel has remained in use since the 8C BC.

Visit. Two flights (17 + 16) of stone steps, of uncertain date (Byzantine to modern), give access to an irregular, partly artificial cave containing the spring. Off this cave open a series of partly natural galleries; to the W they connect with Warren's Shaft and Hezekiah's Tunnel; and to the S with the Siloam Channels and other galleries (Parker and Vincent, 1909–11). It is possible to walk through Hezekiah's Tunnel, but the visitor should bring lights, and be prepared to walk through shallow water in a narrow and occasionally rather low tunnel for 533m.

Continuing S down the Kidron Road for some 100m we arrive at the second area of excavation where remains are still visible on the SE ridge. (Shiloh Areas B–D–E). Here a further section of the 8C BC City Wall (c 90m in length) overlies a stretch of the 18C BC City Wall about mid-way up the slope. To the W of the wall, against the inner face, structures of nearly all periods from the Early Bronze Age (c 3000 BC) have been uncovered.

Access is by a steep and rough path up the slope at the S end of the large dump created by the excavations, and thence by a track N through the excavations. The earliest structures pre-date the building of a city wall, and consist of the stone foundations of broad-roomed houses with interior benches and other installations which were founded on bedrock c 3000 BC. These were succeeded by houses within the 18C BC city wall. Structures of later date including Iron Age and Hellenistic houses have also been found.

In the area immediately to the S of these remains, which was cleared to bedrock by Weill and re-explored by Kenyon, are numerous cuttings in bedrock mostly of Hadrianic date, but including some long narrow cuttings of uncertain date and purpose which were thought by Weill to be the **Tombs of the Israelite kings**, including David and his sons and successors, who were buried within the walls of the city (I Kings 2:10) up to the time of Manasseh, after which the 'Garden of Uzza' (probably near Silwan) was employed. The most impressive of Weill's tombs was entered by a shaft which led to a vaulted tunnel 16.5m long and 4m high. At the end is a stone bench with a niche, perhaps intended for a coffin. Another tomb (discovered by Weill in 1923–24) also seemed to reflect a Phoenician influence. These tombs had been looted anciently as well as quarried in the Roman period. Josephus writes that the Hasmonean ruler Hyrcanus took 3000 talents from the Tomb of David, which he used partly to buy off Antiochus VII Sidetes (138–129 BC) and partly to pay a mercenary force (War I:61).

As the visitor descends again to the road, on the left approximately 20m above the road are the remains of a round tower excavated by Weill in 1912–13 and probably of Hellenistic or Roman date. The area adjacent to the Hellenistic or Roman round tower was certainly used in the Iron Age for burial and the location of the royal tombs in the area just above is therefore not impossible. This area is at least a more likely site than the traditional Tomb of David on the W hill (Rte 8), which was not inside the walls in the time of David.

S, along the Kidron road, there are parts of the Hellenistic-Roman-Byzantine walls for 120m at the S end of the Tyropoeon Valley on either side of the road (see History); a section of the overflow tunnel from the Pool of Siloam can be seen on the right (see Pool of Siloam, Rte 9).

11 The Kidron Valley

Topography. The Kidron Valley bounds the E side of the city of Jerusalem. It starts to the N of the city, where it is comparatively broad and open, and is today called the *Wadi Jauz*. This is an àrea of olives and vineyards, now being given over to houses and hotels. The valley narrows and deepens opposite the Old City, where it becomes known as the Valley of Jehoshaphat, and S of the Haram deepens to a shallow gorge with steep Turonian limestone scarps on either side which were much used for burial in the past. At the points where it is joined by the Tyropoeon and Hinnom valleys the floor widens, and alluvial soils and plentiful water create a garden area. Above the E bank is the village of Silwan. The Kidron contained only a winter torrent, apart from the spring of Gihon and well at Bir Ayyub, and the ancient floor was deeper than today. Since Herodian times the main sewer of Jerusalem ran down the Tyropoeon to the Kidron. Below Silwan the valley turns to the E and continues a steep descent through the Judaean wilderness past the monastery of Mar Saba (Rte 17) to the Dead Sea.

History. The Kidron is mentioned in the Old Testament, mainly as the border of the town, or because of its springs and fields and its use as a cemetery. Absalom, son of David, is said to have set up his memorial pillar in the King's Valley (II Sam. 18:18) which, like the King's Garden, is identified with Kidron. The destruction in the Kidron of the paraphernalia of foreign gods by the kings of Judah is also recorded (e.g. I Kings 15:13). Monumental tombs were located here from the Iron Age onwards. Following texts such as Jer. 31:40 and Joel 3:2 and 12 the Kidron was identified with the Valley of Jehoshaphat (literally 'Yahweh judges'), and with the site of the Last Judgement, a tradition accepted by both Jews and Christians and one reason for the location of the modern Jewish cemeteries here. The Kidron Valley was occupied extensively by Byzantine hermits.

Visit. A short walk in Kidron provides an interesting view of the city, with a number of ancient monuments along the way. It is possible to continue from Rte 10, from Gihon and the SE ridge and walk up the Kidron; but preferable to continue from Rte 12, the Mount of Olives, and progress downhill from Gethsemane. If following the latter route, take the track which leads SW from the JERICHO ROAD at a point just S of the CHURCH OF ALL NATIONS and leads in a few minutes to the Tombs of Jehoshaphat and Absalom. Buses 43, 45 from the Damascus Gate Bus Station serve this area.

As we descend the track past the modern Jewish cemeteries the walls of the *Herodian Temple* tower above to the W. The limestone scarp steepens on the left of the track, and set in a rock-cut courtyard is the *Tomb of Absalom. This is the most prominent monument in the Kidron and depending on the eye of the beholder, a graceful addition to the landscape, or a monument in decadent late Hellenistic style. The traditional association with Absalom (who built himself a memorial pillar in the King's Valley) is false but of long standing; de Tollot (1731) records that passers-by threw stones at this tomb because of Absalom's disobedience to his father David. Its construction probably dates to the last half of the 1C BC and it is undoubtedly part of a Jewish burial complex belonging to a wealthy family, perhaps priestly or Sadducee, in the early Roman period. It contains a small tomb chamber but is also part of the Tomb of

Jehoshaphat, which leads off the court at the NE corner. The Tomb of Absalom may have contained the principal burials, and thereafter acted as a memorial cenotaph for succeeding generations of the family buried in the adjacent hypogeum. *Excavations*. Guy (1922) and Slousch (1925).

Description of the Tomb of Absalom. The square open court is c 12.50m in length, quarried from the rock-scarp. The monument, pseudo-peripteral and composite in style, has the lower section as far as the cornice cut from the rock, and the upper part built of masonry. The monument stands on a podium. Each corner has an angular quarter-engaged pilaster ending in quarter-columns, and each side two semi-engaged columns. The capitals are Ionic, with egg and dart motifs, and on them rests an architrave with Doric frieze of triglyphs with late triangular guttae, and metopes with paterae. Above is a roll and cavetto cornice which are clearly close copies of those on the Tomb of Zechariah and the Monolith of Silwan (see below). Above, the built cubical base, tholos drum and concave pyramid are all developed late Hellenistic features, which, allied with Roman style mouldings, indicate a date into the Roman period in Jerusalem. The pyramid is topped by a rope moulding and a circlet or cup of leaves. The total height is c 16.50m. The holes hacked in the sides are those of looters, except for the original entrance high on the S side which leads to the burial chamber. Steep steps descend internally from this entrance to a small squarish chamber, with relief ornament of circles

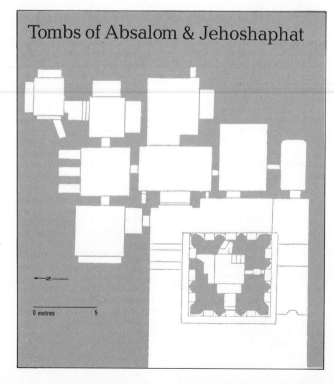

Tombs of Absalom & Jehoshaphat

0 metres   5

and discs on the ceiling and two bench arcosolia. One bench has a ledge above it, possibly for lamps. The tomb was looted in ancient times.

Description of the Tomb of Jehoshaphat. At the N end of the E side of the court is an entrance leading to a burial complex. The portal (2.5m × 3m) has a finely carved pediment. The tympanum contains an acanthus and running scroll growing from a vase. The foliage contains flowers and fruits, with carving and motifs similar to Herodian ornament on ossuaries and Herod's temple. Leaf acroteria survive at the corners of the pediment, but that at the centre has been cut away in later work. All the visible chamber tombs of the Kidron were re-used by Byzantine hermits. Inside the hypogeum is a complex of eight rectangular burial chambers. The plan is cruciform with some later chambers added to the E. The plan of the burial places is unusual: they may have been intended for use with sarcophagi (cf. Herod's Family tomb). The E chambers have bench arcosolia.

Carved pediment of the Tomb of Jehoshaphat, from the west (courtesy of John Kane).

A few metres S the height of the rock-scarp increases, and a further complex of tomb chambers is revealed. The principal monuments are first the Tomb of the Bene Hezir, or traditionally the Tomb of St. James; and slightly to the S the Tomb of Zechariah usually identified as the cenotaph or *nefesh* of the Bene Hezir tomb.

Description of the Tomb of the Bene Hezir. The tomb probably dates to the late 2C BC or the early 1C BC. It is earlier than that of Absalom and in purer Hellenistic style. The tomb of St. James the Less was identified here in the 12C. The tomb is rock-cut, with a Doric façade. Two free-standing and two engaged columns without bases have straight Doric capitals supporting a Doric frieze with triglyphs and diglyphs and conical early guttae (cf. the Tomb of Jason, Rte 14) with cornice above. At the S end of the architrave is an inscription in square Hebrew characters which is probably of Herodian date and may have been added at the time of some of the later burials in the tomb. The inscription is translated: 'This is the tomb and the memorial of Eleazar, Haniah, Jo'azar, Jehudah, Simeon, Johannan, the sons of Joseph son of 'Oreb; also of Joseph and Eleazar the sons of Haniah, priests of the family of the Bene Hezir'.

This family is associated with the Hezir of I Chr. 24:15 who being of the descent of Aaron was among those who drew lots for taking charge of the service in the temple. Behind the façade is a portico off which lead steps at a high level to the N and a rough cut passage to the S which are of uncertain date and purpose. At the back of the portico a rectangular doorway leads to a hypogeum with cruciform plan, in which bench chambers have unusually shaped kokhim which may also be of early date. The rear chambers have bench arcosolia and may be later additions. Like most family tombs, the hypogeum was probably used for at least three generations.

Adjacent to this tomb are various other rock cuttings. On the N side is a finely dressed façade with a long recessed panel containing a

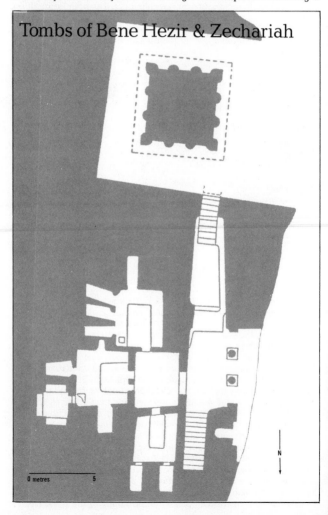

Tombs of Bene Hezir & Zechariah

0 metres   5

N

rectangular doorway which leads only to a small niche. The rock above has been removed, and may once have been capped by a pyramid. This monument shows no Hellenistic influences, and may be associated with the little square cuttings beneath the Tomb of the Bene Hezir, perhap tombs of the Iron Age.

Description of the Tomb of Zechariah, usually identified as the memorial or *nefesh* of the Bene Hezir tomb, and not associated with Zechariah, lies c 10m S of the tomb of the Bene Hezir, in a square rock-cut court connected to the tomb by a rough passage. The solid cubical monument stands on three steps and a podium. The roughly cut chamber below the steps is probably not part of the original plan. Like the tomb of Absalom, the monument has angular quarter-engaged pilasters at the corners (with mouldings which are finer and were clearly copied by the builders of the tomb of Absalom), which end in quarter-columns; each side has semi-engaged columns with Ionic capitals with egg and dart motifs and good profile. Unlike the tomb of Absalom, the tops of the columns have the beginnings of Ionic fluting, and the capitals of the N, E and S sides are unfinished. The architrave is much plainer, with no triglyphs or metopes, and above is the roll and cavetto cornice which seems to be particularly popular in these Kidron tombs. The monument is capped by a plain high pyramid with square base, again probably copied from the Monolith of Silwan. The detail of the tomb design is early and appears to complement that of the adjacent Bene Hezir hypogeum.

Immediately to the S is a very crudely cut façade with two columns which is not connected with the Bene Hezir-Zechariah complex.

The visitor can then descend the lower Kidron to visit the Gihon Spring and the SE ridge (Rte 10) or if interested in very destroyed tombs of Iron Age date, continue along the higher track S into Silwan village. As one enters the village, on the right at the edge of the top of the rock-scarp in a prominent position is the monument variously known as the **Monolith of Silwan** or *The Tomb of Pharaoh's Wife or Daughter*. Because it now has a flat top it looks like a small village house. It is however a funerary monument of great antiquity, probably to be dated to the 9C–7C BC and constructed under Phoenician-Egyptian influence. It has the remnants of an old Hebrew inscription, discovered by Clermont-Ganneau in 1870. Its style clearly influenced the later monument of Zechariah.

The monument is entirely hewn from the rock scarp as a free standing cube (c 5.5m × 4.8m) once capped by a square-based pyramid. The walls of the cube, unlike those of the tombs of Absalom and Zechariah, slope slightly outwards to the base. At the top of the façade a pronounced roll and a deeply undercut cavetto or Egyptian cornice project. The original doorway was small (only 0.82m × 0.685m) and was set high in the façade. Above it was a slightly recessed panel wider than the door, with a single-line inscription, perhaps originally of 20 characters. In later times (Roman?) the pyramid was quarried from the roof, and a Byzantine hermit enlarged the door removing most of the inscription in the process. Only a fragment with 1½ characters survives at the top left corner of the doorway. Inside a passage leads to a small squarish chamber (2.25m × 2.18m); traces of a projecting rock-cut bench survive against the left side, the rest of which was probably cut away by the hermit. Probably at the same time the niches in all three walls were added and the entrance passage enlarged. The gabled roof, cut at approximately 130° on either side of the apex, seems to be typical of other tombs of the Iron Age in the Silwan necropolis.

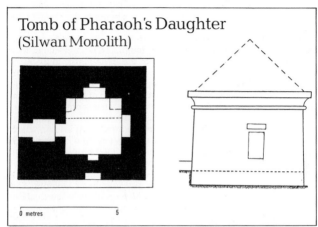

Tomb of Pharaoh's Daughter
(Silwan Monolith)

0 metres   5

Two other tombs of this type and date were found slightly further S in the village. Following the same street into Silwan, c 50m further on the left are the remnants of two more *monolithic tombs*. The first was noted by Clermont-Ganneau in 1870, an inscription was discovered by Reifenberg in 1946, and the monument studied by Ussishkin and Barkai in the early 1970s. It is hard to see, being partly covered by a house and steps; the opening is blocked and the tomb chamber in use as a cistern. It was also partly destroyed during Roman-Byzantine quarrying. The monolith is 4.75m wide, and is preserved 4.25m high. In the centre of the façade a deep niche 2.42m high, 1.50m wide, and 0.50m deep had a small opening cut at a higher level than the hewn entrance porch. The stone was very smoothly dressed. The inscription was located above the niche and almost nothing survives. It may have been worded like that of the tomb immediately to the S. Above the inscription are traces of a projecting cornice, but the upper part of the monument is destroyed. It was perhaps the tomb of a high official in the court of Judah who had his tomb constructed in Phoenician style at a prominent spot.

The last of these tombs is located immediately S on the left and was also discovered by Clermont-Ganneau in 1870. The inscription is better preserved. The façade is flush with the modern street, c 8m wide, and had a rectangular door and window (subsequently enlarged) in a perfectly dressed surface. The small door (1.90m × 1.44m) was set high in a recessed niche, and had a recessed panel (1.32m long) with a three-line inscription in Old Hebrew above it. It was translated by Avigad: '(the tomb of)...]yahu who is over the house. There is no silver or gold here but rather (his bones) and the bones of his wife(?) with him. Cursed be the man who should open this'. It seems to be the tomb of a high steward or chamberlain of the Judaean period, and Avigad and Yadin suggest it was that of the Shebna mentioned in Isaiah 22:15–25 as Clermont-Ganneau had hardly dared hope.

Shebna was a high official, the palace governor who was denounced by Isaiah because of his pre-occupation with the building of his tomb 'cutting out your grave on a height and carving yourself a resting place in the rock'. He is often identified with the Shebna who was adjutant-general in the court of Hezekiah, who was one of the officials sent by Hezekiah to negotiate with the Assyrian army in 701 BC (II Kings 18:18–19:7; Isaiah 36:3). A defaced single-line inscription of the same length was located in a panel over the window. Clermont-Ganneau had both inscriptions removed and sent to the British Museum. The N wall was at least 6m in length and a return seems to indicate that this was also a monolithic tomb. The chamber, trapezoidal, 4.65m × 2.25m, with a height of 2.95m had a flat ceiling, but a sort of rough console or cornice projecting 0.60m below the ceiling of the S side may be reminiscent of Iron Age practices elsewhere (École Biblique, Rte 13).

Along the scarp below Silwan, S from the Silwan Monolith, are numerous small *square cuttings in the rock*. They open onto small *chamber tombs*: some have gabled ceilings and are probably all part of the extensive Iron Age necropolis of Jerusalem. Clermont-Ganneau entered many, and described their general features. Vincent estimated there were between 40 and 50 visible, but others still hidden by the debris of the village. They are mostly used for storage by the modern villagers.

The extensive modern village of Silwan (from the ancient name of Siloam) occupies the E side of Kidron overlooking the gardens of Silwan. The villagers were notorious in the 19C for their aggressive behaviour to foreigners, but provided most of the workforce for the foreign archaeological expeditions which have worked on the site of the ancient city.

The spring Gihon lies opposite the village (Rte 10) and channels at least as early as the Iron Age led the spring water down the E side of the valley to irrigate the gardens.

Further down, c 250m S of the SE hill, on the W side of Kidron just beyond the junction with the Hinnom Valley (Rte 15) is the other ancient water supply of Jerusalem, *Bir Ayyub*, or *Job's Well*, and also traditionally associated with the *en-Rogel* of I Kings 1:9, near which was the stone Zoheleth where Adonijah the half-brother of Solomon held a sacrifice of sheep, oxen and buffaloes and declared himself king. It was a point on the border between Benjamin and Judah (Jos. 15:7) and perhaps is also the Dragon Spring of Neh. 2:13.

Description. A well sunk over 38m deep, with stone-lined upper shaft (small stone lining in upper 12m, huge blocks in lower 9.5m), and rock-cut lower shaft and collecting cave at bottom. The water supply is directly linked to the winter rainfall, and in a wet January the water used to well up and overflow the shaft; in summer it had to be drawn up, and in modern times pumped up. The water collects from the adjacent limestone strata underlying the Kidron and Hinnom valleys, but had a mixed reputation probably linked to a degree of surface contamination. According to Vincent the lower part may date to the Iron Age, when the valley floor was 10m lower than today, and may have been damaged by an earthquake in the days of King Uzziah (Zech. 14:5). The large masonry lining the lower part of the upper shaft may be of Roman date. About 1880 a ruinous stone building with low dome covered the well which was one of the principal water supplies for Ottoman Jerusalem. The water was carried up to the city in goatskins by the Silwan villagers who sold it for up to six pence a skin. They also recounted a legend that the well was a miraculous creation resulting from the healing of Job in a nearby cave and pool. Modern constructions above were due to later pumping installations but the system was supplanted by the new British pipelines which supplied Jerusalem after 1918.

Warren (1868–69) found a *tunnel aqueduct* running down the Kidron c 27.4m to the W of Bir Ayyub, which extended for 548.6m to the S, was 1.8m high and 1.06–1.28m wide and lay 21.3m below the surface. It was approached by seven staircases from the E side which were all 12.1m to 15.2m deep, and mostly 0.9m wide. The system included a large rock grotto fed by aqueducts from the N and leading out to the S, all cut at the cost of enormous labour and apparently intended to improve the supply of water.

Further down the Kidron other caves and tombs of the Herodian and Byzantine periods have been noted.

12 The Mount of Olives

Introduction. The Mount of Olives, the hill opposite Jerusalem on the E above the Kidron Valley; also called Olivet in the King James Version (II Sam. 15:30, Acts 1:12). It is mentioned in the Old Testament in connection with the Ceremony of the Red Heifer (Num. 19: 1–10), in the New Testament as the location of many events in the week before the Crucifixion, and as the Place of the Ascension. On Palm Sunday the Franciscans and pilgrims walk from Bethphage on the Mount of Olives to Jerusalem. Zechariah (Zech. 14:4) foretold the coming of the Messiah to the Mount of Olives, and some Christians following this text saw it as the place of the Second Coming of Christ. It has many olive groves, now giving place to new housing, and very extensive Jewish cemeteries, for it is the desire of many Jews to be buried in Jerusalem.

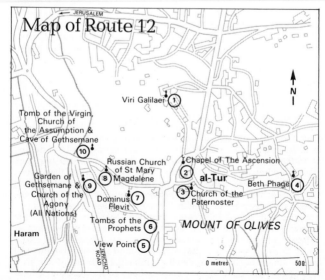

Topography. A ridge of soft limestone with many terraces and scarps, just over 4km long, with three main peaks. The higher NW part of the ridge is properly called Mount Scopus, 903m high, and is the location of the Hebrew University and the Augusta Victoria Hospital (Rte 13). The central area, the Mount of Olives proper, is 806m high and is called *Jabal al-Tur* (from the Syriac *Turo Qedisho*, the Holy Mountain), with the village of Kafr al-Tur, and lies directly opposite the city of Jerusalem. The S area, *Jabal Batn al-Hawa*, which is the lowest peak and stands above the village of Silwan, is identified with the Mountain of Corruption (II Kings 23:13).

History. Apart from a Palaeolithic handaxe discovered on the E slopes in 1965, the earliest traces of man on this ridge are of the late third millennium when shaft-grave burials were located on the S and E slopes of the central ridge (Warren, 1867; Saad, 1961; Kenyon, 1965). The E and W slopes were used for burial in the Middle Bronze Age (Warren, 1867; Saller, 1954), and the W slope also formed part of the cemetery of Jerusalem in the Late Bronze Age (Saller). There are hints of its use as a high place of worship in the Iron Age (David's place of worship mentioned in II Sam. 15:32, uncertainly identified with Nob; and the high places dedicated to foreign gods built by Solomon on the right hand of the Mount of Corruption in II Kings 23.13); the W slopes of the S peak were also used for burial at this time (Clermont-Ganneau, 1870).

The Mount of Olives continued to be used as one of the major cemeteries of Jerusalem in later periods. In Roman times the road to Jericho crossed the saddle between the N and central peaks, and according to the New Testament a path led by Gethsemane up the central peak and on towards Bethany.

Many of the events of the last days of Jesus' life were enacted here: the route of his triumphal entry into Jerusalem before the Passover started from the Mount of Olives; his arrest in the Garden of Gethsemane took place low down on the E side of Kidron; and the place of his Ascension is located on the top of the central peak. The sites of most of these events were commemorated by churches from the 4C onwards.

Between 370 and 378 St. Basil founded a monastery here in which were relics of St. John the Baptist. Theodosius (c 518) records 24 churches on the Mount of Olives, and c 570 the Piacenza Pilgrim notes vast numbers of monks and nuns. Many buildings were destroyed by the Persians in 614, and hundreds massacred; some churches were rebuilt by Modestus, and later by the Crusaders. By the 19C little except ruins and gardens remained, but in the second half of that century a reflorescence of building took place.

Visit. To avoid a steep climb, go by bus (75 from the DAMASCUS GATE) or taxi to the top of the Mount of Olives (c 2km), and return on foot by the steep path to Gethsemane. By road turn N at the junction near the NE angle of the Old City wall, descend to the right to the WADI JAUZ and then up to the Mount of Olives. From this road the tower of the Augusta Victoria Hospital can be seen to the N (Rte 13). Turn right at the crossroads at the top of the hill towards the village of al-Tur. At c 300m on the right is the lane to the traditional site where the disciples were called 'Men of Galilee' by two men in white immediately after the Ascension (Acts 1:11). The site of the **Viri Galilaei** (**1** on p.254) is marked by a Greek Orthodox church established in 1887 on a 17C house. Nearby are remains of a Byzantine chapel over a tomb. The tradition locating this site may go back to the early 6C, when the Breviarius notes 'and from there (the valley of Jehoshaphat) you come to Galilee, where the disciples saw the Lord Jesus after the time when he rose from the dead'. The tradition seems to have developed in the 11C–13C principally in the Eastern Church. The Latin name was first used in the 16C.

Returning to the main road and continuing to the S to the centre of the village of al-Tur, on the left and marked by a small minaret and a mosque is the ***Chapel of the Ascension** (**2** on p.254), the traditional site of the Ascension of Jesus (Luke 24:50–52) 40 days after the Resurrection (Acts 1:2–9). According to the Old Testament (II Kings 2:11) Elijah ascended in a whirlwind with chariots and horses of fire; by contrast in the New Testament Jesus was lifted up and hidden by a cloud as he blessed the disciples.

History. Tradition maintained that the site of the Ascension was first venerated in a cave on the Mount of Olives, but c 384 Egeria records that the place of the Ascension was located at the *Imbomon* higher up the mountain above the cave and church of the Eleona. The Imbomon was then included in the liturgy of the bishop on the first Sunday of Holy Week; from midnight on the Thursday till near dawn on the Friday; and at Pentecost rather than at the Ascension on the 40th day after Easter.

The first church on this site was built slightly later, before 392, by Poimenia a pious Roman lady. It was sacked by the Persians in 614, restored afterwards by Modestus, and described by Arculf in 680. His description is of a round building with three porticoes entered from the S. Inside it was open to the sky, with the indestructable footprints of Christ in the dust inside a railing. Eight lamps shone brilliantly every night through windows facing W towards Jerusalem. In the 9C the Commemoratorium notes that it was served by three clergy and presbyters. This shrine was restored by the Crusaders in 1102. The entrance was then from the W and approached by 20 steps. Inside was a single vaulted portico with wall paintings and sculptures. The central area was open to the sky with an unroofed edicule in the middle. The exterior was fortified. In 1198 Salah al-Din gave the site to two pious followers (Wali al-Din and Abu'l Hasan), for the Ascension of Jesus is recognised in Islam, and it was restored c 1200 re-using much of the Crusader material.

The present domed edicule over the footprints marking the Ascension bears a close resemblance to the Qubbat al-Mi'raj on the platform near the Dome of the Rock (Rte 2) which was also erected c 1200. The footprints of Christ in the rock were venerated, and the left footprint about this time was transferred to the Aqsa Mosque where it is still located (Rte 2). The building became more ruinous by the end of the 15C, and the E section was walled off to form the asymetrical shrine we see now. Excavations were carried out by Corbo (1960).

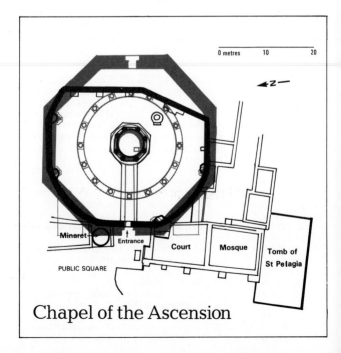

Chapel of the Ascension

Visit. On the right of the entrance is a small mosque *(Zawiyat al-Adawiyya)*, with court and gallery from whence there is a good view of both the Chapel of the Ascension and the surrounding countryside. On the left is a small *octagonal minaret*. Mosque and minaret date to 1620.

The central entrance gives directly onto an open court with paved path to the small Chapel of the Ascension of Christ (c 1200). The chapel has a stone dome on an octagonal drum. The octagonal walls, with fretted cornice, have piers flanked by small marble columns at the angles which are of Crusader date. The columns support a fine series of *12C Crusader marble capitals*, some with elaborately entwined and deeply-cut foliage, two with fantastic animal motifs depicting winged quadrupeds with the heads of birds. Entering the chapel from the W, the interior contains a mihrab in the S wall, and, in an asymetrically placed frame on the floor, the imprint in the rock of the right footprint of Jesus. Outside, the W side of the court is enclosed by a much rebuilt octagonal wall of varied masonry; a wall of the 15C reducing the earlier octagon bounds the E side. Bases of columns are visible in the ground which probably belong to the 12C Crusader round portico, as do some trefoil half-bases against the wall itself. The rings set high in the walls are used to attach tents and awnings at the Feast of the Ascension when Arab Christians come, especially from Bethlehem and Ramallah. Altars for these services are built against the E wall: in the 19C there were Armenian, Coptic, Syrian, Greek and Latin altars.

Medieval capital at the Chapel of the Ascension (courtesy of Kay Prag).

To the left of the entrance and on the S side of the Mosque is the site of a tomb: in Jewish tradition it is the *Tomb of Hulda*, a prophetess in Israel in the days of Josiah (640–609 BC) (II Kings 22:14–20); in Christian tradition it is that of *St. Pelagia the Penitent*, a dancing girl from Antioch who spent the rest of her life as an anchorite in a cell on this site and was buried there. The place was visited by the Piacenza Pilgrim c 570, and was much visited by Christian pilgrims in Crusader times too; according to Muslim tradition it is the tomb of a 9C Muslim holy woman, *Rahibat Bint Hasan*, and in the 19C was located in the SW corner of a Dervish monastery. Vincent notes that the cave had a Greek epitaph with the name 'Dometila'.

Turning left or S as we leave, the **Church of the Paternoster** or **Eleona** (3 on p.254) is just to the S at the junction of the lane to Bethphage.

History. A cave on this site was venerated as the site where Christ taught the disciples, and also at first as the Place of the Ascension. Eusebius and the Bordeaux Pilgrim (333) record that a church was built here by the order of Constantine, called the Church of the Disciples and the Ascension, or the Eleona, the church of the Olive Groves. It was one of three churches that Constantine constructed over a cave: that of Christ's birth at Bethlehem, of his death and Resurrection at the Holy Sepulchre, and of his teaching and Ascension here. The site of the Ascension was moved up the hill by 384 when Egeria mentions the church of the Eleona frequently as the site of liturgical visits during Holy Week: on Palm Sunday; on the Tuesday evening when the Gospel of Matt. 24:1–26:2 was read; and on Thursday. The church was destroyed by the Persians in 614, and not specifically mentioned in the restorations of Modestus.

After 614 pilgrims seem to have visited the Church of the Ascension and not to mention the Eleona, but the Commemoratorium (early 9C) lists 'The Church where Christ Taught his Disciples' with three monks and one presbyter, next to that called 'The Ascension of Christ'; c 870 it is not mentioned by Bernard the Monk. Possibly it was in ruins by the Crusader period, when the cave was associated in particular with the teaching of the Lord's Prayer, and with the place where Jesus spent the nights during his last days in Jerusalem (Luke 21:37). In 1102–06 a modest oratory was built, and improved in 1152. The church was damaged in 1187, repaired following the treaty of 1229, still existed at the end of the 13C but was in a poor state by 1345; traditions concerning it shifted in the following years. The church of the Credo (where, it was said, the disciples composed the Creed) was also located here.

In 1851 the stones of the 4C church were being taken down to the Valley of Jehoshaphat and sold for tombstones to the Jews. In 1857 the Princesse de la

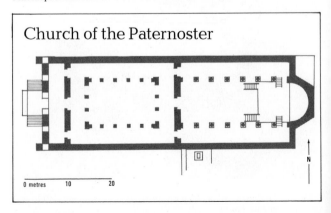

Church of the Paternoster

0 metres   10   20

N

Tour d'Auvergne bought land and started a search for the site of the cave; in 1868 she built a cloister modelled on the Campo Santo at Pisa, and founded a Carmelite convent to the E in 1872. The inner wall of the cloister commemorated the teaching of the Lord's Prayer in the cave with 32 copies of the prayer in different languages. The Byzantine foundations over a cave were discovered in 1910 partly beneath the cloister, which was then moved; and from 1915 an attempt was made to rebuild a basilica on the ancient foundations over the ruined cave: the half-built enclosure today marks this endeavour.

Visit. Hours: 8.30–11.50, 15.00–16.30 daily.

Entering from the N, on the left of the door is a plaque with the Lord's Prayer in Aramaic and Hebrew. The large court opposite is the unroofed, partly reconstructed Byzantine basilica built above the cave, with steps down to the place of the Lord's teaching. The cave was partly collapsed when discovered in 1910, and is now a curious combination of ancient rock cuttings, concrete supports and marble furnishing difficult to associate with the ancient place of prayer and teaching. The cave cuts part of a 1C AD rock-cut kokhim tomb.

Continuing up the steps opposite, turn left at the top, to the cloister containing the *68 copies of the Lord's prayer* in as many languages, inscribed on Palestinian tiles set in the walls. The *tomb of the founder* is located on the S side of the cloister.

The lane to the right of the entrance to the Paternoster leads left to the *Russian Orthodox Convent on the Mount of Olives* (established 1887, no admittance). Its prominent tower can be seen from the Jordan Valley on a clear day. Byzantine tomb chapels N of the Russian church contained some fine *Armenian mosaics*. The finest has a splendid border enclosing elaborate designs with fish, fruit, birds, and animals and an inscription in Armenian at the edge 'Susannah, mother of Artaban'; another, less elaborate mosaic, mentions the Armenian Bishop Jacob, and a third names St. Isaiah. A more complete and very fine Armenian mosaic can be seen just N of the Damascus Gate (Rte 13).

A right turn leads c 500m to **Bethphage** (**4** on p.254), the site mentioned in Mark 11:1 as the beginning of the triumphal procession of Jesus into Jerusalem commemorated on Palm Sunday. The precise location of Bethphage is uncertain but the modern Palm Sunday procession begins from the Latin Church. The Franciscan monastery was built in 1883 on the medieval ruins of a church found in 1876. It contains a stone with paintings showing the meeting of Jesus and the sisters of Lazarus (John 11:20–30). The remains illustrate the 12C tradition that this was the site of Bethphage. A new Greek Orthodox Church has been built nearby, and a footpath on its N side leads to Bethany (Rte 16).

Returning to the Paternoster, and continuing around to the left, the road leads to the INTERCONTINENTAL HOTEL; opposite, on the right is an excellent ***viewpoint overlooking the Old City** (**5** on p.254). To the SW can be seen the site of the *ancient city* on the SE hill. Looking a little to the N and W is *Mount Zion* with the dome and tower of the *Dormition church*; in front the S end of the *Haram platform* with the grey dome of the *Aqsa Mosque*, and a view over the recent excavations S of the Temple Mount; further N on the Haram platform is the golden *Dome of the Rock*; and behind it at a distance and more difficult to see in the midst of the Old City, slightly to the NW, is the grey dome of the *Church of the Holy Sepulchre*, with the square tower of the *Lutheran Church of the Redeemer* just S of it. An excellent view of the *E walls* of the city, including the *Golden Gate* (the closed E gate of the Haram) can be had from this point; and below on the slopes of the Mount of Olives, the golden onion-shaped domes of the *Russian Church at Gethsemane*. Returning a few metres in the direction of the Paternoster, a steep lane descends on the left towards Gethsemane.

On the left at the top of the lane are the *Tombs of the Prophets Haggai, Zechariah and Malachi* (6C–5C BC) of the three last books of the Old Testament (**6** on p.254). Though venerated as such by Christians and Jews, this is in fact a *catacomb of 1C BC/AD date* of unusual plan with central circular chamber and radiating fan-shaped corridors with burial places (kokhim). It was used for the burial of foreign Christians in the 4C–5C as shown by inscriptions above the burial places (Clermont-Ganneau 1870, 1874).

Open Mon–Fri 9.00–15.30. Torch necessary.

0 metres   10

N

Tombs of the Prophets

Continuing down the steep lane, on the right is the Franciscan property with the **Church of Dominus Flevit** (**7** on p.254), the place where Jesus wept over the city as he rode towards it on Palm Sunday (Luke 19:41).

History. Excavations (Saller, 1954) revealed a cemetery used in the Middle and Late Bronze Ages (c 1600–1300 BC), and used again 1C–4C AD. A 5C monastery was built here, and a chapel of the 14C was superseded by a 17C mosque to the N (al-Mansuriyya) the ruins of which were visible to the N in 1873–74. The N part of the property was acquired by the Franciscans in 1889, who built a chapel in 1891. They acquired more land to the S during World War II and a new church was built over the 5C chapel in 1955.

Visit. Open October–March 8.00–12.00, 14.30–17.00; April–September 8.00–12.00, 14.30–18.00.

Some tombs preserved from the excavations are visible on both sides of the path. Eighteen tomb complexes of the 1C–2C AD were excavated, all of which contained sarcophagi and ossuaries, some of which were re-used in the 3C–4C, employing trough arcosolia in which the rock was carved to form a sarcophagus, rather than placing a separate sarcophagus on a rock-cut bench. The pressure for space in the 1C AD tombs was such that sarcophagi were piled up to 3m deep in some chambers. The Bronze Age burial place is not preserved, but was 6m SW of the SW corner of the present church. It contained over 2000 objects, including pottery imported from Cyprus. The church is built over the 5C Byzantine monastic chapel, with part of the apse preserved. A Greek inscription on a partially preserved mosaic records the name of the 5C founder; other Byzantine fragments can be seen. The windows frame the view of the city over which Jesus wept.

Lower down the hill on the right is the **Russian Orthodox Church of St. Mary Magdalene at Gethsemane** (A. *al-Moscobiyya*) set in a garden (**8** on p. 254). Open Tue and Thu 9.00–12.00, 14.00–16.00, admission charged.

This picturesque church with its seven golden domes reminiscent of the Kremlin was built by Czar Alexander III in 1888. The yellow stone work and fretted lead barge boarding lend a stolid 19C tone to the architecture, but the agreeable series of shallow round arches at the top of the façade make a bridge for the eye between the building and the delightful domes. The church, with iconastasis, icons and paintings, has services at 6.00 and 16.30.

Descending the lane the visitor arrives at the entrance on the left to the **Garden of Gethsemane** (from Aramaic words meaning oil vat) and the **Church of All Nations (Church of the Agony)** (**9** on p.254).

History. The site, by early tradition, is that where Christ prayed, was betrayed by Judas and was arrested by the soldiers sent by the chief priests and elders on the night before his Crucifixion (Matt. 26:36–56). The Bordeaux Pilgrim (333) says that in the Valley of Jehoshaphat there was a vineyard with the rock where Judas betrayed Christ, and a palm tree connected with Palm Sunday; Egeria (384) says there was a graceful church at the place of Jesus' prayer above Gethsemane, which was visited before arriving at Gethsemane during the liturgy on the morning of Good Friday. This church of Jesus' prayer at Gethsemane is probably the Byzantine structure with three aisles and curious external towers flanking an open portico rather than a narthex, beneath the present Church of All Nations. It was probably built by Theodosius I and dedicated c 385. All the churches on the site incorporated the traditional rock on which Jesus prayed, as noted by the Bordeaux Pilgrim. The 4C church was destroyed in the earthquake of 747/8. The Crusaders built first an oratory on the site, then another church with three apses c 1170 on a slightly different orientation. This church seems to have been abandoned in the 14C. Excavations were carried out by Orfali (1909–20). The present church was built by the Franciscans in 1924.

Visit. Bus 43 from the Damascus Gate. Hours: April– October 8.30–12.00, 15.00–19.00; November–March 8.30–12.00, 14.00–17.00.

The Franciscan walled garden is a pleasant spot, with large and venerable olive trees, estimates of whose age range from 300 to 1000 years. The olive is a tree which bears fruit only after some years, and lives a long time, but it is unlikely that any survive from the time of Christ. Undoubtedly olives were cultivated in this area, but many of the groves were cut down by Titus in AD 70. The garden is planted with rosemary and other flowers. A walk around it brings the visitor

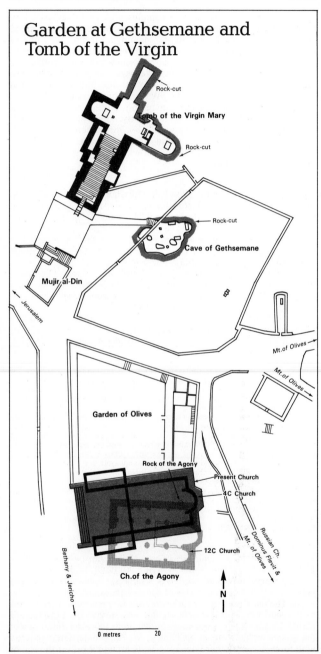

Garden at Gethsemane and Tomb of the Virgin

Rock-cut

Tomb of the Virgin Mary

Rock-cut

Rock-cut

Cave of Gethsemane

Mujir al-Din

← Jerusalem

Mt. of Olives →

Mt. of Olives →

Garden of Olives

Rock of the Agony

Present Church

4C Church

Russian Ch.
Dominus Flevit &
Mt. of Olives →

12C Church

Ch. of the Agony

← Bethany & Jericho

N

0 metres   20

to the W end of the Church of All Nations (1924). It has a porch with mosaics on the façade representing Jesus offering his suffering to God, fronting a basilica covered by 12 low domes; inside, the three aisles and three apses are decorated with mosaics on blue and green backgrounds; the light is dimmed by the purple glass in the side windows ('the hour when darkness reigns' of Luke 22:53). The church preserves sections of Byzantine mosaics, the outline of the Byzantine basilica and some cuttings and fragments of the Crusader church; the latter include small fragments of a fresco of Christ and an angel now preserved in the Museum of the Convent of the Flagellation (Rte 3).

In the vicinity there are also commemorative gardens of the Greek and Armenian churches.

Descending to the main road, turn right. On the left is the reputed *Tomb of Mujir al-Din* (1456–1522), an Arab writer who is best known for his book on the history of Jerusalem and Hebron (1495). It is marked by a 20C dome in a square enclosure at the bend of the main road.

A few metres further, on the left, is the ***Tomb of the Virgin Mary** (**10** on p.254), the Armenian, Greek, Ethiopian and partly Latin *Church of the Assumption.*

History. Traditions about the death of Mary in Jerusalem, her burial and Assumption ('Transitus Mariae') in the Valley of Jehoshaphat may date as early as the 2C–3C and were stronger by the 5C when the claims of Ephesus to this honour were hotly disputed. A church may have been built c 455, when an early tomb with kokhim and arcosolia was isolated by quarrying, to leave the kokhim chamber partly destroyed at an upper level, and a lower chamber with bench arcosolium to be venerated as the Tomb of Mary. This quarrying process was similar to that carried out around the Tomb of Christ in the Church of the Holy Sepulchre. An upper round church which surpassed the lower for grandeur was built by Mauritius (589–602) and destroyed in 614 by the Persians.

By the 7C the place of Mary's death had been localised on Mount Zion (Rte 8). The Church of St. Mary in the Valley of Jehoshaphat was described by Arculf in 680. He says this was on two levels: the upper contained four altars, and like the lower was round. In the lower level at the E end was an altar, and on the right was the empty rock-cut tomb of Mary. The Commemoratorium (9C) says it was served by 13 presbyters and clergy, 6 monks and 15 nuns. The ruins of this church were rebuilt by the Benedictines c 1130, and Queen Melisande was buried here in 1161.

The Abbey Church of St. Mary of Jehoshaphat had an adjacent monastery which was excavated by Johns (1937). It had a court and porticoes, halls with early Gothic columns, and frescoes in red on a green background. The complex, being outside the walls, was fortified by three towers. Most of the superstructure but only part of the lower storey of the church were destroyed by Salah al-Din after 1187 when the stones were used to repair the city walls (Rte 2, Bab al-Asbat). The lower 12C church on Byzantine foundations has survived virtually intact.

Visit. Open daily 6.00–11.30, 14.00–17.00; closed Sunday.

Descending steps to an open square courtyard, the only part of the church visible is the portal of c 1130 with a pointed arch supported on eight marble columns. Inside a wide staircase of 47 steps descends to the lower storey of the Byzantine church. In the upper section of the stairs the walls are of 12C date, and contain 12C windows blocked to keep out the Kidron floods to which the site has been vulnerable. At the seventh step on the right is the Tomb of Queen Melisande (died 11 September 1161). An arch over the step is carved with a lily-bud motif, and the tomb (4.49m × 1.68m with cupola) was once protected by iron bars. The body was moved in the 14C to a place at the foot of the stairway and is not mentioned after 1483. Since the 14C this tomb has been identified as that of Joachim and Anne, the parents of the Virgin.

A few steps lower on the left, were the tombs of some other members of the Crusader royal family. This was later identified as the tomb of Joseph. Towards the bottom of the stairs the masonry is Byzantine, as is most of the church itself. The floor is 10.6m below the level of the entrance. It has a built apse to the W and a longer rock-cut apse to the E. Various cuttings and passages on the N side relate to truncated tombs of the 1C BC/AD. The Tomb of the Virgin is marked by a small square chapel in the centre of the E apse. In Crusader times it had an edicule with arcade supported by 16 columns on a marble socle, and still has a medieval lintel over the N door. The present altar inside the Tomb hides the remnants of a bench arcosolium tomb of perhaps the 1C AD. The niche S of the tomb is a mihrab, installed when the Muslims had joint rights to the church (in Muslim tradition Muhammad saw a light over the tomb of Mary according to Mujir al-Din, and 'Umar prayed at Gethsemane in 638). There are altars belonging to the Armenians and the Greeks in the E apse, and one of the Ethiopians in the W apse with a cistern adjacent. The dimness and the blackened walls add to the sense of antiquity within the church.

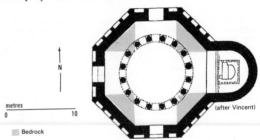

N

metres
0   10

(after Vincent)

Bedrock

Byzantine Ch. of the Virgin restored
(upper storey)

Returning to the courtyard, to the left is a passage leading to the *Cave of Gethsemane* or the *Grotto of the Agony*. Probably a natural cave originally, which may have had many uses and has been several times re-cut. The channels in the floor, the traces of mosaic and of 12C wall paintings, the hole in the roof all hint at such uses as a burial cave, as a workshop for processing olives, a Byzantine shrine connected with the location of the place where the disciples slept while Jesus prayed, the place of his prayers, or of his arrest, or where he spent the night. A Crusader Church at Gethsemane was located in this cave. Like the Church of All Nations, the chapel is cared for by the Franciscans and has the same hours of opening.

Returning to the road, to the right on the opposite bank of the Kidron valley is the modern Greek Orthodox *Church of St. Stephen*, which marks one traditional site of the stoning or burial of St. Stephen, the first martyr, outside the city gate (Acts 7:58). In Crusader times it was the N, not the E, gate of the town which was named for St. Stephen (see École Biblique, Rte 13).

It is possible to descend further down the Kidron Valley from this point to visit the fine rock-cut tombs (Rte 11) or to return up the hill to our starting point near the NE corner of the Old City.

13 The Northern Suburbs

Introduction. This section covers the area N of the Old City of Jerusalem, mainly to the E of the Nablus Road but also including the Mandelbaum Gate and the Tombs of the Sanhedrin. There is no single route for the various scattered monuments and places of interest, grouped below according to accessibility.

The N suburbs beyond the walls of the Old City were only developed during the 19C. Pierotti (1864) notes that from the Muslim cemetery on Karm al-Shaikh (near Herod's Gate) to the Tombs of the Kings there was earth, vegetation and bare rock, with no trace of an ancient city. From the 1870s small settlements grew up here, and from the 1880s various foreign institutions were established, such as the American Colony in 1881, the Dominican Convent of St. Stephen in 1884 and the German Catholic Hospice and College in 1886. The rate of building increased in the 20C, and especially from the 1950s. Today, as well as various institutions, there are hotels, consulates and hospitals situated here, and it is a populous suburb with the main shopping area along Salah al-Din St. It is mainly inhabited by Christian and Muslim Arabs, with, further out, new Jewish suburbs linking the western city with Mount Scopus.

Places of interest close to the Old City.

*The Archaeological (Rockefeller) Museum.

The former museum of the Department of Antiquities of Palestine is located on the N side of SULAIMAN ST, opposite the NE corner of the Old City, two minutes' walk E of Herod's Gate. Bus 27, 43. Open Sun–Thu, 10.00–17.00; Fri–Sat, 10.00–14.00; closed on Jewish holidays. Admission charged.

History. The Department of Antiquities of the Mandate Government was set up in 1920, and the objects inherited from the Ottoman government collection, supplemented by objects from excavations from 1920 onwards were in the charge of the First Keeper of the Palestine Museum, W.J. Phythian-Adams. The present museum was built (1927–29) as the Palestine Archaeological Museum with funds from J.D. Rockefeller, to house the antiquities of Palestine, and was formally opened in 1938. It was administered by an international committee of trustees until nationalised by Jordan in 1966. It was annexed by Israel in 1967 and now houses part of the Israel Department of Antiquities as well as an excellent systematic display of antiquities which is largely unchanged since Mandate times. Designed in a distinctive local style by Austin Harrison (1881–1976), Chairman of the Public Works Department of Mandate Palestine, who combined ideas drawn from Byzantine and Islamic palaces and caravanserais with a neo-Gothic style influenced by his Lutyens training (see also the main Post Office, and the old Government House, Rte 14).

It is built of local stone. The vestibule leads to a hall under the central tower, and the building is arranged symmetrically around a rectangular pool in a cloistered court. Study rooms were designed adjacent to the long exhibition galleries, and a lecture theatre and library located in the front wings. It has a fine garden with interesting local plants and trees.

Visit. The Tower Hall is used for temporary exhibitions; the permanent display begins in the **South Octagon** to the left of the entrance and continues into the **South Gallery**. Here the objects illustrate the archaeological sequence in stone, pottery, metal-work and other materials from the Palaeolithic to the Iron Age. Most of the sites represented are those of the major excavations in Palestine up to 1948, and include the caves at Mount Carmel (Garrod and Bate), Jericho (Garstang), ʿAi (Marquet-Krause), Megiddo (Fisher, Guy,

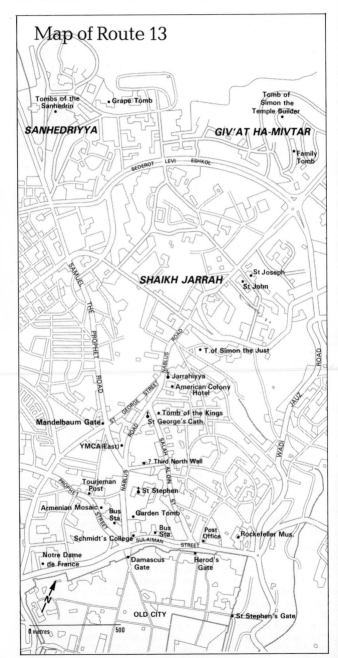

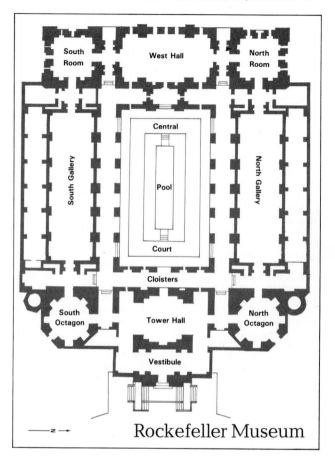

Rockefeller Museum

Loud), Tell Beit Mirsim (Albright), Lachish (Starkey), Ajjul, Fara and Jemmeh (Petrie) and Beth Shan (Rowe and Fitzgerald). In the **South Room** are some of the *great wooden beams from the Aqsa Mosque* (see Aqsa Mosque and Islamic Museum, Rte 2) which were removed during the 1938–42 restorations. They date mostly from the 7C–8C.

In the **West Hall** are *stucco relief and sculpture from Khirbat al-Mafjar* near Jericho. This Umayyad palace was built by the caliphs Hisham and al-Walid II after c 724 and destroyed still unfinished in the earthquake of 747/8. Delightful and rare Islamic depictions of the human figure should be noted, including a probable statue of al-Walid himself; and a lively procession of painted quail. Complex geometric and floral patterns cover the entire surfaces, and reflect developing early Islamic art influenced both by Sassanian traditions and those of the local schools of craftsmen. It was the first time in Palestine that carved stucco was used extensively as a surface ornament.

Continuing beyond the hall, a small room to the left contains a display of jewellery from the Hellenistic to later periods.

In the **North Room**, among other important pieces of 12C Crusader sculpture, are the *lintels from the entrance doors of the Church of the Holy Sepulchre* (Rte 4). These derive from a French Romanesque school, and were removed from the church to preserve them following the earthquake of 1927. In the **North Gallery** is pottery and sculpture of the Roman and later periods. More sculpture is placed in the cloister.

Leaving the museum, turn right along SULAIMAN ST, passing Herod's Gate on the left, and on the right are the *East Jerusalem Post Office* and the entrance to Salah al-Din St (the main shopping street of East Jerusalem). After another 200m on the right is the Damascus Gate Bus Station, with Solomon's Quarry opposite (Rte 1). Behind the Bus Station can be seen *Jeremiah's Grotto, A. Zawiyat al-Adhamiyya*, a complex of caves and a cistern in which tradition holds Jeremiah (a Jewish prophet at the time of the Babylonian destruction in 586 BC) wrote his Lamentations and was buried. It became a Muslim shrine c 1361.

Continue 150m to the Damascus Gate, turn right for 200m up PROPHET ST to the *Armenian Mosaic located in a house at the corner of a short street on the right. Open 7.00– 17.00. The 5C–6C mosaic, found when the foundations of the house were being dug in July, 1894, measures 6.4m × 3.9m It was set on bedrock inside rough rubble walls with plastered surfaces. At the E end there was a small apse; under the SW corner a small natural cave contained human bones and lamps of the 5C–6C. That the room was a mortuary chapel is indicated by the inscription at the E end which reads: 'For the memory and salvation of all those Armenians whose name the Lord knows'. The building is identified by some with the church of St. Polyeucht. The mosaic is elaborate, with tesserae of many colours. Within a guilloche border is a vase from which springs a vine with many branches and grape clusters. Peacocks, ducks, storks, pigeons, fowls, an eagle, a partridge and a parrot in a cage are depicted in the branches.

By continuing c 100m further along Prophet St a visit can be made to the *Tourjeman Post* at 1 REHOV HEL HAHANDASA. An exhibition on the 'Reunification of Jerusalem' is shown in a house which was used as an Israeli frontier post on the edge of No-Man's Land between 1948 and 1967. Open Sun–Thu, 9.00–15.00. Admission charged. Bus 11, 12, 27.

Returning along Prophet St the area of No-Man's Land from 1948–67 is on the right, and rising above to the left is the newly restored bulk of *Notre Dame de France*. This was founded by the Augustinian Fathers of the Assumption as a pilgrim's hospice in 1887, and being on the front line, was badly damaged during and after the 1948 war. In the vicinity was located the 12C Church of St. Lazarus Outside the Walls, with a leper house attached. The Latin Patriarch sent an appeal to Louis VII of France on behalf of this establishment c 1130; and in 1144 Baldwin III (whose nephew was a leper) confirmed the grant of a vineyard made by King Fulk for its endowment.

Returning towards the Damascus Gate, take the left turning into the NABLUS RD (also called the Shechem or Ramallah Rd), which runs N from the Damascus Gate. The large building on the opposite corner is *Schmidt's College*, founded as the German Catholic Hospice and College in 1886; used temporarily as the British governorate immediately following the surrender of the city in 1917, and later as the British Royal Air Force Headquarters. The *Church of St. Paul* adjoins it.

Continuing c 150m we arrive at (left) part of the East Jerusalem Bus Station, and opposite, a small lane between walls leads up to the **Garden Tomb**. This was identified as the Tomb of Christ by General Gordon (of Khartoum) in 1883. There is no early tradition to support the proposal, but it retains an atmosphere fostered by the garden in which it is set. Many visitors find this site more readily identifiable with the Gospel scene than the dark and urban context of the Church of the Holy Sepulchre, and it is preserved as an interdominational place of prayer for Christian pilgrims. Open daily except Sunday, 8.00–12.30; 15.00–17.00.

Visit. The Garden Tomb is cut in a quarried scarp approached through a garden. The quarrying may date to the time of Herod Agrippa I (AD 37–44). The door and windows in the tomb façade are due to later re-working, probably in Byzantine or Crusader times. The deep channel along the ground, sometimes identified as the groove for a giant rolling stone to seal the entrance, is of uncertain date and purpose. The square tomb chamber inside, with three much-destroyed projecting benches with troughs but no arcosolia which would be typical of the late Roman period, may well date to the 8C–6C BC when there was a nearby cemetery (see École Biblique, below). The idea of locating the Tomb of Christ in this area was current in the 19C when the knoll immediately to the E and above the garden was identified with Golgotha, the Place of the Skull. This was a popular belief, based on the resemblance of the prominent knoll to the shape of a skull, with bare rounded top and two caves marking the eyes and also drew on a Jewish tradition that this was the place of stoning just outside the city on the road to Damascus. This identification of Golgotha was adopted by Thenius (1842), Fisher Howe (1871) and Conder (1878); and thus in 1883 Gordon's adoption of the nearby tomb as the site of the Tomb of Christ had ready followers.

As one leaves the site of the Garden Tomb, the wall on the right encloses the grounds of the *Dominican Convent and Church of St. Stephen* which is entered a little higher up the Nablus Road.

History. In about 415 a village priest discovered the bones of Stephen, the first martyr of the Christian church, and in 438 Eudocia was present when the relics were deposited in their first shrine. She built a church on this site c 455–60 to house the relics, on the traditional site of Stephen's death by stoning (Acts 6:5–8:1) and later was herself buried here. A large monastery occupied the site in the 6C, but was destroyed in the Persian sack of 614. A chapel was built in the 7C, and the site was extensively redeveloped by the Knights Hospitallers in the 12C. This Frankish complex was pulled down for strategic reasons in the face of Salah al-Din's advance in 1187. A hospice was created in the 'Asnerie' (the stables of the 12C complex) after 1192 for Christian pilgrims who were not permitted by the Ayyubids to lodge within the walls. This rule was relaxed in 1229 but re-established after 1244. In 1881 part of the 12C stable complex and a chapel with an altar painted with saints were uncovered near the road; to the E the Byzantine church was discovered. The Convent of St. Stephen was built on the site in 1884; the École Biblique et Archéologique Français de St. Étienne (with fine library) was established in 1890. The present Church of St. Stephen was built in 1900.

Visit. The church is built on the foundations and preserves some of the *mosaic floors* of the 5C Byzantine church. The court contains *ancient cisterns* and *tombs*. The latter include one previously sealed by a Byzantine tombstone inscribed: 'Tomb of the deacon Nonnus

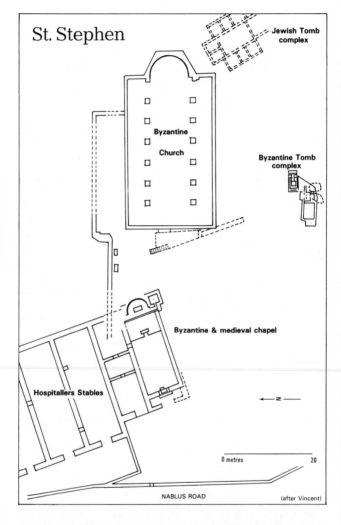

St. Stephen

Jewish Tomb complex

Byzantine Church

Byzantine Tomb complex

Byzantine & medieval chapel

Hospitallers Stables

N

0 metres   20

NABLUS ROAD

(after Vincent)

Onesimus of the Holy Sepulchre of Christ and this monastery'. One tomb had a round blocking stone. Two tombs may have originated in the Iron Age. They have central rectangular halls leading to burial chambers with benches. The chambers are very well cut (cf. the Iron Age necropolis at Silwan village, Rte 11), and were designed to take up to 20 primary burials with small lower chambers for secondary burials. The features which support an early date are the cornice and panel mouldings on the walls, the square chambers with projecting benches, some with troughs but without arcosolia, the head rests carved on the benches (cf. the tombs below the Church of Scotland, Rte 14) and small parapets along the edge of the benches. Both tombs were re-used in the Byzantine period. The first is at the SE angle of the church, discovered during construction work in 1885; the second, found a few years after, is incorporated in a building used as a cemetery by the monastery since the 19C and is about 50m S of the church. If the tombs originate in the Iron Age, they are the largest tombs of that date known in Judah, and their style and size have suggested to some that they should be identified with the Royal Caverns mentioned by Josephus (War V:147; see also Solomon's Quarries, Rte 1).

Continuing up the Nablus Road, at the next crossroads a diversion to the NW brings one at c 250m to the area of the *Mandelbaum Gate*, at the S end of PROPHET SAMUEL ST. This was the only crossing point between East and West Jerusalem between 1948 and 1967. It was named for the owner of a nearby house, and a plaque now marks the site. A fortnightly convoy starting here was permitted through Jordanian territory under UN supervision to maintain the Israeli enclave on Mount Scopus. In the area immediately S of the crossing of Prophet Samuel St, St. George's and Shivte Yisrael roads, a small Byzantine monastery was excavated in 1935 (Baramki). The chapel had a coloured mosaic with floral patterns dated to the 8C.

Returning to the crossroads on the Nablus Road, and walking a few metres E on the N side of ST. GEORGE'S ST (opposite the garage) are the remnants of a major *ancient defensive wall* excavated in 1965 (Kenyon). It was c 4.30m wide, constructed variously of fine drafted ashlar stones, large, roughly squared stones without marginal drafts, and also smaller rubble masonry and mortar. It is part of a wall which stretches parallel to and opposite the central part of the present N wall of the Old City for c 600m, lying c 450m to the N of it. The most easterly point discovered lies in the garden of the Albright Institute (see below), and other sections can be seen W of the Nablus Road. The foundations of seven N-facing towers have been found; probably it was never finished, and it has been robbed since for building materials.

The wall was first studied and identified as the Third North Wall of the city (see p.30) by Robinson (1841); some sections have been excavated: Sukenik and Mayer (1925–27, 1940); Kenyon (1965); and Ben-Arieh and Netzer (1972–74). It is now variously identified as: (1) the Third North Wall of the city of Herod Agrippa I (AD 41–44) described by Josephus (War V:142–160), which Agrippa left unfinished but was later hurriedly improved by the Jews during the First Revolt; (2) a forward defence barrier at the time of the First Revolt (AD 66); (3) a siege wall built by Titus in AD 70. Only the beginning and end of the course of the Third North Wall can be identified with any precision. It was built to enclose the houses that had begun to extend beyond the Second North Wall, including the new suburb of Bezetha. The first theory is supported by the length of the wall as given by Josephus (33 *stades*) and the mention of the adjacent monuments of Helena of Adiabene; the second by the lack of any evidence for domestic occupation of this period N of the present Old City; and the concurrent evidence for burials of the 1C AD in the area outside the Damascus Gate. The beauty of the Herod Agrippa masonry, which Josephus describes, also fits that of the lower courses of the Roman gate at the Damascus Gate and favours the identification with Agrippa's work. The identification is not yet resolved.

North of St. George's St the Nablus Road and Salah al-Din St converge. Just up the Nablus Rd on the right is the *Palestine Pottery*, for many years manufacturing colourful ceramics with designs based

on old Turkish patterns, made originally by Armenians who came to
Jerusalem in 1919 to make tiles for the repair of the Dome of the
Rock. A short distance further on the left is the YMCA (East).
Continuing to the E end of St. George's St, opposite in SALAH AL-DIN
ST is the *Albright Institute of Archaeological Research*, founded as
the American School of Oriental Research in 1900. Fragments of the
'Third North Wall' and a possible Byzantine chapel have been
excavated in the garden.

Turning left up Salah al-Din St, pass the Law Court (left), and at
275m on the right are *The Tombs of the Kings. Identified as the
Tomb of Queen Helena of Adiabene (died c AD 65) and cut c AD 50,
the tomb complex is a large and interesting example of a monumental Jewish family tomb in the Graeco-Roman tradition. Open daily
8.30–17.00. Admission charged. A torch is useful if visiting the burial
chambers.

History. The tomb is identified with that described by Josephus (Antiq. XX:17–
96, 101; War V:147) as the tomb with three pyramids built by Helena of
Adiabene three stadia from the town. Adiabene was in the NE of modern Iraq,
where members of a Jewish merchant community had converted the royal
family to Judaism. Following the death of her husband, and the accession to the
throne of her son Izates in AD 41, Helena came to Jerusalem, arriving at the
time of the famine in AD 44. Her generous gifts to relieve the famine endeared
her to the people of Jerusalem, and she stayed on, built a palace in the SE part
of Jerusalem, and a tomb for her eventual burial. She returned to Adiabene on
the death of her son in AD 65 and died shortly after. Another son, Monobazes,
became king, and sent the bodies of Helena and Izates to Jerusalem for burial,
which must have taken place shortly before the beginning of the First Revolt.
The disturbed times may have been a factor in placing the principal burial, in a
sarcophagus inscribed 'Queen Saddan' in Aramaic (which is thought to be her
Aramaic rather than Greek name) in a concealed lower chamber. The fortunate
effect was that it escaped the attentions of the looters who devastated the upper
burials.

The tomb seems also to have been used for burial after the First Revolt, as de
Saulcy found an urn with ashes in the tomb in 1863, which were perhaps those
of a Roman, as cremation is forbidden in Jewish law. It was probably looted
again c 1483 during the reign of al-Ashraf Qa'it Bay and a number of sarcophagi
were then perhaps taken to be used as fountain troughs at the Tariq al-Wad, the
Bab al-Sakina, the Mahkama and in the Haram itself (Clermont-Ganneau; see
Rtes 2 and 3). One of these is now placed outside the Islamic Museum in the
Haram (Rte 2). Two similar sarcophagi were found by de Saulcy in the tomb
itself. The monument was wrongly identified by de Saulcy in 1863 as the Tombs
of the Kings of Judah (the origin of the present name). The tomb was bought as
such by a wealthy French Jewish family in 1878, and in 1886 given by them to
the French Republic, by which it is still administered. A Jewish tradition locates
the tomb of the 1C AD Kalba Savua' (father-in-law of Rabbi Akiva) here.

Visit. Entering from Salah al-Din St, turn right to the top of 24 broad
descending rock-cut steps. Channels at the side and centre collect
rainwater to fill two cisterns located at the bottom of the stairs. That
on the right is smaller; that ahead has two round-headed windows
and a rock-cut pillar. To the left a rock-cut arch with a single incised
moulding leads to an enormous, almost square court. It measures
nearly 26m a side, and both the court and the steps may have
originated as a quarry. To the W is the damaged ornamental façade
of the burial complex. The columns, two free-standing, and two
engaged end-columns, are missing; the capitals were probably of the
Corinthian order. Several fragments of Corinthian capitals were
found in the excavation of the court and compare with those found at
the Family Tomb of Herod (Rte 14). Above, a flat architrave has a
frieze of leaves, citrus and almonds with a central rosette. Above that
a frieze with triglyphs, dentils and round metopes with paterae flank

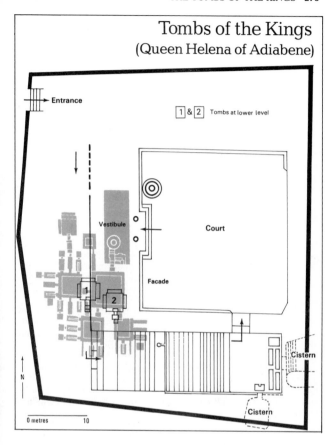

Tombs of the Kings
(Queen Helena of Adiabene)

Entrance

1 & 2 Tombs at lower level

Vestibule

Court

Facade

1
2

Cistern

Cistern

N

0 metres   10

the central motifs of two acanthus sprays, two wreaths and a bunch of grapes. The dentils continuing under the acanthus emphasise the remoteness of the Hellenistic ancestry of the Doric style in this Roman-Jewish setting. The frieze is capped by a cornice. Above, the façade has been reconstructed (on paper) as crowned with three pyramids or memorial monuments, which have not survived. Behind the façade is a vestibule where some architectural fragments discovered in the excavations are displayed.

On the left side of the vestibule are steps leading down to the burial chambers. At the top, and also just outside the vestibule on the right side of the façade, are two rock-cut basins, probably used for ablution in the funerary ritual. The entrance steps were once blocked by a large round stone (cf. Convent of St. Stephen, above, and Herod's Family Tomb, Rte 14). They lead to a large square hall off which four doors lead to a complex of seven large chambers with numerous kokhim; smaller passages exist at various levels. The two chambers on the S lead to chambers on a lower level. A fine sarcophagus, now in the Louvre in Paris, was located in the first chamber on the right of the entrance. It has a curved lid carved with leaves, flowers and fruits in rather stiff, stylised forms. The sacrophagus of Saddan (also in the Louvre), was found by de Saulcy in a lower chamber near the centre of the complex. The corners had been knocked off in order to get it into the burial chamber. This burial chamber had bench arcosolia and may have been cut a little later than the upper chambers. Many of the stone sealing doors had relief carved panelling.

Opposite the entrance is the rear of **St. George's Anglican Cathedral**, college and hospice, which is entered from the Nablus Road. The church was built in 1898. The Protestant interests in Palestine were first served under a joint Anglo-Prussian agreement (for details, see Christ Church, Rte 6), which was dissolved in 1887. Bishop Blyth was then appointed to the Anglican see. The new establishment included the collegiate church of St. George, boys' and girls' schools, an episcopal residence and a clergy house all on the N side of the town. The 'Jerusalem Association Room' of the London-based Palestine Exploration Fund met at St. George's College early in the 20C. The cathedral, stone-built and with an English character, has a hospice with pleasant garden adjacent. A painted tomb, probably of late Roman date, was discovered during the construction work but not preserved. About 30m N of the Tombs of the Kings, at the side of the road, a sculpted head of Hadrian was found in 1875. In the 1860's Warren and Wilson noted a very large reservoir pool to the W of the Nablus Rd in this vicinity, which was filled by surface run-off, but was then nearly full of debris.

Following the Nablus Road down the hill to the N, after a few metres is a small cemetery (right), and beyond (also right), the **American Colony Hotel**. Originally settled by Swedish Protestants and American missionaries in 1881, the American Colony is one of the historic entities of 19C Jerusalem. The hotel remains in the ownership of the family. The central building is a fine example of a princely late Ottoman house with courtyard and many details lovingly preserved. The decorations include tiles made in Jerusalem by craftsmen from Turkey in 1919–20. An upstairs room contains a fine Ottoman ceiling.

25m N of the hotel is a small mosque marking the site of the *Zawiyya Jarrahiyya*, a domed tomb of the Amir Husam al-Din al-Jarrahi (c 1201) which used to be specially venerated by country people for the granting of prosperous expeditions, good harvests and good luck, especially with hens and egg production. The mosque was added in 1895–96. From here the road descends into a valley, and then climbs the hill of Shaikh Jarrah, a Muslim village established c 1900, now with many institutional buildings, including consulates and St. Joseph's Hospital. *St. John's Ophthalmic Hospital* is also located here. Originally founded in 1882 by the revived English Order of the Knights of St. John for research on the endemic Palestinian problems of trachoma, and formerly occupying a building just S of the Sultan's Pool on the Bethlehem Road (opposite the House of Quality). That building was damaged in 1917 and 1948, and the present site was developed after 1948.

(A more distant excursion is possible from this point if travelling by car or bus, by continuing on the Nablus Road to the N beyond Shaikh Jarrah and Shufat: at a distance of c 4.5km N of the Old City is the site of Gibeah of Saul, see below.)

Below the S side of the hill of Shaikh Jarrah is located the so-called **Tomb of Simon the Just**. Descending the hill from the American

Colony, take the first right turn, then fork left and turn left to the end of the road. A tomb set among other rock-cut tombs on the N side of the Wadi Jauz was identified in Jewish tradition as that of Simon the Just, (H. *Shimon ha-Zaddiq*) who was High priest in Jerusalem in the late 4C BC and renowned for piety and goodness to his people (Josephus, War XII:ii:5 and Ecclesiaticus 50:1–21). It was investigated by Clermont-Ganneau in 1871, who noted a Roman inscription on a *tabula ansata* on the rear wall of the antechamber above the low doorway. Though much damaged, it named Julia Sabina, a Roman lady, perhaps related to a Julius Sabinus who was a first centurion of the Tenth Roman Legion. The tomb should date well into the Roman period, and is therefore not the tomb of the High Priest Simon. The site was bought by the Jews in 1876 and is a place of pilgrimage. The damaged façade had already been filled with masonry in the 19C; two of the five chambers within have bench arcosolia. One has been converted into a cistern at some past time. Many other undecorated tombs of this period exist around the outskirts of Jerusalem, usually fronting on to a small court.

Sites on the more distant northern fringes of Jerusalem.

To the NW (c 2.2km NW of the Damascus Gate) in the new suburb of Sanhedriyya is the complex of tombs around the **Tombs of the Sanhedrin**. They are now mostly preserved in a small park just N of Samuel the Prophet St. Bus 2, 16, 39 and 40 from the Central Bus Station in West Jerusalem; the park is open daily until sunset.

These tombs are part of a huge cemetery stretching across the outer edges of the N side of the city. All those known were pillaged in ancient times. The best known of this group of about 20 Jewish family tombs of the first half of the 1C AD is the monument called the Tombs of the Sanhedrin or Judges (**Tomb 14** towards the NW of the group) which was discovered at the beginning of the 17C. The tomb is falsely associated with the 70 judges who maintained Jewish religious law and met in the Temple Area, because the number of burial places it contains (actually only 55 kokhim, 4 arcosolia and 2 cave/ossuaries). Nothing is known of its real ownership, and there is no evidence that it was used for other than family burial over several generations.

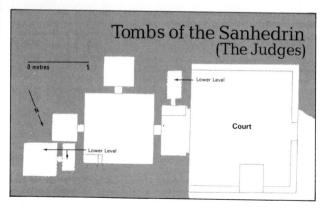

Visit. That the site was an ancient *malaki* quarry is attested by the marks in the floor of the forecourt (9.90m × 9.30m × 3.50m deep).

The court was used in medieval times as a caravanserai. On the E is a rectangular door having a triangular pediment with dentils. The acroteria at the sides are rather rigid palmettes or acanthus, the central acroterion has gone. The tympanum contains a rather flatly carved all-over design of acanthus scroll, with fruits (no grapes) restricted to the central area. The ornament is copied on the doorway of the hypogeum inside the vestibule, on a reduced scale. The entrances to the burial chambers themselves were generally small, with a rebated edge into which the blocking stone fitted fairly precisely. Inside this tomb is even larger than that of Helena of Adiabene (see above). The first great chamber has two storeys (which is a unique feature), with very dense alignments of straight and long kokhim. The openings are arched, with rectangular rebates for the blocking slabs. The upper levels of kokhim are set back in pairs within arcosolia. There are six chambers behind the vestibule, three on the upper level, and three at a lower level reached by stairs.

Tomb 8, to the E, is an interesting rock-cut tomb which has a court with benches and columns which are distyle in antis with pilasters as wall ends (cf. Helena of Adiabene, above). The capitals are late Doric with concave profiles. The pilaster capitals have very degenerate late mouldings. Inside is a central hall with three chambers leading off, one containing four kokhim beneath three arcosolia.

Other tombs are located in the park, and a few outside in nearby buildings. Some, which have been destroyed during the last century, had interesting ornamental details such as metopes with paterae, triglyphs, dentils, late-style guttae, anthemia, egg and dart moulding, and one tomb had a two-storey façade, with shortened columns on the upper level and late Doric capitals.

The **Grapes Tomb** is c 200m NE of the Tomb of the Judges, in the Doris Weiler Gdn in YAM SUF ST. This has a very large court (6.7m), again probably originally created by quarrying. The tomb entrance has a triangular pediment with dentils, and three large, rather stiff acroteria over an Ionic T-framed doorway (2.7m × 2.4m) with broad jambs; the tympanum is very flatly carved with a central rosette and a running vine scroll with grapes. The soffit of the entrance has relief carving of rosettes and foliage in coffer-like panels. The vestibule is large (3.4m × 5.2m) with a cavetto cornice and Doric-type capitals with ornament in more local style on the pilasters. The interior has a fairly regular plan with three chambers leading off a central hall, each with six kokhim, except that the middle kokh on the S side forms a passage to a further chamber which has three arcosolia and a sunk circular panel on the ceiling containing a star rosette in relief. It probably dates to the beginning of the 1C AD.

The monumental tomb furthest to the N in this great cemetery, (c 3km NW of the Damascus Gate, c 1km to the NW of the Sanhedriyya Tombs) is known as the **Tomb of Umm al-'Amud** (or 'Mother of the Column'), and is cut into a long rock scarp. The columns for which it is named disappeared long ago, and only parts of the façade are preserved in the angles of the rock-cut forecourt. Probably also originally *distyle in antis* with late Doric capitals, the tomb has a Doric frieze with rosettes in the metopes. An interesting feature is the carving of the rock façade to imitate drafted masonry.

Approximately half-way between Sanhedriyya and Shaikh Jarrah is *Ammunition Hill*, an Israeli War Memorial dating from 1975 and commemorating the Six Day War. Park and museum on the S side of Sederot Levi Eshkol. Closed Sat and Jewish Holidays.

Continuing along Sederot Levi Eshkol, in the NW angle of the junction formed by this road with the Nablus Road, is the new suburb of Giv'at ha-Mivtar, where another section of the Jewish necropolis of rock-cut tombs was found during construction work. At the S end of the suburb the *Family Tomb* was discovered, already partly destroyed. A square chamber had nine remaining kokhim cut into three walls, and another loculus for a secondary interment of bones cut from a central pit. In this complex the bones of up to 40 adults and children were discovered, 20 in ossuaries, five in the central pit, five in the kokhim; study of the bones showed that at least four people were genetically related, illustrating the family nature of these tombs. Six ossuaries were placed in front, and ten inside, the kokhim. Many of the ossuaries were decorated, and some had Greek or Hebrew inscriptions. The pottery dated the use of the tomb to c 50 BC–AD 70.

In the NW part of this suburb was the *Tomb of Simon the Temple-Builder*, a large tomb with 12 kokhim and a pit. Among the ossuaries it contained was one inscribed in Aramaic 'Simon builder of the Temple'. The style of the tomb does not suggest that this was the burial of the 'architect' of the Temple, but rather perhaps someone who had worked on its construction. The same tomb contained an unnamed ossuary with the bones of a man (aged 24–28) who had been crucified (mass crucifixions are noted in the time of Alexander Jannaeus (103–76 BC), in the revolt during the census of AD 7 and again during the Jewish Revolt, as well as the crucifixion of individuals). Other occupants of this tomb included one who had died by burning, a woman who died of a blow from a mace, and a child who died of starvation: all illustrating the unsettled times.

Just over 2km to the N from Giv'at ha-Mivtar on the Nablus Rd is **Gibeah of Saul** (H. *Givat Sha'ul*—the Gabath Saul of Josephus; A. *Tell al-Ful*, or Mound of Beans). This was the home and capital of Saul, first king over Israel. It is 4.5km N of Jerusalem on a hill to the right of the Nablus Rd.

Excavations. Albright (1922–23, 1933); Lapp (1964).

History. Set in an elevated position, the earliest remains on the site date to the Middle Bronze Age. A town was founded in the 12C which is likely to be the town in the centre of the tribal territory of Benjamin involved in the story of the Levite whose concubine was assaulted in Gibeah (Judges 19). It was destroyed c 1100 BC perhaps in the revenge taken by the other Israelite tribes against Benjamin (Judges 20). During the 11C a fortress was built on top of the hill probably by the Philistines, or by Saul.

Historically Gibeah was the home of Saul (I Sam. 10:26; 11:4) who was made first king over Israel, and from whence he ruled. The fortress was constructed of

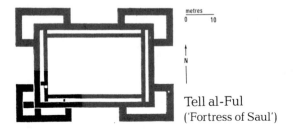

metres
0   10

↑
N
|

Tell al-Ful
('Fortress of Saul')

large roughly dressed and roughly coursed stones. Only one corner was excavated, and reconstructed as part of a rectangular building c 52m × 35m, with casemate walls and corner towers. Later in the same century it was repaired, probably by Saul or David. It was abandoned during the time of Solomon. The site was again fortified in the 8C–5C BC, probably as a frontier-watch tower between Israel and Judah. This small fortress was located on top of the SW corner of the earlier fort. It was probably destroyed by the Assyrians in 701 BC (Isaiah 10:29) and by the Babylonians in 597 or 587 BC. Another fortress, and a small village were located on the E side of the hill in the late 6C. Occupation in the Persian period is indicated by the discovery of some tombs, and of pits in which wine was made and stored in jars. There were few finds of Hellenistic-Maccabean date. A village of the early Roman period was probably destroyed by Titus, for the Roman army is recorded as camping in a valley close to Gabath Saul on the night before reaching Jerusalem in AD 70. (Josephus, War V:51).

Mount Scopus, the N and higher end (903m) of the ridge which includes the Mount of Olives (Rte 12) lies to the NE of the Old City, and is approached by several roads and bus services (9, 28). Mount Scopus has various institutions established in the 20C, including the original section of the Hebrew University and some modern and ancient tombs.

History. A strategic high point from which there is an overview of the city; the name itself means look-out or watch-tower. It is mentioned by Josephus as the place where Cestius pitched camp in AD 66 (War II:528) before setting fire to the suburb of Bezetha and very nearly taking the Temple from the N before making his disastrous retreat. Titus also pitched camp here in AD 70 (War V:67) at the beginning of the siege of Jerusalem. The Crusaders camped here too in 1099; and the British forces after the taking of Jerusalem in 1917. It contained an Israeli enclave around the Hadassah Hospital and the Hebrew University 1948–67.

Visit. Approaching from the S side, the visitor first passes the *Augusta Victoria Hospital* on the right at the lower end of the hill. The tall tower (60m) is a landmark providing good views. Built by Wilhelm II and the Empress Augusta Victoria of Germany in 1898, the hospice and hospital were opened in 1910. At first it was under the protection of the Order of St. John: it is sponsored by the Lutheran World Federation and the United Nations; open 12.00–16.00 daily. Bronze statues of the founders (by A. Wolf) have been set up in the courtyard.

Continue up the hill to the NW to the expanding complex of the **Hebrew University**.

History. Proposals for a Jewish university in Jerusalem were first made in the 19C and plans were formulated in 1902. The house of Sir John Gray Hill with 50 acres of land was purchased in 1913, and foundation stones laid in 1918. The first part of the university was officially opened in 1925, with Institutes of Chemistry, Microbiology and Jewish Studies. It expanded up to 1948, with more land purchase, the opening of faculties of Humanities and Science, a pre-faculty of Medicine, and sections for agriculture, education, Jewish antiquities, a museum of botany, and a printing press (now the Magnes Press). In 1926 the Jewish National and University Library was built (architects Chaikin and Geddes). Cut off from its staff and 1027 students in 1948, the university and hospital were maintained by a caretaker force until 1967. A new campus was set up at Giv'at Ram (Rte 14).

After 1967 the Mount Scopus campus was re-opened, extensively renovated and expanded: the Faculty of Law occupied the building of the former library; the Harry S. Truman Research Institute; dormitory, cultural and cafeteria facilities for 3000 students in residential complexes; School of Education; Institute of Archaeology; Saltiel Center for Pre-Academic Studies; Martin Buber Adult Education Centre; Rothberg School for Overseas Students and the Hillel House. In 1981 a 'Return to Mount Scopus' was celebrated with the relocation of the Faculties of Humanities and Social Sciences etc. The modern Mount Scopus Synagogue (architect Ram Karmi) is a central feature.

Visit. Free tours of the University are available from the *Bronfman Family Reception Centre*, daily at 11.30. Three ancient Jewish tomb complexes are located on the university campus, which formed part of the very crowded necropolis in the 1C AD. At the NE end of the central road, located within the Botanical Garden of the university, is the **Five Tombs** complex discovered in 1972. The tombs were cut as separate entities but so close together that they are interconnected by breached kokhim. With slight variations, each tomb had a small door leading down to a square chamber with pit, and benches with kokhim in the other three walls. One tomb contained one ossuary and another eight ossuaries, some of which were decorated with rosettes and vines. One was incised with a fluted column with Ionic capital, a device not uncommon on ossuaries of the 1C AD. The tomb was looted and many of the ossuaries broken in antiquity.

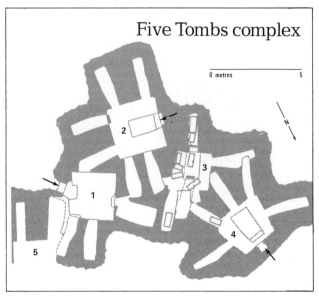

Five Tombs complex

0 metres 5

About 70m SE is the **Tomb of Nicanor**. This is a more monumental tomb, with an intricate catacomb and a façade. It belonged to one of the wealthy and well-known families of Jewish Jerusalem in the 1C BC–AD, being identified by an inscription on one of the ossuaries. The Greek and Hebrew inscription named Nicanor and Alexa, the sons of Nicanor the Alexandrian who is noted in the Talmud (as well as on the ossuary), for giving the bronze gates of Herod's temple. The tomb has a large court, with columns *distyle in antis*, and a corridor with four branches of burial chambers on several levels.

A little to the NW is the **Tomb of a Nazirite**, discovered in 1967, cut in very soft rock and interesting for its internal ashlar walls, round vaulting and façade. The ashlar walls compare with the masonry in the Tomb of Herod's Family (Rte 14). The tomb, with small entrance and four chambers, was looted in antiquity, and contained more than ten ossuaries and two very fine sarcophagi cut with excellent workmanship in hard limestone. The ossuaries are decorated in common style with rosettes. The inscriptions on them named 'Hanania son of Jonathan the Nazirite' and his wife Salome. A Nazirite was one placed under a vow.

Beyond the University, to the NW is the **Hadassah Hospital** on Mount Scopus. The Jewish Rothschild-Hadassah University hospital was opened in 1938 (E. Mendelson, architect: massive blocks with coursed stone and proportioned fenestration were employed), and renovated and expanded after reoccupation in the 1970s (Y. Rechter, architect). (See also Rte 14, Hadassah Hospital). Tours are available Sun–Fri, hourly 9.00–12.00.

On the NE side is the Arab village of Isawiya. On the NW side is the World War I British Military cemetery. Adjacent is a Jewish cemetery.

Decorated Jewish (Jerusalem style) ossuary, 1C BC/AD (courtesy of John Kane).

14 The Western Suburbs

Introduction. The greater part of modern Jerusalem lies W of the Old City and few remains of earlier times can be seen there, apart from some tombs of the Roman and medieval periods and the Monastery of the Holy Cross.

Prior to the 19C the population lived within the walls for safety and the rocky land outside was used for grazing, gardens and burial. By the mid-19C occupation was beginning to extend along the routes to Jaffa, Gaza and Bethlehem. The Greek Orthodox Clerical Seminary was established in the Monastery of the Holy Cross in 1852; various houses were built in 1855 when Montefiore bought land SW of the city, and Consul Finn and Bishop Gobat built summer homes SW and NW of the city; Bishop Gobat's house lay N of the Jaffa road, but conditions were still unsafe and the adjacent house was abandoned in 1860 because of bandits.

Building, particularly for institutional use and with a somewhat defensive architectural style, was much more extensive in the 1860s. The Montefiore houses were put up in 1860, as was the German (or Schneller) Orphanage; the Russian Compound was opened in 1864, the Talitha Kumi Girls' School (German) in 1865; the Lepers' Hospital in 1867; the carriage road to Jaffa was finished in 1868 and the Nahalat Shiva Jewish Quarter established in 1869. The following 20 years saw a torrent of building, and by 1914 much of the area around the Jaffa Road was built up, the more westerly sections occupied predominantly by new Jewish quarters, with a number of Christian and Muslim Arab quarters to the N, E and S. During the Mandate period many more administrative buildings were located in this area, such as the Romema Reservoir and new water pipe lines in 1918, the Electric Power Station in 1926, Government House and the Palestine Post Building in 1931, the Palestine Broadcasting Service in 1936, the Central Post Office in 1938, as well as cinemas and hotels. Considerable thought was given to the planning and development of the entire city, as exemplified in the Zoning Plan of 1922 which incorporated a large area of park land around the Old City itself. The war of 1948 created havoc between the various ethnic quarters, and many Arabs abandoned their homes W of the armistice line. Since 1948 the expansion of building activity has been considerable and since 1948 buildings appropriate to the capital city of Israel, including the Parliament or Knesset, have been located here.

The following tour of the western suburbs is divided into subroutes: **Rte 14A**, the central area; **Rte 14B**, the northern area; **Rte 14C**, the southern area; and **Rte 14D**, the outskirts. Most of the places of interest are located in the central area.

A. The Central Area of the Western Suburbs

(Bounded approximately by the Jaffa Road, the Hebrew University (Giv'at Ram campus) and the Railway Station.)

The heart of the NE area of this section is **Independence Park**, located at the old Mamilla Pool and Muslim Cemetery. Numerous buses pass the park, including 6, 7, 15, 22.

History. The oldest feature is the Mamilla Pool, 88.5m × 58.5m × 5.8m deep. Its original date is uncertain, but it may well have started as a rain-fed pool in a quarry at the head of the Hinnom Valley in the time of Herod the Great, and later been incorporated in the Upper Aqueduct system from Solomon's Pools. It is sometimes identified with the Upper Pool of the Bible. It was certainly incorporated in the Mamluk water system in the 15C and later, when a channel linked it to the Pool of the Patriarch's Bath (Hezekiah's Pool, see Rte 4). Theophanes links it with the site of a massacre of Christian captives by the Jews in 614 (Eutychius says by Jews and Persians). The description of Bernard the Monk c 870 also pursues this theme: 'A mile west of the city of Jerusalem is the Church of St. Mamilla, which contains the bodies of many people whom the Saracens martyred and whom she buried' (Wilkinson). Bernard refers to a 'Saracen' synagogue, and clearly over-estimates the distance. The site of a massacre is also commemorated in the nearby Lion's Cave, though in Jewish tradition it is the location of a massacre of Jews by Greeks. The cemetery was also used by Christians, in particular as the burial place of the Canons of the Church of the Holy Sepulchre (Clermont-Ganneau). A Church of St. Mamilla was located here in the 12C.

In the 13C it became the largest Muslim cemetery in Jerusalem, mentioned by Mujir al-Din in c 1495 and in use up to the 20C. According to Mujir al-Din, it 'contains the graves of men who were illustrious for their learning or their piety, or who fell in battle against the infidels'. Clermont-Ganneau identified the ancient church of Mamilla with the *Zawiyat al-Qalandariyya* which still stood in ruined state in the middle of the cemetery c 1495 when tradition held it had been a Byzantine church. The cemetery has been largely ruined since 1948 and the Independence Park established more recently.

View of the Mamilla Pool and cemetery in the late 19C (C.W. Wilson, Picturesque Palestine, *Vol. I, p. 102: Virtue and Co., London, 1880).*

Description. The *Zawiya Kubakiyya* is an elegant Muslim chapel of c 1289, located in a grove c 100m E of the Mamilla Pool. It is the burial place of the Amir Aidughdi al-Kubaki, who was the Governor of Safed under the Mamluk ruler Baybars, but who was later banished to Jerusalem where he died on 22 September 1289, aged about 60. It is the only Mamluk tomb still standing outside the Old City. The original building may have been the mortuary chapel of the Crusader Canons of the Church of the Holy Sepulchre, as it incorporates a number of typical 12C Crusader features (Clermont-Ganneau), taken over by the Muslims in the 13C.

Essentially a cube supporting a cylindrical drum surmounted by a dome, the entrance on the NW side has a trefoil horseshoe arch, and on either side of the recess, re-used Crusader elbow consoles of different sizes support an arch with voussoirs which are also re-used Crusader work. The dated Mamluk dedicatory inscription is placed above the lintel. The drum also contains a series of brackets supporting a cavetto cornice that are probably of Crusader origin. The interior is lit by windows in three walls. The SE wall contains the mihrab. The transition from square base to circular drum is effected by a series of arches with muqarnas niches and small fluted conches acting as squinches.

In the centre of the mausoleum is a fine Romanesque Crusader sarcophagus with gabled lid and blind arcading on the sides rather than the usual Muslim tomb and headstone. The sarcophagus and the hoodmould of the outer entrance have very similar diaper work, suggesting a common source for both. Another such sarcophagus was noted not far away in the cemetery. Clermont-Ganneau speculated that both sarcophagi once belonged to high dignitaries of the Church of the Holy Sepulchre. Restored in the late 19C, the doorway has been recently blocked.

On the N side of the Mamilla Cemetery and S of Ben Yehuda Road, at 27 REHOV HILLEL, is the **Nahon Museum of Jewish Art from Italy**, also called the Italian Museum or the Italian synagogue. It contains the interior and objects from an Italian synagogue dated 1701. Open Sun 10.00–13.00; Wed 14.00–19.00. Admission charge. Free guided tour sometimes available. Numerous city buses.

Further W is the *Bezalel School of Art and Artist's House* at REHOV SHEMU'EL HANAGID 10–12, just S of Ben Yehuda St. This was founded by Boris Schatz in the early years of the 20C to train Jewish artists; it contains exhibitions and a restaurant. Open Sun–Thu 10.00–13.00; 14.00–17.00; Fri 10.00–13.00; Sat 11.00–14.00. Bus 4, 7, 9, 17, 19.

On the W side of the Mamilla Cemetery, nearing the S end of KING GEORGE ST, is the building of the *Jewish Agency*, head office of the World Zionist Organisation and containing the Zionist archives, the Golden Books recording donations for land purchase, the Jewish National Fund and the United Jewish Agencies. From 1921 the Jewish National Council, and from 1929 the Jewish Agency, were set up to establish a Jewish national home in Palestine. The building, designed by Y. Ratner in 1927, is regarded as one of the earliest in the modern architectural movement in Palestine, and the design reflects the architect's German training. Thirteen Jews were killed in a terrorist attack here on the 11th March, 1948. Further S, near the junction of King George St with Gershon Agron, are located the Chief Rabbinate (H. *Hekhal Shelomo*) at 58 King George St, named for Shelomo Wolfson, father of Sir Isaac Wolfson who donated the building. It has a *museum of Jewish liturgical art and folklore* and a *Torah library*; adjacent is the new **Jerusalem Great Synagogue**, which is used mainly for festivals. Free daily tours are available Sun–Thu 9.00–13.00; Fri 9.00–12.00. Bus 4, 7–10, 14, 16.

To the NW along the S side of the Jaffa Rd and just over 1km W of the Old City is the *Mahané Yehuda (Jewish) quarter*, founded in 1887, which has an oriental style market on the S side of the Jaffa Road, busiest on Wed and Thu. Bus 6–8, 10–12, 18, 20. Less than 1km further W, on the N fringes of the Sacher Park, are the Convention Hall (H. *Binyené HaUmma*) near the Jerusalem Hilton Hotel, and to the SE the Soldiers' House (H. *Yad LaBanim*) and Soldiers' Memorial, both designed by D. Reznik. The latter complex, pyramidal in concept to symbolise the soul rising to heaven, contains a Memorial Hall with basement lecture hall and archives.

At the S end of the Sacher Park the **Israel Parliament** or **Knesset** building is located off REHOV RUPPIN. Bus 9, 24, 28. The visitors' gallery is open to the public when the Knesset is in session, Mon–Tue 16.00–21.00; Wed 11.00–13.00. Tickets can be purchased from the office, free tours of the building in English are available Sun and Thu 8.30–14.30. Passports are required.

Opposite the entrance is a very large *bronze menorah* (seven-branched ritual candlestick) with scenes from Jewish history, presented by the British Government. Inside the building, opened in 1966, are tapestries, wall and floor mosaics all designed by Marc Chagall. Adjacent is the Wohl Rose Park, containing many species of roses.

A little over 0.5km to the W is the Giv'at Ram campus of the **Hebrew University** (for early history, see Mount Scopus, Rte 13).

Following the suspension of activity on the Mount Scopus campus in 1948, the Hebrew University at first rented premises from the Franciscan Monastery of Terra Sancta in Jerusalem. In 1958 a new campus was established at Giv'at Ram with Faculties of Medicine, Dental Medicine, Law and Social Sciences; also a Graduate Library School, School of Pharmacy, and School of Social Work; in 1963 a new medical school was opened at 'Ain Karim (see below, Hadassah Hospital).

After the 1967 war and the renewed access to Mount Scopus, the faculties of the University were re-organised, and an intensive programme of rebuilding, restoration and expansion began. Some faculties moved back to Mount Scopus, and the Giv'at Ram campus now houses the Faculty of Science, the Science Library, the Institute for Advanced Studies, the Institute for Life Sciences, dormitories for 3000 students, and has the central building of the Jewish National and University Library. The library has a collection of Hebrew manuscript codices from the 10C onwards, and also some in Arabic, Samaritan, Syriac, Persian, Armenian and Latin; it also houses about 16,000 rare books. Guided tours are available Sun–Fri 9.00–11.00, starting from the administration building. Bus 9, 24, 28.

As well as the university buildings and synagogue, the campus contains the *Williams Planetarium* and *Wise auditorium*.

Near the University campus a Byzantine basilica church (17.5m × 14m) was excavated in 1949 (Avi-Yonah). On the S side were several rooms, including a chapel with a mosaic dedicated to St. George; on the W side were remains of monastic cells and a burial chamber. It may be identified with the 5C church of St. George in Nikephoria, which had a monastery and hospice for the aged *(gerocomion)* with a chapel, built by the Empress Eudocia and mentioned by John Zosime in the 10C (see also below, St. George's Chapel).

On the same side of REHOV RUPPIN, and S of the Knesset, is the **Israel Museum**. Open Sun, Mon, Wed, Thu 10.00–17.00; Tue, Archaeological Museum 16.00–22.00, Shrine of the Book and Billy Rose Art Garden 10.00–22.00; Fri and Sat 10.00–14.00. *Holiday times vary.* Tickets for Saturday and festivals to be bought in advance from agencies or the museum. Guided general tours of the Museum (in English) are available Sun, Mon, Wed, Thu, Fri at 11.00; also on Sun at 15.00 and Tue at 16.30. Special tours of the archaeological galleries, Mon 15.00; of the Shrine of the Book, Sun 13.30 and Tue 15.00. For other tours, lectures, current exhibitions, concerts and activities, information and monthly programme leaflet ask at the information desk. Admission charge. Bus 9, 24.

Planned to house the growing national art and antiquities collections in an expandable complex of low, interconnected buildings and pavilions in a pleasant and relatively informal setting, the large area of hillside contains a number of separately housed collections, and sculpture in a garden setting. It contains the Israel Department of Antiquities and Museums and the national archaeological collection since 1948. The displays also utilise some items from the collections of the Palestine Archaeological (Rockefeller) Museum (Rte 13) from excavations up to 1967. As well as the antiquities of Israel and neighbouring cultures, the museum contains ethnography and Judaica, period rooms, contemporary art and design, sections on distant cultures and a youth wing. It was opened on 11 May 1965; the Youth Wing was completed in 1979, the Impressionist and Pre-Columbian wings in 1980. The main museum complex was designed by Mansfeld and Gad.

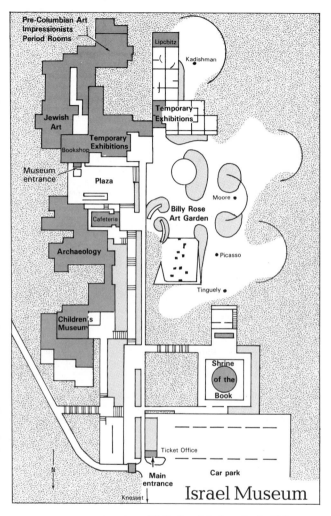

Visit. * The Samuel Bronfman Biblical and Archaeological Museum.
At the top of the main approach, cross the plaza to the left past the
cafeteria; in front of the entrance there is a fine view of the
Monastery of the Holy Cross in the valley to the E (see below). The
entrance foyer contains an excellent bookshop as well as cloakroom
and information desk. The central stair descends to the exhibition
halls.

The *first hall* contains temporary archaeological exhibitions, some
relate to current excavations; the collections of the Bezalel Art
Museum lie ahead and to the right (see below).

On the left the permanent archaeological exhibition begins with an
excellent and recently re-displayed guide to the earliest traces of

man in Israel and abroad, with displays relating to environment and chronology. Illustrations of the sites, flint tools, flora and fauna, many of the latter exhibiting species long extinct in Israel, and ancient climatic conditions are shown. Finds from 'Ubaidiya in the upper Jordan Valley, around one million years old, as well as from Middle and Upper Palaeolithic sites can be seen. This hall also contains Mesolithic material of the Natufian culture (c 15.000–9000 BC), from sites such as **Eynan**, the Hayonim Cave in W Galilee, and the **Mount Carmel** caves, with evidence for the earliest beginnings of agriculture and more complex food-processing. The bone and shell beads and pendants are beautifully polished.

Of the *Neolithic material* (8th–6th millennia BC) the plastered skull from Beisamun is of interest, and compares with those found at Jericho. The increasing social complexity attested is matched by the progress in agriculture, at a time when various cereals and food animals were domesticated. A model of early Neolithic stone hut-circles at **Nahal Oren** illustrates a small village of the period.

At the lower end of the gallery are notable finds of the *Chalcolithic period*, late 5th–4th millennia BC. These include stone and pottery ossuaries from **Azor, Ben Shemen** and **Givatayim**. Many of the pottery ossuaries seem to be models of the houses of the living and have interesting details in the doors and gable ends. An enormous storage jar of this period, of unique size c 1.60m high, testifies to the need to produce and the capability to store food in optimum conditions. Finely worked basalt, flint, ivory and haematite objects prepare one for the magnificent *copper treasure from Nahal Mishmar*, found in a cave W of the Dead Sea.

Most of the 429 objects discovered are on display; they include copper maceheads, sceptres, 'crowns', axes and adzes, many cast by a sophisticated lost wax process using copper alloys, indicating high techological achievement as well as fine craftsmanship. Abandoned in a cave, the hoard with its enormous weight of copper and fine ivory may represent the treasure and offerings associated with a contemporary temple.

The successive rooms are arranged in chronological sequence through the Bronze and Iron Ages. The *Early Bronze Age* (3rd millennium BC) is represented by finds from **Khirbat Karak, Kfar Monash, Arad, Gath (Tell Shaikh Ahmad al-'Uraini)** and other sites, when sizeable towns were normally defended by stone or mud-brick walls. A rather dark mezzanine gallery exhibits pottery from the succeeding non-urban interlude (c 2350–1900 BC), the most interesting object being a *silver cup* from a tomb at 'Ain Samiya (in the hill country N of Jerusalem) with crude relief and incised scenes, the iconography of which derives somewhat remotely from Mesopotamian mythology. Some bone beads from **Beth Shan**, and a range of copper (occasionally bronze) weapons often deposited in the tombs of this period are exhibited from various sites.

A range of pottery and other artefacts from the *Middle and Late Bronze Ages* (2nd millennium BC), the period of the **Canaanites**, include votive offerings from a seaside temple at **Nahariyya** on the extreme N coast. Some of the finer pottery of this period is imported from Cyprus, and notable finds from **Tell Nagila** include a Black-on-Red Ware *Cypriot jug* probably imported during the 17C–16C BC; of slightly later date, is a fine Cypriote Base Ring Ware pottery *model of a bull*. Both indicate an increase in mercantile contacts between Canaan and the adjoining countries.

A small mezzanine gallery has an exhibition of artefacts from

Hazor, Megiddo, Beth Shan, Lachish and **Tel Mevorakh** illustrating Canaanite cult and religion. Evidence of Egyptian influence is strong.

At the N end of the galleries, a more monumental display of *Iron Age architecture* supplements the exhibits; these include the restored 9C–6C window balustrade from **Ramat Rahel**, sculpture from the gates at **Hazor**, and a proto-Aeolic capital from **Jerusalem**.

The next gallery contains a display of objects from later periods, in particular an exhibition of *alphabets and inscriptions*, and *sculpture of various periods*. Noteworthy is a *bronze head of Hadrian*, part of a life-size statue found at **Tel Shalem** near Beth Shan. From this gallery the visitor may either return to the entrance through a gallery with a fine exhibition of glass, or may continue on to the Childrens' Museum.

The **Children's Museum** in the Youth Wing has lively and much-used displays relating to the past, using a variety of subjects and means to convey ideas. There are also workrooms and a playground. The visitor may leave at a point midway down the main central path, and either return up the hill towards the Bezalel Art Museum and the Billy Rose Art Garden, or continue down towards the entrance and turn left for the Shrine of the Book.

The **Bezalel National Art Museum** has a collection of Jewish liturgical objects mainly from countries outside Israel, including the *ark of the synagogue* of Old Cairo. As well as a permanent exhibition of works by Israeli artists there are works by Cezanne, Chagall, Gauguin, Picasso and van Gogh; also period rooms of Old Masters from France, Italy and Britain; and temporary exhibitions.

The **Billy Rose Art Garden.** Sculptures donated by Billy Rose are displayed in a terraced garden exhibition designed by Isamu Noguchi. Included are works by Lipschitz, Maillol, Henry Moore, Picasso, Rodin, David Smith, Tinguely and others.

The **Library**, donated by A. Springer and opened in 1968, contains c 50,000 books. Open Sun, Mon, Wed, Thu 10.00–17.00; Tue 16.00–20.00. The hall, with seating for 400, is used for concerts and films.

The Shrine of the Book is located in the lower N part of the complex, to the right of the entrance, and is easily recognised by the gleaming white tiled roof designed to resemble the lid of a jar of the type associated with the storage of the manuscripts called 'The Dead Sea Scrolls**'. The building was designed by F. Kiesler and A. Bartos.

History. The scrolls were discovered between 1947 and 1956 in caves near the shore of the Dead Sea, preserved by the extremely dry conditions. They were owned by a community of Essenes, a Jewish sect, living at and around the site of Qumran, which was destroyed c AD 69 in the Roman suppression of the First Jewish Revolt. The manuscripts include complete (Isaiah) or very fragmentary pieces of all the books of the Old Testament on prepared skins, written mainly in Hebrew and Aramaic between c 225 BC and c AD 69, and are important for comparison with the books of the Old Testament in their present form, being copied at the time when the Old Testament was receiving its final written form. Altogether fragments of nearly 500 manuscripts were discovered, and in addition to the books of the Old Testament, the finds included commentaries, apocryphal and sectarian works, among which is an order of battle for an apocalyptic war between the Children of Light and the Children of Darkness. They are important for the light they shed on sectarian Jewish beliefs in the time of Christ.

Various controversies arose over this aspect of the documents during the years following their discovery. A number of the manuscripts are preserved in this museum. The *Copper Scrolls* (in the Museum in Amman, Jordan) were found in a separate cave and probably date to the period between the two Jewish Revolts. The period of the Second Jewish Revolt (AD 132– 135) is also well represented in the Shrine of the Book. Led by Bar Kosiba or Bar Kochba, a second attempt at Jewish revival and independence from Rome was suppressed by 135. A group of refugees hid in a cave in the Nahal Hever above the W shores of the Dead Sea, taking their most important possessions and documents with them, including deeds of ownership and marriage contracts, but their place of refuge became their tomb. The state of preservation of the organic remains, including textiles, makes a poignant and superb display of contemporary life.

Visit. Descending through the forecourt, the entrance to the Shrine of the Book leads to a corridor in which the display cases contain documents, and fragments of manuscripts from the *Psalms*, the *Temple Scroll* and *apocalytic works*, as well as *scroll jars*. The principal display area, in a circular gallery under the 'jar lid' is on two levels. On the upper level, in the round central case, is a copy of the great **Isaiah scroll**. The wall cases, from the left of the entrance, contain parts of the Habbakuk Commentary, apocryphal works and psalms, letters of the time of Bar Kochba, the Habbakuk Commentary, tefillin (phylacteries containing set texts from Scripture) from Qumran, parts of the manuscripts of the War of the Sons of Light against the Sons of Darkness, and the Qumran Manual of Discipline (some manuscripts are copies of the originals). Stairs descend to a lower level, where objects from the cave in the Nahal Hever (Wadi Murabba´at) of the time of Bar Kochba are displayed. Notable for their fine state of preservation, baskets, metalwork, tools with wooden handles, cosmetics, textiles, door keys, jugs and a magnificent glass dish are on display, all deposited in the cave c 135.

The Monastery of the Holy Cross. Located approximately 400m E of the Israel Museum, on the W side of SEDEROT HAYYIM HAZAZ, is the picturesque and strongly built monastery on the site in the Valley of Rehavia where tradition holds that the tree grew from which was made the cross of the Crucifixion. Still with sufficient undeveloped land around it to permit the illusion of a rural landscape just under 2km from the City Walls, and to retain the perspective of a medieval building strong enough to protect the monks from brigandage, one of the best views of the Monastery is from the Israel Museum terrace.

History. Built by the Lazes, a kindred people of the Georgians (in modern S Russia) under the encouragement of Peter the Iberian (Georgian, not Spanish) in the mid-5C, the present building was constructed on the site in the 11C by the Georgians under King Bagrat. As the Georgian fortunes declined in the 16C under the Ottomans (when they no longer occupied the favourable position enjoyed under the Mamluks), the monastery was sold to the Greeks and repaired in 1644. From 1852 it was used as a clerical seminary.

Visit. Open Mon–Fri 8.00–12.00. High stone walls, strong buttresses and windows well above ground level remind one that the monastery lay outside the city walls and suffered from the attacks of brigands on various occasions. Forming an irregular rectangle it contains several courtyards, with monastery, library and church. The church dates mainly from the 11C and has nave and side aisles with pointed vaulting, and a dome supported by four pillars. A section of the floor with mosaics dates to the original 5C church. The much-repainted late medieval frescoes on the walls tell the story of the Tree used for the Crucifixion. Behind the high altar is a round opening which marks the site where the tree grew. The library of the seminary is incorporated with that of the library of the Greek Orthodox Patriarchate in the Old City.

Approximately 0.5km ENE of the Monastery of the Cross is the ***Tomb of Jason** located in a small park on the N side of ALFASI ST in the Rehavia suburb.

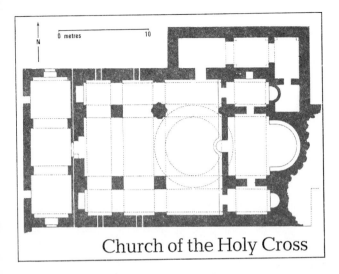

Church of the Holy Cross

History. Excavations (Rahmani 1956) indicate that this Hasmonean tomb was cut c 100 BC about the time of Alexander Janneus for Jason who may have been involved in the Jewish naval exploits recorded by Strabo. The pottery found in the tomb implies that it was in use for two or three generations, with c 25 burials of persons aged between 3–50. It was robbed, perhaps at the time the Hasmonean dynasty was ousted by Herod the Great in 37 BC. It was damaged in an earthquake, probably that of 31 BC, and used for a final burial c AD 30.

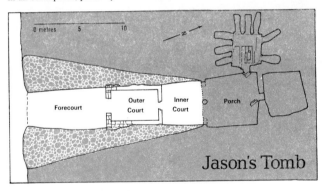

Jason's Tomb

Visit. Open Mon, Thu 10.00–13.00. Bus 9, 17, 22.

The tomb has a rock-cut forecourt divided into three, the inner section being entered through a built round-arched portal, with a vestibule on the N side. The tomb itself is restored with a single column *in antis* (which is unique in Jerusalem at this period). The Doric capital has a straight profile, an early feature paralleled on the Tomb of the Bene Hezir (Rte 11). The tomb is topped by a pyramid (restored on the evidence of a few fragments found in the excavations). The plastered walls of the vestibule are decorated with drawings, graffiti and inscriptions. The drawings, in charcoal, show

three ships: on the right is a swift warship with ram, 14/15 oars and a
rudder, pursuing a fishing vessel, and on the left is a smaller warship.
On the N wall is a stag, on the W wall a palm branch; and scratched
on the E wall are a chalice and a seven-branched menorah, which
are probably later than the charcoal drawings. Aramaic and Greek
inscriptions are placed near the ships, of which the principal is a
funeral lament in Aramaic 'A powerful lament make for Jason, son of
P.... Peace. Who hast built thyself a tomb...'.

The burial chamber to the left has eight rather irregular kokhim in
the walls with stones to close them, and two others partly cut and
partly built in the floor; opposite is a roughly and irregularly cut
ossuary chamber, also with ship drawings in charcoal. I Macc. 13:29
refers to another Hasmonean tomb at Modin which was also decorated with pyramids and ships. Another ship drawing was discovered
in the Church of the Holy Sepulchre (Rte 4).

Approximately 0.4km to the S, at 2 HAPALMAH and the corner of

Tomb of Jason, from the south (courtesy of John Kane).

HANASI ST is the *Mayer Institute for Islamic Art. Named after Professor L.A. Mayer, the noted orientalist and archaeologist, it has a fine and varied collection of Islamic art. Open Sun–Thu 10.00–13.00, 15.30– 18.00; Sat and eves of holidays 10.30–13.00; closed Fri and holidays. Admission charge. Tickets for Saturdays to be bought in advance from the Museum, or from the King David, the Moriah or the Plaza Hotels. Bus 15.

The terrace has a 13C basalt lintel from the diwan in the City Wall of Tiberias, carved in relief with two confronted animals of uncertain species attacked by lions. Inside there are displays on three floors, with a library and archive on the top floor.

The basement contains a lecture hall and displays of books, paintings, tiles, printing, clocks, puppets and the *Salomon Collection of Turkish shadow figures.*

The main ground floor: *Room 1* (left) contains Sassanian and Early Islamic Art, including some beautiful pottery and metalwork; chessmen and ivories; textiles from 7C–10C Egypt and from 10C Yemen; and Kufic inscriptions from 11C Iran. Also displayed are three sculptures from Khirbat al-Mafjar, the 8C Umayyad palace at Jericho (cf. Rte 13, Rockefeller Museum). *Room 2* contains exhibits of the high period of Islamic art. To the right is the *Treasury Room 3* which contains glass vessels from the 7C onwards, some goldwork and textiles, including objects from Iran and India dating to the 19C and earlier.

First floor: *Room 1* (left) contains Late Iranian art, including calligraphy, textiles, tiles, metal, leatherwork, some very fine illuminated manuscripts; textiles decorated with wax colours; armour; and blue-and-white lustreware. In the centre, *Room 2* contains Ottoman Art with coins, illuminated manuscripts, textiles, leather, mostly of the 18C–19C; some fine tiles and bowls, guns, armour, astronomical survey instruments. *Room 3* (right) has Moghul art: fine Moghul jade inlaid with gold and rubies used for dagger handles, cups and other objects. The exhibition also includes silk and textiles from 17C Turkey; inlaid jewelled and enamelled work; laquer-decorated papier maché work; a large brass astrolabe; horse harness, elaborately inlaid with turquoise and coral; fine armour; inlaid wood; a fine teak window from India; a shawl from Kashmir; brasswork; 17C–19C Indian minatures; and 19C embroidered cloth from India.

Approximately 250m to the E along CHOPIN ST is the *Jerusalem Theatre.* On REHOV MOHILEVER, c 600 to the ESE, is the **Museum of Natural History**. The exhibition is devoted to local wildlife, with models. Open Sun–Fri 10.00– 13.00; Mon and Wed 16.00–18.00; Sat 10.30–13.00. Closed during August. Admission charged, except on Sat. Bus 4, 18.

Leaving the museum and park on the S side on to HaMaggid St, and continuing E to ʿEmeq Refaʿim, one enters the quarter established as the German or 'Templers' colony in the Valley of Refaim, founded by south German Protestant Christians from Würtemberg in 1871. A religious community of 'the Temple' or 'Friends of Jerusalem', founded in 1860 to found the ideal Christian community in the Holy Land, their first colony was established at Haifa in 1868, and the second shortly after in Jaffa. The community was evacuated in World War II.

S of the junction of the ʿEMEQ REFAʿIM and the BETHLEHEM ROAD, is the **Jerusalem Railway Station**. The line to Jaffa (Tel Aviv) was opened in 1892.

N of the station is the *Khan Theatre*, formerly an Ottoman khan or inn for travellers staying outside the town, or arriving after the city gates were locked for the night. Now used as an entertainment centre. Bus 4–8, 10, 18, 21. Nearly 300m E of the station is the **Abu Tor Observation Point**, from which there is a fine view over the Hinnom Valley and the Old City. At Dair Abu Tor is located the site of a 12C Church of St. Procopius (see p.304).

N of the Khan Theatre at the main intersection of roads to N, E and S and on the crest of the watershed, is *St. Andrew's Church of Scotland* and Scottish Hospice, built in 1927 to the design of Clifford Holliday. It reflects his interest in Armenian monastic architecture.

Below the church on the E side, is the old road to Hebron and Bethlehem, still in use in Mandate times, and between it and the church in the rock scarp are some **Iron Age rock-cut tombs**. Dating to the 8C–6C BC, the entry gives onto a chamber with rock-cut benches on two or three sides at waist height or higher. The benches are flat, well-dressed and have carved head-rests showing the position in which the bodies were laid, some singly, others up to four in a row, and sometimes alternately head to foot. Below the benches deep caves were cut for use as ossuaries or favissae. The tombs were robbed anciently, but parallels from Lachish, Silwan (Rte 11), the Convent of St. Stephen (Rte 13) and other sites in Judah suggest the date (1978–79, Barkai).

On the N side of the Scottish church, walls of uncertain function but Byzantine date were excavated at the same time as the tombs. Continuing to the NW to King David St, the *Liberty Bell Park* is on the left. This garden, funded by the USA and Israel to mark the bicentennial of the USA, contains a replica of the Liberty Bell in Philadelphia, as well as a small amphitheatre and a sports ground. On the right is the *Bloomfield Park* established with funds from Canada.

On the E side of the park, facing Mount Zion and the walls of the Old City, are the **Montefiore Windmill and Houses**. Bus 4, 6, 7, 8, 10, 15.

History. Among the earliest structures to be built outside the city, they were founded by Sir Moses Montefiore, an Anglo-Jewish philanthropist who attempted to relieve the poverty of poor immigrant Jews in the 19C. The land was purchased in 1855; the houses, called Mishkenot Sha'ananim, were built in 1860, designed by the British architect William Edmund Smith as two long rows of attached housing with entrance porches. The houses were damaged in the war of 1948, and remained in the front line until 1967 after which they were reconstructed (1973) by the Jerusalem Foundation as a music centre and guest house, with ten self-contained apartments in the long building for the use of visiting artists, musicians and scholars. The music centre, with recording studio, is located under the windmill square (1975). The windmill itself is now a museum and memorial to Sir Moses Montefiore. To the N of the windmill is the Yemin Moshe Quarter, established in 1891 with 130 houses which were rehabilitated in 1969.

Just N of the Montefiore houses is the site of *St. George's Chapel*, also identified with the Byzantine and Crusader Church of St. George in Nikephoria.

In the N end of the Bloomfield Park, E of the King David Hotel, is the **Tomb of Herod's Family**. From the outside this is a much-destroyed and rather insignificant-looking monument, though the interior is worth a visit and the site is interesting for its associations. Herod the Great was buried at his fortress at Herodium to the S of Jerusalem, but members of his family may have been buried here. The attribution is circumstantial, depending partly on references in Josephus to the location of Herod's Monuments and Herod's Tomb in this area (War V:108—Titus in AD 70 flattened the land from Mount Scopus to Herod's Monuments. V:507—Herod's Tomb lay on the line of Titus' siege wall in AD 70); partly to the traces of its former grandeur; and partly to its position on the E side of the Hinnom Valley directly opposite to and visible from the palace built by Herod the Great, 400m to the E.

History. Josephus records the deaths of many members of Herod's family (War I:228 when Antipater was poisoned by Malichus, Herod 'performed the funeral rites for his father with magnificent ceremonial'. War I:581 on Herod's brother Pheroras 'Herod had loved him till his dying day, but for all that it was rumoured that he had poisoned him'...'and honoured him with a most magnificent funeral' in Jerusalem. Other possibilities include Herod's wife Mariamne I whom he executed; and his brother Phasael who died at the hands of Antigonus in Jerusalem during Herod's flight. But the date of the tomb is uncertain: it could be of the second half of the 1C BC (Antipater died c 43 BC) but some features seem later and it might have been intended for the later Herods. It was robbed in antiquity, and entered again by a breach in the S entrance in 1891.

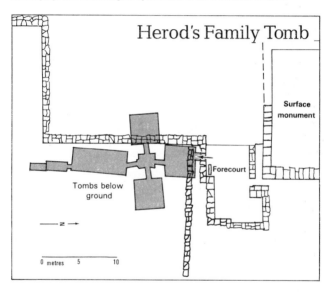

Visit. The rock cut forecourt measures 10m × 6.50m. On the NW side are traces of a massive podium 18m × 20+m constructed of high quality masonry set 2m deep into the rock, which may be the base of a nefesh (memorial monument), perhaps with a pyramid similar to that of the Tomb of Absalom (Rte 11). The fragments of masonry excavated included bits of cornices and capitals, all of the Corinthian and Roman order and apparently of later date than the architecture of the Tombs of Absalom (2nd half of 1C BC) and the Bene Hezir (late 2C or early 1C BC) (Rte 11). They compare with the Corinthian capitals found at the Tombs of the Kings (mid-1C AD) (Rte 13).

The entrance corridor to the tomb leads down fairly steeply from the SW corner of the forecourt and was blocked by an enormous round blocking stone (also cf. the Tombs of the Kings, Rte 13). This gives access to an antechamber, and on the S side to another corridor with blocking slabs which leads to a small rectangular chamber with asymmetrically placed doors in each wall. This chamber is built with four massive masonry piers, and vaulted. An unusual feature in the construction of the tomb is its excavation in the *malaki* beneath a harder band of *mizzi* limestone which has been left rough as the ceiling. The internal walls of the tomb chambers were then constructed of finely cut, flat-dressed and polished white masonry (cf. the Tomb of a Nazirite, Rte 13). The rock floor was levelled.

The complex consists of four main chambers. Another long chamber to the S gives access to a thin chamber with another entrance to the S. The N entrance was for mourners, that on the S for the sarcophagi and the dead. The tomb contained no benches, kokhim or arcosolia. The dead were placed in sarcophagi and ossuaries. When entered in 1891 the tomb contained only two sarcophagi and some ossuaries, the former in the long S chamber. They are well-carved in fine stone, one with a modest moulded panel, the other with an acanthus vase, vine scroll and rosettes. These are in the Museum of the Greek Orthodox Patriarchate (Rte 4), and the site itself is owned by the Greek Orthodox church.

Returning to King David St, and continuing N, on the left at a short distance is the **YMCA**. Built in 1933, the tall tower with cupola is one of the Jerusalem landmarks. The tower is open Mon–Fri 9.00–15.00, Sat 9.00–13.00, closed Sun. Admission charge. Bus 6, 15, 18.

The YMCA has tennis courts and other sporting facilities, and is a hotel. It also contains the Herbert Clark Collection of Antiquities. In 1932 a cemetery of the 5C–7C was discovered 100m W of the building. It contained simple rock-cut tombs covered with stone slabs, all oriented E–W. Walls nearby were perhaps those of a monastery. An incription in one of the buildings states that it was the tomb of S(amuel) bishop of the Georgians, and the complex may therefore have been a Georgian monastery. Opposite, the *King David Hotel* was built in 1930. It was damaged and 90 people killed in a Jewish terrorist attack on 22 July 1946.

A short distance to the N, on the right is the *Hebrew Union College* with the Nelson Glueck School of Biblical Archaeology. At the top of King David St, on the left at 32 AGRON ST, is the **Taxation Museum**, which illustrates the history of the taxation of the Jews in Palestine and in the Diaspora. Open Sun, Tue, Thu 13.00–16.00, Mon, Wed, Fri 10.00– 14.00. Free. Bus 6, 15, 18, 20, 22, 30.

Back at the starting point of the tour of the central section of the new city, the determined sightseer can still continue W down Gershon Agron St, with the Mamilla Cemetery to the right, passing the large hospice of the Sisters of the Rosary on the left to the crossroads at Kikkar Zarefat. Between Ha Yessod and the Gaza Rd, leading SE and SW respectively, is the Franciscan Terra Sancta College. South of it, on Smolenskin St, is the **Musical Instruments Museum** (the Rubin Academy of Music). It contains an exhibition of ancient and modern musical instruments. Open Sun–Fri 9.00–13.00. Admission charge. Bus 4, 7, 9, 14, 22.

B.   The Area North of the Jaffa Road

The N section of the new city, N of the Jaffa Road, contains some places of interest for the history of Jerusalem in the late 19C and early 20C. At the E end of the Jaffa Road, on the N side, is the *Town Hall*. At 250m on the left is the *Central Post Office* (architect, A. Harrison, 1938). The area opposite is part of the old **Russian Compound**, which was established in the 19C for the care of the pilgrims from Christian Imperial Russia, and today contains the Russian Cathedral, the Municipality Information Office, the Police District Headquarters, and the Law Courts. An ancient, probably Herodian, column lies in a quarry in the grounds.

History. In the early 19C when the numbers of Russian pilgrims coming to Jerusalem each Easter were relatively small, they were accommodated in the Greek Orthodox hospices and monasteries of the Old City. By the mid-19C the numbers were increasing, and the Grand Duke Constantine Nicholaevitch visited Jerusalem in 1859 to assess the situation. With a grant from the Imperial Treasury, and private donations, ten acres of land were bought on the N side of the Jaffa Road, just outside the city walls, and building commenced. In 1864 Trinity Cathedral was consecrated, and hostels for monks, priests and 800 lay pilgrims, men and women, were provided. A hospital and consulate were also located inside the walled compound. Within 20 years 2000 pilgrims were coming annually to visit the holy places, mostly poor peasants travelling by ship from the Black Sea to Jaffa. In 1881 further action was taken by the Imperial family, and Grand Duke Sergei Alexandrovitch founded the Imperial Orthodox Palestine Society which built the great Sergievsky hostel in 1889. This contained a refectory and bath house, with drainage, cisterns, ventilation, stoves, and heating, and at the same time some much-needed repairs were carried out. By the early 20C up to 9000 pilgrims were coming every Easter (see also Rte 4, the Russiam Mission in Exile). The mass pilgrimages and the need for the hostel ceased at the time of the Russian Revolution. The compound was used as police headquarters and prison during the Mandate, was purchased by the Israeli government in 1955 and continues in use as a police headquarters and Law Courts.

Visit. The **Cathedral of the Holy Trinity** lies at the centre of the compound. Its cluster of domes evokes the Russian church at Gethsemane, but they lack the charm and elegance of the latter. Near the back of the church, and lying nearly parallel to it, is a great *monolithic column* which was found during building work in 1871. It still lies in the quarry bed; length 12.15m, mean diameter c 1.75m, but greater at base than head; it was abandoned because it split near one end. Clermont-Ganneau suggested that the size agreed with that of the columns of the Royal Portico of the temple of Herod the Great (1C BC), and may have been intended as one of the engaged columns placed adjacent to the wall. As so many of the large tombs in the area N of the city seem to have started life as quarries (Rte 13), and as Solomon's Quarries may have been in use in Herodian times (Rte 1), it seems likely that much of the *malaki* stone used by Herod may have come from the N side of the city. The compound today houses the Police District Headquarters and the Law Courts in the former men's hospices NW and SW of the cathedral, and a *museum* to the E commemorating Jewish terrorists is in the building which was in Mandate times used as the central prison and was the Women's Hospice in the 19C.

  N of the Police Headquarters, on the opposite side of the road at 13 QUEEN HELENA ST is the **Agricultural Museum**, on the site of the Russian Palestine Society Hospice which lay opposite the N entrance of the Russian Compound. There is an open-air display of ancient farm tools. Open summer Sun–Fri 8.00–13.00; winter Sun–Thu 8.00–14.00, Fri 8.00–13.00. Bus 6, 8.

Turning left up Monbaz St, left into Prophet St, and right into Ethiopian St, brings one to the domed Ethiopian Church and monastery built 1896–1904. This is located at the S edge of the **Me'a She'arim Quarter**, a quarter for strictly Orthodox Jews, built in 1874 and of local architectural interest. The name means '100 gates' and is also a play on the words of Gen. 26:12 'Isaac sowed seed in that land, and that year he reaped a hundredfold...'. Like the Montefiore houses (see above) the Me'a She'arim houses were constructed as row houses, but enclosing common courts, with the outer walls forming a continuous protective façade. The main court leads to semi-private courts which in turn lead to the houses. The courts contained communal kitchen and toilet facilities. The thick masonry, with decorative features, especially to the doorways, the outside stairs, and the European red tile roofs bear some resemblance to the ghettoes of Europe.

At the time this formed the largest private building project in Jerusalem. It is now a centre for religious items, books, and scribal work, with many synagogues and Torah schools. The costume of the medieval ghettoes of Europe is retained, with black garments and round fur-bordered hats.

To the N is the *Bokharan Quarter*, established in 1892 by Jews from central Asia. To the W in the *Zikhron Moshe Quarter* (established 1906, named for Sir Moses Montefiore) is Strauss St where the Strauss Health Centre (both named for an American-Jewish benefactor, Nathan Strauss) is located on the E side, and the Bet HaHistadrut (headquarters of the Labour Union with sport, recreation, theatre and concert facilities), the Medical Academy and the Biqqur Holim Hospital (neo-classical style, 1907) on the W.

A Muslim shrine of Ayyubid origins is located in Strauss St, 50m SW of the Mitchell Cinema. This is the *Qubba Qaymariyya*, a walled sanctuary or shrine with a dome, built in rather sober style but with good proportions, before 1251.

History. This Muslim burial chamber was built to house the tombs of five princes of the al-Qaymari family of Damascus, who were martyred between 1250 and 1267, according to Mujir al-Din. Later tombs were added to the shrine, as were the dwelling house and tomb of Shaikh 'Ukasha, and a minaret. Other rooms were added perhaps to shelter pious visitors, and the enclosure wall was fitted with tethering holes for horses. The tomb was still maintained in the first quarter of the 20C, with the five tombs parallel to each other, each with a headstone and green coverings.

Visit. The tomb is a cube with dome, with a projection in the centre of each wall containing a narrow window. The drum also has four windows, with concave moulding at the base of a rather flat dome. The entrance is on the N side. *Interior:* a wide, slightly pointed arch in each wall has a well-defined moulding and window beneath each apex. The arches rise from groups of engaged columns, with treble rebates to the squinches with fluted conches in the corners. There is a smaller arch to the mihrab in the S wall. Fragments of re-used Crusader decorative masonry are placed between the tops of the columns, and include a frieze of variegated leaf or flower patterns. The architecture has parallels in Damascus in the Ayyubid period. Now badly damaged, but the bases of the five tombs remain.

Just over 1km to the NW is the *Biblical Zoo*, located off YIRMEYAHU ST, in Shikkun Habad. Open daily 8.00–sunset, except Sat 8.00–16.00, closed Sun. Tickets for Saturday to be bought in advance from the Cahana Ticket Agency, 1 Dorot Rishonim St, Bus 15. The zoo has a collection of birds, animals and reptiles mentioned in the Bible.

Approximately 250m to the NW is the *Museum of Jewish Art* off SOROTZKIN ST, on the campus of Girls' Town. Open Sun–Thu 13.00–17.00. Bus 3, 7.

To the S is the suburb of Romema, established in 1921. On the N side of the Jaffa Rd, a little before the junction with Sederot Herzl, the Romema (meaning 'elevation') Reservoir was installed on high ground in 1918 as part of the new Mandate system to provide Jerusalem with a good water supply. 280,000 gallons of water per day were piped from Solomon's Pools S of Bethlehem to the Romema Reservoir, and then distributed by pipe to the Old and New City, and as far as Mount Scopus and Bethany. From 1934 the water was pumped from Ras al-'Ain down on the edge of the coastal plain to the Romema Reservoir. The **Central Bus Station** is located on the N side of the Jaffa Rd, and just to the NE at Kikkar Allenby at the end of Romema Road, is the *Allenby Memorial* commemorating the entry of Allenby into Jerusalem in 1917. Bus 6, 12, 18, 20.

C.   The Southern Section of the New City

The southern section of the New City contains relatively few places of interest. The first suburbs were established here in the later part of the 19C, including the Arab quarters of Katamon, established 1875, and Abu Tor also founded in the 1870s. The Beit Josef Jewish suburb was established in 1888, and other Jewish suburbs such as Talpiot from 1922 onwards. Some of these were attacked during the height of Muslim-Jewish tension in 1929. Government House was built to the SE in 1931. The buildings in the E part of this area were much damaged in the fighting in 1948, when the Arab occupants fled eastwards. From 1949– 67 the border between Jordan and Israel ran through the E part, with the old Government House in a demilitarised zone used as the UN Headquarters. There has been much development of new Jewish suburbs in recent years.

2km S of the Old City, the British Mandate *Government House* was built in 1931, as the High Commissioner's Residence; architect A. Harrison, whose design, employing concepts drawn from local styles of architecture, is recognisably from the same hand as the Rockefeller Museum (Rte 13). It was taken over in 1949 by the United Nations Truce Supervision Organisation, and is now UN headquarters. 1.3km to the SW in the suburb of Talpiot is the *Bet Agnon*, at 16 KLAUSNER ST off the Betar Road. This is the house of S.Y. Agnon, a winner of the Nobel Prize for Literature, in which his study, books and pictures are preserved. Open Sun–Thu 9.00–12.00. Bus 7. To the E is the new suburb of East Talpiot, established in 1976, with more urban development in hillside apartment blocks.

The Betar Rd continues S to *Ramat Rahel*, the Hill of Rachel (0.9km). Bus 7. The site of a modern kibbutz (collective settlement), occupying a high and strategic position (818m above sea level), it has a view of Jerusalem and Bethlehem. It contains a recreation centre and swimming pool, and is the site of an ancient Judean palace.

History. Excavations (Aharoni, 1954–62, with the University of Rome for the final three seasons) showed that the site was first settled in the 9C–8C BC when a royal citadel within a casemate wall was built and surrounded by gardens and farmhouses. It has been identified with the biblical Beth-hakkerem. This first settlement was followed by a larger one, with a massive enclosure c 186m × 165m containing a palace c 75m × 50m. Fragments of at least six Proto-Aeolic capitals were found on the site, and a stone window balustrade (now in the Israel Museum). The palace may have been built for King Jehoiakim at the end of the 7C BC, and destroyed not long after in the Babylonian destruction of 586 BC. Another citadel on the site existed in the 4C BC and a poorer domestic settlement in Herodian times. Burial caves of the 1C and 3C AD were found in the vicinity. A villa and a bath house built by the Tenth Roman Legion c 250 were also found on the NW and central parts of the site, which were re-used in the Byzantine period. Also of the Byzantine period, built c 450, were the Church of Kathisma and monastery. The basilica church with patterned mosaic floor lies at the NE of the site. The name of the church is preserved in the name of the well of Bir Qadismu, c 400m to the W. According to a Christian tradition, Mary rested here on her way to Bethlehem (Rte 17). There was a poorer settlement in the early Arab period (7C–8C), after which the site was abandoned.

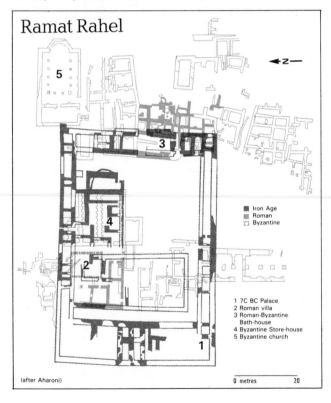

Ramat Rahel

1 7C BC Palace
2 Roman villa
3 Roman-Byzantine Bath-house
4 Byzantine Store-house
5 Byzantine church

Iron Age
Roman
Byzantine

(after Aharoni)   0 metres   20

The kibbutz at Ramat Rahel was founded by the Jewish 'Labour Legion' in 1926. It was attacked in 1929 and largely destroyed. Rebuilding by Russian immigrants began in 1930, and more immigrants from Germany and East Europe came in 1934. Attacked again in 1936–39 and destroyed in 1948, it was then just on the Israeli side of the border. Rebuilding began in 1949; it came under fire in 1956 when four archaeologists working on the site were killed, and being on the border was damaged again in 1967. The kibbutz is now an independant settlement within the municipal borders of Jerusalem producing fruit, vegetables and meat, and offering guest house, hostel, camping and other facilities.

2.2km to the NW is the suburb of Gonen, formerly Katamon (Greek meaning 'near the monastery'), a Christian and Muslim Arab quarter founded in 1875, and abandoned when captured by Israel in the 1948 war, with the area of **St. Simeon** at its heart. A Greek Orthodox church and monastery marks the supposed site of the tomb of the upright and devout Simeon of Jerusalem who recognised the child Jesus as the Messiah when Mary and Joseph came to present him in the Temple and make the customary offering. Simeon had been told by the Holy Spirit that he would not die until he had seen the Lord's Messiah. 'Lord, now lettest thou thy servant depart in peace, according to thy word. For mine eyes have seen thy salvation, which thou has prepared before the face of all people; to be a light to lighten the Gentiles and to be the glory of thy people Israel' (Nunc dimittis, Luke 2:29–32).

History. The site of the Tomb of Simeon was located in the 4C, but it was principally in the 14C that tradition located the house of Simeon here. It was sketched by de Bruyn in 1681. The ruins were bought by the Greek Orthodox Patriarchate in 1859; and the Patriarch built his summer residence here in 1870, 2.5km from the walls of the Old City. The ruins of Simeon's house were incorporated in the present church in 1881.

Visit. In the NE part of the interior a rock-cut tomb with rebates for a covering slab is venerated as the *Tomb of Simeon.*

1.6km to the SW, at the S end of the suburb of Bayit WeGan, is the Holyland Hotel, in the grounds of which is a large **model of ancient Jerusalem** in the time of Herod the Great. It is updated as excavations reveal new insights into the ancient history and topography of Jerusalem and the model is well worth a visit by those who wish to visualise the ancient city and the temple of Herod the Great. Open summer 8.00–17.00; winter 8.00–16.00. Admission charge. Bus 21.

D.   Other Places of Interest on the Outskirts of the City

Mount Herzl, with *Military Cemetery*, the *Holocaust Memorial* and the *Jerusalem Forest.* Located approximately 7km W of the Old City off Sederot Herzl; Bus 12, 17, 18, 20, 23, 27.

At the E end of the hill is the *Tomb of Theodore Herzl* (1860–1904), founder of the modern state of Israel. He summoned the first Zionist Congress in Basle in 1897 which established the political ideal to found a national home for the Jews in Palestine. His remains were brought here in 1949. A museum contains documents relating to his life and work. Open April–October 8.00–18.30; November–March 8.00–17.00, guided tours on request but not 12.30–14.30; museum open daily 9.00–17.00 except Wed, Fri, Sat 9.00–13.00.

The Military Cemetery to the N is open daily until sunset.

At 0.6km to the W is the *Holocaust Memorial*, (*Yad VaShem*, monument and memorial). The main Israeli memorial to the six million Jews who died under the Nazi regime in Europe, the complex built in 1957 contains a Hall of Remembrance with mosaic floor with the names of 21 concentration camps, a light of remembrance, exhibitions and archives. Open Sun–Thu 9.00–16.45; Fri 9.00–13.45.

To the W is the extensive *Jerusalem Forest.*

The ʿAin Karim road descends SW from Kikkar Holland for c 2km to the village of ʿ**Ain Karim** or ʿ**Ain Karm**. Bus 17.

Christian tradition (but not a more positive identification) regards this attractive village as the birthplace of St. John the Baptist, the home of his parents Zechariah and Elizabeth, and the site of the meeting between the Virgin Mary and Elizabeth (Luke 1:5–25, 39–66). The village contains a number of churches commemorating these events. Like Ramat Rahel (see above) it is identified with the biblical site of Beth-hakkerem (Jer. 6:1), but this is doubtful. There is a modern Jewish suburb nearly 3km to the NE also called Bet HaKerem after the biblical site, which was founded in 1923.

History. Pottery of the late third millennium was discovered in the vicinity of ʿAin Karim (now in the YMCA Jerusalem, see above). There was occupation here in the Middle Bronze Age and the Iron Age, and numerous remains of Herodian, Roman, Byzantine and the early Arab periods indicate almost continuous settlement. Pagan objects give hints of a shrine or temple in the Roman period before the development of the Byzantine traditions. There are references to a church here in the 6C–8C and 10C.

From the time of the Russian Abbot Daniel (1106–07) there were references to two churches at ʿAin Karim, but both existed earlier. Charters of 1110 and 1154 show the land belonged to the Knights of St. John; an edict of 1166 transferred rights to the Templars. The place was abandoned in 1187 though the churches survived. A Muslim shrine was built in 1242 by Abu Yusuf, 200m WNW of the Church of St. John. In 1336 Jacobus di Verona found Armenian monks at the Church of the Visitation, and Muslims at St. John, but by 1480 Muslims occupied both sites. In 1621 the Franciscans made an attempt to re-establish themselves at St. John, which was successful in 1674. In 1681 they persuaded four Christian families from Bethlehem to settle at the village.

In 1860 the Sisters of Our Lady of Sion arrived and built their convent from 1862–90 at the W end of the village. In 1871 the Russian Orthodox arrived, and converted the S ridge above the village into a community with church, and many beautiful cottages for nuns. In 1881 ʿAin Karim was a flourishing village with c 600 inhabitants, of whom 100 were Latin Christians and the rest Muslim. In 1894 the Orthodox community also built a church dedicated to St. John the Baptist.

At the turn of the century ʿAin Karim had a population of c 2000 of whom 200 were Orthodox Russians and Greeks, 300 Latin Christians and the rest Muslim. In 1911 the Sisters of the Rosary opened a house near the Church of the Visitation. On 7 July 1948 Israeli forces captured the town from the Egyptian army who had been holding it for the Arabs, and the town was abandoned. There is now a Jewish artists' colony in the village, with commercial development, attracted by the setting.

Visit. This was once an attractive traditional Palestinian village set amid terraces with vines, now neglected, and increasingly hemmed in by suburban expansion. On the N near the centre of the village is the *Franciscan Church of St. John the Baptist*, the reputed home of St. Elizabeth and St. Zechariah, and birthplace of St. John the Baptist.

History. Fragments of a marble statue of Venus dating to the Roman period discovered in the foundations of the church gave rise to hypotheses that there may have been an earlier shrine of Venus or Adonis on or near this site possibly in Hadrianic times. Ruins of a 5C–6C church underlie the present building, which is mentioned in the 6C and 8C. It was damaged in the 7C and 11C. The Crusaders rebuilt the church which at first belonged to the Knights Hospitallers, and then to the Templars, who had to leave it in 1187. The Muslims are noted as occupying the church in 1336, and other pilgrims commented that it was partly ruined by 1610–11 and 1616. The Franciscans got possession and repaired it in 1621, but a month later had to leave and the doors were sealed; in 1624 the doors were removed, and the building was used as a stable. By 1638 there was renewed pilgrimage to it, but by 1672 the wall behind the high altar had collapsed. In 1674 the Franciscans finally managed to return and rebuild the church. The monastery around the church was also rebuilt on Byzantine and Crusader foundations in 1694–97; another storey was added in 1860, and further enlarged in 1897. In 1895 a new bell-tower was built on the site of the previous one of 1857 which itself had an earlier predecessor.

Visit. The church dates to 1674, standing on sections of earlier churches of the 5C and 11C–12C with later additions and repairs. It has a tall thin tower with small spire (1895). The bells (from Venice) were blessed in 1896. The W façade preserves the N Byzantine door, which was discovered in 1941. The main doorway at the W end was built in 1885.

The interior has a nave with side aisles divided by piers. The high altar is dedicated to St. John; the altar on the right is dedicated to St. Elizabeth, his mother. A 17C–18C painting in the style of Murillo can be noted above the sacristy doorway, which was much prized by the mostly Spanish Franciscan monks in the late 19C. The present sacristy was converted from a large storerooom in 1850; previously it lay to the SW. At the E end of the S aisle is a niche containing a stone with Latin inscription which tradition associated with St. John and which stood half way between ʿAin Karim and the desert of St. John. When Muslims attempted to destroy it in 1721 it exploded and in superstitious fear they presented part of it to the church. It was placed in its present position in 1897.

Steps descend from the N aisle to the *Grotto of St. John*, traditionally his birthplace, where reliefs depict scenes from his life. The altar was made in Livorno and donated by Isabella of Spain.

17C and 19C building operations as well as archaeological work by Saller in 1941–42 revealed fragments of the earlier structure, including two 6C chapels on the SW side of the church. Of these part of the N *Chapel of the Martyrs* was revealed in 1885 during the building of the W door of the church, some further fragments were discovered in 1939, and the rest was investigated by Saller in 1941–42. The chapel is 17m × 12.5m, but only the E, W and N walls were found; the discoveries included an apse, a raised chancel, and a mosaic with geometric patterns containing doves, plants and peacocks, set in an acanthus border; the mosaic also contained a Greek inscription 'Greetings, Martyrs of God', but whether these are the Forty Martyrs of Cappadocia, the Holy Innocents, the monks of St. Saba (Rte 17) or others is unknown. There are two rock-cut tombs in the apse.

In 1941 a second chapel was discovered S of the first. It is 13.1m × 8.3m, also with raised chancel, geometric mosaic floor and traces of a chancel screen.

To the S (at c 400m) is the *Spring of the Virgin* (A. ʿAin Sitti Maryam) which rises in a cave. Over it is built a small mosque, mentioned as a vaulted place of prayer in 1881; it was abandoned in 1948, but is attractive despite its dereliction. Since the 14C a tradition held that Mary, on her visit to Elizabeth her cousin, drew water from the spring.

Continuing W along the hillside from the spring, the road leads past the buildings of the *Russian Convent* (1871) which include two churches. One is dedicated to St. John the Baptist.

Further W is the Franciscan *Church of the Visitatio Mariae* on another traditional site of the home (or summer residence) of St. Elizabeth (or the summer residence of Zechariah), where Mary visited for about three months.

History. Byzantine remains and a cave have been located here, which are perhaps the setting commemorating a legend found in the 'Protoevangelium of James'. Tradition may have located here the place in which Elizabeth hid John from Herod. The church is not mentioned before the visit of Abbot Daniel in the 12C. 19C excavations revealed the lower storey of the Crusader church, mentioned also by John Poloner in 1422, and ruins of a former monastery and upper chapel. The interior once had frescoes, probably dating after the 12C. The site was purchased by the Franciscans in 1679 who constructed a monastery, and in the 19C built the lower church over the 12C Crusader building.

The present upper church was built in 1955, and has a mosaic on the façade depicting Mary's arrival at the home of Elizabeth. The interior has frescoes and mosaics, with lines from the 'Magnificat' on the pilasters ('My soul doth magnify the Lord, and my spirit hath rejoiced in God my Saviour. For he hath regarded the lowliness of his handmaiden...' Luke 1:46–55). The lower church is decorated in similar fashion.

Approximately 2km to the W of 'Ain Karim is the Franciscan *Monastery of St. John in the Wilderness* or First Desert of St. John. A spring, a grotto and a chapel mark the 12C traditional site of John the Baptist's sojourn and preparation in the wilderness (Luke 1:80). The church and monastery were built in 1922 on the site of the 12C monastery.

1.2km SW of 'Ain Karim, but nearly 7km SW of the Old City, lies the *Hadassah Hospital* and the *Hadassah Hebrew University Medical Centre* at 'Ain Karim. This modern teaching hospital was built with funding from the Hadassah Women's Zionist Organization. The original Hadassah Hospital was opened on Mount Scopus in 1939 but was not accessible between 1948 and 1967. In 1963 new facilities were opened at 'Ain Karim; these included a School of Nursing, and Public Health and Community Medicine as part of the Faculty of Medicine. The synagogue contains magnificent **∙windows by Marc Chagall**. Tours of site and synagogue, audio-visual presentation, Sun–Thu each hour 8.30–12.30; Fri 9.30–11.30. Synagogue also open 14.00–16.00. Admission charged. Bus 19, 27.

2km to the N is the holiday village of Bet Zayit. Fossil *dinosaur footprints* were discovered here. Bus from Central Bus Station.

8.2km NW of the Old City, on a hill top visible from many of the northern suburbs and from the countryside around, is *Nabi Samwil*, the traditional location of the **Tomb of the Prophet Samuel**. Open summer 8.00–17.00, except Fri 8.00–16.00; winter 8.00–16.00. No bus.

History. 'Father of the Prophets' and the leading religious personality of Israel in his time (11C BC, the Old Testament Books of Samuel), the son of Elkanah, an Ephraimite of the town of Ramah, Samuel is linked with the sanctuary of Shiloh and the story of Eli; he anointed both Saul and David kings over Israel; but there is no evidence that he died or was buried here (I Sam. 25:1 records that he died and was buried at Rama). The hill-top may have been an earlier place of sacrifice for the people of near-by Gibeon (al-Jib), and only later by the 6C did the cult traditions linked with a high-place of sacrifice come to be associated with Samuel.

The site was called Mountjoy by the Crusaders, because from the top of this hill they first saw Jerusalem in the morning of 7 June 1099 on their way to the conquest of the city. They built a church here in 1157 which was destroyed in the 18C, though the ruins, with groined arches supported by brackets were still extant in 1874 and partly incorporated in a mosque built over the aisles, with a minaret in the SE corner of the S transept and the cenotaph of Samuel in the centre of the earlier nave. The present mosque was begun in 1911.

Following almost the same route as the Crusaders, British forces captured Nabi Samwil during their advance in 1917, and a British position here which controlled the road from Jaffa played a strategic part in the capture of Jerusalem on 9 December 1917. There is a fine view from the mosque.

15 The Valley of Hinnom

Introduction. The Hinnom Valley (Valley of the Sons of Hinnom, A. *Wadi al-Rababi*) begins in the vicinity of the Mamilla Pool (see Rte 14) and descends steeply from a height of c 770m above sea level at the NE end of the Old City, to c 600m where it joins the Kidron Valley. Descending as a steep-sided valley, it formed the defensive W and S boundary of the city in Herodian and Byzantine times.

History. From the period of the Judges the valley marked the boundary between the territory of Benjamin and that of Judah (Jos. 15:8; 18:16). The Old Testament has frequent references to the cults of non-Israelite gods during the period of the monarchy, who were worshipped here by some of the inhabitants of Jerusalem: Baal, and Molech to whom cremation offerings of children were made at Topheth, at the bottom of the Hinnom (II Kings 23:10; Jer. 32:35). According to Jeremiah, it was to be the 'Valley of Slaughter' on the 'Day of Vengeance' (Jer. 7:32). In this tradition lies the origin of the Jewish Gehenna, the hell of fire, (*gehenna* being the Greek and Latin form of Hinnom Valley) which developed in Roman times under Persian influence. The S section of the valley was used for burial in Roman and Byzantine times; and from then developed the tradition of the Potter's Field, bought as a foreigner's burial ground by the chief priests with the 30 silver coins with which Judas betrayed Jesus (Matt. 27:3–10); alternatively the Aceldama or 'Field of Blood' which Judas bought with the silver after the betrayal (Acts 1:18–19), and where he fell and burst open (though probably 'Field of Sleeping' is a more correct rendering of the Aramaic). Many incidents seem to be confused in the background to these traditions. The S part of the valley certainly became a place to bury strangers (Matt.27.7) and Antoninus Martyr c 560 also mentions it thus. It was given to the Knights of the Hospital of St. John in 1143 for burial of those who died while on pilgrimage, and some time after 1187 to the Armenians. The traditional location of this field has remained constant at the SE end of the valley, and it was used for burial at least until the 17C.

Visit. The road descends S from the Jaffa Gate into the Hinnom Valley, with the walls of Sulaiman above to the left, and the area which formed the border from 1948 to 1967 down on the right. Many houses were destroyed in the fighting, and some, like the row of shops in the Arts and Crafts Centre down to the right and the Montefiori houses above to the SW have been restored in recent years. At the bottom of the valley, just before it swings to the E and above the road bridge, is the low-lying *Sultan's Pool* (A. *Birkat al-Sultan*) formed by a strong masonry dam closing-off a section of the valley. It was c 178m × 80m, up to 12m deep and the solid dam wall over 18m high. Its original date is uncertain. It may have been an early rain-fed pool in the valley, or more probably part of the Herodian low-level aqueduct system from Solomon's pools which ended at the Temple (at the 735m level); it was the 'Germain's Pool' of Crusader days, named for a benevolent inhabitant of Mount Zion; probably restored by al-Nasir Muhammad late in the 13C when he restored the aqueduct; again in 1399, and probably in the late 15C when more work is mentioned by Felix Fabri; restored by Sultan Sulaiman in the 16C, after whom it is called today. It was already ruinous by 1723, and by the 19C only a muddy pool in the wet season remained.

Continuous work must have been required to clear the debris and silt washed down in the winters. In the early 20C a cattle market was held by the pool on Fridays. Filled in, it now contains the Merrill Hasenfeld Amphitheatre (1980–85), converting one of the great pools or reservoirs of Jerusalem into a modern park-like public place. A fine *Ottoman fountain* is located on the N side of the road bridge. It was built by Sulaiman II in 1537, with ornately carved pointed arch, muqarnas semi-dome and inscription.

At the curve of the valley to the S, St. Andrew's Church of Scotland stands above to the right (see Rte 14), and below it the original site of the British St. John's Ophthalmic Hospital founded in 1882, located here until 1948 (for the present buildings, see Rte 13). The hill to the S, Abu Tor (see also Rte 14) probably had a 6C church of St. Procopius at the top: some columns and mosaics were excavated on the Greek property in 1914. It was called in Crusader times the 'Hill of Evil Counsel', as a tradition located a house of Caiaphas here, where the decision to kill Jesus was taken. The site was given to one of Salah al-Din's warriors in 1187. He was noted for riding into battle on the back of a bull, whence derives the present name of Abu Tor. He was buried there and the tomb became a place of Muslim pilgrimage.

A road curving to the E leads further down the Hinnom valley. Many ancient rock-cut tombs, principally of Hellenistic, Roman and Byzantine date, are located in this area. Towards the lower end of the valley, above the rock-scarp to the right, is the Greek Convent at the site of Aceldama.

The site of **Aceldama** is marked most clearly by the Greek *Convent of St. Onuphrius*, a Byzantine hermit. It contains the 'Apostles's Cave' now used as a chapel. Like most of the caves in the vicinity, it was a Jewish rock-cut tomb of the Roman period, re-used in the Byzantine period. It has a frieze (1C BC/AD) above the entrance, carved with eight panels with rosettes and grapes similar to that on the Tombs of the Kings (see Rte 13). There were traces of frescoes in the forecourt. A 16C tradition says eight of the apostles hid here during the arrest and crucifixion of Jesus. Adjacent to the convent are two burial places which the Orthodox associate with Aceldama. Above, and outside the convent to the W, is the complex associated in western tradition with Aceldama.

History. In 1143 the Patriarch of Jerusalem gave the church and some land at Aceldama to the Order of the Knights of the Hospital of St. John (see Rte 4, Muristan) for the burial of pilgrims. A 13C map marks 'carnel(ium) Johannis ubi sepeliuntur Anglici' (the first word comes from old French into modern English as 'charnel house'). Later the site was given to the Armenians, whose ownership is preserved in the A. name of the site *al-Firdaws (al-Armani)*, 'the (Armenian) paradise'.

Visit. Descriptions exist in late 19C books of a deep chamber, partly rock-cut, partly masonry, with a massive central pillar supporting a domed masonry roof. Much Crusader masonry and a great pointed arch survive of what was the pilgrims' charnel house of the Knights of St. John. On the W wall are crosses and Armenian inscriptions. A deep layer of bones survived into the early 20C.

Further W are many more rock-cut tombs in the cliff, mostly Jewish but re-used in the Byzantine period. The convent site overlooks the junction of the Hinnom with the Kidron Valley, and the gardens of Silwan (see Rte 11). Buses 43, 44, 45 from the Damascus Gate Bus Station serve this area.

16 Bethany

Introduction. The village of Bethany may be reached by Bus 43 from the Damascus Gate Bus Station, and by car following the Jericho road 3km SE; or by minor roads over the Mount of Olives, from the village of al-Tur. Following the route by the Jericho Road, one descends first into the Valley of Jehoshaphat and passes the churches at Gethsemane to the left (see Rte 12). From the top of the ascent there is a magnificent view back towards the Haram area before the road turns the corner. The carriage road to Jericho was first completed in 1889. In former times the old road crossed over the Mount of Olives and descended via the Wadi Kilt. Just beyond the corner a minor road to Bethlehem (the main road 1948–67) turns to the S, and after another 400m a turning to the SE gives onto the minor road to the village of Abu Dis and beyond to the Monastery of Mar Saba (by a poor, steep road) (see Rte 17).

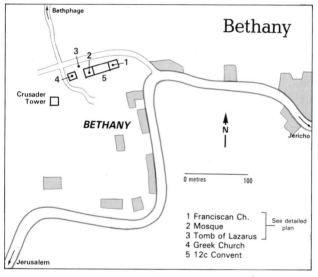

At 3km we reach **Bethany**, a Muslim and Christian Arab village, population 3600, A. *al-Azariyya* from the name of Lazarus, located on the SE slopes of the Mount of Olives. Bethany was by tradition the home of Lazarus, whom Jesus raised from the dead (John 11:38–44), and his sisters Martha and Mary, where Jesus stayed often; also of Simon the Leper, at whose house Jesus was anointed (Mark 14:3); it was also the place to which he returned after his triumphal entry into Jerusalem (Mark 11:11), and from near which the New Testament notes his Ascension (Luke 24:50), though no other tradition supports this. Excavations by S.J. Saller (1949–53).

History. Remains in the vicinity of the modern village suggest that a village stood here at least from Roman times and that there was an earlier settlement of the Iron Age. This is equated with Ananiah in the territory of Benjamin (Neh. 11:32) from which the New Testament name is derived (Beth Ananiah = Bethany). There is little trace otherwise of the events of the New Testament.

There seems to have been no church here in the early 4C, though Eusebius and the Bordeaux Pilgrim (333) mention the tomb in a vault or crypt. St. Jerome c 390 records visiting the Tomb of Lazarus and the guest room of Mary and Martha, which is the Lazarium mentioned by Egeria in the liturgy on Saturday in the seventh week of Lent: 'Just on one o'clock everyone arrives at the Lazarium, which is Bethany...by the time they arrive there, so many people have collected that they fill not only the Lazarium itself, but all the fields around' (Wilkinson); at the end of the service, the start of Easter was announced. This church was destroyed in an earthquake and a larger one built in the 5C. Theodosius (not later than 518) mentions the place, as does Arculf in c 680.

Queen Melisande, whose youngest sister was a nun in the Convent of St. Anne in Jerusalem, purchased the village of Bethany from the Patriarch of the Holy Sepulchre in 1143 in exchange for estates at Hebron. She built at Bethany a Benedictine convent fortified with a tower, in honour of St. Lazarus and Mary and Martha, endowing it with the large estates of the village of Jericho. Not long after her sister Joveta was elected abbess, thus becoming at the age of 24 the head of one of the richest convents in the Kingdom of Jerusalem. At this time the Byzantine church was restored and strengthened, a chapel built over the tomb of Lazarus itself, and extensive convent buildings built adjacent. Joveta died c 1173–78, and the nuns went into exile at Acre in 1187. The village seems to have been abandoned in the 14C; the ruins are mentioned by Poggibonsi in 1347. In the 15C the place was still associated with Lazarus, and the Mosque of al-'Uzair (Ezra) was built in the 16C in the forecourt of the Byzantine church in front of the entrance to the tomb, for Muslims also venerate Lazarus; not long afterwards the Franciscans were permitted to cut a new entrance from the road on the N side of the tomb. In 1697 Maundrell noted the ruins of 'the Castle of Lazarus'. In 1952 a Franciscan church was built to the E, and from 1965 a Greek church was built to the W.

Visit. Ascending from the bend of the Jericho road in the village of Bethany, the most visible structure is the *Franciscan Church*, built 1952–55, architect A. Barluzzi. Open March–October 8.00–11.30, 14.00–18.00; November–February 8.00–11.30, 14.00–17.00. Ascend to the W end either through the Franciscan garden or by the road, and enter the *forecourt* **(1)**. The *modern church* **(2)** is cruciform in plan, has a mosaic of Mary, Martha and Lazarus on the façade and the interior decorated in polished stone and mosaic work. Under trapdoors just inside the church doorway can be seen parts of the apse of the *4C church* **(3)** (which was 13m shorter than that of the 5C). The apse of the *5C church* **(4)** is outlined in white marble near the modern E altar. Under other trapdoors and grids in the church and the court are fragments of the *Byzantine mosaics* of the 4C and 5C churches. Much of the nave mosaic of the first church still existed at the time building work began in 1952. It has geometric patterns. The W wall of the court **(5)** contains the W façade of the *5C basilica*, with three doorways. Passing through the S doorway **(6)** the angle opposite to the right contains a pillar of the *Byzantine atrium*. In this atrium is now placed the mosque **(11, 12)** built against the entrance to the Tomb of Lazarus.

On the S side of the Byzantine atrium, to our left, was a long room **(7)**, part of the *12C Benedictine convent*. This monastic complex S of the church, c 62.5m × 50m, was partly cleared by Saller. Part is still occupied by the ruined or inhabited houses of the village. The room, with rough vaulted masonry, contains an old olive press and mill, and at the E end a pilgrims' dining room. At the W end the stairs **(8)** lead to the upper part of the Crusader convent. Leaving the courtyard of the Franciscan church, on either side of the entrance **(9)** is some 12C buttressing of the 5C wall.

Turning left up the hill, the first entrance on the left **(10)** is that of the *Mosque of al-'Uzair*, the courtyard **(11)** of which is part of the

Byzantine atrium; the *16C mosque* **(12)** (not usually accessible) contains the original entrance to the Tomb of Lazarus in the W wall.

A further 25m up the hill on the left is the small modern entrance **(13)** to the **Tomb of Lazarus** cut by the Franciscans in the late 16C or early 17C. A flight of 24 very uneven stone steps descends to the antechamber of the tomb. Probably originally a rock-cut tomb, very little trace of its original form remains. It is assumed that the rather rotten rock has collapsed, perhaps at the time the Crusader chapel was built in the 12C. The present sides are of masonry, and even the floor levels may not be original. The original blocked entrance is visible in the E wall of the antechamber (towards the mosque). The alignment suggests the tomb pre-dated the Byzantine churches. The small tomb chamber itself can only be entered by a very low passage.

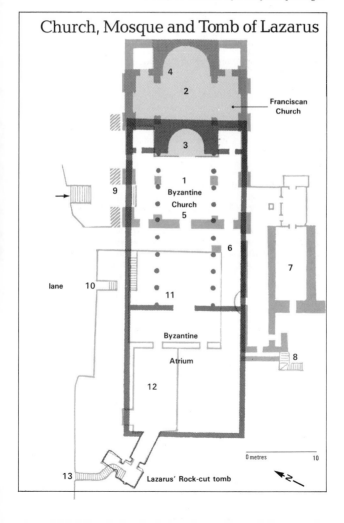

Church, Mosque and Tomb of Lazarus

4
2

Franciscan
Church

3

1
Byzantine
Church
5

9

6

7

lane
10

11

Byzantine

Atrium

8

12

0 metres   10

13   Lazarus' Rock-cut tomb

Continuing up the hill, on the left is the new *Greek Orthodox Church*, begun in 1965, which incorporates a wall of the Crusader chapel built over the Lazarus tomb. Turning left at the crossroads beyond brings one to more substantial ruins which belong to the *Greek Orthodox Patriarchate*. One tradition identifies them with the House of Simon the Leper, another with the House or Castle of Lazarus. The podium contains drafted masonry of the Roman period re-used from some earlier structure, but the remains of a tower belong to the fortified Crusader Monastery of the 12C. The tower is 14.60m × 14.80m and has a cistern beneath its floor. Returning to the cross-roads, the track ahead (on the right as one ascends) leads up to Bethphage (see Rte 12).

Descending again to the road, other excursions to places further E on the Jericho Road can be made. At c 7km is the new West Bank Jewish settlement of *Ma'ale Adummim*, above the Jericho Road to the E (Bus 74). Established to increase Jewish settlement in the area and as part of the new industrial complex, it is also linked by a new highway to the new N Jewish suburbs of Jerusalem. It is planned for a future population of 35,000 on 1300 hectares of land in modern dwelling units with park and recreation facilities. Located 500m above sea level in the Judaean wilderness, the modern apartment blocks and single units have a splendid view over the Judaean hills, and provide an unexpected element in the otherwise superb wilderness landscape. The settlement is named for the biblical site of Ma'ale Adummim, literally 'the ascent of the red rocks', a pass leading up from Jericho to Jerusalem, on the border between Benjamin and Judah (Jos. 15:7), which lies further to the E.

The pass is located at c 18km from Jerusalem (Bus 74) in the vicinity of the traditional site of the Good Samaritan Inn. Eusebius in the 4C notes that 'Maledomni' was a fortress midway between Jericho and Jerusalem, and later a Crusader stronghold was also built to guard the E approaches to Jerusalem. The remains of this fortress lie above the site of the Inn of the Good Samaritan (see below), on the hill on the N side of the present road. It is surrounded by a rock-cut ditch and approached by a ramp at the NW corner. The ditch is 7m deep and between 5.8 and 7m broad; the site within has a trapezoidal shape, 62.5m × 55m × 66m × 47m, with the remains of a keep (over 9m²) with a barrel-vaulted roof at the SE, and vaults at the NW. It has been identified as the *Tour Rouge* built by the Templars to protect the Jericho pilgrims, and mentioned in the 14C by M. Sanuto.

The Inn of the Good Samaritan on the S side of the Jericho Road, at c 18km from Jerusalem, was early located in this vicinity (Jerome and Paula, c 385). The parable (Luke 10:29–37) has been localised with the continued passion of pilgrims to have a site for every event noted in the Bible, but is not authenticated other than as a likely place for travellers to be attacked by robbers. A caravanserai, with buildings and enclosure wall, which served as a police checkpoint at various times this century, now has a tourist shop and no remains of particular note; some re-used small blocks of drafted masonry can be seen in the enclosure wall; the buildings themselves are of the Ottoman period, the Khan Hathrurah, described as being in a ruinous condition in 1873 (Survey of Western Palestine). The entrance and the road then lay to the S.

Returning c 4km towards Jerusalem, the turning to the S to Mishor Adummim (once the road to Nabi Musa) takes one to the new industrial complex. At 1.5km on the left is the site of **Khan al-Ahmar,**

*Coaches at the Good Samaritan Inn on the road to Jericho,
c 1907 (courtesy of the Manchester Museum).*

the 5C Monastery of St. Euthymius. It is difficult to appreciate this
Byzantine monastic complex once set in the wilderness, and now in
ruins amidst modern industry. A further 6.5km to the E is the sister
site of **Dair al-Mukallik**, once the Monastery of St. Theoctistus. Both
were investigated by Chitty and Jones (1927–28).

History. Two Byzantine hermits, Euthymius and Theoctistus, occupied a cave at
Wadi Mukallik in 411, and were joined by others. A monastery grew up around
a church in a cave, and people from the Arab tribes around were converted,
including Shaikh Peter Aspebet who was baptised with other members of his
tribe c 421 (and later became Bishop of the Arab Camps at the Council of
Ephesus). Euthymius preferred the life of a solitary, and he and a pupil,
Domitian, moved W to live at the site now called Khan al-Ahmar. Here another
community developed, for which Peter Aspebet built a cistern, a bakery, cells
and a church which was dedicated on 7 May 428. Both these monastic centres
became great strongholds of Orthodoxy in Palestine. Euthymius sent Saba (see
Mar Saba, Rte 17) as novice to Theoctistus.
    Euthymius died in 473, and is remembered as one of the major founders of
monasticism in Palestine. A tomb was built on his cell at Khan al-Ahmar. In
479–82 the deacon Fidus turned this *laura* into a *cenobium* or monastery, and
built for it a church, a fortified tower and monastic cells. The church was
consecrated in 482. The two monasteries separated after 485, and the older
Theoctistus monastery retained the' hospice they had previously shared in
Jerusalem. Much is known of the monastery of St. Euthymius because Cyril of
Scythopolis wrote a life of St. Euthymius after being himself a monk in this
monastery in 544–54.
    St. Theoctistus was destroyed in 614, but Khan al-Ahmar was re-established
in the 7C. It was damaged in the earthquake of 747/8, but seems to be
mentioned in the Commemoratorium in the 9C when it contained 30 monks. St.
Theoctistus seems to have been revived briefly in the 11C, when unsatisfactory
monks from Mar Saba were sent there. St. Euthymius seems to have survived

until destroyed by Salah al-Din or Baybars in the late 12 or 13C, quite possibly when the latter was making the road through to Nabi Musa, one of the reputed tombs of Moses, just NE of the Dead Sea.

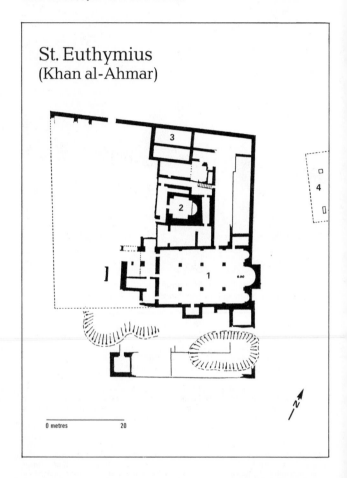

St. Euthymius
(Khan al-Ahmar)

0 metres   20

Visit to St. Euthymius, Khan al-Ahmar. There is an enclosure with a three-aisled *basilica* (1) in the SE corner. This church is built over an undercroft with barrel vaults, which according to St. Cyril was the refectory established in the earlier church. The S aisle has a *mosaic* of c 5C–8C, with geometric and arabesque patterns; on the piers and pilasters of the S aisle were traces of frescoes depicting saints, probably of the 12C–13C. The sacristy is placed near the centre of the S wall. The surviving barrel vaults may be 8C. Parts of a chancel screen and marble floor under the dome were also uncovered. To the N near the centre of the enclosure is the *tomb/cell of Euthymius* the founder (2), a chapel with an altar on the E. On the N side of the monastery was a defensive tower **(3)**, and outside to the E a very large cistern **(4)**, presumably that built by Peter Aspebet in the 5C. The other rooms contained the domestic facilities of the monastery. **Visit to St. Theoctistus, Dair al-Mukallik.** (Map reference 186 131). This is a remote and inaccessible site, set in a gorge. The hermits originally entered caves by climbing ropes up the sheer wall of the gorge, which have since become even less accessible due to rock falls. A large cave complex is located over 8m above the path. It includes a *cave chapel*, with a large *mosaic fish* on the floor, some *frescoes* (poorly preserved) of the 6C–8C and others of the 11C, in at least three layers. The oldest showed Christ between saints and angels; 13 saints around the apse, of which the faces are destroyed, are probably 13C. Other more recent paintings of red crosses were done by a monk called Teofan in 1884. There are other cuttings, for cells, granaries and cisterns.

17 Bethlehem

The town of Bethlehem to the S of Jerusalem has several places of interest in and around it, the most notable being the Church of the Nativity. Take Bus 22 from the Damascus Gate, or private transport by the Bethlehem Road. Following the Bethlehem (Hebron) Road, which runs S passing the Sultan's Pool (see Rte 14) and passes the railway station, continue past the turning to Talpiot. The housing at this end of the town contains many poor modern apartment blocks and some ruins. In a few minutes, at c 6km from Jerusalem, the road passes the site of *Bir al-Qadismu*, a well and pool on the left of the road at which tradition placed the site where Mary rested half-way to Bethlehem. The commemoration of this event included the building of a church called the Kathisma or Seat by a wealthy matron of Jerusalem, named Ikelia, c 451–58, the name of which is preserved in the present Arabic place name. It is usually identified with the Byzantine church and monastery 400m to the E at Ramat Rahel (see Rte 14).

Bir al-Qadismu is also sometimes identified with the Well of the Magi, and a tradition that the light of the star that led the wise men to Bethlehem was reflected in its waters. Other ruins of the 4C–7C and of medieval date in the vicinity, in particular on a hill to the right of the road, are sometimes connected with these stories, and were also identified by 15C pilgrims with the house of Habbakkuk, a cultic prophet of Judah in the days of Josiah and Jehoiakim (7C–6C BC).

Approximately 600m further up on the left, 6.5km from Jerusalem, is the Greek Orthodox *Monastery of Mar Elias*, an interesting semi-fortified three-storey building with square bell-tower capped by a tiny dome. The Cretan John Phocas made a pilgrimage to Jerusalem (c 1185) and notes that in 1160 the Emperor Manuel Comnenos rebuilt the monastery from its foundations on the site of the 6C monastery of St. Anastasius, but its name (Mar Elias, St. Elijah) only dates from this time. A 12C tradition identified the site with the spot where the prophet Elijah paused on his flight to the S. Elijah had challenged Ahab, the King of Israel (871–852 BC) and the priests of Baal to a confrontation at Mount Carmel. When God proved more powerful, Elijah slaughtered all the prophets of Baal. Jezebel, the Phoenician Baal-worshipping wife of Ahab, threatened vengeance, and Elijah fled S to Beersheba (I Kings 19:3) pausing here on the way.

The monastery was restored in the 14C and renovated in the 17C. On the opposite side of the road a stone seat was placed by his wife for Holman Hunt, the Pre-Raphaelite painter (1827–1910): he is particularly noted for scenes with a strong religious inspiration. At a short distance on the right is the road to *Tantur*, a Christian Arab village, with the Ecumenical Centre for Advanced Theological Studies founded in 1972 on the initiative of Pope Paul VI. The town had an old church dedicated to St. Sergius (perhaps mentioned by Grethenios c 1400), later incorporated in the Tantur Monastery where the Knights of Malta founded a hospital.

At nearly 8km from Jerusalem on the right is the **Tomb of Rachel**, A. *Qubbat Rahil*, an open cupola of possible 12C date modified in the 19C.

History. Rachel was the younger daughter of Laban of Haran (in N Syria), for whom the patriarch Jacob laboured 14 years before receiving her as his second wife; the mother of Joseph and Benjamin, she died giving birth to Benjamin between Bethel and Ephrath (Gen. 35:16–21) and was buried near Ephrath in the territory of Benjamin (I Sam. 10:2) probably somewhere in the vicinity of al-Ram (N of Jerusalem). A late gloss on Gen. 35:19 put the site of Ephrath near Bethlehem, and this was accepted by the early Christians.

Various pilgrims (Paula and Jerome c 385 and others later) mention the tomb at the present site, then marked by a heap of stones, and perhaps an altar, up to Crusader times. Benjamin of Tudela (1163) describes 11 stones covered by a cupola on four pillars at the site; Maundrell (1697) mentions 12 stones.

It is venerated by Christians, Muslims and Jews, but in the 19C was visited particularly by the latter. It was purchased by Sir Moses Montefiore in 1841, who added an antechamber with a mihrab for Muslims on the E side, and as the tomb chamber was kept locked by the Jews presumably the open arcades were also filled in by Montefiore. This would agree with Conder's observations in 1883 when the square building (7m) had an open arch in each façade supporting the dome which had recently been blocked. The antechamber with mihrab on the E side was also a recent addition to a probably 12C domed shrine. The key of the inner chamber was then kept by Jews who visited the site on Fridays.

Visit. Open summer 8.00–18.00; winter 8.00–17.00; Friday and Jewish Holidays 8.00–13.00; closed Saturday. Bus 62 from the Central Bus Station.

The small square shrine with whitewashed dome, and cenotaph of no great antiquity, was restored in 1967. It is much visited by Jewish pilgrims, especially women.

Beyond, the roads to the right make a diversion to the Christian Arab village of *Bait Jala* (1km); population 6500. It is identified with the Giloh of Jos. 15:51 and II Sam. 15:12. In 1873 it was described as a flourishing stone-built village, depending for water on cisterns and a well in the adjacent valley, with a population of 3000 of whom 420 were Catholic, the rest Greek Orthodox, and was served by a Greek and a Latin church. The Latin church is near the E end of the village, the Greek church further W. In 1925 a subterranean Byzantine crypt or cave-tomb was discovered in the church of St. Nicholas, which had been used as a reliquary. It is a vaulted chamber, 2.3m square, 2m high, with side vaults.

Above Bait Jala to the W at 2km is a hill with viewpoint. The observation point is at 923m. Below it a road leads NW for just over 1km to the *Cremisan Convent* (Salesian Order) which is noted for its wine production. At 1.4km to the NW of the convent is the site of the *Fountain of Philip*, now called 'Ain Hanniyya (map reference 165 127). The tradition which associated the spring and ruined church on this site with the baptism by Philip of the eunuch who was a high official of the Queen of Ethiopia (Acts 8:26–39) only dates to the 15C. The Byzantine tradition linked Philip with a more likely spot on a route to Gaza, at 29km on the Jerusalem to Hebron road, at 'Ain al-Dhirwa. The ruins of this church between 'Ain Karim and Bethlehem were sketched by de Bruyn in 1681. There is a niche above the spring, and ruins of a 5C–6C *basilica* cleared by Baramki in 1932. The atrium (12m × 10m) had a white mosaic floor, and porticoes. The narthex (12m × 3m) had a mosaic with scale-pattern enclosed by a border of small flowers. The basilica (12m × 16m) had a wide nave (5m) with a narrow aisle to each side, separated by two rows of five columns. The nave mosaic had a vine trellis growing around medallions. The S aisle floor had a scale-pattern mosaic, the N aisle had a design of squares containing flowers. A chancel, raised one step above the nave, led to an inscribed apse. Traces of an altar (with marble reliquary beneath it which contained bones) were discovered. The Byzantine dedication of this ruin is unknown.

Returning to the main road, just beyond Rachel's Tomb at 8km from Jerusalem the road divides, continuing straight ahead to Hebron. Take the left fork into Bethlehem and continue up the hill to MANGER SQUARE on the right at the centre of the town (9.5km), passing at 9km the turning to the Fountain of David (mentioned by de Bruyn in 1681). In the 19C three large ancient cisterns on a flat rock terrace were called Bir Da'ud in accordance with this tradition.

Bethlehem. Pop c 20,000. Located on ridges in the hill country of Judah, with steep descents to the wadis on the E, Bethlehem is noted as the home of David and the birthplace of Christ, and is set amidst fertile land with the wilderness of Judah not far to the E. It also lies beside the main road from Jerusalem to the S hill country. The name derives from the A. *Bait Lahm*, place of meat (classical) or bread, food (colloquial A. and H.). It has no spring, and originally depended on cisterns until water was brought by aqueduct from Solomon's Pools in the Herodian period. A largely Christian market town for the Bedouin and the surrounding villages, in a region of agricultural, meat and dairy production, it also has vineyards and wine production, and a thriving industry in olive wood and mother-of-pearl carving (various items of religious significance for pilgrim souvenirs, and jewellery) which can be seen in the many shops.

History of the town and the church. Evidence for a varied, extinct Lower Pleistocene fauna were recovered in excavations in Bethlehem by Bate and Gardener (1935–37) and Stekelis (1940). The site of a Late Bronze Age and an Iron Age town has been noted on the E side of the Church of the Nativity. The town may be mentioned in the Amarna letters (14C BC), but this is not certain. Following the Israelite conquest it was part of the territory of the tribe of Judah (12C–11C BC). It was also the home of the Levite who became priest for Micah in Ephraim (Judges 17–18), the home of the concubine of the Levite of Ephraim (Judges 19), and the setting for most of the story of Ruth.

It was the home of David (c 1004–965 BC), the son of an Ephrathite called Jesse (I Sam. 17:12, 15). Here Samuel annointed David king over Israel (I Sam. 16:1–13). A Philistine garrison occupied the town during the early wars of David (II Sam. 23:14–16) when David longed for a drink of water from the well by the gate of Bethlehem (see above, David's Fountain). Later a town of Israel in the time of David and Solomon, and then of Judah during the divided monarchy, it was refortified by Rehoboam (928–11) (II Chr. 11:6). The prophet Micah in the days of Jotham, Ahaz and Hezekiah (8C BC) foretold the coming of the Messiah to Bethlehem (Micah 5:2).

There is no reason to suppose that any major interruption in its history occurred till the time of the Babylonian destruction, but then in 586 BC many of its leading citizens were exiled to Babylon; 123 men returned under the Persian dispensation (Ezra 2:21). Following the depopulation it was taken by Edomites who in turn were expelled by John Hyrcanus.

The New Testament records two versions of the birth of Jesus in Bethlehem (Matt. 2:1–16 and Luke 1–2), which various authorities think occurred c 4 BC on the basis of the date of the census of Augustus when Quirinius was Governor of Syria (Luke 2:1–2) in the time of Herod the Great, who, according to the story, ordered the Massacre of the Innocents, and following whose death (4 BC) Archelaus succeeded as ruler (Matt. 2:19–22). The New Testament genealogies place Jesus in the descent of Abraham and David. The town certainly acquired greater importance at this time, partly because it overlooked the main roads to Herod the Great's fortress palaces at Herodion and Masada.

Very few remains of the 1C–3C AD have been recovered. Following the suppression of the First Revolt (AD 70) and the Second Revolt (AD 135) Jews were proscribed from living in the area. Some later writers (Jerome) maintain that from the time of Hadrian there was a grove sacred to Adonis (Tammuz) in the vicinity of the Cave of the Nativity. The tradition of Jesus' birth in a cave at Bethlehem dates back to at least the 2C (Justin Martyr and the Protevangelium of James), and soon after 246 Origen noted a cave and a manger. From the 4C many Christian pilgrims came to Bethlehem, and the desert on the E became one of the great centres of Byzantine monasticism. Eusebius, Egeria and Jerome (4C) also mention a tomb of David in Bethlehem. In 325 Constantine built a great basilica with octagonal chapel over a series of caves, which was dedicated on 31 May 339.

The Constantinian basilica. Excavations beneath the present structure have shown that this was fronted on the W by a flagged court or street, which led to a square court (27m) with porticoes on all sides (partly under the present narthex). The porticoes had mosaic floors, with geometric designs, and corner columns with heart-shaped cross-sections. As the 4C basilica was shorter than the Justinian church, the W wall of the basilica was 2.8m E of Justinian's, but the N and S walls lay on the same lines. The W wall had three doors and was approached by three steps from the court. The church itself was a square basilica (26.5m), divided by four rows of nine columns into a 9m wide nave, and four side aisles (the inner ones 3m wide, the outer 3.5m wide). The floor level is 60cm below that of the present church. The mosaics, which have a technical similarity to those in the Imperial Byzantine palace in Constantinople, appear to date to the 5C.

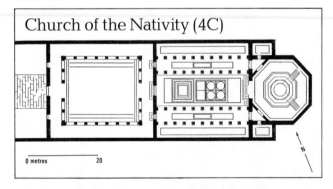

Church of the Nativity (4C)

0 metres   20

To the E an octagon built over the cave of the Nativity was 7.9m on each side. It was approached from the basilica by three stairways, the central one being 5m wide. The two side entrances may have been indirect approaches through a diaconicon and prothesis. In the prothesis part of an early black and white mosaic with crosses was found. Within the octagon pilgims were permitted to approach a railing from which the cave could be viewed from above. It is not certain how the cave itself was entered at this time. The plan had close parallels with other Constantinian martyria, including the basilica and Anastasis in Jerusalem, and may well have been similar to the structure depicted on the right side of the apse mosaic in the Church of St. Pudenziana in Rome.

The church was visited by the Bordeaux pilgrim in 333, whose description includes the traditional cave with manger. At the end of the 4C St. Jerome (c 340–420) settled in Bethlehem with a group of matrons, including Paula whose pilgrimage he described, and founded two monasteries. Here also he translated the Bible into Latin, his work becoming the Vulgate as used by the Latin church. Various repairs to the basilica were carried out in the 5C. The Constantinian basilica was destroyed in the Samaritan Revolt of 529.

A new basilica was built in the 6C, usually attributed to Justinian (527–65). It was larger, and with a slightly different plan to the previous church, but on the same site and incorporated parts of the previous building. This basilica has survived to the present day.

Justinian's basilica. A legend noted in the writings of Eutychius, patriarch of Alexandria in the 9C, maintains that the architect sent by Justinian to rebuild the church was beheaded on imperial orders for unsatisfactory work. It has been speculated that this was due to a failure to carry through a design involving a

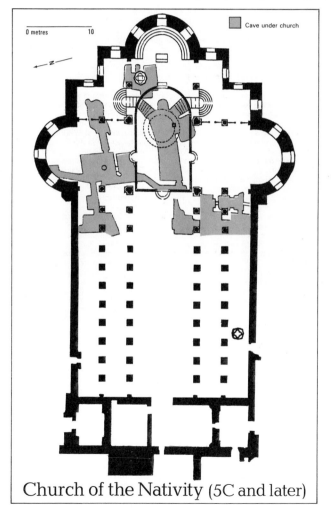

Church of the Nativity (5C and later)

dome 33.6m in diameter over the cave. Instead a clover-leaf triple apse was built in the form visible today. At the W end the atrium was extended and formed a rectangle; a narthex was constructed above the 4C E portico. The basilica itself was lengthened to 33m, the nave widened to 10.25m and the side aisles narrowed. The columns and capitals of the earlier building were used, as well as ten new columns, and four new columns at the crossing beneath the dome.

The church was dedicated to St. Mary Theotokos, and beneath it the cave with the manger was lined with marble. Sophronius, describing the church c 614: 'And when I see all the glistening gold, the well-fashioned columns and fine workmanship, let me be freed from the gloom of sorrows. I will also look up at the design above, at the coffers studded with stars, for they are a masterpiece, brilliant with heavenly beauty. Let me go down also to the cave, where the Virgin Queen of all bore a Saviour for mankind'. In 570 St. Jerome's tomb was supposed to be near the mouth of the main cave in the church, and though the site moved later, it was still regularly shown in the 12C. Jerome also recorded that he buried the matron Paula beside the cave, where she and her daughter Eustochium continued to be remembered. As well as the church, perhaps built c 531, Justinian rebuilt the walls of Bethlehem. By this time there was clearly an extensive complex of monasteries and guest houses in the town. The Persian sack of 614, which wreaked such havoc on the Christian monuments of Jerusalem, spared the Church of the Nativity, because, it was said, the Byzantine mosaics of the façade showed the Magi worshipping the infant king, and the Persians recognised and respected the familiar dress of Persian holy men.

In 634 Bethlehem surrendered to the Arabs, and the church was again spared. In 638 'Umar prayed in the S transept and it was given to the Muslims as a place of prayer. However in the 10C when Muslim tolerance of the Christian shrines lessened, the mosaics in the S apse were taken down. The presence of this Muslim shrine again saved the church from destruction by al-Hakim in the 11C. In c 675 Epiphanius the Monk on his visit was shown the family home of David to the left of the Church of the Nativity. The town of Bethlehem was clearly badly affected by the earthquake of 747/8, as it was mostly in ruins in c 750; the Commemoratorium notes that in the early 9C the church was served by 15 presbyters, clergy and monks. In c 870 Bernard the Monk noted the Church of the Blessed Innocents on the S side. The Commemoration of the Holy Innocents (Matt. 2:16) is first noted in the 4C, and a chapel on the S side of the main church is recorded in 417–39.

Just before the capture of Jerusalem in 1099, on 6 June, Tancred and Baldwin of le Bourg rode to secure the church at Bethlehem on the plea of the mainly Christian population of the town. In 1102 Saewulf found that Bethlehem had been largely destroyed by the Muslims, but the church had survived. It was richly restored in the time of the Crusader Kingdom of Jerusalem (1099–1187). On Christmas Day 1101, Baldwin I, the first king, was crowned in the church. The restoration of the church included Byzantine mosaics given by the Emperor Manuel Comnenos (1143–80). The Crusaders also built a monastery on the N side. The town itself prospered. The Latins left in 1187, but Salah al-Din allowed two priests and two deacons to return in 1192 as a favour to the Bishop of Salisbury. Various modifications were made in the Middle Ages, especially after 1244 when the town was devastated by the Khwarizmian Turks and again came under Muslim jurisdiction. These included the progressive narrowing of the W door for defensive purposes.

In 1350 von Suchem described the church as fortified like a castle: the remains of a wall and gatehouse at the W end of the present forecourt have been excavated. The roof was replaced in 1482: Edward IV of England gave the lead, Philip of Burgundy the pinewood; the Ottoman Turks removed the roof lead for bullets in the 17C. The plan drawn by Amico in 1609 shows a massive walled complex containing church and monastery. In 1672 the Greek Orthodox managed to gain rights to most of the building; the Armenians acquired some rights in 1810; and the Latins were only re-admitted to a share through the intervention of Napoleon III in 1852 and the present division of the church among the different sects has remained largely in this 19C state. The church and town were damaged in the earthquake of 1834, and the church in a fire of 1869. Many monasteries, convents and schools were built in the town.

Excavations. R.W. Hamilton, 1932; W. Harvey, 1934; Bagatti, 1948–51. The Franciscans cleared an area adjacent to the church in 1926, when 13 bells dating from the 14C were discovered. They had been removed in the 15C–16C when the ringing of Christian church bells was forbidden by the Muslims.

Visit to the Church of the Nativity. Approaching the church from the W from Manger Square, the present paving (1932) overlies part of the *Constantinian atrium*. The wall to the right is part of the Armenian Orthodox monastery. The massive church ahead with its tiny door reminds the visitor of the unsettled times through which the 6C structure has survived. Subject to depredations in times of invasion, weak central government or anti-Christian fanaticism, only traces of the original three wide doors of the time of Justinian may still be seen. Progressively narrowed from the great 6C lintel, the main door has a blocked pointed arch which may be 13C or later; the smallest blocking may be of Mamluk or Ottoman date. The N door of Justinian is mostly hidden by a buttress of 1775, and the S door by the Armenian monastery. Parts of moulded lintels and a baluster capital can be seen. Through the present door (1.2m high), the visitor enters the now dark and partitioned narthex of the 6C church. It extends the full width of the basilica but only a short central section is visible; the partitions are of various dates. The vaulted roof is medieval. The central door to the basilica has the remains of a great carved wooden door presented to the church by two Armenians in 1227.

Entering the basilica one is confronted by the splendid wide *nave of Justinian*. On either side are the double rows of 11 columns (6m high) which separate the side aisles; most of the capitals and columns are re-used from the earlier 4C Constantinian basilica (the capitals are Byzantine Corinthian with crosses); the columns themselves are of local white-veined red limestone and have the *remnants of 12C and later paintings* on their upper surfaces. These depict the Virgin and Child and saints, including Canute of Denmark and England done in the 12C. There are also grafitti representing the crests and mottoes of Frankish knights which mostly date from the 14C to the 17C. The soffits of the architrave have carved timbers some of which probably date to the 6C: some designs are paralleled in the oldest timbers from the Aqsa Mosque in Jerusalem (see Rtes 2 and 13). The great timber gable roof of the 14C was restored in the 19C. The main lighting comes from the round-arched clerestory windows. The paved floor contains trapdoors, which can be lifted to reveal large sections of the **5C mosaic floor** beneath the present level. Those in the central nave are the best preserved, and have parallels in the Imperial palace in Constantinople.

The walls now only bear fragments of the splendid series of **12C mosaics** which once covered them; they are best seen on the N wall. They were arranged in five registers against a background of gilded tesserae: the lowest illustrated the genealogy of Jesus; the next showed the churches of the towns of the 13 Great Councils of the Church, with texts relating to the decisions made at them. They include, on the N wall, that of the Council of Antioch in 272 which expelled Paul of Samosata as an heretic; of Sardica (Sofia) in 343 which judged the Athanasian heresy; the S wall had Nicaea (325), Constaninople (381), Ephesus (431), Chalcedon (451) and Constantinople (680); the register above has a frieze with jewelled acanthus plants and vases, Byzantine motifs similar to those used by the Umayyads in the Dome of the Rock in Jerusalem in the 7C; the next register shows angels (winged and haloed) between the clerestory windows, with the name of the artist (Basil) at the foot of the third angel from the E on the N wall. At the top was another frieze. The W wall was also originally covered with mosaics depicting the prophets. The 6C octagonal font in the S aisle is not in situ. Its Greek inscription reads: 'For the memory, repose and forgiveness of the sinners of whom the Lord knows the names'.

Steps lead from the nave to the raised choir over the grotto, and side entrances to the transepts. The wall blocking the transept from the basilica was built by the Greeks in 1842.

The main altar at the E end, and that on the S (the *Altar of the Circumcision*), are the property of the Greek Orthodox and are lavishly ornamented with an 18C iconostasis crowned with gilded angels, icons, gilded chandeliers and lamps. On the N side of the High Altar is the Armenian Altar of the Three Kings. The altar in the N apse is dedicated to the Virgin and is also Armenian Orthodox. Trap doors in this area can also be lifted to reveal the fine **5C mosaic** which surrounded the Constantinian octagon above the grotto. Complex guilloche, rosette and trail patterns form geometric designs, with floral borders and vine trellises; medallions with birds, flowers, fruits and more patterns make a rich and elaborate carpet. **12C mosaics** showing scenes from the life of Christ can be seen on the E wall; on the N section Christ shows his wounds to Doubting Thomas; a fragment depicts the Ascension; on the S section Christ rides on a donkey through the countryside during the Entry into Jerusalem.

Steps lead up from the S apse or transept to a doorway to the courtyard of the Greek Othodox monastery. On the S side is the bell tower. In the NE corner of the court is the Greek Orthodox *Chapel of St. George* (12C). On its outer wall is a lively carved plaque depicting St. George slaying the dragon. To the W is the Armenian monastery.

St. George and the Dragon, Church of trhe Nativity, Bethlehem (courtesy of Kay Prag).

Returning to the church, on the S side of the high altar a flight of steps leads down to the **Grotto of the Nativity**. The *6C bronze doors* at the N and S entrances to the Grotto are those of Justinian, and should be noted before one descends the rather steep dark steps. The rebated pointed arch and columns framing the entrance are 12C. The cave where the birth of Jesus is commemorated is c 12m × 3m. In an apse on the E side a silver star (1717) set in the paving, many lamps and marble lining mark the birthplace of Christ. The cave was splendidly adorned in the 4C. Steps on the left of the entrance lead to the *Roman Catholic Grotto and Altar of the Manger*. A passage at the W end of this complex used to connect with the caves now entered from the N (see below).

Ascending the steps on the N side, and continuing NW past the Armenian altars to a door in the N apse, we come to the W end of the Latin *Church of St. Catherine* built in 1881 on the N side of the Church of the Nativity. It is said to be the site of Christ's appearance to St. Catherine of Alexandria, and the prediction of her matryrdom c 310 (she is buried in Mount Sinai). The modern basilica has three aisles, with piers separating the central and side aisles. The ceiling is groined and plastered. It was built with funds from the Emperor of Austria, and replaced a smaller church of the same dedication. To the N and W is the Franciscan monastery.

Immediately to the right on entry, steps descend to more of the cave complex beneath the Church of the Nativity. (A guide and map are located on the right side of the steps). Here *rock cuttings, including ancient tombs,* with various modern additions, chambers and blockings, commemorate various people and traditions. In the first large chamber are said to be the tombs of the children killed in the Massacre of the Innocents, when Herod the Great attempted to kill the infant Jesus by slaying all the babes of Bethlehem (Matt. 2:16); a chapel is dedicated to St. Joseph, the husband of Mary; the tombs said to be of the devout Roman matron Paula and her daughter Eustochium who made a pilgrimage with Jerome c 485, later settled in Bethlehem and were buried near the Cave of the Nativity; and to the right the double cave of St. Jerome the first containing his tomb, and the further one a chapel marking the site where he is said to have translated the Bible. Another tomb is said to be that of Eusebius, Jerome's successor as head of the monastery at Bethlehem. It is unlikely that these locations are authentic. Parts of the Constantinian and Justinian foundations may be seen.

Returning to the church of St. Catherine, and leaving by the W door, the *cloister* was restored in 1948 by A. Barluzzi using columns and capitals of the 12C Crusader monastery on the site, where traces of an earlier 5C monastery associated with Jerome also exist. A modern statue of St. Jerome is placed here. The Amico map of 1609 shows that pilgrim accommodation and the refectory were located on the N side of the cloister. Return by the W entrance of the cloister to the courtyard before the Church of the Nativity.

Manger Square contains some of the principal buildings of the town, as well as shops. Passing the Mosque of 'Umar at the NW corner, 100m along the street leading W, a right turn leads to the *Old Betlehem Museum*. Open daily except Thu afternoon and Sun. It reconstructs an old Bethlehem house. The street running E from Manger Square along the S side of the Church of the Nativity leads to the *Milk Grotto* (at c 250m on the right), a cave (5m × 3m × 2.5m) where legend proclaims the Holy Family once sheltered, and a drop of the Virgin's milk fell on the cave floor as she suckled the child Jesus. This has given rise to the superstition that the rock itself (here rather soft and chalky, not uncommon in the Bethlehem region), ground into dust and eaten, will increase the milk of women. The chapel, in the Franciscan Convent, is open 8.00–11.30, 14.00–17.00.

The roads descending to the E of Bethlehem lead through the village of Bait Sahur, a mainly Christian village with a number of churches, which tradition equates with the home of the shepherds, and with the fields in which Ruth gleaned. A burial cave of the Early Bronze Age was discovered here. Just to the E are the sites where the traditions connected with the **Shepherds' Fields** are localised (Luke 2:8–10): 'And there were in the same country shepherds abiding in the field, keeping watch over their flock by night. And, lo, the angel of the Lord came upon them, and the glory of the Lord shone round about them, and they were sore afraid. And the angel said unto them, Fear not: for, behold, I bring you good tidings of great joy, which shall be to all people'.

History. Many accounts have been given by early pilgrims to the site. Egeria's account of the church called 'At the Shepherds' (c 381–84), is recalled by other writers who mention the church, a large walled garden and a 'very splendid cave with an altar'; Paula in 385 went to the Tower Eder ('of the flock') which was associated with both the patriarch Jacob and the shepherds; Arculf (c 680) also visited the tower mentioned by Paula at the Shepherds' Fields, where he says were the tombs of the three shepherds; Willibald (724/5) also came, and Bernard (c 870) mentions a monastery of the Holy Shepherds a mile from Bethlehem.

Visit. The Greek Orthodox site at the Shepherds' Fields is at KANISAT AL-RU'AT, 2km a little to the S of E of Bethlehem in the midst of fields. Open 8.00–11.30, 14.00–17.00. Here an old tradition and some Byzantine and medieval ruins mark the site, which may be that visited by the early pilgrims. The ruins at al-Ru'at include a cave used as a church in the 4C, of which the barrel-vaulted roof survives and which is approached by a flight of 21 steps. It has three apses with traces of mosaic and old frescoes. The church remained in use to 1955. A Byzantine chapel was built above the cave church; and was in turn replaced by a larger church which was destroyed in 614. It and a monastery were rebuilt in the 7C and survived to the 10C. A new, large church has been built on the east; the 4C lower church restored; and the remains of the upper church and monastery preserved. (Key is with the priest.)

At 0.6km to the N is the Franciscan site, at KHIRBAT SIYAR AL-GHANIM. Open 8.00–11.30, 14.00–17.00. Here, in pleasant surroundings with a fine view towards the hills is a low natural cave or rock shelter with soot-blackened roof, partly enclosed to make a modern chapel. Above is a very modern church designed like a tent, with a sculpted bronze angel; just to the N are *ruins*, excavated by Guarmani in 1934, and Corbo in 1951–52. These contain a rectangular monastery (80m × 42m), with an early phase dated to the late 4C–early 5C, and a second phase of the 6C–8C. The complex was poorly preserved, with just the apse of the church remaining, and among other fragments, a large lintel decorated with crosses. The monastery, with courtyard, had various domestic remains with wine presses, bakery, querns, cisterns and animal pens. The W wing was best preserved. The Franciscans identify this monastery with that at the Shepherds' Fields.

Further excavations by Corbo in 1952 at KHIRBAT ABU GHUNAIN c 3km NE of Bethlehem also revealed a small walled monastery (24.75m × 18.4m) with a court and cistern. A church (16.7m × 5.1m) with two steps up to a chancel screen and single apse lies on the N side. The floor was covered by a floral mosaic, mostly destroyed by later occupation in the Islamic period. Corbo considers that this may have been the Monastery of Photinus-Marinus, founded in the 5C by the brothers Marinus and Lukas, disciples of Euthymius. It formed one of very many Byzantine monasteries in the area; another exists just 2km NE of Bethlehem at BIR AL-QUTT (also excavated by Corbo, 1952– 53). This is a larger complex (35m × 30m) with a church on the N side, dated to the 6C and with Georgian inscriptions indicating a dedication to St. Theodore; it has a colonnaded court and a refectory with geometric designs in the mosaic floor.

11km directly E of Bethlehem, but by a progressively more poorly surfaced and then unsurfaced steep road (c 14km) is the Greek Orthodox monastery of **Mar Saba**. Though a lengthy and uncomfortable drive, the expedition is a pleasant one for those admiring views of the wilderness and fortified medieval monasteries. *Women are not admitted to the monastery.* Earlier visitors used to approach on horseback down the Kidron Valley from Jerusalem by a precipitous path; Curzon, who did this in 1834, gives a lively account of being ambushed and captured by Arabs in the ravine, who were convinced the Curzon party were Egyptians rather than Franks because of the dress they affected. The modern road from Bethlehem winds NE past several small villages, before turning SE along the ridges into the less habitable regions.

About 0.6km S of the road at c 6km E of Bethlehem are the ruins of another Byzantine monastery at KHIRBAT AL-MAKHRUM (map reference 175 123). Surveyed by Corbo in 1950, who noted a monastery of rectangular plan (c 50m × 33m). The courtyard had a cistern and rooms around it, and an attached church. In the same area c 0.6km further E Corbo excavated another 6C Byzantine monastery in 1954, at KHIRBAT JUHZUM (map reference 176 123). A long room with a geometric patterned mosaic was cleared. A dormitory was defined on the N side, which contained stone pallets; in a room to the E a slab with Greek inscription on one side, and a relief showing a cross flanked by peacocks and columns on the other was discovered. Corbo identifed these ruins with the monastery of Marcianus.

Returning to the road, and continuing to the NE at c 8km just before entering the village of 'UBAIDIYYA is the Greek *Monastery of St. Theodosius*, or *Dair Ibn 'Ubaid*, or *Dair Dosi*; a legend says that the Magi stayed in a cave here on their way home from Bethlehem. It housed 400 monks when its founder St. Theodosius died in 529 and his tomb lay beneath the church. Modestus, who restored so many of the Jerusalem churches after the Persian invasion in 614, was abbot of St. Theodosius. The Commemoratorium c 808 says there were 70 monks here, but Saracen brigands burnt the monastery and slaughtered many monks, and the rest fled. It was described in 1185 as fortified with towers, was still mentioned in 1250 and in 1400, but was deserted by 1620. Conder visited the ruins in 1879 which were then used as storehouses by the 'Ubaidiyya who also had a *maqam* or shrine there. The Greeks renegotiated their rights and took possession in 1893. They rebuilt the monastery and uncovered a considerable amount of Byzantine masonry.

The road forks in the village, continue to the right for Mar Saba on an unsurfaced road: views down to the Kidron Valley to the left, and a notice reminding the visitor that women are not admitted to the monastery at Mar Saba. The steep descent has a surfaced road for a short distance, and one can have a first sight of the two great towers of the monastery ahead. Only as one arrives can the monastery itself be seen, as it hangs on the near side of the Kidron Ravine.

History. St. Saba or Sabas was one of the most famous monks in Palestine, and is still commemorated by both the Greek and the Latin churches. He was born in 439 in Cappadocia, and after an unhappy childhood joined a local community of monks. He came to Jerusalem at the age of 18, and being already attracted to the life of a solitary, he joined Euthymius (376–473) who was one of the great founders of Byzantine monasticism in Palestine. Euthymius sent him as novice to Theoctistus, in the monastery to the E of Jerusalem (Dair al-Mukallik, see Rte 16), and eventually Saba settled in a cave in the sides of the Kidron, in the type of wilderness gorge, picturesque, solitary and defensible that the Byzantine monks of Palestine preferred. There was no water in summer, until a source was excavated near the bed of the wadi. Other monks joined Saba, and the community grew to 150 and needed a priest. Saba was ordained priest, and the first, or 'God-built' church was consecrated by Sallustius, Bishop of Jerusalem, on 12 December 491. A larger church was built and dedicated on 1 July 501.

Saba was made archimandrite over all the hermit monks of Palestine in 493, and was a distinguished theologian, noted for his attacks on the Monophysites whose doctrine was condemned at the Council of Chalcedon in 451. He was twice sent on embassies to the Emperor in Constantinople, first in 511 to persuade the Emperor (who supported the Eutychian heresy) to stop persecuting the Orthodox; and again in his 91st year to gain support in putting down the Samaritans, and to seek redress for the Orthodox sufferings during the Samaritan Revolt. Saba also set up two hospices near the Citadel in Jerusalem for the use of the monks from the monastery. He died in 532, and was buried at the monastery, where his relics were venerated. He is also remembered for the lion who tried to drag him off and eat him, but whom he managed to tame. It remained a troublesome pet, and finally he told it to be at peace or leave: it left. It is also noted that he vowed never to eat apples because Eve tempted Adam with this fruit; that his date palm still grows at the monastery and its fruit has no stones; and the monks still feed his birds daily (the Tristram's grackles of the locality). His life was written by Cyril of Scythopolis.

The monastery was plundered by the Persians in 614, and suffered from Bedouin attacks in 796, 809 and 842. Nonetheless in the 8C–9C the monastery was one of the most important in Palestine, notable for the number of scholars, including St. John Damascene (8C) who was another distinguished theologian, noted particularly for his attacks on iconoclasm; also St. John the Silent, St. Aphrodisius, St. Theophanes of Nicaea, St. Cosmas of Majuma and St. Theodore of Edessa. It was visited by Epiphanius the Monk, and by Hugeburc in 724/5, who mentions both the monastery and many rock-cut cells. The Commemoratorium c 808 says that there were 150 monks at St. Saba. In 1102, in the early years of the Latin Kingdom, there were more than 300 monks at the monastery. The relics of St. Saba were removed from the monastery by the Venetians, but the Orthodox monastery survived the upheavals of the 12C.

The monastery was pillaged by the Arabs in 1832 and 1834. When Curzon arrived in 1834 as a captive of the Arabs who had ambushed him, it was to find the Arabs lining the walls of the fortified monastery and clearly in control of the monks and the surrounding area. Having established that they were Franks, the Arab captors appear to have treated Curzon's party with great civility.

Curzon had been attracted by accounts of the fine library which the monastery was said to possess. By scrambling up a ladder in the church to a small door about 3m above the floor, he managed to inspect the library; but was disapppointed to discover that the 1000 manuscripts it contained were all works of divinity, mostly of the 12C, including some enormous folios. There were another 100 manuscripts on a shelf in the apse which he was not allowed to examine but he was assured they were liturgies in use during the year. He also saw a further 100 manuscripts in the base of the great N tower which included a copy of the Iliad. Having purchased three manuscripts, he departed on a visit to the Dead Sea in course of which he used one of the folios he had purchased as a pillow.

Curzon returned on two subsequent occasions, and eventually acquired what he deemed to be the most interesting manuscript in the monastery, a 9C–10C copy of the first eight books of the Old Testament.

Severe damage was caused by the earthquake of 1834, and in 1840 the monastery was enlarged and restored by the Russians. Conder visited it in 1873, 1881 and 1882. He noted that the library had recently been removed to Dair al-Sahb, near Jerusalem; and that the refectory was new and painted with very poor and gaudy frescoes. In the early 20C there were only about 50 monks at the monastery, who led an austere life, tending their gardens and living mostly on vegetables. The monastery was supported by donations, the small charges for accommodating pilgrims and travellers, and by a few estates, including some near Bethlehem.

Visit. There are even fewer monks living there today, but the blue painted domes give the complex a lived-in look on a human scale which softens the dramatic situation of the only monastery which has had a virtually uninterrupted occupation by its Orthodox monks since it was built in the 5C. It ranks with St. Catherine's in Sinai as being one of the oldest inhabited monasteries in the world. In 1965 the body of St. Saba was given back to the monastery by Pope Paul, and made the long journey from Venice by way of Jerusalem. A lively, joyous procession met the tiny embalmed body of the saint in the square inside the Jaffa Gate, near where his hospice must have been in the 5C, and priests and monks, bands of musicians, Boy Scouts, and members of the Orthodox community escorted the saint to the Church of the Holy Sepulchre, where he lay in state for some time before venturing on the last stages of the rough journey to his home at Mar Saba. The blackened feet in tiny slippers provided an extraordinary contrast between human fragility and the spiritual triumph and tenacity of the monastery and its founder over the centuries.

Open 8.00–17.00 daily.

The visitor approaches from the W. The monastery is supported on massive terraces up the cliff-like edge of the Kidron Ravine. The two great towers are the first visible sections. That on the S, St. Simeon, built in 1612, which is detached from the monastery, was used to accommodate women pilgrims, but is rarely open. It appears to have a cistern in the base. The great rectangular N tower forms the NW bastion of the high stone walls. The whole monastic complex dates from the 5C onwards, but much of what is visible was restored c 1840. The entrance is by a low door in the W wall. Within, a stepped passage descends to the main court: in the centre stands the empty *Tomb of St. Saba*. The main church to the E with large blue dome and adjacent small bell tower is dedicated to the Annunciation. Five tremendous buttresses support it on the S side. It has five aisles, apse and dome, and frescoes which Curzon noted as ancient in 1834, now mostly modern; parts of an old carved and gilded iconostasis survive in a solid but not very interesting building. It is now the resting place of the saint.

On the NW side of the court is the *Church of St. Nicholas*, built against a grotto in the rock which may be the cave where Saba founded the first church. The royal doors in the iconostasis are 15C. Behind a grille are the skulls of monks slain by the Persians in 614. At a higher level to the N is a chapel with the empty *Tomb of St. John Damascene*—his relics were also removed during the Crusades but are now lost.

The monastery contains many cells; the terraces, once cultivated as gardens, ascend in steep steps to the NW corner-tower. All around the monastery are the cuttings of many other ancient hermit cells. Many are or have been occupied in the recent past by Bedouin. On the E side of the wadi, protected by a metal grille, is the cave said to be that of St. Saba. Downstream the approaches to the gorge are further fortified by walls and two towers, the ruins of which can be seen from the monastery. The road climbs past the exterior NW corner of the monastery and continues along the W bank of the Kidron. A path descends to the ravine near the corner, and another from the S tower. Below the monastery is a feeble spring, but most of the water needed is collected in cisterns during the winter.

The *cell of St. Sophia*, the mother of Saba, who eventually followed him to Palestine, is 300m to the N low in the wadi. It has remnants of 12C frescoes. The road (track) crosses the wadi upstream to the N and continues down to the Biqaʿ where another Byzantine monastery was located.

The return to Jerusalem can be made via Bethlehem; alternatively turn right at ʿUbaidiyya, and descend to the crossing of the Kidron. A steep climb up the other side leads to the village of Abu Dis and eventually to the Bethany Road, not far from Jerusalem.

INDEX

Place and site names are in **bold**, persons in *italics*, ancient names in SMALL CAPITALS, other entries in Roman type.

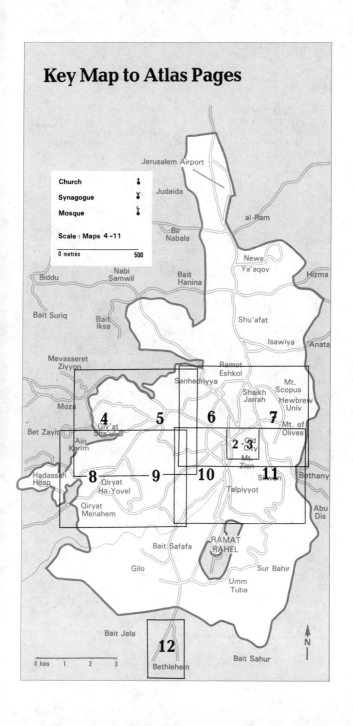

Key Map to Atlas Pages

Church	⛪
Synagogue	✡
Mosque	☪

Scale : Maps 4–11

0 metres — 500

Jerusalem Airport

Judaida

al-Ram

Bir
Nabala

Newe
Ya'aqov

Hizma

Biddu

Nabi
Samwil

Bait
Hanina

Shu'afat

Isawiya

Anata

Bait Suriq

Bait
Iksa

Mevasseret
Ziyyon

Ramot
Eshkol

Sanhedriyya

Shaikh
Jarrah

Mt.
Scopus

Moza

Hewbrew
Univ

4   **5**   **6**   **7**

Mt. of
Olives

Bet Zayit

Giv'at
Sha'ul B

Ain
Karim

2 -3 Old
City

Hadassah
Hosp

8   **9**   **10**   **11**

Mt.
Zion

Silwan

Bethany

Qiryat
Ha-Yovel

Talpiyyot

Abu
Dis

Qiryat
Menahem

Bait Safafa

RAMAT
RAHEL

Gilo

Sur Bahir

Umm
Tuba

Bait Jala

12

Bethlehem

Bait Sahur

N

0 kms   1   2   3

2

NABLUS ROAD

Bus Sta.

PROPHET STREET

Damascus Gate

HARAT
Mawlawiyya
Shaik
Lu'lu'
A.AL-HINDI

St Spyridion

HA-ZANHANIM

T.AL-WAD

New Gate

al-Qaymari

NEW GATE ST

Christian Brothers Coll.

St Saviour

St George

St Basil

ST FRANCIS

St Theodore

Casa Nova

St Nicholas

St Demetrius

Greek Cath. Patriarchate

St Catherine

St Michael
STREET

Greek Patriarchate (Orth)

Great Greek Mon.
(see Route map 4)

Coptic Khan

St George

Pool

Petra Hotel

St Euthymius

Mikra Panagia

TARIQ AL-KHANQAH

al-Khanqah

CHRISTIAN QUARTER STREET

Holy Sepulchre

Mos.of 'Umar'

NEW BAZAAR

Muristan

St John
the Baptist

Gate of Judgement

St Caralambos

Coptic Patriarchate

Khan al-Zait

Russian Mission

Ch.of the Redeemer

SUQ AL-LAHHAMIN
SUQ AL-'ATTARIN
SUQ AL-KHAWAJA

FRED WILLIAM ST

Austrian Hospice

Polish Cath.Chap.

T.AL-SARAY

St Veronica

Dar al-Sin
Tunshuq

al-Qirimiyya

al-Lu'lu'iyya

T.AL.

Khan al-Sultan

T.BAB

al-Qaymari

T.KHAN AL-ZAIT

T.AL-TAKIYYA

A.AL-TAKIYYA

JAFFA ROAD

◁ **6**

Jaffa Gate

ℹ

DAVID STREET

Christian Info.Centre

ST MARK'S ST

Ya'qubiyya

Christ Church

Dar Disse

Citadel
(see Route map 5)

PATRIARCHATE ROAD

H.AL-ARMAN

St Thomas

(see Route map 6)

ARMENIAN

St James
Cath.

Armenian

Garden

Gulbenkian Library

Mardigian Mus.

St Mark

HABAD STREET

Folklore Museum

AL ZAITUNA

St George's Convent

Con.of the Olive Tree

JEWISH QUARTER LANE

Israelite Tower

Israelite Wall

(see Route map 7)

Hurva & Ramban

Jami'Kabir

Synagogues

Rothschild Bld.

Nea Church

cistern

Batei Mahse

S.

BETHLEHEM ROAD

Sultan's Pool

Zion Gate

Ch.of the Holy Saviour ↕ (see Route map 8)

Dormition Ch. *MOUNT ZION*

Ayyubid Tower

7
▽

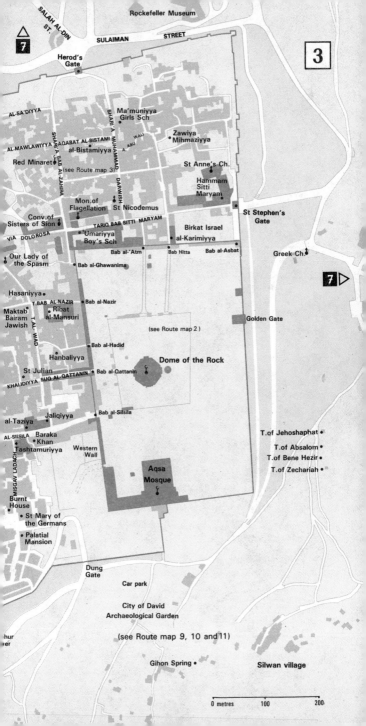

4

JAFFA ROAD

SHEUNAT HAR NOF

Military
Cemetery

MEGADIM

MOUNT HERZL

T. of Theo. Herzl

Holocaust Mem

HA-ZIKKARON

KIKKAR
HOLLAND

TIRZA

TEFE-NOF

SHA'ARAY

HA-RAV UZZI'EL

BAYIT

HIDA

WE-SAN

HA-PISGA

'AIN KARIM

'AIN
KARIM

St John

NEIDITZ

'IMMANU'EL

OLSWANGER

BRAZIL

HANTKE

BORUCHOV

YISRA'EL ZANGWILL

QIRYAT

HA-YOVEL

TORA

WA-'AVODA

of the Virgin

8
▽

6

Grape Tomb
Tombs of the Sanhedrin
YAM SUF
PARAN
LEVI
SEDEROT
SANHEDRIYYA
RAMOT ESHKOL
MA'ALOT DAFNA
Mus. of Jewish Art
MAHANAYIM
ZALMAN
Biblical Zoo
TEL-ARZA
SHIKKUN HABAD
SHEKHUNAT HA-BUKHARIM
ROMEMA
ZEFANYA
MEQOR BARUKH
Mandelbaum Gate
ME'A SHE'ARIM
Bet HaHistadrut Qaymariyya
MAHANE YEHUDA
Ethiopian Ch.
PROPHET
Soldiers' House
JAFFA ROAD
Agricultural Mus.
MORASHA
RUSSIAN COMPOUND
Cath. of the Holy Trinity
Sacher Park
NAHALAT AHIM
Bezalel Sch of Art
Nahon Mus. of Jewish Art
Notre Dame de France
New Gate
Kubakiyya
Knesset
QIRYAT WOLFSON
Independance Park
Jewish Agency
Mamilla Pool
Taxation Mus.
Jaffa Gate
Chief Rabbinate
Hebrew Union Coll.
King David Hotel
Arts & Crafts Centre
YEMIN MOSHE
Monastery of the Cross
REHAVYA
Tomb of Jason
Musical Instruments Mus.
YMCA
T. of Herod's Family
Sultan's Pool
Montefiore Windmill
Bloomfield Park
Museum
QOMEMIYYUT
Liberty Bell Park
St Andrew's
Khan Theatre
Jerusalem Theatre
Mayer Inst. (Islamic Art)

10

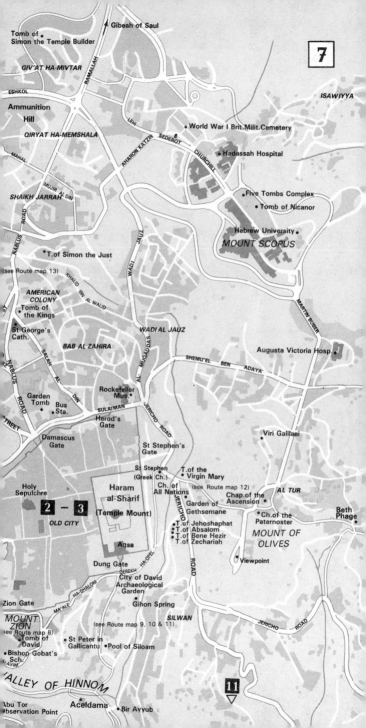

Tomb of
Simon the Temple Builder

Gibeah of Saul

GIV'AT HA-MIVTAR

ESHKOL

ISAWIYYA

Ammunition
Hill

QIRYAT HA-MEMSHALA

World War I Brit.Milit.Cemetery

LEHI

SEDEROT

AHARON KATZIR

CHURCHILL

Hadassah Hospital

MAHAL

MUJIR
AL-DIN

SHAIKH JARRAH

Five Tombs Complex

Tomb of Nicanor

NABLUS
ROAD

T. of Simon the Just

Hebrew University

MOUNT SCOPUS

JAUZ

WADI

KHALIL

IBN

AL WALID

(see Route map 13)

AMERICAN
COLONY
Tomb of
the Kings

WADI AL JAUZ

AL-
MUQADDAS

MARTIN BUBER

St George's
Cath.

BAB AL ZAHIRA

SHEMU'EL

BEN

ADAYA

Augusta Victoria Hosp.

NABLUS
ROAD

SALAH

AL-

DIN

Rockefeller
Mus.

JERICHO
ROAD

SULAIMAN

Garden
Tomb
Bus
Sta.

Herod's
Gate

STREET

Damascus
Gate

St Stephen's
Gate

Viri Galilaei

Holy
Sepulchre

St Stephen
(Greek Ch.)

T.of the
Virgin Mary

Ch. of
All Nations

(see Route map 12)

AL TUR

Haram
al-Sharif

(Temple Mount)

JERICHO

Chap.of the
Ascension

Beth
Phage

2 – 3

OLD CITY

Garden of
Gethsemane

Ch.of the
Paternoster

Aqsa

T.of Jehoshaphat
T.of Absalom
T.of Bene Hezir
T.of Zechariah

MOUNT OF
OLIVES

Dung Gate

HA-OFEL

DEREKH

City of David
Archaeological
Garden

Viewpoint

ROAD

Zion Gate

MA'ALE HA-SHALOM

Gihon Spring

MOUNT
ZION
(see Route map 8)
Tomb of
David

SILWAN

St Peter in
Gallicantu

Pool of Siloam

(see Route map 9, 10 & 11)

JERICHO

ROAD

Bishop Gobat's
Sch.
HIVIM

VALLEY OF HINNOM

Abu Tor
Observation Point

Aceldama

Bir Ayyub

11

BET ZAYIT

8

△4

MOUNT HERZL

Military Cemetery

T. of Theo.Herzl

Holocaust Mem.

HA-ZIKKARON

'AIN KARIM

QIRYAT

NEIDITZ

'AIN KARIM

St John

'IMMANU'EL

OLSWANGER

TORO

YISRA'EL ZANGWILL

BORUCHOV

HANTKE

BRAZIL

Spring of the Virgin

Russian Convent

Ch.of the Visitatio Mariae

QIRYAT HA-YOVEL

Hadassah Hospital

SZOLD

THON

CHILE

E.SERENI

FLORENTIN

KORCZAK

HANNA SZENES

DEREKH

HENRIETTA

ICELAND

MEXICO

GUATEMALA

URUGUAY

NICARAGUA

COLOMBIA

QIRYAT MENAHEM

HA-KARKOM

MEXICO

DAHOMEY

BOLIVIA

AVRAHAM STERN YA'IR

KALLANIT

COSTA RICA

HA-NURIT

AYVIT

COSTA RICA

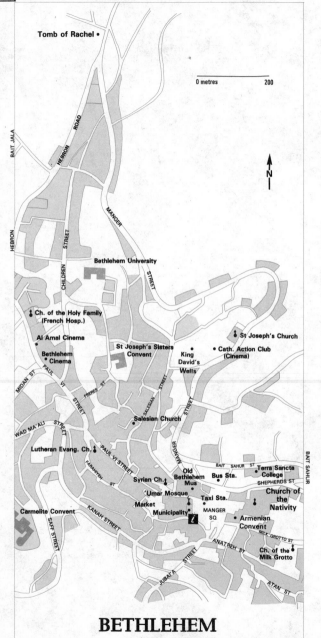

12

JERUSALEM

Tomb of Rachel •

0 metres   200

BAIT JALA

HEBRON ROAD

HEBRON

MANGER STREET

CHILDREN STREET

N

Bethlehem University

• Ch. of the Holy Family
(French Hosp.)

• St Joseph's Church

Al Amal Cinema •

Bethlehem
• Cinema

St Joseph's Sisters
Convent

King
David's
Wells

• Cath. Action Club
(Cinema)

MIDAN ST

PAUL VI STREET

FRERES ST.

SALESIAN STREET

WAD MA'ALI STREET

• Salesian Church

FARAHIYEH ST.

Lutheran Evang. Ch. •

PAUL VI STREET

MANGER STREET

BAIT SAHUR ST

Syrian Ch. •

Old
Bethlehem
Mus

Bus Sta.

• Terra Sancta
College

BAIT SAHUR

SHEPHERDS ST.

Carmelite Convent

KANAH STREET

'Umar Mosque •

Taxi Sta.

Church of
the
Nativity

SAFF STREET

Market •

Municipality •
ℹ

MANGER
SQ.

• Armenian
Convent

MILK GROTTO ST

ANATREH ST.

JUBA'I A STREET

• Ch. of the
Milk Grotto

ATAN ST.

BETHLEHEM